INDIA AS IT MAY BE

INDIA AS IT MAY BE;

AN OUTLINE OF
A PROPOSED GOVERNMENT AND POLICY.

GEORGE CAMPBELL

GYAN

Published by

GYAN

Gyan Publishing House
5, Ansari Road
Daryaganj, New Delhi-110002
Phone: 011-47034999, 9811692060
E-mail: books@gyanbooks.com

Distribution Network
gyanbooks.com
India, USA, Canada, UK, Australia, France

ISBN: 978-81-212-8806-4 (PB)
First Published, 1853

2nd Impression 2023

Printed at: Gyan Press, Delhi.

INDIA AS IT MAY BE
Author: George Campbell

INDIA AS IT MAY BE;

AN OUTLINE OF

A PROPOSED GOVERNMENT AND POLICY.

BY GEORGE CAMPBELL,

AUTHOR OF 'MODERN INDIA.'

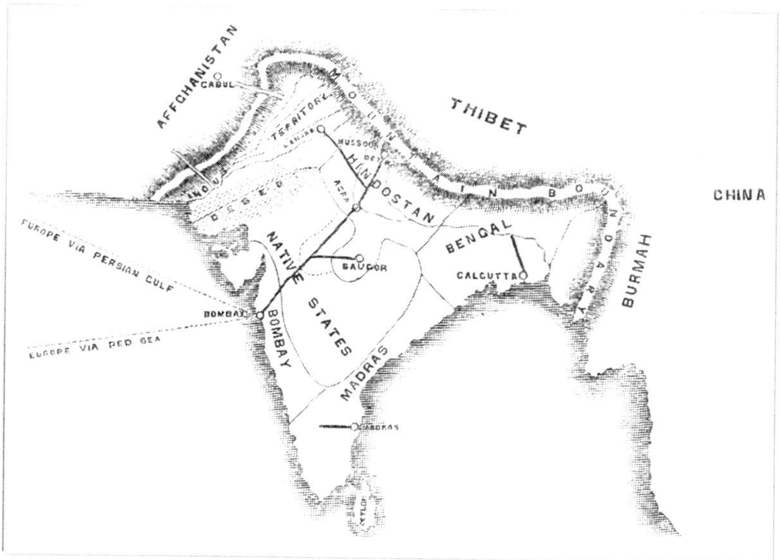

LONDON:
JOHN MURRAY, ALBEMARLE STREET.
1853.

CONTENTS.

CHAPTER I.

HOME GOVERNMENT.

CHAPTER II.

INDIAN GOVERNMENT.

CHAPTER III.

OUR POLITICAL RELATIONS.

CHAPTER IV.

THE CIVIL ADMINISTRATION.

CHAPTER V.

THE CIVIL SERVICE.

CHAPTER VI.

MILITARY ESTABLISHMENTS.

CHAPTER VII.

FINANCE.

CHAPTER VIII.

MORAL AND MATERIAL IMPROVEMENT.

DIRECTIONS TO THE BINDER.

PREFACE.

WHILE analysing and comparing things as they are I have been led into determining, completing, and setting in order certain views with regard to the future management and prospects of India. The result is contained in the following pages, which comprise a general outline of a projected administration and policy, and which I now with all deference and humility submit to the public.

It is more necessary that the British Parliament should provide an efficient government for India than that it should prescribe particular measures. The details of the administration may be better and more conveniently regulated by the Indian Government. But as the nature and strength of the machine must be determined with reference to the work to be done, I hope that it will not be out of place at this time shortly to review the requirements of the country.

The scope of my plan doubtless embraces some subjects in respect to which my qualifications as an adviser may justly be called in question, and I should hardly have ventured to travel over so large a field did it not seem to me that as the time for legislation approaches there is still a want of definite and connected general plans. Various suggestions have been put forth on particular points, but the whole subject has not been so brought together in one view as to enable us to estimate the *relative* bearing of different suggestions.

We want as it were a map of the ground to be operated upon. I do not pretend adequately to supply this want; but if my rough sketch may in any degree render intelligible the relative positions of the most prominent questions, and facilitate the more perfect and detailed plans of more skilful artists, my object will be accomplished. I hope that my plan is so far complete that I shall not be liable to the imputation of proposing some things to the entire disregard of others possibly incompatible, or of suggesting ends in an Utopian spirit without providing the means. For instance, I do not with some people propose, on the one hand, to abandon great part of our revenue in favour of princes or people, and, on the other, to spend large sums on magnificent works without making any provision for the wherewithal. So far as in me lies I have tried to look at both sides of each question, and to render one part of my scheme consistent with another. I do not claim originality in all the parts of my plan. I have without scruple availed myself of every suggestion which has seemed to answer my purpose. I have endeavoured to select, convert, and fit together the best materials from whatever quarter derived—to supply such things as were wanting —and to connect and put in array the whole. I fear that I may not fully meet the views of either of the two extremes into which opinion is divided—that I shall not propose so total a subversion of the existing order of things as will satisfy those who see nothing but evil in the present system; and, on the other hand, that the changes which seem to me to be necessary may appear to those who, admiring things as they are, would let well alone, to contain the elements of innovation, and to be on that account dangerous and inexpedient. I have steered a middle course. It will be seen that some of my proposals are founded on the same main principles as those suggested by that distinguished ex-Governor General whose experience and knowledge of Indian affairs are, above all others, so great and so admirable, while on other questions, in which I believe that his intellect is not unprejudiced, I have taken wholly opposite views. If my arguments are in any degree just, the materials selected from different and even opposition workshops are not inconsistent or irreconcileable.

In my former publication on Modern India I have attempted succinctly to describe the country, the people, and the government as they exist. Suffice it now to say that we have reached the natural limits of a great and undivided empire; that we have peace within those limits,* and are not threatened with any *defensive* war; that the country is fertile and populous, the people personally most capable, and in many respects civilized—politically submissive; and that our Government possesses materials which, judiciously reconstructed, are capable of great and beneficial efficiency. Under an efficient government, occupying a situation of singular advantage, I believe that the social and material wants of the country may be very fully supplied, and that the personal character of the people may be immensely

* I speak of India, not of Burmah.

elevated. In truth, an infinite field of improvement lies before us.

Certain political characteristics are indelibly stamped on particular races, but the ordinary social civilization of this ancient hemisphere seems to have had everywhere much in common. Our western society has in fact sprung by gradual progressive changes from that elder civilization which a few centuries ago was common to the East and the West, but more highly developed in the former. Whether we go historically back or geographically east, we travel very much in the same direction, and most of the manners and customs which now seem peculiar to the East have had their parallels in the earlier days of the West. Then why should not the East be also capable of progress? Why, commencing from a similar level, should it not be raised as the West has been raised? After all, we are but Orientals among whom the old leaven of Greek and Roman civilization has fermented into progress, and I see no reason why we should not introduce in the East a similar progress. I believe that we might and should do so; that India is fully capable of the very highest civilization; and that Heaven has imposed on us a task which we may not neglect.

Hitherto the country has not been fortunate. Repeatedly a prey to conquerors by no means the most civilized or the most forbearing of mankind, its best dynasties have been very shortlived. We seem now to have greater advantages, and we may hope, if we use these advantages well, to attain greater stability. We have rescued the natives from anarchy and confusion, and, doubtless, years of peace have done much to fill up the gaps caused by years of war; but it is fairer to compare our government with the more prosperous times of the better native dynasties, and in this view there is a good deal to be said on both sides of the question. Our administration is pure, and we have every desire to do justice; but our armies are expensive —our government is wanting in concentrated energy—its policy has often been mistaken—and our judicial system is inappropriate and inefficient. The natives in some respects prefer indifferent justice, easily procured, to the most perfect system if complicated and difficult of access. The whole native system of government is but a delegation of absolute power from one official grade to another. To the people one man is their ruler, and he has full and prompt power for good or for evil. He may be neither pure nor disinterested; but there is a limit to the capacity of one *pool* (as Lord Ellenborough would call it), and, his own interests satisfied, he may be not disinclined to do substantial justice among a people whom he thoroughly understands. He is bound by no inflexible general rules, which, while designed for the good of the majority, may inflict hardship on individuals, and are apt to be slow and difficult of application. He can, if he will, do popular justice in each case. We, on the other hand, go altogether on the principle of setting aside individual will and discretion, trusting nothing to any man, but regulating everything by strict rules. Up to a certain point this system is most beneficial, but it may be carried too far; and in India especially its over refinement is not appreciated. The evils are patent to all, while the good is seen only by philosophers. Good, simple, and discreet codes of essential law must be the greatest of blessings to any country, and are particularly required in India, but a too tight tying of the hands of public officers is only necessary when we must guard against political tyranny. Such a system was once necessary in England, but a change is now taking place, and the essence of all our present administrative and judicial reforms seems simply to consist in trusting to the discretion of individuals many things which were formerly determined by the strictest rules of law. It is now found that public opinion and the press are sufficient checks on the conduct of great officers, and that a large latitude may, with much advantage, be allowed.

I do, then, think that the natives of India very much prefer large individual power, easy and popular justice, even at the risk of a little abuse of that power; and that, in comparing our present administration with that of a good native government, we must set against the many acknowledged advantages of our rule not only the obvious evils resulting from the expense of our system and the necessary ignorance of foreigners, but also the injuries and inconveniences caused by the cumbrousness and inflexibility of our machinery, and which I believe to be for the most part remediable.

Of course, the individuals lately dominant have suffered by our rule, and some others who would like to be dominant are excluded from that position; but neither do I think that we are bound to govern the country for the benefit of the highest classes, nor (if the term be used in our sense) do I admit the existence of the ill-used "native gentry" so often expatiated on by philanthropic and imaginative people. The only persons who have any good claim to that title are the better classes connected with the land, and their position (except in the Ryotwar territories) is unquestionably far more favourable under us than it was under other conquerors. But as regards general social rank there is no well-defined line between gentle and semple. Our European notions in this respect spring from a feudal origin. The organisation of the Rajpoots and other Hindoo conquerors is undoubtedly feudal; but the Mahommedan empires being, in the territories fully conquered by them, the purest of Oriental despotisms, and in no respect feudal in their character, exaltation or degradation but depended on the imperial will or the caprices of fortune. Slaves became Emperors, and Emperors became slaves—men rose like mushrooms, and like mushrooms decayed. True, individuals of all classes were elevated to high posts. There were prizes in the lottery which any of the people might draw, and of the chance of which they are now deprived. But no particular classes of society, except some of the latest Mahommedan rulers, can complain of special degradation.

If the supposed nobles and gentry are not subjects of just sympathy, still less are the recent princes. The old patriarchal chiefs and clans, never completely conquered, and who retained a feudal tenure under the Moguls, are at least as well off under us.

As concerns the general people, I believe that, upon the whole, the best administered of our provinces are now, taking all advantages and disadvantages together, about upon a par with the best administered of the small native states blessed with a good individual ruler. I have had a good deal to do with petty transfers, both one way and the other: I have generally found that neither were the subjects of the very best of these patriarchal governments averse to be brought under our rule, nor did our subjects in every case think it an insuperable hardship to be made over to the rule of the native chief; petty local circumstances might turn the scale either way.

This, then, is the case as regards the best of those small states which are under our feudatory supervision and control; but as concerns the majority of native states, their subjects are undoubtedly infinitely worse off than in the worst of our territories, and would be delighted to be brought under our government. Almost all the large states, and those whose feudatory tenure has not been sufficiently regulated, are thus ill managed.

Upon the whole, then, the natives owe to us not only the blessings of protection from external war, and, what is still more important, from internal anarchy, but a considerable *average* improvement in the civil administration. But I do also think that that improvement is far from being so great or so general as it might be, and ought to be, if we make the most of our peculiar opportunities. In particular, there seems to be strong evidence to show that the results of our administration of the Madras and Bombay territories is by no means so favourable as could be wished.

Most people are agreed that there are many deficiencies in our system; but there is a very wide discrepancy both in the statements of present facts and the opinions as to future policy.

I believe that the great cause of these very contradictory statements and opinions is the want of uniformity in our system. In truth, our management of different racter of the administration which are or may be raised shall be finally settled, we may wait a very long time indeed. I believe that the best plan would be to act like a jury assessing damages—to take the average of the various irreconcileable opinions; and we may thus arrive at the conclusion that the Indian government is in fact by no means so black as some people paint it, but that there is very great room for amendment. Amendment then I trust that we shall have and have quickly. It will be hard indeed if it is denied either because as an English political question the matter does not seem very pressing, or because the opinions of various persons cannot be reconciled. I fear that there is too great a disposition to avoid fully grappling with a difficult subject. Yet the question is not one which a powerful ministry need shrink from dealing with. The ends are of vast importance, and will not be attained without considerable improvement in the government, but the present task is not to define ends, but to provide an efficient governmental constitution—a difficult question, no doubt, but not so very large and intricate as it appears when we discuss the details of the administration. We only want some general idea of the character of the present government, good, bad, or indifferent, and a rough *notion* of the work which lies before a new government. There are then to be decided but two or three main points, important, but lying in comparatively narrow compass.

The grand want of our present system is a central government of some kind. Improvements of detail will be of little use if we do not somehow so arrange that it shall be possible to answer the question who governs

India? That is what no one now can tell, and I believe the truth to be that *nobody* governs it, or, at best, that things are left to the varying chances of individual local officers, and that our whole establishment of Indian Governments, Court of Directors, and Board of Control, are but checks on the progress of those local officers. For instance, it is on all hands admitted that the Madras land revenue system is a failure. But whose business is it to institute a new system? No one does so. The fact is, that under the present constitution things will in each department, and each local division, go on as they are till some local officer designs something new. The difficulty will then be to obtain the sanction of each of the various powers to a change, and if a change is in the end sanctioned, it will be not on any large and general principles, but in deference to the pertinacity of the applicant and without reference to its consistency with other plans similarly sanctioned.

I have formed the opinion, in which I am every day more and more confirmed, that most things are in the main identical in all parts of India as we found it; and I think that it is most necessary to introduce some *general* principles and general system. So far as any general government of India is concerned, nothing would have been done in the last fifty years. We have in fact a quadruple government, whose sole duty is to prevent the executive officers from doing too much. It is this then that we must strive to remedy. We must vest somewhere sufficient administrative functions, and we must institute a proper system of gradation, instead of many parallel mutually checking authorities. One authority must direct another, instead of merely checking the proceedings of another. We are altogether wanting in progress, and the means of progress we must supply through some body actually and ostensibly governing India, and fairly responsible to public opinion.

A great want, and one which may be without disadvantage supplied, is publicity. Some things must, no doubt, be secret, but the great mass of our business is such as will well bear the light and would be every way the better for public airing. We not only keep the public in the dark, but we contrive so completely to mystify the servants of Government, that one knows not in the least what another is doing.

In regard to the constitution of the Government, the points which seem to me to be most important are—the transfer of the whole central executive power to a sufficiently constituted Supreme Government in India; the improvement of the Court of Directors, and especially the introduction of a certain proportion of members selected otherwise than by popular election; arrangements for securing a nearer and better understanding between the Indian Minister and the Court; provision for the formation of good laws and a good judicial system; and the abolition of appointments and jurisdictions emanating from any source other than the general Indian Government.

Of separate matters requiring legislation, the most pressing are the colleges for the education and testing of the young men nominated to the services, and the legal restrictions in regard to the leave and other rules affecting those services which have become inapplicable to the present day.

I have always looked with great admiration on much of the education supplied at Haileybury to those who like to learn, and personally I feel exceedingly indebted to it. Insufficient as it is in quantity, I believe that it is not to be had elsewhere, and would, of all things, deprecate the abolition of a special place of education for the civil service and the reliance on ordinary education. Till the educational system of the country is very much changed indeed, this cannot with safety be done; and if it *could* be done, it would be, I think, in several ways most undesirable. But I think that the special education is not carried far enough, that the duty of plucking is evaded, and that the tone of the college is not what it ought to be. I think that it was a mistake to build it isolated on an out-of-the-way heath—that an academic site and academic atmosphere would have been infinitely preferable. I would transfer our special college from Hertford Heath to Cambridge, and would very much raise the tests of admission to the civil service. I would also institute a great military school, or expand Addiscombe into that character, and would send no cadet to the Indian army who has not received a military education.

There will be, I believe, no hesitation fundamentally to alter the rules for the regulation of the services prescribed in a former age.

In glancing at the general principles of future policy which I recommend, I hope it will be seen that I am by no means inclined to carry to an impolitic extreme principles which I believe to be in the main sound. In describing facts, I have only generally and incidentally alluded to, without fully explaining, views which may have been therefore, in some degree, misconceived. I very much deprecate the advance of our frontier. Believing that the natural limits of India have been fixed by nature in the clearest and most insuperable way, I rejoice that we should have reached those limits, but I deeply regret that we should overstep them by an offensive war; and I think that, if England will enter on a fresh career in a new continent, she should do so at her own costs and charges, and that India should not be called on to pay if loss should accrue. I am by no means in favour either of an immediate general absorption of all native states, or of any general rule for the assumption of the direct management of *every* territory which we can from time to time, without breach of faith, appropriate; very far from it. Not only would I keep substantial faith, but I have both a very good opinion of the management of *some* small native states, and a conviction of the policy and advantage in several ways of maintaining certain native feudatories and governing a portion of the country *indirectly*. I do sincerely trust that we shall not sacrifice our good name or appropriate countries which do not pay; but for these very reasons I advocate the formation of a good feudatory system, through which those native states which we maintain may become useful members of the empire, and may answer the purposes of faith and policy without inducing anarchy, confusion, and misrule. I draw a wide distinction between different states according to the circumstances of each. There are, after all, comparatively few of which I would covet the direct rule; but I think that the appropriation of Oude, Gwalior, and one or two others, would be most beneficial in every way, both to the empire and to the people of those states, without entailing any disadvantage whatever; and that we should lose no opportunity which occurs of obtaining possession of these large, rich, and convenient territories. The Rajpoots and other clans I would, without doubt, maintain, and would only by a more discreet and equitable policy make them more directly subservient to our uses, and thus in some degree relieve the finances of the empire.

In our own territories I confess that I should prefer the interests of the people to those of the mushroom official nobles of the former dynasties, and would be just before being generous.

Our administration should be avowedly despotic; but I would be far from introducing severities which are no necessary part of despotisms. In spite of all the faults of the Indian press, I by no means propose to gag and silence it; no man would more deprecate such a course. I would above all things render our laws systematic, simple, and clear, but would not carry them into too great detail; would not regulate minor matters by too precise laws; but, enforcing among the servants of Government an efficient discipline and subordination, I would place much trust in them, and would leave a good deal to individual discretion. As the best means of obtaining a supply of good and trustworthy servants, I would fully maintain a profession devoted to the civil service of the state; and while relaxing its monopoly of office in some respects, would even extend its field of employment in others; but I would use the most stringent means to render that profession in the highest degree efficient, and would make admission to its ranks to depend on fitness more than on favour. I would particularly study economy in our enormously expensive military system; and I would strain every nerve to put our finances on a healthy footing. As I have already said, I do not propose to sacrifice revenue with one hand and to spend money with the other; but, first providing a surplus, I then spend it on the improvement of the country.

I would not retard, but in every way encourage, colonization, conversion, and the introduction of European morals, manners, and arts; I am even more sanguine than most people as to the aptness of the people to receive these benefits.

With a view both to colonization and to the efficiency of a European government, I strongly advocate a regard to considerations of climate in fixing our administrative stations and our political and social capitals.

If then we have but an efficient government, such as Parliament may now supply, the union of the advantages of freedom in constituting, and despotism in executing, a great imperial administration will be such as no other country possesses. India should be the best governed country in the world; and I fully believe that we might make it one of the most civilized and advanced countries in the world. I picture to myself India as it may be under an enlightened patriarchal empire, peaceable, prosperous, and Christian—its arts developed—its sciences perfected—its surface covered with useful works—its people educated, refined, and rich.

London, Feb. 15, 1853.

INDIA AS IT MAY BE.

CHAPTER I.

THE HOME GOVERNMENT.

Nature of question and main principle premised; nature of present defects; shall India be actively governed in India or in England? the controlling power of the Crown as at present exercised; evils to be remedied; proposed remedy; minor changes; the administrative board and its defects; proposed modes of election; proposed mode of joint nomination and election; summary of proposed Home Government; suggested changes in regard to India House establishment; the Court of Proprietors; proposed Court of Experts; patronage.

Nature of the question.

IT may be presumed that the public now sufficiently understands that the question as to that part of the administration of her Majesty's Indian territories which is conducted at home is in no wise involved in the rights or claims of what once was, and still in name is, the East India Company. Those rights have long since been determined: the part still played by the proprietors of East India stock in the election of an administrative board is merely intrusted to them for the public advantage; and we are now simply to discuss the form and mode in which India may be best and most conveniently governed, reference being had to English politics and facts as they exist, rather than as they might be under the most perfect theory.

Assumed main principle.

From the peculiar circumstances attending our acquisition of India has arisen a system of government, the main principle of which seems to be so well approved by all parties, as, under present circumstances, better and more practicable than any other, that there can be little doubt of its retention; and it were useless here to argue the matter. That principle consists in the exercise of the right of initiation and the management of details by a permanent board free from direct party influences and mutations, and the possession by her Majesty's Government of an absolute power of control over the proceedings of this administrative body, hitherto called the Court of Directors. Measures of ordinary administration do not necessarily or generally originate with the ministry of the day; and by the aid of the independent non-political and experienced Court our Indian policy is more uniform, better considered, and less exposed to the vicissitudes of party warfare, than that of other departments of the state. Indeed, the more one learns of the mode in which matters are conducted by parliamentary ministers, and of the influences to which they are subjected, the more one is convinced of the excessive good fortune of India, in being comparatively free from such evils. It is agreed, then, that on the one hand some such body as the Court of Directors must be preserved, and on the other, that as, under our constitution, Parliament, and the ministry which commands a majority in Parliament, must of necessity be all-powerful, the cabinet of the day must retain an absolute power of control.

Name of Crown or Company.

Whether this conjoint government is carried on in the name of the Crown or under the traditionary appellation of the Company—whether the Directors render fealty to the Crown or the Crown exercises authority over the Directors—is of little importance as concerns the Home Government; but I shall afterwards have occasion to notice the advantages to be derived from the use of the name of the Crown in India.

Premising, then, that no radical change can be made with advantage; that on the whole the Indian administration has not been abused; and that comparatively, at least, it is infinitely to be preferred to (for instance) the Colonial Office, we must consider what improvements can be made while we preserve the main principle. I think it will be found that there are considerable imperfections and weaknesses which in no way involve this principle. Although the present machine, complicated as it is, may seem in this country to work tolerably well, it is in India that its defects are felt; it is there that the results of its cumbrousness and slowness are every day practically experienced, acting as a clog and drag on onward progress. We should therefore, even whilst satisfied with the present solution of an English political difficulty, consider the claim of the government and people of India to an improvement of our machinery and acceleration of our pace. In truth, I believe that with all its faults the Home Government deliberates wisely and well, and that the greater part of all that emanates from it is worthy of much commendation. But it is in matters referred home from India for *previous* sanction that the difficulty of obtaining a prompt and decisive answer is found to be an evil of the most serious description, and one which is the subject of much local complaint. Whatever may be the rule in future, it is certain that hitherto it has been considered necessary to refer almost all important measures of internal administration for the previous orders of the Home Government, and that such a reference is apt to be looked upon as a sort of postponement *sine die*. The matter may or may not be revived by answer from England in from one to ten years, but for the present there is an end of it. Many important measures are

Nature of present defects.

discussed and changes suggested—all parties seem to approve—but at last comes the too often fatal and conclusive announcement—"the matter has been referred for the orders of the Court of Directors." Now, I by no means impute it to the fault of the Directors that this reference should frequently be, in fact, an indefinite postponement. That it should be so follows, and must follow, from the nature of the Home Government, from the complicity of the arrangements, the unbusiness-like construction of a large, nearly unpaid, and heterogeneous body, the great division of authority, and the intermeddling of a separate establishment in Cannon Row. However well inclined each individual may be, it is not to be expected that, regarding a great Indian question which gives scope for much difference of opinion among professional men, and to English minds is infinitely complex—it is not to be expected, I say, that the Chairman and Secretaries at the India House, the Clerks at the Board of Control, the President and Secretaries of the Board, and four-and-twenty easy-going elected Directors* in a constant state of rotation, and without any permanent division of business, or any fixed and professional leaders, that they should all, in any moderate time, come to a business-like decision on such a question. There is great security for their doing nothing rashly, but a very great temptation to let things remain as they are; while in fact there is immense scope and necessity for progress. This is the evil which, if we cannot altogether remedy, I believe that we may at least greatly mitigate. As it now stands, it does, beyond all question, very much retard the advance and improvement of the Indian administration; and it is on this

* I give the different authorities in the order in which business comes before them, commencing with the Chairman of the Directors and ending with the Directors collectively.

account that I fear the too great disposition now prevailing in this country—"*quieta non movere*"—to suppose that, because nothing goes excessively wrong at home, we may let well alone. I am far from wishing to see too active a Home Government, but I think that we should render it competent to keep pace with and abet Indian progress, and should secure this much, that it shall not act as a drag and over-check on an efficient Indian Government.

The Supreme Government has at present, according to the letter of the Act of Parliament, full power to act in everything, subject only to the subsequent orders of the Home Government: for instance, it may make any law, but is bound to repeal it if ordered to do so. In practice, however, the communication being now so speedy, and the inconvenience of reversal of accomplished acts so great, it has happened, as I have already stated, that most measures of importance (wars excepted) are referred home for previous sanction; and especially if an expenditure exceeding a very moderate sum is to be incurred, such a reference must be made even in matters of comparative little importance. Now, if it is necessary to wait for the decision of the Home Government, and that decision is not very promptly given, this practice is in fact a deprivation of the power of acting, and it is useless to give the Supreme Government a general authority over the several presidencies if it have not itself sufficient power.

The prodigiously detailed form in which everything is sent home, both by the Supreme and by every local Government, is one great cause of the slowness of the Home Government. Such masses of papers are received that the essential information is almost lost, or can only be gathered by intense labour. This practice, no doubt, originated in the detailed information of commercial matters necessary to a commercial company, but should now be materially altered.

Antecedent question – Shall India be governed in India or in England?

An important question then arises at the outset, of which we must first dispose. Is the General Government of India to be really in India or in England? Are the minor presidencies to be supervised by the Supreme Government or by the Home Government direct; and what is the degree of control which should be exercised by the Home Government over the Supreme Government in India? I think that this subject has not been sufficiently considered. It seems to me that there is not so much question of the relative power of the Board of Control and Court of Directors as of the Home Government generally and the Indian Supreme Government.

It is of the very utmost importance in every way that we should have one efficient central moving power for the whole of India, an active initiative centre, and we must decide whether this power is to be vested in the Governor-General and Council or in the Home Government. We may either intrust the Goverment of India to the former, and leave to the latter only the task of checking, controlling, and supervising its proceedings; or we may vest in the Home Government the imperial power—the direction of the several different presidencies—and merely give to one local government a political power of control in emergency, when time does not admit of a reference home.

When the presidencies in India were detached and separate settlements in different parts of a great continent, they were supposed to have no internal connection with one another; each was governed separately, and the Governor-General of Bengal had merely an exceptional power of control. But when India became one great country, subject to our universal rule, it was apparent that a central government was proper and necessary. It seems to have been the intention of the last Act of Parliament to vest this power in the Supreme Government; but then the Home Government still retained a simultaneous and parallel authority. While our empire has been consolidated in India, the means of communication with England have been so much expedited that it is now possible to refer things home in a comparatively short time. The subordinate presidencies correspond both with the Government of India and with the Home Government direct at the same time; and it has happened that, while the Government of India has by law an absolute control over the legislation and finance of the inferior presidencies (the very subjects which might, with least injury, be referred home), it does not, in fact, interfere much in executive matters. The latter are, for the most part, carried on by the local governments in correspondence with the home authorities, whose position, however calculated to digest laws or regulate finance, does not fit them for active executive functions. Now this division of authority is very injurious. What is several people's duty is no one's duty, and there seems to be a great want of executive generalization in the management of India. We must now determine either to make the Government of India thoroughly efficient for the management of *all* India, to relieve it from the clashing of a parallel authority, to subject the local governments to it completely, exclusively, and in everything, and to leave it to manage the empire, rendering an account to the Government at home; or we must relieve the local governments from a system of double checks and controls which hinder and embarrass them in some things, without prompting them or pushing them forward in others, and place them directly under an efficient Home

Government. We have altogether in the whole Indian system too many checks and too little to urge forward and ensure combined and uniform action. Everything is done disjointedly by individual efforts. A Sir Thomas Monro starts up as a great prophet in one age and place, a Mr. Thomason in another; but the results of their experience are nowhere united. They differ in many and important points: opposite systems are followed at the present day, and the right hand of the empire does not even know what the left hand doeth. There is intense centralization of checks, but no centralization whatever of execution beyond the limits of each separate Governor or Lieutenant-Governor. It was clearly the intention of Parliament to remedy this evil, but the object was not sufficiently effected, and another effort to the same end must be made. Meantime steam has raised the question (which has rendered it necessary for me to discuss the matter in this chapter), Shall the central executive be in India or in London? If we lived under an efficient despot, who could at once select, appoint, and maintain a Board of the best working-men in the empire to sit in Leadenhall-Street, there would be, if not a preponderance, at least a very strong array, of arguments in favour of London. We ought to be, and I hope may be, pretty free from wars in future; and for matters of internal administration, the time now consumed in the actual transit of despatches between the presidency Governors and Leadenhall-Street would be (supposing a centralized and untrammelled Home Government, which would answer as promptly and decidedly as the Governor-General) no overwhelming objection. It would seem a good and natural arrangement, that the best of tried Indian talent—now most lamentably thrown away after retirement to England—should be made available; that first-rate Indian ex-officials, whose health has failed in India, or who claim in a cessation of exile the reward of their labours, should be employed in that portion of the government which can now be conducted at home. We should thus obtain a permanence and a concentration of the ability of successive periods, such as we have not had in the constantly changing Governors-General and Councils. Recent practice would from time to time be added to matured experience; the assistance of jurists, too, would be more accessible than in India; and a very efficient government might be formed. It is true that men might hardly be the same exclusively-devoted and energetic public servants in this country as in India, where, isolated as they are, their whole souls are in their official duties; it is true that in lapse of time personal Indian knowledge and Indian associations might wane; it is true that, while in India a man's physical energies generally decay before his mind, and he retires before he ceases to be efficient, in England a great and good man might decline into senility, and it might be difficult to get rid of him; but still, all things considered, I believe that London might be the seat of government if, as I have said, we lived under a despotic constitution, and could in any way secure the appointment of the best men. This, however, is the difficulty; England is not a despotic country, and it would be difficult to maintain a good despotic government in England. The Court of Directors, as at present constituted, is not at all of the nature of an executive body. Executive efficiency is always in the inverse ratio to numbers; it would be necessary very much to reduce the numbers and to form a permanent Board of paid men of business. Is it possible, under our political constitution, to secure the impartial appointment of such a Board? It is generally supposed that it is not. The number being limited, we must have not only some, but *all*, good men—and not only good men, but the very best men. It may be doubted whether we could depend on so much public virtue; still more may it be doubted whether, if such a Board were formed, they could, in this country, be preserved free from various personal influences. Yet, with all the disadvantages, I confess that I should much prefer to intrust the central administration to a Board at home, constituted as I am about to propose, rather than to the present Council of India, located in Calcutta, in a bad climate, always separated from the Commander-in-Chief, and generally from the Governor-General, and constituted in a manner inconsistent with executive efficiency. But if, on the other hand, the Council of India be posted permanently and advantageously in a healthy climate, where the presence of the Governor-General, the Commander-in-Chief, and the heads of departments may be secured, and if it be rendered strong and efficient enough in its constitution, then it will be infinitely preferable to intrust to the Governor-General and Council the initiative and general executive direction of all things; and to make the Home Board merely a deliberative and controlling body, to whom the Indian Government should be responsible for its acts.

What would intrust to Indian Government;

Still it is impossible and undesirable altogether to free the Indian Government from a practical obligation in some degree previously to ascertain and consult the wishes of the Home Government. The latter must have entire power over the Government in India, and, if efficient, its policy in large and lasting questions is likely to be more uniform and better considered than that of successive governors of varied views and experience. It would be, therefore, highly inconvenient that, in very important matters which admit of a reference home, the Indian Government should act without the knowledge of the

and what leave with home Government.

Home Government, or without giving it an opportunity of expressing its views. I would not attempt to abrogate the reasonable and discreet use of a wholesome practice. I would transfer the executive direction of the minor presidencies and the management of details to the Supreme Government in India. I would remedy the evils which have hitherto accrued from continual and minute references by confining these references to really important *principles* and large expenditure, by putting them into convenient form, and ceasing to oppress the Home Government with such masses of manuscript and detail, by providing that the Indian Government should sufficiently perform its duty by announcing important measures contemplated by it, and giving reasonable time for an expression of opinion, and that it should not be bound to wait an unreasonable time in the absence of decided and intelligible orders; and more particularly, I would obviate the difficulty by so simplifying and improving the Home Government that it may be expected in reasonable time to arrive at a sound, clear, and conclusive decision on matters so referred to it.

It is with this view that I would consider the details of the Home Government.

First, then, let us look to the form and mode of exercising the controlling power of the Crown.

Controlling power of the Crown, as at present exercised.

It appears that at present, although this power is nominally vested in a board composed of the chief members of the Cabinet, it is practically exercised by one minister alone. The President of the India Board is a cabinet minister, who, in most instances, has had little previous experience of Indian affairs. He has two parliamentary secretaries, who like himself are unprofessional, coming in and going out with a party; but he has no other responsible and constitutional advisers. His office is at Westminster, at the opposite end of London from that of the Court of Directors. He seems to be under no obligation of personally consulting either his colleagues in the ministry or the Directors.

Board of Control, constitution of.

When he happens to be in town he generally sees the Chairmen of the Direction once a week, but beyond this he is not necessarily brought into contact with the Directors; and it rests with the President personally how far he admits them into his confidence. All business between the Court and Board is transacted in writing, which involves the copying, transmission, and retransmission of every paper. For the transaction of this business there is in the Board of Control an establishment of clerks under head clerks of departments, who have risen, by a long course of service, to that situation. Some very efficient persons are known to have held these latter appointments; but this fact must be principally attributed to good fortune; for I find from a return attached to the report of the Committee of the House of Commons (p. 344) that the subordinate offices of the Board of Control constitute a strictly seniority service, each officer, from the highest to the lowest, ranking and being paid according to length of service. The scale of salary seems to be about 100*l.* per annum for every four years' service. The senior has served forty-eight years, and receives 1200*l.*; the first assistant, thirty-two years, and receives 800*l.*; the juniors, six years, and receive 150*l.* each. The experience of all must be exclusively confined to the office in Cannon Row. I am not aware that there is any test of qualification on appointment to this service.

The Board thus constituted has absolute power over the proceedings of the Court of Directors, with certain exceptions; but that power is very differently exercised in the ordi-

Powers of; and mode of conducting business.

nary internal administration, and in matters involving external politics. In the former the Directors have both a constitutional and a practical part; in the latter, three Directors, bound to secrecy, act as little more than mere ministerial officers of the Board.

In ordinary matters the customary mode of transacting business I understand to be this:

Drafts of despatches proposed for transmission to India are prepared at the India House under the orders of the Chairman and Deputy Chairman, and are sent to the Board for approval, in the form of a previous communication, which is not a mere general note of what is proposed, but a detailed draft, and frequently a very bulky document, accompanied by masses of enclosures. A previous communication goes into the hands of the head clerk of the department, and is by him submitted, with his own suggestions, first to the Secretary, and afterwards to the President. The draft is not only formally approved or negatived, but is varied and altered as the Board sees fit, and is then returned. It appears that nearly one-half of the previous communications (including probably most of the long and important despatches) are more or less altered by the Board of Control; but a large proportion of these alterations are said to be of a verbal and unimportant character.

A proposed despatch now, for the first time, comes under the cognisance of the Committee of the Directors to whose department it belongs; so that if they would make any change they must commence the discussion *de novo*, in opposition to what has been proposed and approved by the Chairs and the Board, and considerable delay and difficulty may probably ensue.

The matter being considered in Committee, the formal despatch is drawn up and submitted to the Directors collectively; but it is not surprising, under the circumstances, that the previous communication, as corrected, is seldom, and only in very particular cases, deviated from. The despatch is now again sent to the Board of Control for official sanction, and this time the proportion of cases in which alterations are made does not exceed five per cent., and in case of alteration the President must give his reasons in full. The Court may remonstrate against alterations, but, having once done so, and received the President's answer, the discussion is closed. The Court may record a protest, but, as a body, have seldom done so.

Everything is supposed to originate with the Court, but the Board may direct the preparation of a despatch on any subject, and when it is prepared may alter it even to the extent of cancelling it, and writing another, which the Court must adopt. The Board has, therefore, *practically* the power of initiating measures, but this power is comparatively seldom exercised.

Time consumed.

Considerable delay necessarily occurs in so complicated a system, but the establishments are efficient, and the delays in current business are not greater than might be expected. Ordinary current despatches from India are said to be disposed of in some six or eight months on an average, and in cases of urgency, if all parties agree, the matter may be settled much more quickly; but there can be no doubt that considerable administrative questions occupy a *very* much longer time, and sometimes in the end no definite decision is arrived at.

Political and secret power.

In all questions of peace and war, or of our external relations and connections with native states in which the President of the Board may think secrecy desirable, he has, in fact, the power of setting aside the Directors altogether, and of sending and receiving despatches through the Secret Committee of the Direction, whose functions are, as has been observed, purely ministerial, who have not even the power of remonstrance, and who can only object if the order be actually contrary to law. In like manner, the Indian governors may send despatches to the Secret Committee for the orders of the President. The Secret Committee in no way consists of the members of the Direction most qualified to advise on political subjects, but is in practice a sort of *ex-officio* committee composed of the Chairman, Deputy Chairman, and Senior Director.* It appears that this power of the Board has been very freely exercised. The Affghan war, the occupation of Scinde,† the Burmese war, are all subjects in which the Court of Directors had no opportunity of interfering, and they have even been kept for years without information on matters in the secret department, or have been indebted for it, in common with the rest of the public, to Parliamentary blue books. On these subjects the President of the Board is constitutionally just as absolute as the Colonial Minister or the Commander-in-Chief of the army in their respective departments, and, in practice, a great deal more so, from the much smaller amount of knowledge and interest acting on public opinion in this country in regard to Indian affairs, and from the secrecy of his proceedings.

Appointments to the offices of Governor and Commander-in-Chief are made by the Directors, but must be sanctioned by the Crown, and are practically determined by the Crown, with the consent of the Directors.

The only exceptions of any importance to the ultimate power of the Board of Control are—the recall by the Directors of any servant from the Governor-General

* Young merchants and bankers are sometimes elected to the Direction—young men of Indian experience never: hence the senior Director (in order of election) is hardly ever of the latter class.

† Even *after* the occupation of Scinde the administration was for three years carried on in the secret department. This was a great abuse.

downwards—the appointment of Members of Council —the inferior patronage—and perhaps certain disbursements from the home treasury. In these things the Board cannot interfere. They may limit the number of inferior appointments (cadetships, civil appointments, &c.) made by the Court, and enforce the prescribed rules, but can neither name nor veto the persons appointed.

Exceptions to controlling power.

The fact seems to be, that in the ordinary internal administration, the India House, generally exercising the initiative, and possessing a knowledge of details which the Board has not, does in reality form to a great extent the effective Home Government of India, and that serious difference of opinion seldom arises between the Court and Board; but that an unnecessary interference in minute details is practised by the Board, and that the efficiency of the Court is thereby checked and impaired. In political matters, on the other hand, the power of the Board is absolute, undivided, and unchecked. There results from the complication of the system this important circumstance, that it is sometimes very difficult or impossible officially to ascertain the real authors of particular measures, and no one exactly knows on whom to charge the responsibility.

General result.

The extent to which the Indian Minister may consult his colleagues is, of course, one of those cabinet and personal secrets which cannot be made known to the vulgar; but we have the authority of an ex-President for saying that he never consulted even Sir Robert Peel when that great man was at the head of the Government. The same high authority informs us that he would not consult the Chairman or any Director rather than any other individuals in the kingdom on account of their filling those offices. If he wanted advice he would go

Relation of President to his colleagues in the Cabinet.

to the person he thought most competent in or out of office.

The exercise of a divided authority is necessarily attended with some disadvantages; but having observed the manner of the power now exercised by her Majesty's Ministers, let us see whether those disadvantages can be any way mitigated.

The present evils seem then to be as follows:—

1. The delay and expense of the double system.
2. An excess of check in the transaction of ordinary business.
3. The want of competent counsel in the transaction of extraordinary or secret business.

Disadvantages of present system.

These evils may be attributed not so much to the nature of the power vested in the Ministry as to the form in which it is exercised. It is evident enough that a double and sometimes treble reference from one place to another, and from one power to another, the voluminous manuscript thereby involved, and the maintenance of a separate establishment in Cannon Row, must cause delay and expense. The expense is not in so great a matter a very pressing consideration; and although the delay is an important drawback, I do not think that the evil thus directly caused is so great as the indirect effect in checking to excess, and acting as a drag on the administrative machine. It has been held that the great advantage of the present system consists in the multitude of checks, by which it is insured that nothing shall be precipitately done. But I believe the fact to be, that in everything except making war (the only subject in which there is no check whatever) we stand much more in need of spurs than checks. Caution and consideration have never been wanting to the Court of Directors, and the only complaint is, that they do not move fast enough. Much of this *vis inertiæ* is owing to the separation of authority. It has been mentioned that the Board in ordinary matters seldom initiates—that duty is, for the most part, left to the Directors—but it is not unnatural, and is, I believe, the fact, that the latter are less willing to undertake important measures involving extensive alteration on account of the uncertainty as to the adoption of their plans by a separate office constantly liable to change, and with which they are not in personal communication. Much of the inconvenience has, no doubt, been obviated by the personal character of the Presidents, and their disposition to avail themselves of the experience of the Directors and to maintain a good understanding; but under the most favourable circumstances, advance is much retarded, and there may again be a President who will pride himself on consulting none of those officially connected with him. It is not the legitimate exercise of their own judgment by the President and secretaries which is to be deprecated so much as an undue interference with details. As I understand it, it is no part of the scheme of conjoint government that the President or secretaries should be professionally acquainted with or informed of details. The object is, that over the proceedings of expert persons reasonable control should be exercised by an English gentleman of superior talents and acquirements bringing merely sound common sense to bear on the subject, and rather controlling what he sees to be amiss than directing what he does not sufficiently understand. He is, therefore, not provided with any constitutional and responsible professional advisers. His establishment is one of clerks, and there is no officer corresponding to the permanent under-secretaries attached to the other departments of the Government. An inexperienced President assisted by a Cabinet of irresponsible clerks can by no means with advantage meddle in details. Such interference must be at the same time inefficient for practical good and offensive to an important body charged with important duties. Yet it would appear that, while there is seldom material difference of opinion between the President and the Court, nearly one-half of the previous communications are more or less altered in details, or what are called *verbal* alterations are made. Now, by whom are these petty and verbal alterations made, and what are they? A Cabinet Minister need hardly be employed to correct the grammar of the Court of Directors. That respectable body can either write English themselves or pay some one else to write it for them. Still we may assume that the Minister can generally write better English than the Directors, and, being qualified to correct their composition, no great harm would come from verbal alterations made by him. But is this the real nature of the alterations, or is it the case that the clerks of the Board of Control are permitted to use their pens upon and alter the details of the drafts emanating from the India House? If it is so, I should say that the practice is an exceedingly bad one, and very unfair to the Directors. The fact is, that some system of previous communication is probably under present arrangements necessary, in order to avoid jarring and official complications; but the result of the present method must be to give to the Board a power over details not intended by the law. It is one thing to draw a pen through a sentence here and write another there in a previous communication, and another officially to alter a despatch for reasons assigned. Yet the Court may find it easier and more expedient to submit to the one in fifty, than to let it come to the other in ten out of a hundred cases.*

* Here is a specimen of the kind of interference exercised. The Governor-General in council lately applied to the Court of Directors for two dozen

All this is the disadvantage of over-checking; but the third evil which I have noticed is the absence of counsel or check of any kind in the secret department. Wars are no doubt generally determined by the Governor-General in India, and in sending orders promptitude is very necessary; but still, if these matters are to be controlled at home at all, it seems very undesirable that they should be left so completely in the hands of the President, without the knowledge, assistance, and constitutional advice which is generally available in other departments. If a secret cannot be trusted to a large body, surely the President should at least be bound to consult and have the constant opportunity of consulting some smaller number of selected and qualified advisers, whose opinions should be recorded whether acted on or no. It is certain that in such unfortunate instances as Affghanistan and Scinde the Directors have always held views which in the end turned out to be just.

Such then are the evils of the present system of double government. But in devising remedies we must be careful to avoid any change which will interfere with the independence of the inferior administrative body, or throw a larger share of the practical administration into the hands of the Minister of the Crown. In fact, the present distribution of functions must be maintained without material alteration. Can we find any means of mitigating the acknowledged evils of the existing system which will not violate these indispensable conditions? One very simple remedy seems to me to suggest itself, and that is to bring the Minister of the Crown into personal communication with the Directors; so to arrange that he shall exercise his

Proposed remedy.

of Bramah's patent locks for his offices. The Court proposed to grant the same. Remark by Clerk of Board of Control:—"I think one dozen and a half would be quite enough." Order altered to one dozen and a half. Such is the story as told to me.

functions, not by written correspondence and through a separate office establishment, but in the same building and in immediate contact with the body charged with and responsible for details, and his legitimate advisers in all things. I draw a distinction between a double and a conjoint government. I fully admit the necessity of a division, or rather distribution, of power and of administrative functions; but I think that the separate functions may be exercised simultaneously as it were; that we may have two workmen in the same workshop, instead of sending every piece of work backwards and forwards; and in this way we may retain all the advantages of a distribution of labour, while we avoid the delay and complication of separate establishments. We may still, if we please, call it a double government; but we shall no longer have two altogether separate governments—one to do and another to undo. The proposed transfer of a great part of the present functions of the Home Government to the Supreme Government in India would also much facilitate the arrangement, and take away much ground of objection.

If then, by merely removing the President with all his powers from one building to another some three miles off, we save all the delay, expense, inconvenience, and injury of a separate office—if, while we continue the absolute power of the Ministry, we avoid much of the undue interference with details and impediments to forward progress which result from divided authority, and at the same time insure that the Indian Minister shall act with the assistance and counsel of those best qualified to give him information and advice, we have a great gain very easily acquired.

Why then should not the President be under the same roof and make use of the same office establishment as the Court of Directors? Why should he not exercise his powers in immediate personal communication with the Court, urging rather than checking their progress, fully learning their views, and deriving from them proper and constitutional assistance? It seems at first sight that it would not be difficult to arrange such an amalgamation. Whatever be the relative powers of the President and the Court, it would be a great thing that they should be exercised, as it were, in the same atmosphere. The separate establishment of clerks in Cannon Row to supervise the proceedings of the India House is by no means an advantage, but quite the contrary. Unless the Directors were suspected of abusing their functions (which they are not), why should the President see matters with different eyes from theirs—why should not the same persons who have put in shape their views expound them to the President—and why should he not verbally receive projects of future improvement? Are the Directors such dangerous people that the President cannot be trusted within their influence? Knowledge is to a certain extent power, and so far I believe that the Directors would exercise, and it is very desirable that they should exercise, an influence over the President such as the fixed employés in all public offices exercise over their political superiors.

Objection thereto.

I confess that I have always looked on this plan as practicable and highly desirable in every way, and that I do not yet understand any insuperable objection to it. The influence of authority in matters of opinion must however be respected, and there is no doubt that some of the best qualified persons seem at present to hold the necessity of continuing the separate office of the Board of Control. It is said that the separation of the offices is required to protect India from the evil influence of party politics. The authority ranged on this side of the question I will not presume to dispute; but I may be permitted here to explain briefly the plan which I would advocate.

Explanation and arguments in favour of.

All must concur in considering it a most indispensable object to exclude as much as possible the influence of political party and parliamentary pressure, and I have commenced by assuming the retention of an independent Board charged with the initiative of administration, and the principle of a conjoint exercise of power. But I cannot see the advantage of separating by a few miles, and thus detaching the working of, the two parts of the machine of Government. Parliament must always have the power of demanding information regarding, and it may be interfering in, Indian affairs; and if this power has been little exercised, it is simply because the members have known and cared little about the matter. Of late, however, things have considerably altered: information is constantly called for,* and Indian affairs are sometimes discussed. This disposition must and will go on increasing, as a knowledge of and interest in India becomes more general; but it will be (I should have thought) by no means greater or more dangerous if the Indian Minister exercises his power in Leadenhall-street, than if he does so in Cannon-row. The only objects are that our Indian policy should not be attacked by one party, because the acts are those of another party; that power should not be used for party purposes; and that the Minister should not absorb the initiative management. He should be able to say, "This is not my capricious doing; I have acted with the advice and consent of the same important body who exercised the same functions under other Ministries." Hitherto there has been indeed this supposed advantage already

* For example I may instance the two enormous volumes published on the Outram affair. The whole essence of the matter, so far as concerns Outram, lies in half a dozen pages.

alluded to, that in ordinary matters, when a despatch is signed by the Directors and sanctioned by the President, it is difficult to fix on any individual the responsibility of its authorship, and a Radical seeking for a victim may sometimes be at fault. But this would equally be the case if measures were settled in friendly verbal discussion. The responsibility would be collective. If the President officially overrules the fixed and recorded opinion of the Court, he must bear the responsibility, and it is right that he should do so. Besides, it is not often that our Indian revenue or judicial measures are made the subject of stirring harangues in the House of Commons. Those subjects are far too dry, and, if need be, the Government might be well prepared to meet the light. The acts most likely to be called in question are those of the secret department. Till within the last year or two, an idea may have popularly prevailed that the Company had something to do with the Company's political transactions, but that veil is at last finally torn off. We now know positively that the Burmese war, for instance, lies as much between Lord Dalhousie and the President of the India Board, as the Cape war between the Governor of the Cape and the Colonial Minister; and the policy of the Government is as open to attack as in any other department whatever.

The real question consists in this,—whether by the proposed change the actual power and influence of the President will be increased. I believe that not only it would not be so, but that the President would be brought so much more under the salutary influence of the Directors, that some of the present restrictions on his ultimate power of control might in compensation be with safety and advantage removed. I would combine with the proposed arrangement such a remodelling of the Court of Directors, that the President should be no nearer to the initiative than before. I would by no means unite his present functions with those of the chairman of the Court of Directors, but would transfer the initiative and executive duties of the latter to chairmen of committees, and drafts would come before the President only when duly digested by competent persons. They might verbally ascertain his views, and impress on him theirs; but there would be an end to the practice of cutting and carving previous communications.

If then the alteration be made with due precaution to prevent the minister's absorbing too large a share of the initiative and executive business, I cannot see that he will be more answerable to Parliament than at present. I would transfer him to Leadenhall-street, and he should exercise power as minister of the Crown presiding over the Court of Directors, or body substituted in their place. The government would be conducted in the name of the Crown (for Indian reasons to be afterwards mentioned), through the President and Council, or Senate* of the Indies.

Proposed arrangements.

There would be no farther necessity for a separate establishment. All despatches received from India and all proposed measures would be in the first instance referred to the committees of the Senate, and by them everything would be initiated, and drafts of despatches and orders would be prepared before being submitted to the President and Senate collectively.

The signature of the President would be necessary to all proceedings, and he would exercise a general power of veto, by refusing, in his place at the head of the

* I shall use the term Senate to distinguish the English from the Indian Council, not as claiming any originality. In this I humbly follow Lord Ellenborough.

Senate, his sanction to measures approved by the majority; record of the circumstance and of the President's reasons being made. I would make no exception of any kind to this right of veto. It would also be necessary (unless the present power of the ministry were to be materially limited) that the President should retain the power of ultimately altering and superseding, on the ministerial responsibility, the drafts proposed by the committees, and approved by the majority of the Senate.

He might, much in the same way as at present, require the committees of the Senate to prepare a despatch or resolution on a particular subject, alter despatches so prepared by them, for reasons recorded by him, and require of the Senate to execute the amended orders. But if the majority of the Senate protest, I would make the Cabinet collectively distinctly responsible, and with this view would require the signature of the First Lord of the Treasury and two Secretaries of State. The method of putting in force absolute power makes a great difference. If the President were permitted simply to present orders for execution in the name of the Crown, he might absorb the initiative, whereas, by the system of suggesting and altering, and in case of irreconcilable difference obtaining the signature of his colleagues, though he may, if necessary, attain his object, he will comparatively seldom exercise that power, and the present checks on the ministerial proceedings will be retained and increased, the more from the President having no longer a separate establishment for the express purpose of assisting him in intermeddling. I would except, as at present, patronage and grants of money from the power of the President to substitute and increase, giving him the veto in these things, as in others.

In regard to the business of the secret department, I would limit it strictly to those things in which secrecy is really necessary, and would have a properly qualified secret committee of the Senate, who must be consulted, and whose opinion must be recorded, leaving it in the power of the President to overrule that opinion on his own responsibility; and if the committee protest, requiring the signature of the three other members of the Cabinet, in the same way as in case of protest by the Senate.

Anticipated results.

I cannot help thinking that on this system, while the ultimate power of the ministry in great things would not be curtailed, or might even be somewhat extended, the facility of intermeddling in details would be considerably abridged; both the administration would be more speedy, energetic, and systematic, and there would be less opportunity for the interference and influence of party politicians than at present. It is now impossible to say how much the President may have interfered, and he becomes in a measure (when an active person is in office) responsible for everything; whereas, in future, his duties would be well defined, and the chief responsibility would rest with those not obnoxious to party.

My argument is that it is not the power of the President, but his separate establishment, that does the mischief, and that, if, instead of living in a separate official atmosphere of his own, he was transferred to that of the India House, he might retain as great real and useful power, and at the same time less habitually exercise a pernicious interference.

I cannot apprehend that the President could in any way encroach upon or absorb the initiative or executive, seeing that the committees who would exercise these powers would be quite independent of him. The only change in this respect would be that the President and Senators would be in personal communication with one another. In such communication it seems to me that well-qualified Senators would be much more likely beneficially to influence the President, than the President to influence the Senators to an undue extent; and when they agree or differ, it is much better that the members of the committee should know at once how the matter stands, than that they should be under the continual apprehension of disapproval or interference in everything which they may send up.

I have said that I would give the President full power of veto in *all* cases without exception, to be exercised in a deliberate, constitutional, responsible way, for recorded reasons. But I do not mean to include in this clause acts of dismissal, which are rather negative than positive acts. The principle of appointment being joint confidence, a cessation of that joint confidence terminates the appointment, and it is on this principle that either the Directors or the Crown may recall a servant.

Power of recall.

This involves the much-disputed question of the present power of the Court of Directors to recall the highest servants, and especially the Governor-General. The danger to be apprehended from allowing the President to veto a vote of the Senate for the recall of a Governor-General is that a refractory Governor-General, and a consenting or collusive President, might set the wishes and legal orders of the Senate altogether at defiance in an irregular way, the Governor disobeying orders, and the Minister refusing to recall him. There would be great danger in taking the matter altogether out of the hands of the Senate. Considerable, however, as are the immediate advantages of the present limit of the power of the ministry in this respect, it is a constitutional anomaly which might possibly cause considerable embarrassment. And I shall not venture to solve that constitutional question. I shall only say, that, if the anomaly can be got over, it is very desirable that both the Senate and the Crown should separately have the power of dismissing any servant either in India or in England. In any case the rule must be reciprocal, either that each may dismiss or that both must concur in dismissing. I think, however, that it would be well to require a concurrence of three-fourths of the Senate in a vote for the dismissal of a Governor-General, if they are permitted to exercise that power independent of the Crown.

I should say that a control or veto over all inferior appointments made by the Senate might be exercised by the Minister without danger and with considerable benefit, and that it should be his special charge to see that no unfit persons are sent out.

If remedy rejected, minor improvements suggested.

If, however, it be decided that it is impossible to unite under one roof the Board of Control and Court of Directors, that the President must still be kept apart, and must still have a separate office establishment, it might be well to do something either to limit the practice of interfering in details, or to provide responsible advisers of the President in such interference.

Some previous communication of intended measures may, no doubt, be advantageous, but it should be confined to a general note of the proposed arrangements to pass between the heads of the India House Committees and the President and Secretaries of the Board, whose *English* intellects are to be brought to bear on it. The *detailed* previous communication of a despatch, to be subjected to the *professional* criticism of the Board of Control establishment, might, I should think, with advantage be discontinued; and when a despatch is officially sent up for sanction, the Board's duties should be confined to approval, disapproval, or material alteration, for written reasons assigned. There should be no interference, without specified reasons, in smaller matters, or in anything in which the President and Parliamentary Secretaries do not think themselves, *unaided*, competent to overrule the judgment of the Senators. The chairmen of committees should have every facility of personally communicating with the President.

Or if it be considered right that every despatch should be *professionally* revised and criticised by a separate establishment, there should be added to the Board either additional paid and professional members, or permanent competent and responsible secretaries, who might stand forth to the world as exercising a large share of the government of India, instead of being shrouded in the mysteries of a bureaucracy.

In the secret department, an efficient secret committee being provided at the India House, their opinions should be given and recorded as formerly proposed, the President having the option, in case of emergency, of transmitting orders after hearing their arguments for the space of one hour and considering for one day, of which proceeding minutes should be made.

The Administrative Board.

Next we are to consider the constitution of that administrative Court, or Council, or Senate, which all agree must continue to form an essential part of the system. A great part of the present functions of the Court of Directors (especially in regard to the inferior presidencies) being transferred to the Indian Government, and business being only reported or referred home in a more advanced stage, great part of the objection to the present Court would cease to be tenable, and it would undoubtedly be a good deliberative body, containing within itself a great mass of Indian knowledge and experience. But the question is, can it not be made better? Its constitution is in many respects faulty.

It may be no great evil that there are many members of the Court whose absence would not be felt. If they do no good, they also do little harm. But a very great and crying evil, and one which most assuredly demands a remedy, is that fact which is admitted on all hands, viz. that, while a numerous Board for the management of Indian affairs exists, the majority of the most efficient public servants who come from India in the prime of life and intellect are by the present system absolutely excluded from any share in Indian affairs. It is quite lamentable to see the men who, after surviving five-and-twenty years of incessant labour in exile in a tropical climate, think themselves entitled to retire to their native country before it is too late—the very best men of a great profession, trained to business from their youth upwards—men who have ruled kingdoms and determined the destinies of millions of their fellow-creatures — to see them at five-and-forty sinking down into small country gentlemen with nothing to do, or into careless water-drinking old Indians. One feels that there must be something wrong when one reads *obscure* among obscure Buckinghamshire magistrates such a name as that of Robert Mertins Bird, familiar as their household gods to some five-and-twenty millions of Asiatics whose all-important interests have been regulated by him, but whose existence is almost unknown in this country. There is no lack of work for men of business in the service of England. The civil service of the state in its higher departments was never a regular profession, and since the Reform Bill has ceased to be professed at all. We depend for everything on accidental or amateur talent. But Indians (who alone of Englishmen have

Evil of exclusion of most fit men.

followed this profession) do not make fortunes now-a-days. Parliament is seldom open to them: the avenues of occupation and advancement are therefore closed, and they live but on the past. Surely the Indian home administration should from so great a supply be well filled. Here, at least, should be a useful occupation for the great men of the East. Unfortunately the Direction can only be entered by election. Election can only be attained by canvassing for years the most sweet voices of the proprietors of East India stock; by continued harassing labour, personal humiliation, and city connection. The best men generally think that they have purchased exemption from the first of these requisites; they have little taste for the second; they are seldom possessed of the third; and I may add, that the position of a Director, partly owing to the vexatious power exercised by the clerks of the Board of Control, and partly to the constitution of the Court itself, is not such as to make it, except as a source of patronage, the great object of ambition which it ought to be to the most distinguished of retiring Indians. It is therefore a fact beyond dispute, that in most cases they prefer to subside into insignificance.

A canvass for the East India Direction generally lasts about seven years. It is sometimes asserted that eminent men have got in, and may get in, with comparatively little trouble; but that statement is not borne out by facts. There are a few instances of very distinguished men who have come in, not with little trouble, but with less than the average labour. One in particular is adduced of a man very eminent in the Indian service, who was elected before he had been three years at home; but I believe that in every such instance the eminence will be found to have been combined with the accident of connection and interest, and that these cases are the exception, not the rule. As the instance to which I have most particularly referred has been quoted to the Committees of Parliament, and is the strongest—indeed, I may say, the only one—on that side of the question, I would venture to recommend that that eminent man should himself be sent for, and asked—first, whether, even in his case, the canvass was a light matter; and, second, whether in his opinion he would, with all his eminence, have come in nearly so soon if he had not been powerfully backed by a strong personal connection and interest among the voters. No one has a more lively sense of the disagreeables of the approach to the Direction than those who have surmounted them and got in; and I believe the fact to be, that the difficulties are increasing every day; that the evil is a rapidly growing one. Indeed, the canvassing system is now carried so far, that the electors have it not in their power to elect the best man when a vacancy occurs. They are pledged five or six deep; and when a new candidate comes from India they may be obliged to say, "I admit your claims; I would vote for you if I could, but I am already pledged to so many that I cannot do so for a number of years to come."

In practice, it is the fact that the majority of the Directors are now men who have had more or less experience in India, and that there are among them some highly distinguished and many very good and much to be respected men, but still they are not elected, by any means, according to the measure of fitness; nor can any man get in except by a most protracted and unpleasant struggle (to which the patronage is the principal inducement), and till the very years in which, fresh from the scene, he might be most useful have passed away. There are also a considerable number of Directors who have no Indian experience whatever. Their holding the office is justified on the ground of the advantage of having an admixture of the leaven of English minds in the Court. And the argument is doubtless a very sound one, if we suppose working English men of business to be introduced as active members of the Court. But what is the fact? I believe that the English Directors are, without exception, merchants and bankers of the city—men who have affairs of their own to attend to, which are to them infinitely more important, who take office for the sake of the patronage, and through city influence. They were, no doubt, the most fitting directors of a commercial company; but I confess that for the government of India I can see no advantage in their filling many places at the Board while so many experienced men are excluded. It is every way desirable to have in the Direction one or two Englishmen from each of several classes, but not a large number of one particular class.

Much of what is wanting to the efficiency of the Court of Directors, and to the position of a Director, is owing to the internal constitution of the Court; and the defects principally arise from arrangements which were very proper for the management of the affairs of a great joint-stock company, but which have become quite inappropriate to the government of an empire. The Directors are nominally elected for four years, but virtually (by a system of combination) for life. Each must remain out one year in five; so that there are really thirty Directors, of whom six are always out by rotation, and all are continually changing their relative positions (as if they were annually shaken up together in a hat or a kaleidoscope) in a way which must go far to destroy their efficiency. The body is too numerous to do busi-

Evils resulting from commercial constitution of East India Direction.

ness, in the first instance, collectively. It is divided into committees, who take up different subjects; but these committees are every year appointed by rotation, so that a financier is one year on the judicial, and the next on the military committee, and no one has any chance of a continued supervision of a particular department. Even the committees, such as they are, are only, as it were, consultative committees. The whole initiative and executive seem to be nominally in the hands of the Chairman and Deputy-Chairman, and practically for the most part (except when there happens to be a remarkably efficient Chairman) in those of the subordinate establishment. The Chairs are elected each year by the Directors, and are almost invariably changed each year. I think I may say that they are elected rather with reference to their personal qualifications to preside over a miscellaneous body of Englishmen, and to make a good figure in transactions at home, than as signifying an opinion that they are the Directors most qualified to govern India, and also that most Directors have some time or other their turn of filling the Chair, whether they have Indian experience or not. I understand that the Director who will occupy that post in the ensuing last year of the present term has never been in India, and that the business of the East India Direction is not his profession or his most important avocation.

For the transaction of business there is at the India House a large and efficient establishment of secretaries, examiners, and clerks. This home service of the Company does not seem to follow any strict rule of seniority; but I do not know that there is more than one instance of a retired Indian servant now employed. It generally consists of English men of business employed by the Court of Directors, most of whom make it the profession of their lives;

East India House establishment.

while others are specially entertained. To all despatches received from India answers are prepared by the departmental officers of the India House establishment, under the direction of and in communication with the Chair and Deputy Chair; and this is the previous communication which, as I have before noticed, is sent to the Board of Control, there corrected, and generally settled between the Board and the Chairs, before the Committee see it at all. If the Chair and Deputy Chair do not happen to be Indian professional men, acquainted with the particular subject under discussion, it must be of necessity that the management of details is much more in the hands of the subordinate officers than in those of the Committee, to whom a matter goes after all other parties have expressed their opinion, and with whom therefore, in fact, rests only a power of remonstrance, very useful, no doubt, when the object was to see that their money was not misspent, but hardly sufficient for the duty of managing a great department.

Remedies for exclusion of best men from Direction.

For that part of the system which excludes from the Direction all Indian officers, whatever their qualifications, who do not care to canvass for years, and do not canvass with success, some remedy is absolutely necessary. What shall it be? You must first, by diminishing the patronage and raising the official position of a Director, make a seat in the Direction less an object to ordinary influence—less a valuable subject of canvass, and more an object of honest ambition to official men. Then as to the mode of appointment. The only two methods of constituting Directors are election and nomination. First, then, can the mode of election be altered for the better? and secondly, can any plan of nomination be substituted? I must say that I much doubt the possibility of devising any very greatly improved system of popular election, for this reason: that all kinds of schemes have been propounded, and there is not one which meets any degree of general favour as an improvement, while in most there would be a decided deterioration. All these schemes propose alterations either in the qualification of voters, or the mode of voting.

Proposed changes in qualification of voters.

It has been proposed to give votes to retired servants of the Company, and also to holders of stock in the Indian funds. But to both of these plans there is this insuperable objection—that it would inevitably lead to men laying themselves out for the Direction, if not openly canvassing for votes while still in India. The army forms the great numerical majority of the Indian service, and, under Lord Ellenborough's proposed plan, the Directors would be simply the men most popular with the army. Not only is there a constant stream of retirements, but those out of the service are so intimately connected with those still in it, that the opinion and influence of the army in India would be all powerful with the retired body at home. Popularity is not always the best test of efficiency; and can anything be conceived more prejudicial to discipline and injurious in every way than a general officer, holding high office in an army, striving to secure his return to the Direction a few years subsequently, like the American Commander-in-Chief canvassing and inspecting at the same time? Again, take the other plan. The holders of Indian stock are principally in India, and a large proportion are natives. Conceive a member of Council, or the head of a department in a Government constituted like that of India, devoting his time to canvassing the voices of the Baboos in order to secure his election on his retirement! Nothing could be more pernicious. This objection, however, does not apply to holders of Indian funds resident in England.

Another proposition is to give votes to English fund-holders. There would be no objection on principle to that plan, but it would only make the canvass a more serious affair than ever.

In short, seeing that whichever way we turn to look for an improved constituency we only make matters worse—or, at any rate, no better; that the proprietors of East India stock are just as good a constituency as we are anywhere likely to find; that they have in their favour the prescription of having long exercised this power; and that the desire to possess a vote has doubtless attracted to this description of stock many persons interested in India, I think that we had better be content with the voters that we have, than fly to others that we know not of. But I should see no insuperable obstacle to adding to the constituency the holders of a certain sum (say 20,000 rupees) in the Indian funds resident in England, and such an arrangement would go far to mitigate the exclusive power now possessed by the *City* interest.

Proposed changes in mode of voting.

It may still be a question whether the mode of voting can be improved. It seems that proxies are only permitted if executed a certain number of days before the poll; and it is proposed to extend the time, that natives of India may become voters. To this the same objection applies which I have urged to the plan of the Indian fund-holders being intrusted with votes. There would be no harm in natives having votes, but there would be the greatest possible harm in officers of Government soliciting their votes.

A Director has propounded a scheme of electoral colleges, and, when I first heard of it, I fancied that it was one for dividing the electors into separate constituencies, instead of electing the Directors collectively; but on looking at the plan, as explained to the committee, it turns out to be something quite different, and so far beyond my poor comprehension that I cannot venture to hint a decided opinion concerning it. I confess that the difficulty of making apparent to ordinary understandings how the best men are to be thereby secured seems to me a *primâ facie* objection; and as to its operation in the Royal Society, it must be remembered that that body has no cadetships to dispose of, and that the same practical value does not attach to its offices as to an East India directorship. Though I am not sure that it has been authoritatively put forth, I cannot help thinking that the division into constituencies might be the only practicable improvement; so that the present system of *combination* might be in some degree interfered with, and the canvass might be more limited and less protracted. I am supposing each constituency of proprietors to elect a Senator for life, or for a very long term of years, and, on a vacancy, that constituency to elect another, so that it might be more like canvassing a small borough. If the tenure be for life, the plan might answer, and, when a Senator unexpectedly dies, the candidates would have a short vigorous fight, and have done with it. But if re-elections take place at stated periods, I confess that I think the value of the patronage would make it altogether unlike a parliamentary election, and that there must be one unceasing canvass and barter of patronage for votes.

Insufficiency of all these proposals.

Take it as we may, the fact then is simply this—that by no form of popular election can you possibly secure the best men. You may get a proportion of good men, but can never depend on always having the best. Irresponsible electors will never, when electing a distributor of patronage, choose *solely* on public grounds (why should they?); and there are many men eminently fitted for the business of government, but eminently unfitted for a popular candidature.

Nomination can only be vested in the Crown, that is in the ministry of the day, and valid objection would no doubt be made to intrusting to the ministry an unlimited power of this kind.

It is certain, however, I repeat, that it is urgently necessary to devise some plan for securing the admission into the Senate of the most fit men, at the fit period of their lives, and without the necessity of a most protracted and objectionable popular candidature. The way towards such an object will be very much smoothed and facilitated by a reduction of the value of the patronage; but it seems to me that the object itself cannot by possibility be effected in any other way than by combining a very limited system of nomination with *responsible* election by a small number of known responsible and independent electors; and thus filling not all, but some of the seats in the Senate.

Proposed system of joint nomination and election.

It might be difficult to constitute a separate college of electors, whether like cardinals or like aldermen, whether composed of ex-governors and ex-presidents, or the result of indirect popular election. I think that the duty of responsible election as a check on nominations of the Crown might be best intrusted to the Senate for the time being. My plan then would be to combine a scheme of modified nomination, and a narrow limit of choice, with an election by the existing Senate, and a tenure of office which should render the holders thoroughly independent. The independence of the Senators must be an essential part of any scheme.

The mode of appointment of Governors-General is in

fact a system of joint nomination and election, which has upon the whole worked tolerably well; but in the appointment of Senators I would put greater checks on the power of the ministry. At present the Court of Directors nominally elect a Governor-General, and the Crown exercises a right of veto; but in practice the ministry nominates, and the Directors have a power of veto. I would prefer this order of proceeding, because the Directors have a great influence in the ordinary elections (and I propose to leave a certain number of seats to election); and if the nomination were to rest with them, the Crown having merely a veto, the Senate might be too much of a close corporation.

My plan is, then, that on the occurrence of a vacancy, from a list of qualified persons the Crown should present a name or names, which it should rest with the Senate to accept or reject within a certain time, and in the event of non-acceptance fresh nominations would be made till one is accepted. The number of the Senate would be so considerable, that the existence of one or two vacancies would not affect its efficiency, and no ministry would delay too long to nominate an acceptable person, lest it should go out and lose the nomination altogether.

I must say that I do not see the force of the insuperable objection which many people entertain to intrusting a very limited power of this kind to the Government of the day. I do not see why, as vacancies occur, the Government should not present to a certain proportion of the seats from among persons of a certain service and prescribed Indian qualification—that is, in fact, from a limited profession; a subsequent power of election or rejection being left to the existing Senate.

May it not be that, in a feeling of reaction from the abuses of the past, we run to the other extreme of too much distrusting the Government? Do we not, in some degree, confound abuse of patronage in the creation of unnecessary offices and emoluments, or the omission of necessary duties for the sake of patronage, with its use in filling, under proper restrictions, in the light of day, and subject to the judgment of popular opinion, legitimate and necessary offices? Though most anxious to see a radical reform of abuses, I am conservative enough to wish for a strong Government; and it strikes me that Governments of the present day, far from having too much power, have too little; that they have, as it were, too little ballast; that the *ins*, as a matter of course, become gradually unpopular, and the wheel revolves more and more speedily. In this view, the exercise of *legitimate* patronage by the Government is anything but a disadvantage, and is the best safeguard against the creation and abuse of illegitimate patronage. You cannot altogether muzzle the oxen that tread out the corn. The only question is, how far the proposed arrangement is liable to abuse? Now, we must admit that *non-professional* appointments—those to which any one may be appointed—are still, even if not grossly abused, most frequently given away rather by personal favour than by merit; but wherever the choice is limited, and the candidates are known, in all professional appointments, I believe that public opinion is now an amply sufficient safeguard, and that gross abuse is rarely met with. Take all the higher legal, and I will even go so far as to say clerical appointments. Of two qualified candidates for a judgeship, one on the right side may, no doubt, be generally preferred (and even this consideration is, I imagine, in some instances little attended to), but the appointment is never made matter of mere patronage and never abused. Is there any recent case in which any Ministry have been even accused of wilfully making a bad judge? Have not even the bishops been generally looked upon as respectable men, till they attained that elevation so dangerous to all human virtue? And great as is the patronage held by bishops, it is by no means indirectly exercised by the Ministry; bishops may use their patronage for personal, but not for political objects. Why might not Senators be nominated in the same way as judges are nominated, even if we had not the additional check of subsequent election? From a limited profession, from persons who have served a certain time in that profession, and who can produce testimony of their efficiency, I would constitute a certain number of professional working Senators, and the appointments should be for life—or for so long as the incumbents are fit for the duties—and with a retiring pension. It would follow that no one Ministry would have the nomination of all or of many Senators. When a vacancy occurred, the party in office would nominate; they might consider politics as much as they do in a judgeship; but even this is not probable, as Indians so seldom take part in politics. I hardly think that it would be a disadvantage if there was some additional stimulus to induce retired Indians to get into Parliament, and take a part there. If an unfit person were nominated, he would be excluded by the Senate. I do, then, believe that such a mode of nomination could not be seriously abused in the present day, and that the services would be made available of many distinguished and efficient men, who are now excluded from the Direction. It must be remembered, in addition to other arguments, that, as I would very much reduce the value of a Senator's patronage, and would not make the salary high, there would be much less temptation to job the appointment away. It is urged that public opinion would not tell with the same force on Indian professional appointments as on appointments from professions in this country—and no doubt the press and the public would not be *so* all-powerful; but still there is now a very strong Anglo-Indian public, and it would be amply represented in the press. I believe, therefore, that it would be sufficiently powerful to prevent any very great abuse in so public and important a matter as the appointment of a Senator. I do not suppose that you would get *only* the best men, but I think that, if the position of a Senator were at the same time made what it ought to be, you would have all the *most* distinguished men, and no *very unfit* ones. Under such a system, Elphinstone, Mackenzie, and R. M. Bird, would have been long ago members of the Direction, and, between election and nomination, you would have secured a sufficient proportion of the most fit men.

Whatever be thought of details, some system of joint nomination by concurrence of the Crown and the existing Senate should certainly be devised.

Still it is, no doubt, desirable to limit as much as possible the risk of abuse. A limit of selection to those whose service in India has been efficient would be most useful. Lord Ellenborough's plan, by which Senators are to be nominated in the first instance by the Governor-General in India, is not explained in detail; and I do not see that practically it can come to anything beyond this: that the Governor-General should have it in his power to place publicly on record, when a public servant leaves India, his opinion of that servant's fitness for further service at home; leaving that recommendation to weigh with the Ministry and on public opinion *quantum valeat*. Something of this kind would, no doubt, be very useful. It would not do to permit a single Governor-General to exclude a man for ever from the Senate; but I would make a certificate of fitness indispensable to nominees—would give the power of granting such certificates in favour of persons who have filled certain offices both to the Governor-General in India and to the Senate at home—and would thus form a class of "emeriti," from whom the Government should be bound to select.

If objection be made to nominating Senators for life, because they might get old without retiring, I answer, first, that the present Directors do in fact hold for life, so that nothing is lost in this respect; second, that you don't want *too* much personal activity in the Home Government, the active Government being in India; third, that it is the only possible way of securing the independence of the Senators; and fourth, that by providing a retiring pension you may superannuate Senators as you do Judges, and that I would superannuate them after a certain age.

If the Senators were *all* nominated, a smaller number would suffice: but as it is probable that some elected members will be retained (and it is desirable that it should be so),—as all of these latter will not be working members, and the collective body will be more deliberative than executive,—I think that the present number of twenty-four might, without detriment, be retained. It must not, however, be forgotten that, as the six *out* Directors have, *de facto*, just as much interest in the Direction as the twenty-four who are now in, there are at present thirty members of the Court to be disposed of; but in that number there must be some whose age, health, or avocations prevent them from taking a very active part; and it might either be arranged to name the twenty-four to remain in, in the Act of Parliament, excluding the six who have hitherto taken least part; or a general election might take place, to give the proprietors the opportunity of selecting those among the thirty whom they would choose to retain; or the six might be retained for a time as supernumeraries.

If possible, still more necessary than a change in the mode of appointing Directors, is a reform and remodelling of the internal constitution, &c., of the Direction.

The nature of the improvements in the interior arrangements and mode of conducting business, embodied in the changes which I am about to suggest, will be evident without farther explanation. And I may here say, that all the proposed improvements in the Court of Directors will be equally applicable even if it is determined to maintain the separate office in Cannon-row, and will still very largely influence the efficiency of the Indian Government.

I would propose then as follows:—

Summary of proposed Home Government.

1. The title of the Court of Directors to be changed to that of "Senate of the Indies," the present twenty-four Directors to be the first Senators.

2. The commercial constitution and rules of the Court to be at the same time altogether altered.

3. A minister of Indian affairs, holding office at the pleasure of the Crown, to be ex-officio President of the Senate, and chairman of the political committee.

4. To the twelve next vacancies, other than vacancies by rotation, nominations shall be made as they occur by the Crown, in a *congé d'élire*, from among persons who have served the Government in India for not less than ten years, who have filled certain superior offices (to be afterwards particularised) for not less than two years—who have been absent from India, or retired from the service, not more than ten years—whose age does not exceed sixty years—and who on retirement have been declared to be emeriti either by the Senate or by the Indian Supreme Government. The present Senate and ex-Governors-General to have the power of granting such

certificates to persons already retired. The certificates to state that the recipient has done remarkably good service to the state in a superior office, and is well fitted for farther important service.* The existing Senate must accept and elect the person nominated by the Crown within one month, or the Crown must proceed to a fresh nomination. These Senators to hold office for life (subject to following provision), and future vacancies in their number to be supplied by similar nomination. To be removable on address of Houses of Parliament. A reasonable retiring pension to be provided after long service, and Senators to be pensioned on attaining the age of seventy years, unless Houses of Parliament address the Crown in their favour.

5. The remaining seats to be filled by election as at present (with the proposed addition of resident fundholders to the constituency); the Senators to hold office for five years, to go out by rotation, and to be immediately re-eligible, provided that their age at time of re-election does not exceed seventy years.

6. The Senate to elect among themselves six Committees, "Political," "Home and General," "Finance," "Judicial," "Military and Naval," and "Moral and Material Improvement," and every Director to belong to at least one committee; also to elect a vice-president, who shall be ex-officio chairman of the home and general committee, and four chairmen of the remaining four committees (the president being ex-officio chairman of the political); all these offices to be held for five years, and the holders to be re-eligible.

7. The proceedings of the political committee to be,

* This would give a wide field for selection, while it excludes mere beef-eaters. The Senate and the Governors-General would each prevent the other from obtaining a monopoly of the certificates. The Senate would not certify regarding unfit men, nor would Lords Ellenborough, Hardinge, or Dalhousie.

if the president consider it necessary, secret, and orders to be in that case despatched and received without consulting the general Senate. In case of difference of opinion, the president to have the power of acting on his own responsibility after receiving the opinion of the members; but if a majority of the committee protest, the president must obtain the concurrence and signature of the First Lord of the Treasury and two Secretaries of State.

8. All despatches received from India to be referred to, and all measures to be first discussed in, the committees to whose department they belong. The committees to prepare despatches or drafts of proposed resolutions, which drafts (being other than secret despatches) shall be ready for the inspection of all Senators the day before a general Senate is held. Committees shall also prepare drafts on such subjects as the president shall order.

9. A general Senate to be held weekly. Each chairman to produce the drafts which have been submitted for inspection the day before, and the said drafts to be accepted, rejected, or remitted with instructions, with or without comment. Measures proposed in full Senate to be referred for report of committee.

10. The president may either assent at the time, or retain the draft for one week for his consideration, and then may either assent, or veto in the name of the Crown, or may alter the draft for recorded reasons. If the Senate protest against alteration, the president must obtain the signatures of three ministers, as in rule 7.

11. Two to be a quorum of each committee, and eight of the General Senate. Senate to have power to regulate leave of absence, &c., of members, so that the quorum be made up; and provided also that any

member absent for more than half the year, or not attending regularly during the other half, is to have no pay or patronage for that year.

12. In the exercise of all patronage, and in making all appointments, the president to have a power of veto as in everything else, but no power of substituting another name; and also to have no power of increasing or inserting grants of money.

13. Either the Crown or the Senate may at any time dismiss any servant at home or abroad; but in case of dismissal of a Governor-General by the Senate without the sanction of the Crown, a concurrent vote of three-fourths of the whole number shall be necessary.

14. Each Director to receive 500*l.* per annum, and a limited share of patronage to be subsequently proposed. Vice-president to have 1500*l.*, and chairmen of committees 1000*l.*

Proposed changes in India House establishment.

Supposing the Indian central government to be rendered more efficient, and the business to be sent home in a more advanced stage of digestion than the present crude and unassorted masses of manuscript, the mere mechanical portion of the establishment at the India House might doubtless be very much reduced, and a considerable expense would be saved. But the Senators being still numerous, and paid rather as deliberative statesmen than as working officers, much important work, including the greater part of the laborious business, must still be done by the secretaries or examiners. They might be re-distributed to suit the altered constitution of the Senate, and their liberal remuneration would be as now well earned. They would be appointed by the Senate (or the committees), subject to the veto of the president, in the same way as all other appointments. The president would have a private secretary, and, as chairman of the political committee, the political establishment would be more immediately subject to him.

One question, however, cannot but suggest itself, whether the isolation of an exclusively home service is not a disadvantage—whether, with so large a supply of Indian men of business, many of whom are driven home by the climate while eminently fit for service in a temperate latitude, there might not be some exchange between the Indian and home services—whether great benefit would not result from employing in the India House men of Indian experience, while, on the other hand, there are several appointments in India connected with finance and accounts, the post-office, sea customs, &c., to which the regular course of the civil service does not directly lead, and which might sometimes with advantage be filled by men of business trained in England. Such an arrangement would go a very long way to promote an efficient understanding between the governments in India and at home. At present the evil is just, in a very much enhanced degree, that which would be felt by a governor in India, whose whole staff, secretariat and councillors, had been all their lives exclusively confined to the Calcutta offices, and who had never been in the interior of the country—an evil the partial occurrence of which in particular instances all Indian statesmen loudly deprecate. Yet the Indian government is now carried on in Leadenhall-street with a great staff, of whom I believe that only one individual has ever been in India. This makes it a very close bureaucracy. I doubt whether it is possible for any man to understand any business in which he has never taken an active share from mere paper knowledge; he can only see things from one point of view; but especially it must be absolutely impossible that an Englishman, who has never breathed an Asiatic atmosphere, can really comprehend Asiatic manners,

Asiatic feelings, Asiatic facts, and Asiatic business. He has at best a sort of reflected and negative knowledge. A man may come to accept certain facts and a certain course of things, and he may do excellent service by abstaining from innovation, and from treading ground beyond his depth, but he cannot get beyond this point. Take, for example, the case of Mill, the historian, who continually falls into blunders which the dullest of Indians could correct. Then why should not Indian experience be made available at home in the executive as well as in the deliberative offices? Might not a portion of the home duties be amalgamated, as it were, with the Indian service, and the servants be made interchangeable? Might not a secretary of the East India House, possessed of all the views of the Home Government, possibly be sent with great advantage as financial minister to the government of India, and might he not return not only the ablest of secretaries, but a practical Indian politician? and might not a distinguished secretary to the government of India fill with great advantage a similar office at home, throw a flood of light into the minds of the Senate, and a few years after, with renovated health, an Anglicised mind, and a thorough possession of the views of and accord with the government at home, be sent to manage an Indian presidency?

I may say, without disrespect to the distinguished men who hold office in the India House, that there must necessarily be, in that establishment generally, a want of the practical knowledge which is necessary to eliminate, understand, and collate the facts stated in various forms and various language in the voluminous papers now sent from the different presidencies in India,—and that some admixture of Indian practical knowledge might be of great use to them.

Proposed digestion and publication of official information.

It also strikes me that great advantage might be derived from digesting, extracting, and converting for publication the marrow of the great mass of facts, arguments, and hidden talent now scattered through and buried in piles of papers like the nuggets of gold in California or Australia. Very few official documents are in their original state fitted for publication, because they are not written with that view; and it is one thing to write for an official superior, another for the general reader. But there might be a literary establishment at the India House expressly devoted to compiling papers for publication for the benefit both of the Indian services and of that portion of the public who take an interest in the subject. Nothing can be more striking than the want of information of this kind under a government which has all possible and most minute information in manuscript almost to excess, and the want of the opportunity of knowledge almost justifies the general ignorance which prevails.

The Senate might also with advantage address an annual report to the Crown, giving some general account of its proceedings and views, the whole or part of which the Crown might cause to be published for the benefit of the nation.

The Court of Proprietors.

I have not yet noticed the Court of Proprietors as taking a part in affairs beyond the election of Directors. It seems that they exercise little real power, except the important right of vetoing money grants of the Directors; an appropriate and necessary privilege, when the money was theirs, and their interests were directly involved. Under present arrangements this power is no longer necessary to secure the pockets of the proprietors; and the interests of India might be, I should say, sufficiently secured from abuse by the joint responsibility of the Senate and the Ministry, and by a provision for giving publicity to grants of money. It would not, therefore, seem necessary on this account to continue the existence of the Court of Proprietors; but there is another use, which is urged with considerable reason, viz. the advantage of securing a public vent for grievances, and the means of bringing to light and holding up any real abuse of the powers of an oligarchy sitting with closed doors. Parliament has only sufficient interest in the subject when other feelings are brought into play which are certain largely to influence it, and which leave so little confidence in the verdict that it is generally agreed to be better to avoid such discussions. When only the interests of India are concerned the House is counted out. Public meetings, then, of persons *bonâ fide* interested in and having some knowledge of India, and the opportunity of seeking and giving explanations, might be very useful. But does the Court of Proprietors supply this want? I should say decidedly not. Look at the account of the meetings. What is the attendance? Most miserable. The whole affair is almost monopolised by one or two pertinacious people, who have hobbies which they have long ago ridden to death, yet persist in attempting to galvanise.

To answer the purpose indicated, the meeting must be put on a broader basis. Now, though it would not do to give to Indian servants and residents retired or temporarily at home the power of electing Directors, or any other actual power, I should say that the privilege of talking and expounding their views might, with great advantage, be accorded to them. It is true that at present any one can buy a qualification to talk in the Court of Proprietors; but he cannot buy a respectable audience, with which I think that the following plan would supply him, if he had anything interesting to say. I would propose to substitute for the present quarterly Court of Proprietors a Court of Experts (or experienced persons), which should consist not only of all proprietors of 500*l.* stock, but also of all who are or have been in a respectable position in India.

Proposed Court of Experts.

I would make the qualification as wide as possible. It should include all the servants, or former servants, of the Government, from an ensign upwards; all persons who have ever paid 50*l.* per annum of land revenue, or 50*l.* sea customs, in India; all who have held any considerable offices in the presidency towns; all merchants, planters, &c., of respectability. The servants of the Company are so numerous, that in such a body I do not think that we need fear a democratic majority. I would give to this quarterly Court of Experts the privilege of making presentments of their opinion to the Senate, on which the Senate should be bound to make some deliverance. I do not think that the Indian Government has any occasion altogether to shun the light, and believe that it would be much better that those who allege that they have grievances should have an opportunity of explaining what they want, than that they should be free to abuse the Government in a general way, without suggesting a particular remedy. For instance, the Company's government has always been talked at as if it were to blame for not supplying good and cheap cotton. Let any one who thinks so propound a plan of improvement in the Court of Experts; let him be heard and answered. In any view I am sure that it would be infinitely preferable to have a fair field for the exposition of grievances in this country than that the Indian press should propagate uncontradicted misrepresentations. Freedom is not dangerous or even inconvenient in a free country. How many monstrous accusations are dissipated by a parliamentary explanation? I believe that many horrible things laid to the charge of the Indian Government would be equally dissipated in the Court of Experts. This fitting freedom of speech and explanation would be much more appropriate in this country than in India, the seat of an absolute and military government, where explanations cannot be exchanged on equal terms, and where the government now submits in silence to calumny.

Patronage.

The particular mode of securing a due qualification in the young men sent out to serve the Indian Government will be most properly dealt with in connection with the general constitution of the services; but as something must, under any circumstances, remain matter of patronage, I would here only treat of the disposal of that patronage, properly so called, bearing in mind, however, that I shall hereafter suggest so great an enhancement of the qualifications as very materially to diminish the value of the patronage as patronage. All nominations are now, as it were, the private property of individuals, being divided among the Directors, and each disposing of his share as he thinks fit. It is desirable in the new arrangements,—first, to be rid of the patronage as a political difficulty; second, to provide for the bestowal of appointments in acknowledgment of and reward for public service; and, third, to open the services more to the general public, inasmuch as they have hitherto fallen too much into the hands of particular classes.

The system hitherto pursued, of giving all the patronage to the Directors, has acted well as regards English politics; and there will be no objection to giving to the Senate and to each Senator a limited share of patronage. But we must first provide for the other objects which I have mentioned.

In regard to rewarding public services by appointments, it is very unfortunate that the claim has been somewhat ostentatiously brought forward in the only light in which it is not tenable; and the case attempted to be set up has completely broken down, to the injury of the general cause. It has been alleged that the officers of the army do not receive a due share of Indian appointments, and demanded that a fixed share of all appointments should be set apart for them. It is shown that, in fact, a very large proportion of appointments are now given to sons of officers, as every one acquainted with India must well know to be the case, successive generations filling the services, and there being hardly an officer with a grown-up family who does not get appointments for some of his sons. But the real question is, are these appointments given for public services, or in proportion to public services? and can the best of the servants of Government, serving his country in India, submit his case in a proper quarter, and, without personal interest or importunity, ask for and get an appointment for the son? Very far from it. It is not in the nature of things under present arrangements that it should be so, while patronage is divided among individuals. A very large portion of the appointments are given to the sons of old servants, not, generally speaking, in consideration of their services, but simply and solely because the same interest and personal or clannish connection which got the father an appointment gets one for the son. A man belongs to an Indian family, or he marries the daughter of an Indian family, or he or his friends, or his friends' friends, have known in India a man who becomes a Director. It is by these means that a large share of appointments are secured to the sons. But all who have observed different families must well know that the share of these good things is by no means in proportion to the merits of the father. Many a distinguished man, who remains at his post in India, has the

Application of a portion of patronage to reward of public services.

greatest difficulty in providing for his sons, and does so in a way quite inferior to the father's position and claims; while many another man of no claims at all, but with some particular channel to a Director, gets the best appointments, especially if he comes home and sets himself to sit on the heads* of his friends, and makes his friends sit on the head of the Director. In fact, if a man rests solely on his public services, where is he to go? The evil to be remedied is, not that the Directors are ill-disposed, but that no patronage is retained by the body for public purposes. If the applicant applies to the Court, he is told, We have no doubt of your merits, but the Court have no patronage. If, without personal connection, he applies to an individual Director, he is told, "I admit your claim, but I have several nephews to provide for; I am deeply pledged, and why select me? why not go to any of the other twenty-three Directors?" I by no means say that no appointments are given by individuals from feelings more or less public-spirited, but such cases are certainly the exception; and when they occur, it is still quite wrong that the public-spirited man should sacrifice his private patronage from public feeling, while he who has no public feeling keeps his. The patronage is not in trust, but in private gift. It is not like a duty of filling a responsible office with a fit person. Any boy is considered fit for a cadet, if he can only get an appointment and pass the prescribed tests; and there is no obligation, legal or moral, to be guided by the merits of the father. Whoever wants an appointment must beg it from door to door; and the hardship is chiefly felt by men in India, who have not the same opportunities of doing so that those at home have. Many notable instances might be quoted of the difficulties

* This expression is an Orientalism, but I dare say that my meaning will be understood.

experienced by men holding the first positions in India; and though some cases have ended honourably to individual Directors, all show that the system is faulty.

It may then be assumed that there is no public arrangement for rewarding service by appointments. Yet when these appointments are to be given away as patronage, could they be more usefully employed? It is argued that servants are paid for their services. So they are, and this patronage is undoubtedly an additional payment. But it would be taken into consideration as such, and would be a form of payment in no way burdensome to the State, and saving a world of anxiety and trouble to meritorious individuals. I would put it on exactly the same footing as similar appointments in the royal army, in which commissions without purchase are distributed by the Commander-in-Chief, as a great public officer, on public grounds, and with reference to the father's services. I believe that an officer of a certain rank and service in her Majesty's army can depend on obtaining a commission for his son; and it is one of the avowed advantages of remaining in that service that it leads to appointments to Sandhurst, &c. What more graceful and grateful way of rewarding the services of Indian officers, civil and military, from a fund of patronage which must be given away somehow, and in regard to which the great object is to get rid of it without raising political difficulties?

I would propose, then, that one-third of the whole patronage should be reserved to be distributed by the Senate collectively on recorded public grounds as a reward for services in India—that every servant of the Company should have the privilege of making application and stating his claims—that the president and chairmen of committees should, in conclave, select those having the greatest claims, stating their reasons—and that the matter should be finally determined in full Court—the president having in this, as in other matters, a right of veto. The names of the candidates and of the persons selected to be published.

Question of more general distribution of Indian appointments.

It may be more difficult to satisfy the remaining desideratum of opening the appointments more generally to all classes. At present some appointments certainly find their way into every class; but perhaps the highest classes—those which have been in late times deprived of the large patronage and easy way of providing for their relations and friends afforded by the political abuses which are now so much diminished—these classes, I say, have perhaps not so great a share of Indian appointments as their position in the country, the value of the appointments, and the necessities of the aristocracy, would give them a fair claim to have. For my own part, holding the doctrine that it is by no means undesirable to give to the Ministry some legitimate patronage in exchange for the illegitimate patronage which has been taken from them—and believing that the relation or supporter of a minister, or a peer, or a member of Parliament would make quite as good a cadet as the relation of a Director—and that the President of the Board of Control uses his patronage as well as any Director—I should see no immediate objection to giving—say one-third of the appointments to the Cabinet Ministers; but then there is the danger that the Governor-General in India might afterwards be subjected to undue pressure on account of the persons so nominated; and I am aware that such a proposition is not likely to meet with favour. If the object would be at all effected by selling commissions in the army, I do not know that there would be any great objection. But I doubt whether the purpose, as concerns the aristocracy at least, would be attained by such an arrangement. That class is not in the present day the best provided with ready money, and the effect might be to bring more Jewish than noble blood into the army. In regard to the civil service, any sale of appointments must be injurious. Here the object must be to make the standard of qualification as high as possible, and to let no man purchase with his money what Lord Ellenborough terms a sort of freehold right in his office. It must be much more of the nature of a contract for the highest class of services strictly rendered and paid according to value, and the appointments should no more be sold than English judgeships.

The nomination of a certain number of Senators would have a good effect in making appointments less dependent on the votes of East India proprietors, and in widening the circle of selection; but except in that way, and by selling some cadetships, I do not know that anything more can be done towards this object, if the great English public officers cannot be trusted with a share for distribution among the class to which they belong.

Patronage of Senators.

The patronage not disposed of in the modes already suggested should annually be divided, as now, among the Senators—and I would give the president a quadruple share. The number of the appointments in the individual gift of each Senator will be, however, considerably diminished by these arrangements; and this result, with the diminished value caused by increased qualifications, will remove one great obstacle to the appointment or election of Senators on public grounds.

CHAPTER II.

THE INDIAN GOVERNMENT.

Use of name of the Crown; necessity of one centralised government; deficiencies of present Supreme Government; remedies for those deficiencies; proposed government and rules; expense; explanation of proposals; appointment of unprofessional persons; share of natives in government; permanent location of Supreme Government: why Calcutta should not be the place; why the place should be in Hindostan; suggestion of a locality and consequent arrangements; alternative if plan rejected; local governments; proposed 5th government and 6th political division; constitution of subordinate governments; expense, powers, location, &c.; arrangements failing a centralised government.

The name of the Crown.

I HAVE alluded to the advantage for *Indian* reasons of conducting the government of India in the name of the Crown. In most cases a name is of little consequence, but sometimes it really carries weight; and I think that the time has certainly arrived when the style and title under which we govern India becomes important, and involves considerable principles of policy. Before giving the reasons for thinking the proposed change desirable, I would observe, as an antecedent argument, that there is no real *primâ facie* objection—that no great harm can result. The name, as I understand it, in no way involves either the principle or any important features of the Home Government of India. India is not in fact governed by any joint-stock company whatever, but the details are conducted by a Board, under the superintendence and orders of the Minister of the Crown. The use of the name of the Company confers no material advantage on the proprietors of East India stock. Whatever be the real constitution of the

Home Government, whether it remains what it now is, or whatever Parliament may decide that it in future shall be, we may retain the name of the Company, or substitute that of the Crown, without making one iota of difference in the relative powers of the Crown and the East India Directors, or in the advantages possessed by the proprietors of East India stock. Supposing then that there are other reasons for desiring a change of name, there can be no reasonable objection on the ground of English politics or English interests.

Reasons for adopting.

On the other hand, the reasons for a change are in India strong and numerous. The Turkish leaders early made themselves emperors; and the Moguls, like ourselves foreigners, and for no very long historical period rulers of all India, in occupying the site of the former empire, assumed that imperial title which commands a large share of respect in Asia, and is only claimed by sovereigns of great empires, or of ancient prescription. They so well succeeded in establishing themselves in the opinion of all India as legitimate emperors, that the prescription of their name lasted and retained a very considerable importance for nearly a hundred years after the decline of their power, and for half a century after they had ceased to possess any share whatever of actual sovereignty. Even to this day the honours formerly bestowed by them are much prized, and I rather think that the present shadow of former empire makes some little money by the titles which he confers. We have succeeded to the Mogul, as the Mogul succeeded to the Turk, and we have lately attained such complete dominion in India as Aurangzebe at the very culminating point of Mogul power never possessed. But we have never claimed the imperial rank; we have been content to appear as an upstart race, commencing by trade and ending by a strong but unlegitimised dominion. We have dealt as on equal terms with the inferior feudatories of the Moguls, and they now yield us obedience, but no reverence. Yet we too have a sovereign of greater power and more ancient prescription than the Great Mogul, and as much reverenced by her subjects. Why then have we not put our own idol in the place of the Mogul, and made the subjects of Her Majesty's subjects bow down and render allegiance to her? Why have we not installed her as Empress of the Indies, and the legitimate fountain of power and honour? We did not do so at first, nor could we have conveniently done so, but it is both proper and convenient that we should now do so.

In fact, while the substance of the Company is gone, we are still hampered with the name, the humility, and the undignified character of the Company; and the only way of getting out of the false position into a true one is by introducing Her Majesty, and requiring from the natives that respect to the throne which we pay to it ourselves. In these things example is everything, and we can only expect the natives to respect that which *we* respect. The Company assumes not the form or dignity of a sovereign. The Company is abused by European settlers, ridiculed by newspaper editors, treated on the same footing as the rest of Her Majesty's subjects in the law courts—and the name of the Sovereign never used or heard of. Yet nowhere is the regal dignity so well understood or so much appreciated as by Orientals, and the title once put prominently forward would soon acquire all the strength of prescription.

As concerns the native states.

First, in our relation with native states the name of the Crown would be of the utmost importance. It would not only command their respect, but would be the keystone of the whole policy which should now be adopted towards them. If they are to be maintained, it must be as an integral part of the empire;

and the same allegiance which they or their more worthy predecessors paid to the Mogul emperor, they should pay to our sovereign. That should be an indispensable condition of our protection and support, and would be readily assented to. Some settlement on a definite footing of the real position, rights, and liabilities of those states is urgently necessary (witness again those terrific Outram Blue-books, all arising out of the indefiniteness of our relations). The Company, having dealt as an equal in name, cannot easily in the same name assume the character and command the respect of a superior. But in the name of the Crown the feudatory chain may be easily and satisfactorily arranged, and, theory being rendered consistent with fact, a system might be formed securing to each chief the power which he ought to have, and defining that which he ought not to have, and in fact has not had; a subject to which I shall afterwards have occasion more particularly to allude.

As concerns our own native subjects.

Next, in regard to our own subjects, the effect of the imperial name on their respect, and in rendering comprehensible to them the nature and the stability of our rule, would be great. At present the natives appreciate substantial benefits derived from us, but no great name or intelligible principle of government conveys reverence to their imaginations, or light to their understandings. Our honours, our titles, and our condescensions, carry with them none of the weight which attached to the empty honours and magnificent pretensions of the declining Moguls. All this might be easily changed, and a great Oriental government would assume a more than Oriental dignity, and exercise that moral hold on the mind which gives strength among any people, but especially among Asiatics.

Another advantage in the use of the name of the

Crown is in dealing with Her Majesty's judicial and other establishments, and with her servants and European subjects in India.

When India was really intrusted to a joint-stock company, it was necessary that representatives of the Crown should have the power judicially to check the proceedings of the Company; but now that the distinction between the British Government and the Company in reality no longer exists, the traditions of ancient jealousy and antagonism kept up by the name, situation, and semblance of a separate and superior source of authority, are noxious and objectionable. It is perfectly clear that the authority under which all different servants of the state, courts of justice, &c., act, should be assimilated throughout India. It might be difficult and would seem absurd at this time to put the establishments heretofore rejoicing in the Royal warrant, and pretensions attached thereto, under an unsubstantial company, and it would be as efficacious and more easy to assimilate by making all to hold office and act in the name of the Crown.

As concerns European courts, subjects, &c.

The European settlers have vigorously opposed their subjection to the Company's courts and Company's servants, and asserted their privilege of being judged by Her Majesty's judges. The more free use of the name of the Crown might smooth the way to the inevitable and necessary equalization of justice, and abolition of class privileges, and would put the Government on that footing in its own courts, and in respect to its own servants and subjects, which it is right that it should hold.

An especial advantage which I anticipate from the introduction of the name of the Crown as the source of Indian office and honour is, that it would facilitate a more free communication and interchange of services between the servants of the state

On other grounds.

in India and those in other parts of the empire both in the civil and military departments. It would be well that Indian service should be more and more recognised as no longer the exclusive service of an exclusive company, but the service of the state in India; and the status and just consideration of Indian servants would be increased, while they would be less isolated from European knowledge and communication. Much good might follow from a nearer connection between the Queen's and Company's armies.

Having settled then that the government should be "Her Majesty's Government in India," as in any other part of the British dominions, let us proceed to the constitution of that government.

Necessity of one central government.

I have before alluded to the necessity of uniting in one great central government the guiding reins of all the different parts of that great empire which is now, in fact, throughout subject to our rule—the essential characteristics of which are identical in every part—the people of which are morally, socially, and politically the same—and into the whole of which the Mahommedan rulers introduced the same system of government. The Mahommedans, commencing from one point, extended their conquests and their system to the extremities. We, commencing at different extremities, have gradually closed in till we have united the whole. Our military system does not very essentially differ in different parts (for our military system we brought with us), but we still retain very radical and important differences in the civil systems of different provinces, because the whole civil structure was new to us, and different individuals, acting apart and experimentally, have followed very different courses. These cannot all be right; and the comparison of so varied experiences ought to enable us to attain everywhere much greater perfection of administration than has been yet exhibited in any single province.

A union of all the powers of an absolute government in one common centralization must lead to much greater executive efficiency than when the parts are disjointed. Decentralization may act well in free constitutions of a more or less republican kind, but never in despotisms. No tyrant is so bad as a petty tyrant. Hence the advantage of a really active and competent central government. We must govern from afar and administer from near, as Louis Napoleon has it. The local governments must have ample power to administer, but they must be guided, directed, and propelled by the central power. The necessity of checking them financially and politically, of preventing them from running wild and upsetting the coach, has long been felt. But we must not only restrain them from doing wrong, we must propel them to do right, and it is in the latter that we have chiefly failed. The Home Government, as at present constituted, is altogether unequal to such a duty, and with regard to the Indian Government, if I may take a simile from a subject once familiar, now nearly extinct, I should say that Bombay and Madras are, as it were, the most distant horses of the coach which the Governor-General, as coachman, has under his command, heavily bitted, but which he has not a long enough whip properly to reach; so that, while they are prevented from going forward, they have every opportunity of gibbing and going backward. Bombay, in particular, is a most expensive, ill-conditioned possession, which costs a great deal more than it is worth.

The political atmosphere of England not being suited then to a strong, prompt, and bold absolute government, it is, as I have formerly argued, necessary to trust the central executive to the Supreme Government in India.

So thought Parliament in 1833, and it was imagined that it had sufficiently provided the means for a thorough concentration of power. It must be confessed that the experiment has, in a great degree, failed. The weather has proved unusually tempestuous—the road has been cut up by divers political torrents—the coachman is not yet sufficiently armed—he has exercised but an authority divided with, and much checked by the control of, two guards of different temperaments—the farther horses pull as little as ever—the coach is very much behind time.

Deficiencies of the Supreme Government.

It is necessary, however, to be a little more explicit as to the extent and causes of the failure of the design of 1833.

Parliament then proposed three principal objects :—

First. To vest a complete central administrative power in a Supreme Government, and thus to secure a uniform and efficient administration throughout India.

Second. To secure to the Central Government so complete a control over and management of the imperial finances as should ensure their healthy condition, and prevent one government from spending what another saved.

Third. To obtain through the Central Government and a law commission a complete, uniform, and simple codification of laws for the whole empire.

Have these objects been fulfilled? I fear not. The administrative system has been in practice but little centralised, and rendered little uniform since 1833. In some comparatively minor matters, as sea customs, &c., something has been effected; but, generally speaking, there is almost as great a divergence and separation as ever. In fact, except as regards legislation and the prohibition of expenditure, Bombay and Madras are still much more under the immediate orders of the Court of

Directors than under the Supreme Government. The constitution of those minor governments seems to prove inefficient and unprogressive. They are sufficiently directed and urged forward neither by the Supreme nor by the Home Government, and even if they were to devise anything new it might be long before it is sanctioned by various and divided authorities. Neither have we generally such governors as Mr. Thomason, nor, if we had, could they act so efficiently.

The imperial finances have doubtless been principally deranged by wars; but also as regards the internal finances of the subordinate presidencies the expected advantage does not seem to have been derived. There is no financial improvement in Bombay and Madras. What has been gained in one way they have contrived to get rid of in another; and Bombay is as remarkable as ever for spending more than her income; while at the same time very strong complaints are made by the subordinate presidencies of their inability to spend money for useful purposes—as regards Madras I believe with some degree of justice.

The legislative failure is the most complete of all. We seem to be no nearer codification than ever. Our laws are more uncertain, insufficient, and unintelligible than before. The way that has been gained by partial and patchwork amendment on the part of the legislature has been more than lost by the accumulation of crude and contradictory precedents, constructions, and other judge-made laws; and the absence of result is really (I can call it by no milder term) disgraceful.

In fairness it must be admitted that the members of the commission have not been altogether idle; but they seem, for the most part, to have worked without reference to the real current necessities of the state, and to have done anything and everything except what they were expected to do and paid for doing. One would think that they had been sent to India to speculate more quietly and at their ease on juridical subjects of English and European interest. They have been much occupied by matters relating to the small local jurisdiction of the presidency courts, and have furnished no end of elaborate reports on "the fusion of law and equity," and I don't know what besides, while, practically, they have done nothing. I hope that their researches may be useful to law reformers in England, but "the fusion of law and equity" can have little interest in a country where those branches of law are not separate,* and do not want fusion; and I fear that from the Governor-General downwards no one in India cares even to read all these valuable reports.

From what I have said of the unpractical working of the law commission I must certainly except the Macaulay code. A penal code, though not the *most* necessary or most difficult of the objects proposed, is a highly practical and useful work. Macaulay's code was completed very early in the existence of the commission. It miscarried from attempting too much, and from that time the commission has not advanced one step.

This failure may be traced, in great part, to other causes; but much is also due to the general shortcoming of the Supreme Government, as a propelling power in the internal administration of the country.

And causes.

I shall here, then, sum up what seem to me to have been the causes of the general failure of the Supreme Government, in addition to the impediments resulting from the cumbrousness of the Home Government, to which I have already alluded.

* Except, of course, in the Presidency Courts, which are regulated by English law, and in regard to which such a question will not be determined in India.

First is, no doubt, the unfortunate occurrence of harassing wars and political anxieties which have occupied the greater part of the time and attention of successive Governors-General.

Second, the position of the seat of government, which has caused the Governor-General to be for the most part, and the Commander-in-Chief and head-quarters of the army always, separated from the council, and from all the offices and records of Government; and the climate of which has made the Governors and councillors less healthy in body, and less active in mind, than they would be in a better situation, and has *pro tanto* diminished the value of their appointments and their wish to retain them.

In the position of the seat of Government.

Third, the constitution of the government, the result of which proves to be, that the Governor-General has generally very little *active* assistance from his council in carrying on the administration. He has not only all the power (to which I do not at all object), but also all the labour. Everything seems to fall on him. The council is, in most instances, simply and solely a consultative council; and beyond the duty of warning the Governor-General when he is going wrong, the office of the councillors may be, and most frequently is, nearly a sinecure. In fact, they are paid for merely giving advice, as no councillors ever before were paid for such a duty. In many constitutions we have honorary or slenderly-paid councillors of this kind, who happen to reside at the seat of government; but I doubt whether such a thing is elsewhere known as paying a man on the *active* scale, buying him out and out, body and mind, as it were, and then employing him *passively*, merely to be consulted. In all other governments,

In the constitution of the Government.

whether it be a constitutional monarchy, a despotism, or a republic, persons so entertained on *active* pay are actively employed; acting is combined with advising, on the sound principle that practice is not a disqualification, but the best qualification, for advising; and they are separately the responsible ministers of particular departments, collectively the cabinet council of the chief of the state. But in India things are differently arranged. The highly-paid councillor is but an adviser; and the real ministers of the chief are the secretaries, who may do much of the active work of their respective departments, but are not responsible ministers, and do not hold a distinct position as the initiative heads of those departments. They cannot act as recognised ministers; and a Governor-General who does his duty is supposed to act, not on their responsibility, but on his own, and should (I believe that Lord Dalhousie does) go into everything himself. The consequence is, that the Governor must either in an irregular way make the secretaries *de facto* ministers,* or is himself much overworked and unable to attend to many important matters, while the councillors do as little as may be. I do not object to the councillors hitherto appointed as *passive* councillors. They are, for the most part, excellent good men; and if the fire of their energies is somewhat expended, they are not the less sage and sound negative advisers against rash error. But I say that neither is theirs the position to act, nor are they generally the men to overcome that position. They are appointed by the Court of Directors somewhat late in the day, as the reward of long and tried past services. They have generally nothing farther to look to; they have the

* And even in this case, if the Supreme Government were really to govern India, the Home Secretary alone could not possibly be equal to all the interior duties, including revenue and justice.

initiation of nothing; and there is no call, and very little temptation, to them, to embroil themselves as the advocates of anything new. They all (almost without exception) merely look on their five years in council as the means of quietly and tranquilly accumulating a considerable sum as the reward of past less liberally paid services. Their only personal care is to preserve their health, to make out their time, and to carry home their savings. They give their conscientious, and generally sound, opinions on the questions submitted to them; and it is no matter of blame to them that they do no more. But the system is a reason why the Government is less actively efficient.

The Governor-General has been also saddled with the responsibility of the local government of Bengal, which is simply another heavy load placed on the back of an overburdened beast. If his share in the Supreme Government is already more than sufficient, it may be supposed that to couple with it another office is altogether fatal to his efficient performance of either duty.

In the want of information.

Another great obstacle has been the want of information in regard to Madras and Bombay. While the law commission was in full numbers, there was a Madras and a Bombay servant with the Supreme Government on that duty; but latterly this has not been the case—both councillors and secretaries have been appointed exclusively from Bengal—there has been in the Supreme Government no personal knowledge of the other presidencies, and the Governor-General has had no leisure to visit them. There is a great gulf between the services of the different presidencies. Neither can there be any interchange of appointments, nor is there almost any opportunity of personal intercourse whatever. Abstracts of the proceedings of each government are no doubt received in

Calcutta; but there seems to be the greatest possible want of any general or condensed views and explanations of their operations for the benefit of those not technically acquainted with their present system, and with their official language. I cannot find, for instance, that any annual or general reports of the revenue systems of Madras and Bombay, and of such-like matters, anywhere exist. Their local papers are forwarded in masses, according to the old routine; and even in matters which are radically the same as those already understood, a few of their peculiar terms, and some differences of form and of conventional language, are (unexplained) sufficient to puzzle and confuse. I believe that to master their administrative system from these documents, without personal explanation, requires an amount of labour which neither Governors-General nor secretaries have ever found time sufficiently to achieve while actively engaged in other duties, and in the comparatively short period during which each individual holds the same office. Now, no sound statesman will make radical alterations till he thoroughly understands the facts as they exist, their bearing and results. This information the Supreme Government generally does not possess; and they have consequently refrained from active interference.

With regard to the divided authority over the local governments of the Supreme Government and Court of Directors, it may perhaps be remarked that, if this is partly the cause, it may also be, in some degree, the consequence, of failure on the part of the former, and that, if the Supreme Government took the duty upon itself, the Court might be willing enough to permit it to do so. But then the Indian Government must itself have sufficient power. If a question must be referred home in the end, it may just as well be sent direct.

The recapitulation of what has been deficient in the

Indian Government naturally suggests the remedies. I have already proposed the improvement of the Home Government, and the rendering the Indian Government more free to act without constant reference home. Of Indian remedies the following are the most important. First and chiefly, peace: and believing, as I still do, that we have reached the natural limits of India; that no danger threatens from within; that the Burmese war is no more a necessary consequence of the possession of India than a war with Greece on the Don Pacifico question would have been a necessary consequence of the possession of England; —believing also that the operations against the frontier tribes beyond the Indus, harassing as they are, constitute at worst but a little war, such as has always existed in those parts, and that the state of Asia beyond the Khyber is not at present menacing;—believing all this, I think that it is in our own power to keep our Indian empire free from serious war, and to dedicate the energies of the Government and the resources of the state to a career of peaceful improvement. No limits are so strong or so useful as ethnological limits; and when we find ethnology, geography, and historical prescription all uniting to assign the same limits to India, and those the limits of our present empire, we have in Asia the same good fortune which in Europe we alone of European countries possess, and we shall be rash if we overstep the limits so markedly fixed by nature.

Remedies for these deficiencies.

Peace.

Next we must constitute the government in such a way that the executive may be equal to the task thrown upon it; that all the labour and all the responsibility may not be thrown on one overworked Governor-General, perhaps little experienced in Indian affairs. Let him have not

In the constitution of the Government.

passive councillors and irresponsible secretaries, but responsible ministers of departments; let them be so appointed as to secure the greatest present energy; let them be men fitted to be the active ministers of a great empire; the first working men of the day, men who feel a pride in, and the certainty of deriving just credit from, their duties; men rising, and hoping to rise still higher. Make the Governor-General the absolute and undoubted head of the Government, but not in himself *solely* the executive Government. That is what is really wanting. Could any one man, if ever so able and experienced, do all the work of England, or of any great empire under the sun, without the aid of responsible ministers and officers of state, and some division of labour? Yet so it now is in India. Combine the duties, positions, and qualifications of the members of council with those of the secretaries, and you have something near what is required. At present you pay for two sets of officials, and the object is not effected—those who counsel cannot act, and those who act cannot counsel. Responsible ministers will do both. The Governor-General must be disencumbered of the duties of a subordinate government. You must also have a new and efficient law-commission, forming a department of the Government, and the Government must be responsible that the work is not neglected or perverted. Means must be taken to secure to the Central Government a knowledge of the systems, the circumstances, and the wants of Madras and Bombay. Without fixing any precise rule, it will not be difficult, among the ministers, law-commissioners, judges, and other officers of the Supreme Government, to have at head-quarters persons acquainted with those presidencies; the appointments in the central administration being bestowed indiscriminately on all the servants

In acquiring information.

of the state, with reference to personal fitness, and to the necessities of the Government. Some interchange and intercommunication between the servants hitherto employed exclusively in their own presidencies should be established; and when the whole attention of the Governor-General ceases to be occupied by wars, he, and a deputation of the Central Government, may, with the aid of steam, in three or four months of the cold weather, make tours of the minor presidencies, returning to their regular duties at head-quarters for the rest of the year.

The heads of the subordinate governments, and of the principal departments in each, should be required to condense all the results of their operations of each year, to explain their systems and principles, and elucidate their working: in short, to supply the methodical and intelligible information which has been hitherto so much wanting. I would especially enforce this system of condensation and explanation in all departments. It has always been too much the fashion in India to substitute masses of crude matter for a graduated system of information, by which each official class should condense for that above it. It is easier to make a clerk copy all the papers of a case than to analyze and explain it.*

In the location of the Government.

Finally, the Supreme Government must be fixed in such a place as will afford a reasonable probability that the Governor-General will not be much detached from his head-quarters by his political and military duties or the neces-

* I am sorry to see, for instance, that the Agra Sudder Court, which used to submit a report on the proceedings of the judicial department of that government, has lately stated that, finding that the Calcutta Sudder does not do so, but only sends up a prescribed form of figured statements, it thinks it expedient to act uniformly, and to do the same; wherefore in future it also will submit no report, comment, or explanations, but only the formal papers.

sities of his health, and, to secure the Governor-General, you must also have the Commander-in-Chief and the head-quarters of the army at the same place; for it is quite impossible that the head-quarters of the civil and military administration should be permanently located apart. If the Commander-in-Chief does not come to the Governor-General, the Governor-General must go to the Commander-in-Chief. Political and military considerations must be all-powerful, and it is useless to attempt to make a government efficient if you locate it where the head is likely to be constantly called away. Moreover, as the Governor-General and his ministers must always be but men and exotics, it is a fact that in a tropical climate their health must be most precarious, and that in a situation unfavourable in a sanitary point of view they have been, are, and always will be, drawn away by considerations of climate. If, then, the geography of India admits of posting them in a good climate without causing injury in other respects, we should indisputably obtain a great public gain; and you could more easily and cheaply command better services of better men than by requiring them to serve in a bad climate. Temporary absences on cold-weather tours for business purposes would do no harm and much good, if you can only be sure of your Governors in the hot weather; but if the cold weather be spent in looking after a campaign, and the hot weather in the hills looking after the Commander-in-Chief, the politics of the frontier, and the Governor's health, while the head-quarters of the Government are far away, what becomes of the internal administration?

I think that it will be the easiest arrangement here to give the government as I would propose it, leaving farther comments and explanations to follow.

Summary of proposed Supreme Government.

Constitution of Government.

1. The Supreme Government to consist of the Governor-General and the following responsible advisers :—

Minister of political affairs . . } to be members of a committee
Minister of the interior . . . } of public affairs.
Minister of justice, to be vice-president of a committee of justice.
Minister of agrarian affairs * . . } to be members of a committee
Minister of revenue and finance . } of resources.
Minister of military and naval affairs } to be members of a committee
The Commander-in-Chief, *ex officio* . } of war.
The governor, deputy or lieutenant governor, of the place where the Supreme Government may assemble.

The above to form the cabinet council of the Governor-General.

Two law commissioners subordinate to the minister of justice, and to be members of the committee of justice.

Four committees (of public affairs, justice, resources, and war) to be formed, each composed of the Governor-General and members designated above; and the Governor-General may appoint any local governor a member of any committee within his territories. The committee of justice to act as a law commission.

Appointment and removal.

2. The Governor-General and Commander-in-Chief to be appointed by the Senate.†

The ministers and law commissioners to be appointed by the Governor-General in council, subject to the approval of the Senate, from servants of the Indian Government of ten years' service in India, with exceptions following; and on prospect of a vacancy, such appointments to be made such reasonable time

* I have thought it the best arrangement to devote a department to agrarian affairs, combining the management of the revenue derived from taxes (properly so called) with the department of finance.

† In this chapter, when speaking of the acts of the Senate, I imply all the conditions and restrictions on those acts provided in the previous chapter. For instance, appointments to these offices must be confirmed by the Crown.

beforehand as may give the Senate an opportunity of exercising the veto before entrance on office.

Exceptions.—i. Competent persons, other than those described, may be specially and exceptionally appointed to these offices by special concurrence of the Governor-General and the Senate, provided that not more than one member of any committee shall be appointed under this exceptional rule.

ii. If the minister of justice be not appointed under the above exception, then one law commissioner shall be appointed by the Senate, being a person professionally trained to any European system of law or jurisprudence.

All the above officers (including the Governor-General and Commander-in-Chief) to be appointed for five years as a definite limit; but to be re-eligible. To be removable only by the Senate or the Crown.

Position in regard to Senate.

3. The Government of India to obey the orders of the Senate in all things, but the latter to be interdicted from interfering in the patronage vested in the former. Information of the proceedings, and as far as may be of the intentions, of the Indian Government, and other information, to be transmitted to the Senate, in such form and at such times as they may from time to time direct.

Position in regard to local governments.

4. The Government of India to be absolute over the local governments, but to be authorised to delegate to them such powers in regard to local legislation, executive functions, and finance, as may seem expedient (under an administrative code to be as speedily as possible drawn up); also to prescribe rules for the transmission of information.

Position and power of Governor-General.

5. In the Government of India the Governor-General to be absolute, subject only to the obligation of consulting his responsible ministers, and to the conditions hereunto annexed.

6. No order in any department shall be issued by the Governor-General, except through the minister of that department, and till the matter has been considered in the committee of which the minister is a member. The minister shall express his opinion in writing, and his colleagues shall either assent or record separate opinions.

Position and power of ministers.

Each minister shall be the responsible head of his department, but shall obey the Governor-General in all things. The Governor-General in Council may from time to time delegate to him the power of acting in minor matters within prescribed limits in his own name and on his own authority. In matters beyond these limits he shall be entitled to present proposals to the Governor-General, on which the latter shall be bound to make a deliverance, *e.g.* "The minister of justice proposes so and so," "The Governor-General consents," or "The Governor-General negatives, or orders so and so;" and this document shall remain of record in the office.

The members of each committee shall have access to the offices of the ministers grouped in that committee, and any member may at any time mark any subject for discussion in committee, and there give his opinion.

Ultimatum in political department.

7. In the political department, when a measure has been discussed in committee, the Governor-General shall then be free to act on his own responsibility, and at his own discretion, with the annexed exception; but in case of difference of opinion between the Governor-General and a majority of the committee, copy of the proceedings shall immediately be sent to the political committee of the Senate.

Exception.—The Governor-General shall not make war with more than 1000 fighting men of all arms beyond the geographical limits of India, and of a political arrondissement for the purposes of military police (to be defined by law), without consulting and receiving the opinion of a secret cabinet council.

Power of committees.

8. In all departments other than the political, in the event of a majority of the committee finally differing from the Governor-General, they may remit the matter for the consideration of a cabinet council.

The council.

9. A cabinet council shall be held periodically or specially.

All matters referred to the council under the foregoing rules, including the appointment of members of the Government under rule 2, shall be there discussed, and the opinions of the members shall be recorded.

The Governor-General is authorised to take the opinion of the council on all matters in which he may desire it.

The Governor-General is recommended and enjoined to take the opinion of the council on all radical and highly important subjects, in which public injury is not to be apprehended from such discussion.

The decision of the council shall be determined by vote.

Ultimate power of Governor-General.

Having received the opinion of the council, the Governor-General may act on his own responsibility, but, acting contrary to that opinion, shall by the first post transmit copies of the proceedings to the Senate.

Laws.

10. Laws, the power of making which has not been delegated to the local governments, shall be made by the Governor-General in council; the Governor-General having in this as in other matters the power of finally acting on his own responsibility.

Patronage.

11. All patronage, other than the appointment of members of the Government, shall be exercised in the department to which each appointment belongs, subject to the same rules as any other act of the Governor-General.

12. In the event of the absence or sickness of any minister, the Governor-General in council may either appoint another person to act for him, or may intrust the duties temporarily to another minister.

Provision for absence or sickness.

13. Three members (including the Governor-General), of whom one shall be a servant of ten years' service in India, shall be necessary to form a quorum of any committee—except in the political department when the Governor-General is absent from head-quarters, in which case the Governor-General and one minister, one of the two being of ten years' service, may form a committee.

Quorums.

Four shall be a quorum of the council.

14. When the Governor-General shall have occasion to be absent from head-quarters, he may take with him such members of the government as he thinks proper. Committees and councils may be formed either wherever the Governor-General may be, or at head-quarters in the absence of the Governor-General, with his consent; and when formed in the absence of the Governor-General, shall have the same power as if he were present, in those things which he may intrust to them.

Absence from head-quarters, and power of delegation.

The Governor-General, *with* (but not without) the consent of the council, may delegate to one or more ministers absent from head-quarters the powers and duties of any other ministers within prescribed limits and localities, provided that the rule in regard to quorums be not transgressed.

15. The Governor-General shall be relieved from the labour of a local government, and also from the charge of the various non-regulation provinces now administered by the Supreme Government. Future acquisitions shall be

Relief of Governor-General from local details.

either annexed to existing local governments, or intrusted to a separate commissioner under the Supreme Government till the mode of their government is determined.

Salaries.

16. The Governor-General to be paid as at present. Each minister to receive per annum 8000*l.*; each law commissioner 5000*l.*; the Commander-in-Chief 10,000*l.* consolidated salary, or, in addition to military pay and allowances, 3000*l.*

Provision for extraordinary cases.

17. In extraordinary cases not sufficiently provided for, the safety of the state is confided to the Governor-General, but he is required to take the earliest opportunity of regularly supplying, or obtaining the supply of, that which has been wanting. No inferior shall object to the orders of the Governor-General on the ground of illegality. The head of the government is responsible for his acts to his superiors in England, and not to his inferiors in India.

Expense of proposed government.

This government, while I believe that it will be infinitely more efficient, will be much less expensive than that last provided by Parliament, as the following figures will show:—

By the last arrangement, the yearly cost was, besides the Governor-General—

	£.
5 Councillors, including the Commander-in-Chief, - -	50,000
4 Law commissioners - - - - - - - - - -	20,800
4 Secretaries to the Supreme Government - - - -	20,800
13 persons - - - - - - -	£91,600

By proposed arrangement—

	£.
6 Ministers - - - - - - - - - - - - -	48,000
Commander-in-Chief - - - - - - - - - -	3,000
2 Law commissioners - - - - - - - - - -	10,000
9 persons - - - - - - -	£61,000

Gain—four persons, and 30,600*l.*

It will be seen that although, from the separation of departments, the government proposed by me may at first sight have looked formidable, there is in reality a great diminution of numbers as well as of expense. The under-secretaries and subordinate establishments would be distributed among the ministers without additional expense.

The plan amounts, in fact, simply to this—to raise the political, military, and finance secretaries to the rank of ministers, and, instead of the home secretary and the counsellors, to have three ministers—of the interior, of justice, and of agrarian affairs.

Explanation of proposals.

Character, duties, &c., of the ministers,

I have designated the minister who stands first in my list "Political" in the Indian conventional, rather than in the literal, sense of the word. The recent term "Foreign" is not applicable, because the greater part of his duties are not foreign at all, but connected with the dependent states in the interior of our empire, and which I propose to put on the footing in name as well as in fact of our feudatories. The political minister will be charged with all our relations with these states, and with such diplomatic business with states beyond our frontier as may be inevitable.

The minister of the interior will be charged not only with all general matters not particularly falling within separate departments, but especially with education and public works, and the whole great task of the moral and material improvement of the people and the country—subjects of which the superintendence would give ample employment to the ablest of men.

As external and internal affairs most directly affect one another, these two ministers (of political affairs and of the interior) will be most appropriately grouped as the Governor-General's committee of public affairs.

The minister of justice will have, at present, perhaps

the most important and difficult task of all. He will not only superintend the current administration of his department, but will be the actual and responsible head of the law commission, and to him we shall trust seriously and practically to force through to completion the great system of codification and simplification designed twenty years ago, but never executed. The task of improving our laws can be so fitly intrusted to no one as to him who has the daily opportunity of witnessing from a commanding and unprejudiced position their practical working, while at the same time neither is his time occupied nor is his mind confined by the active exercise of the judicial functions of an existing system. I think that two assistants in the law commission will be an amply sufficient number—more would but embarrass. If the minister be a European jurist, his assistants will be selected from the best of Indian servants; if he be an Indian servant, he must have the assistance of an European jurist.

and of the law commission.

Hitherto it seems that the legislative member of council is not considered to have any *necessary* connection with the law commission. It would appear that he is paid 10,000*l.* per annum for drafting in a uniform and legal form the acts which the Government of India has from time to time occasion to pass—a very useful and necessary duty, no doubt, but one which might be quite as well performed by any clever young man from a special pleader's office. The councillor, however, having nothing else to do, has generally accepted the office of president of the commission. We have seen how completely he and the commission have failed. A good working minister of justice might manage things very differently. I shall reserve for another place the detail of the objects to be set before, and other particulars regarding, the new law commission. Suffice it here to say, that there is every reason to believe that the objects proposed by the last Act, and not attained, may, if rightly set about, be well effected, in a very moderate time, to the immense advantage of the country and the Government. In addition to the permanent committee of justice, the Governor-General will have it in his power to issue special commissions to natives and others, and to employ them in the compilation of particular codes or rules.

I shall also propose a supreme court of justice for all India in connection with the Supreme Government.

The departments of revenue and finance are too large to be managed in all their details by one man. I would, therefore, have two separate ministers—one to superintend the great department of land revenue, and the agrarian interests connected with it; another for ordinary revenue and finance, and to supervise the details of expenditure which now give employment to the financial secretary. And, intimately connected with one another as are these two duties, the two ministers will unite in a committee of resources.

The minister of military and naval affairs will unite the duties of military councillor and military secretary, and this minister with the Commander-in-Chief will form the Governor-General's committee of war (a term which I use for brevity, meaning, in fact, of military and naval affairs). They will also be members of, and assisted by, a military and naval board.

In superintending and sharing all these various duties the Governor-General will have ample employment.

Explanation of plan of committees and council.

I have adopted the plan of grouping the members of Government in committees for advice and discussion, because, while for executive action unity of purpose and power is indispensable, counsel and warning are sometimes necessary to all men.

We cannot always see our own acts as others see them; and the calm assistance of an able unbiassed mind is most important in matters where the active executive officer may be, in some degree, carried away and prejudiced. On the other hand, the whole council would be inconveniently numerous for the transaction of matters of detail. But for the decision of very important measures or obstinate difference of opinion, a cabinet meeting will ensure the amplest discussion and the soundest advice of able men of all departments viewing a matter from many different positions and in many different lights. The local governor will be one of the most practical and important members of the council.

Appointment of ministers, &c.

I think it essentially important that under the new system the *initiation* of the appointment of the ministers, as vacancies from time to time occur, should ordinarily be vested in the Governor-General in India—the councillors having the opportunity of expressing their opinions publicly or privately, and the Senate retaining a veto to prevent abuse. Under the present system the appointment of passive councillors by the Directors is quite unobjectionable, and acts very well. But in regard to active ministers, it is a natural and necessary sequence of the position of the Home Government that their knowledge and appreciation of merit is considerably behind that of the Governor-General on the spot; and that, though they are well qualified to judge, sooner or later, of the most deserving men, they cannot be depended upon to nominate those of greatest present energy and fitness. To do so, they must have not only the usual official documents, but the reports of surgeons, physicians, and mental philosophers. Because a horse won the Derby last year, you will not without inquiry lay your money on him this year for any race. He may be lame, or sick, or sorry; or a better horse, known only to the jockeys, may be coming into the field. So a man who has done excellent service to the state for thirty years past may not be the fittest to undertake a new and more important office, and the interests of the empire cannot be sacrificed to the deserts of individuals. Every man must take his chance, and be estimated at his market value. You must allow your trainer the Governor-General, and his council of jockeys of departments, to place your men, only taking care that he does not cheat you, and interfering when you suspect that your interests are being jobbed or sold.

What I have just said applies to ordinary nominations of persons selected from the Indian service. But a more difficult and debateable question arises in the exception, as to the appointment of other persons from England to fill situations in the Indian Government. Shall such appointments be permitted, and on what terms? I have no doubt that the places can and generally will be well supplied from the Indian service; but still it seems to me to be desirable that some extraneous blood should, if possible, be introduced. My reasons for thinking so are as follows:—

Admission of unprofessional persons.

I have stated, as one advantage and object of a revised scheme of government, and of conducting the Indian administration in the name of the Crown, that there might then be some degree of interchange between the services of the state in India and those at home and in other parts of the empire. An exclusive and class system of government is, on all hands, admitted to be an evil; and while I believe that there is not in the empire any great class of trained professional civil servants of the state at all to be compared to that possessed by the Indian Government, I also think that that class is, in some respects, cramped in its opportunities of acquiring general information; that it may be, in some degree, *too* professional and Asiatic in its feelings, views, and knowledge; and that some sort of community of knowledge and interchange of duties between the trained professional expertness of public servants employed in India, and the enlarged views and information of those brought up in England, might be, with great advantage, established. I do not think that the Indian service would by any means suffer in its personal interests by such an arrangement, if carried out honestly and in good faith. I have proposed that the best Indian servants should be professionally employed in the home portion of the government of her Majesty's Indian territories, independent of the caprice of popular election; and it is a fact flattering to the merits of the Indian service, that, on the mere ground of the market value of their services, several of its members have been employed, and successfully employed, by her Majesty's Government in some of the most important offices under the Government at home and in the colonies abroad. I hope that the frequency of such instances will much increase on better acquaintance; but recriprocity is the soul alike of commerce and of politics; and if it be possible to introduce with advantage into some Indian offices English statesmen or men of business, the Indian services must, in their turn, sacrifice some personal interests to those of the state. In the end I believe that they will be the gainers by free trade in public duties. The strong line of demarcation which has hitherto been drawn, by which, up to a certain point, the Indian service is exclusively privileged, and from certain high offices it is systematically excluded, should be in some degree relaxed. At present the minor governorships of Madras and Bombay are literally the only ground common to English and Indian servants; the Governors-General, Commanders-in-Chief, and legislative councillors being exclusively English: all the rest exclusively Indian. Now I think that, if we are to have English governors at all, it is of the very highest importance that her Majesty's Government should have some men at their command who have not only their personal confidence, but already know something of India and Indian affairs;—that a new Governor-General should not necessarily commence the acquisition of the very rudiments of Indian knowledge *after* his appointment. It should be possible to send a rising man to India in a secondary post in the first instance, where, performing a special duty, for which he has special qualifications, he might acquire a general knowledge of the country and the people, and of the general bearing of all departments: and I also think it but fair and reasonable that the best Indian servants should not be excluded by rule from the very highest appointments, and would open everything to their honest ambition, especially when, by service or residence at home, they become personally known to her Majesty's advisers. I would then arrange that between men rising in England who have seen service in India, and men who have risen in India employed at home, a class of statesmen should be formed, common to the mother-country and her great dependency—a connecting link between them—who would introduce into England some knowledge of, and interest in, Indian affairs, and into India some English progress; and that Governors should be appointed from this class: so that, on the one hand, the English politicians sent to India may possess competent knowledge and skill, and, on the other, the highest appointments may be open to the best of those Indian servants who may engraft European progress on Indian experience.

Governors-General have complained of the want of

the assistance of English minds in their councils. That assistance would be supplied to them by one or two English ministers, and the possession of such assistance would remove one great obstacle to the promotion of the best Indian professional men.

Altogether, then, I think I may assume that some such arrangement as I have suggested is desirable, if practicable and secured against abuse. Let us see how it can be carried out.

Cases in which such appointments may be permitted.

I propose to admit the special appointment of non-Indian persons to the office of minister, provided that there shall not be more than one such person (exclusive of the Governor-General) in any one committee, and no order can be issued without the advice of one or more ministers of local Indian training; such a minister being (I think it will be said with good reason) an essential to form a quorum of each committee. If the Governor-General be a statesman of English education, the political minister must, no doubt, be an Indian officer, both as possessing the necessary knowledge of the natives and of their language, and because, in cases of emergency, the Governor-General and political minister may act alone separate from the council, and the presence of one Indian officer is required to make a quorum of committee. But were the Governor-General, either by previous service or by long tenure of that office, to be himself qualified as Indian, it is not impossible that a rising man might be sent from England, and trained for a future Governor in the office of political minister. As to the ministry of the interior, whoever may be Governor-General, it seems not only possible but probable that an able Englishman might sometimes be of the greatest use in superintending plans of education and material improvement, as well as the general discipline of the interior government, purely professional matters (justice, revenue, &c.) being excluded from his department. He would be of much personal assistance to the Governor-General, and not the less so from being free from personal connection in India. Such an appointment might, therefore, be on some occasions quite justifiable.

It is not likely that an English agrarian minister would ever be appointed, because the requisite knowledge of that branch is only acquired by long personal experience, and it is a department in which the Indian service supplies a great abundance of most able and admirable men. But it is quite possible (as I have, in a previous chapter, suggested) that the Senate might wish to send out, as financial minister, on a particular occasion, and with a particular object, a home servant, fully acquainted with their views of finance, and thoroughly practised in its details by India House experience: the subject being one which depends less on locality than any other. The Commander-in-Chief being an officer of the English army, the minister of military and naval affairs must, of necessity, be an Indian officer (to constitute a legal committee), and, of course, would be so on many other grounds. But, an Indian officer commanding the army, it is *possible* that there should be an English military minister.

A mere legal councillor, to draw up the form of Acts, will no longer be necessary—the law commission will do that; and the ministry of justice will certainly not be an appointment which can be bestowed on any mere English lawyer. I mean—and I say it without any disrespect—that such gentlemen, for instance, as are usually appointed to offices in the Indian supreme courts, would not be fitted for the appointment which I am discussing. But one can well conceive a case in which an accomplished European professional jurist, uniting the technical qualifications of a lawyer with the energy and broad views of a statesman, would fill the office with great advantage, being in himself the soul both of the executive administration of justice and of the professional undertaking of the law commission. One can imagine, for instance, Lord Brougham to have made an excellent Indian minister of justice. If we could obtain such a man we might have everything codified in one quarter of the time that the old law commission have consumed in their reports on the fusion of law and equity, and similar subjects. At the same time, unless such a man should be found, it is not indispensably necessary that the minister of justice should be a professional lawyer in the strict sense of the word; it is enough if he is accustomed to view and superintend the working of laws, and the professional commissioners would supply the rest (though, of course, it would be better if the two qualifications should be found united). Either an Indian officer of enlarged views and some judicial experience, or say a first-rate English under-secretary of the Home Department (who must become, I believe, a kind of *quasi* lawyer), might be appointed with advantage, selection being made of the most fit person, Indian or English; and with the aid of one European and one Indian professional commissioner he might carry through the required codes.

It will be observed, however, that I propose to make every appointment of a non-Indian person to the office of minister a special and exceptional case. The great object is to insure against abuse. When the nomination to an appointment is confined to the limit of an active profession, there is, as I have before argued, comparatively little chance of abuse, because the candidates, their history and qualifications, are well known, and a united profession is strong to expose and decry any gross abuse of its interests. But it is different when your choice is in no way limited; when there is no professional standard by which to judge the candidates; and when the temptation to serve an unprofessional friend is so much greater than in the case of hiring a professional man in the professional labour-market. I have said that most of these appointments might probably be filled from the Indian service, and doubtless they *would* generally be well filled in this way. It is only when in special cases it seems that a particular office might be *better* filled by going beyond the limits of the profession, that an exception should be made; and I would secure this exception against abuse by the provision that the Governor-General and the Senate should, by *previous* correspondence, concur in the propriety of appointing a particular person. It would be open to either party, in anticipation of a vacancy, to make a proposal to the other. If the required concurrence could not be obtained, the vacancy would be filled up from the profession under the ordinary rule. We may be pretty sure that the Senate and the Governor-General will not concur in the appointment of an unfit man when so easy and satisfactory an alternative is before them.

Appointments from minor presidencies.

I have made no special provision for the appointment of a certain number of members of the Government from each presidency, for reasons to which I have before alluded, and because I hope to see established a more intimate connection between the services. I expect that the Supreme Government would, under the new system, become well and personally acquainted with the affairs of all the presidencies, and that the fittest persons would be selected for the offices of the Central Government from all India, reference, of course, being had to the particular requirements of the Government at the particular time, and it being probably so arranged that there should be at head-quarters, in some capacity, some one personally acquainted with the affairs of each part of India, to whom reference could be made for petty explanations, dependent on mere local knowledge. In the law commission, too, I have thought it unnecessary to burden a body intended to act with numbers fitted only to deliberate, by specially providing a member from each presidency. The old commission must at least have collected a mass of information. If more is required, résumés of existing laws or customs might be well and speedily obtained from the local governments; and I have supposed the presence at head-quarters of experienced officers from different parts of India, whom the law commission, as well as the Government, might at any time consult. Besides, at any rate the penal code, which has so long occupied the old commission, has nothing whatever local about it; and, in most things, the less local are our simple general laws the better. It is only when we come to codify the unwritten civil customs of places and classes that we become local or rather personal. Mere local regulations I would leave to the local governments.

Term of appointment.

I propose to appoint all the great officers of Government, distinctly and definitely, for five years, supposing them to remain so long willing and able to serve efficiently. But I would make them re-eligible, and would by no means desire to consider five years the practical limit of their term of office; far from it. On the general principle, that in the public service we must look not to individual deserts, but simply to the market value of the services available, I would never propose to displace a qualified minister (like a member of council under the present system) because he has had a fair share of the sweets of office, and in order that another may have his turn. Experience is an advantage—wear and tear of body and mind a disadvantage; and when a man's term is out, I would simply consider whether the old man or the best new man to be found is likely to do the best future service. Those rare good men who seem to be occasionally sent by Providence for the performance of particular tasks are not so often found that we can afford to lose them when they occur; and especially in India (it is the great misfortune of the Government of that country) it is difficult to retain them so long as we could wish. A good man should be kept as long as he lasts and will stay, and should be cherished as the apple of the state's eye; his health cared for; his personal feelings regarded; his sons, if well fitted, employed by the Government without wearing personal solicitation. It is a great deal too much the fashion in India to work a willing horse to death. The principle seems similar to that in the southern slave States: work a man while he lasts; use him up; and then take your chance of getting another. Many a man is exhausted, or retires, who, well cared for, would have lasted much longer; and I think it a great advantage, if, by the division of labour which I have proposed, as well as by the regard to climate in locating the government, which I shall shortly propose, by the mode of distributing patronage suggested in a former chapter, and in other ways, the services of the best men may be secured for longer periods than at present. On the other hand, many men placed in high office without becoming so incompetent as to be ejected on recorded grounds, disappoint previous expectation. Time, tear, and climate, tell on all men; and it is every way desirable that at certain reasonable intervals an office should be at the unfettered disposal of the Government. It is therefore that not only in practice but in law I would make a new nomination necessary at the end of five years. And then, if the outgoing man be most fit, let him be re-appointed for another term. If such a man as Lord Dalhousie will remain in India, he is now doubly valuable after the experience of five years. Why, then, should he be under a sort of prescriptive obligation to resign, and merely asked to stay from year to year? Why should he not be formally re-appointed? I would apply this principle to all the ministers and law commissioners, and shall afterwards have occasion to suggest it in regard to other appointments. At present the Home Government can continue a man in his appointment; but after the usual five years it is a precarious, uncertain, and temporary tenure, very different from a fresh appointment.

In certain cases it is quite necessary that there should be a power of removing from office, by special order, within the allotted term, but this power must, under any circumstances, rest with the Government at home.

Powers of the Government.

That the Government of India should be in all things subordinate to the Home Government, and that it should be absolute over the local governments, are essential parts of the scheme of administration. But we may hope that the Indian Government will be permitted the fullest scope to initiate and act, and that the Home Government will for the most part confine itself to supervision and control. To permit the interference of the Senate in the patronage of the Governor-General would defeat the object with which the partition of patronage has been proposed, and it is therefore, as now, prohibited. It is to be hoped that the form of transmitting information will be vastly improved, and that the Home Government will be much better informed of all that is passing in India with a very much smaller expenditure of labour, paper, and ink. It is impossible to fix by rule the particular matters in which the Indian Government must inform the Home Government *before* acting—that must be left, to a certain extent, discretionary; but I would make it an invariable rule, that, having announced its intentions, and received in a reasonable time no orders to the contrary, it shall be perfectly free to act. The Governor-General should send home an annual budget, but should not be restricted in comparatively small items of expenditure.

To require every local regulation of the subordinate governments to pass the Supreme Government in the form of a law (and it is at present by no means clear what acts are regulated by law, and what require no laws) is a useless hindrance of business; and it is every way expedient that it should be permitted to the Central Government to delegate to its subordinates the power of declaring certain rules (whether they be called laws or regulations) within their own limits. A check on the expenditure of the subordinate governments is very necessary; but it may be intrusted to the Supreme Government to define the mode in which it is to be exercised, and the degree of licence to be permitted.

Powers of the Governor-General.

That the Governor-General should have the power of acting in all things on his own will and responsibility, when he chooses so to do, is inevitably necessary for the efficiency of an absolute despotism ruling over a conquered country, and to secure the safety of the state. It would never do in a great crisis to admit the possibility of legal and constitutional difficulties. Right or wrong, the Governor-General must for the time do as he will, and answer for his conduct afterwards. At the same time, the obligation of consulting and receiving the recorded opinion of efficient and responsible advisers is a much greater check on abuse or inconsiderateness than any direct limitation which could be put on his power; and I have tried to propose a plan by which due counsel may be secured without the delay, discordance, and other evils attending too great multiplicity of opinions.

Mode of conducting business.

If the Governor-General and minister of a department are agreed on a subject, and the other member or members of the committee do not object, there is no need of farther reference. If a difference of opinion is recorded, the Governor-General must consider it well, as, in case of his proving to be wrong, it stands for a memorial against him; and in the event of the difference being maintained on both sides, a reference to the council is every way reasonable.

Political department.

Many reasons will suggest themselves why in matters belonging purely to the political department the matter should not necessarily go beyond the committee.

Exception to power of political committee.

I do not think that injury can result from the exceptional rule which I have introduced in the political department, and it may save us from future parallels to the Affghan war.

The delay in great and distant operations caused by consulting the council will hardly be perceptible, and is in no way to be weighed against the danger of a rash and ambitious or a weak Governor-General involving us in great difficulties. Parliamentary prohibitions of conquest were useless till we reached the natural limits of India; but having reached those limits, we must stop, or we find again no natural limits short of the limits of Asia—and Asia might not pay. India being geographically almost as much isolated from Asia as Britain is from Europe, it is almost as desirable to restrain the too great disposition of rulers to make and meddle in matters with which they have no concern.

In addition to the limits of India, I would give the Governor-General power within such a line of ordinary operations (to be geographically defined) as should enable him to act against and chastise frontier tribes and robber enemies, and to secure his external defences; but any operation beyond these limits must be extraordinary, and I only wish it were possible without political danger still farther to curb the power of the Indian Government to go to war beyond its own boundary.

Use of the council.

While it is only in exceptional cases that the Governor-General is under obligation to consult his cabinet council, it is to be expected that, under the voluntary and recommendatory clauses, that body will be his advisers on almost all broad and important questions, and in a body so constituted there cannot be wanting the best and soundest advice.

Governor-General's power of legislation.

In the exercise of the Governor-General's power, I doubt whether a distinction can well be drawn between the laws of an absolute government and any other act; between the power of making laws and the power of acting independent of laws. Such a distinction might lead to the dispute on legal grounds of the acts of the Governor-General. It is enough that the Home Government can at any time order the repeal of improper laws.

Patronage.

The rule by which patronage is exercised in the department to which each appointment belongs does not stand in need of comment. Each class of officers, political, revenue, or judicial, will be appointed by the Governor-General in consultation with the minister of the department; and general patronage, not belonging to separate departments, or belonging to several departments combined, will pass through the ministry of the interior, the ordinary executive representation of Government being included in this latter class of appointments.

I have already alluded to the principle on which the committees are formed; and as three persons are essential to that principle, and the Governor-General has the power to supply the place, or provide for the functions, of absent ministers, no inconvenience can arise from requiring a quorum of three; which will always be available for any committee, when any three members of the Government are present. In political matters it may however be sometimes necessary that the Governor-General should have every facility of moving and acting uncramped by too much restriction, and I have therefore provided that in this exceptional case two (the Governor-General and one minister) shall be a quorum. The council consisting of nine members, four is a small quorum, and will be always available at head-quarters. I have fixed it so low, that business may not be stopped by any possible contingency.

Quorum of committees and council.

The only restriction which I have placed on the absolute power of the Governor-General is that which limits his power of acting separate from and without the advice of his ordinary ministers to cases in which the council shall consent to his doing so, and then makes it obligatory on him to take with him at least one minister as his responsible adviser, to whom the powers of other ministers would be delegated. Political difficulty cannot result from this rule, because on an emergency, taking with him the political minister, the Governor-General and minister constitute a committee all-powerful in political affairs, with the salutary exception already noticed. In other matters of interior administration, it may be presumed that the council will consent to all reasonable delegation of power to facilitate local arrangements; and under this rule the Governor-General, one minister, and the local governor, may with the consent of the council constitute a committee on any subject, at

Single restriction on power of Governor-General.

Power of delegation.

any place; or with two ministers the travelling government will be in itself sufficiently complete. If the Governor-General when absent from his council differ from his advisers (including the local governor, whom he may at any time call in) on matters other than political, it is only proper that the matter should be delayed and referred to the council for their opinion.

The Government being properly located, we may expect that prolonged delegation will be the exception, and not the rule: but temporary delegation for other purposes than war and climate will be more frequent than at present, and most useful.

Salaries.

The salary which I have assigned to the ministers is adequate, but, considering the importance of the duties, and the enhanced value of European labour in India, by no means large. It may, perhaps, be inexpedient to pay a man too high when you want him to work. Both men and animals when over fed get lazy; you must rather feed them with liberal moderation, their labour considered, and see that they are well treated, stabled, and groomed. At present, members of council have so little to do, and so much to get, that they are not in working condition. A minister will work, and hope to rise still higher.

It will be found that the provision for relieving the Governor-General from local details is quite necessary to his efficiency as head of the Supreme Government.

Provision for extraordinary cases.

The last article provides for the extraordinary exercise of power by the Governor-General in cases not provided for (of which he must be the judge), and negatives all right of inferior servants to refuse compliance on any ground.

For instance, if, the Governor-General being absent on a political emergency, the political minister were to die, and the Governor-General to be left alone, he must act alone. All extraordinary cases cannot be provided for, and you must trust something to a man in the position of the Governor-General.

Question of share of natives in the government.

Before leaving the constitution of the Supreme Government, it may be well here, once for all, to notice the question, whether it is possible to give the natives any legislative share in the government of India, or to prepare them in any way for freedom. I have all along assumed, and hold as beyond all question, that the idea of giving them any actual power is altogether chimerical and impossible. Our government must be the purest despotism. We have the best securities in our own constitution that the Englishman who represents this country as supreme ruler of India will act to the best of his power for the benefit of the people, without local connection or prejudice; without the obstacles to executive efficiency, and the danger of the tyranny of a dominant majority or minority, incident to all free constitutions; and also without the corruption and tyranny usually incident to despotisms. This is a great advantage; and I doubt whether it is either desirable or possible to alter it. Even if it were desirable, I believe that political freedom may be indigenous, but cannot be cultivated to advantage. Unless you have an indigenous national aptitude for political freedom, and a prescription deeply rooted in the national mind, freedom is but the freedom from all rule, and another name for anarchy. These conditions are not found in India, where there is not even a united nation. They may exist among certain classes, but not in the population in general. If, then, the advantage of our rule should ever be disputed, it will probably be only a question between the relative advantages of a foreign and a native despotism; the one being pure and expensive, the other cheap and probably corrupt. While, therefore, everything should be done to elevate the natives socially and individually, I see no object in attempting their political elevation beyond the limits of small municipalities.

But I can see the very greatest advantage in availing ourselves to the utmost of individual native knowledge and intelligence, as a guide and aid in administering the affairs of a government in which they are interested, and of a people whom they must understand better than we do. There are natives whom I believe to be more qualified, personally, and especially from their position, to give a valuable opinion on the effect of administrative measures and the real working of our system than almost any European. We might at the same time enlist the advice and assistance of such men, and confer on them an honorary distinction, flowing from an avowedly imperial source, which they would highly appreciate.

This brings me to the suggestion of a native consultative council (the proposal that they should have votes in a legislative council being out of the question). To such a council assembling ordinarily for personal discussion there is one positive and one negative objection. The first is, that such an assembly must necessarily be almost entirely composed of natives resident at the seats of the supreme and local governments (supposing the latter also to have consultative councils). But the natives of the present presidency towns are (with a few brilliant exceptions) the worst class whom we could consult: the most Europeanised; the most denativised; the most likely to be influenced by personal interest and intrigue; the least acquainted with what is going on in the country; the most given to call themselves "the natives;" the least in any way representing that class of her Majesty's subjects. To trust to them alone, as exponents of the feelings of "the natives," is most injurious.

The negative objection is, that I doubt the possibility of getting natives to talk freely on doubtful points in a large, and, so far, public assembly.

On matters in which an unanimous opinion prevailed the assent of a respectably-constituted native assembly would carry weight with it; and a dissent would, if the government had been strangely blind to native opinion, probably open its eyes. But practical information and advice on difficult and disputable points is only to be obtained from natives by private conversation, and tested by comparison of arguments.

Proposed native privy council.

I would propose that some distinction, corresponding to our rank and office of privy councillor, should be conferred, in the name of the Crown, on natives of talent and distinction throughout the country, both on our own immediate subjects and on the feudatories of the empire. Perhaps among this latter class would be found some of the best advisers regarding our internal administration, because they alone are in a sufficiently independent position to give impartial opinions. The opinion of a man placed in such a position as the Nawab of Rampore seems to me especially valuable. This privy council, then, I would not ordinarily assemble as a body, or would do so only for nominal purposes, just like the English privy council; but I would give to privy councillors the privilege of addressing written memorials to Government on public matters, and would enjoin on the Governor-General and Governors to consult by circular, on all subjects on which they may think native opinions desirable, all or a portion of the privy councillors, and on special occasions to appoint a time and place of meeting, where all interested in the discussion of a particular measure should be invited, if it so please them, to attend and expound their views. The opinions of privy councillors, being collated and examined, should be recorded in the proceedings of Government, with the reasons for or against acting on the advice given, and should be submitted, in a condensed form, for the information of the Home Government. The Governor-General might also summon particular privy councillors to particular cabinet councils, where their opinions should be recorded, but they should have no votes.

Some such arrangement seems to me to be the proper medium between a Quixotic advocacy of native political rights and a foolish neglect of native intelligence and opinion.

The advantages of privately consulting individual natives are obvious, but cannot be reduced to rule.

An important question remains: where shall the Supreme Government be permanently located? I have already adverted to some of the *necessary* conditions of good government which involve this question, and shall here sum up the various considerations of necessity and prudence which should guide us in fixing a place as the seat of our government and capital of our empire.

Location of the Supreme Government.

It is desirable that the place should be as central* as possible to the different parts of the empire, and the nearer to England *pro tanto* the better.

Objects proposed.

It is necessary that it should be so situated that it shall be the actual and usual residence of the Governor-General, and the permanent head-quarters of the army; and to secure these objects it is not only

* I mention this consideration first, rather as that which first occurs than as attributing the first importance to its exact geographical fulfilment.

desirable, but necessary, that it should be within reach of those vital political and military affairs, duties, and apprehensions in which the Governor-General and Commander-in-Chief must always be personally engaged.

It is necessary that the seat of government should be so placed, fortified, and protected, that, in the possible event of either internal disturbances or frontier invasion, it should run no risk of falling by any sudden *coup* into the hands of rebels or enemies.

It is extremely desirable that it should be in a climate suitable to European health and energy, in order to secure both the uninterrupted presence and the long-continued service of the members of the Government, and their vigorous and zealous performance of their duties; and it will be a most important end of such a situation that we may make it not only a capital, but also a colony.

It is desirable that the seat of the Supreme Government should also be the head-quarters of one of the subordinate governments, and, if possible, of the most important and the best of those governments, the most favourable specimen of our administration, the best model on which to form the ideas of the English members of the Supreme Government, and on the experience of which to improve the other governments.

It is desirable that it should be among the finest people in India—those most extensively employed by us, and whom it is most important to attach to us.

Finally, the expense of a transfer must be taken into consideration.

If there were any city pre-eminently the capital of India, or having any claim whatever to that character, it might be natural and desirable to consider first the possibility of making that city the seat of government; but there is, in fact, no such city. Delhi and Agra have ancient prescription in their favour, but that is hardly sufficient, unless it can be shown that the causes which gave them ancient pre-eminence still exist.

Supposed *primâ facie* claim of Calcutta.

Calcutta is still the nominal seat of government, but there can be no greater mistake than to suppose that, as a city, it has any claim to be a political capital of India; it is the undoubted commercial capital of Bengal, but nothing more. I do not know that there is any good census of the great towns, but at any rate Calcutta is, even in population, in no way very pre-eminent, and is only one of some half-dozen of the most populous places in India. It has no doubt a larger commerce than any other place, but it is a city of recent origin, and exclusively commercial. It contains no other native aristocracy than the aristocracy of commerce, and has nothing political about it. Now, whatever England may be, the empire of India is not (I will make bold to say) pre-eminently commercial, and there is no reason for regarding commerce alone more than any other great branch of industry. There is no stronger *primâ facie* ground for fixing the seat of the government of India at the most important seaport, than there would be for fixing the government of France at the chief port of that empire. Even the prescription which Calcutta had in some degree acquired while yet our empire in India was only partial, it has quite lost, from the practical fact that for the last twenty years it has not been the actual or usual seat of the Supreme Governor and chief power of the state. With respect to the European residents, I believe that it would positively be a very considerable advantage to relieve a man in so great a situation as that of the Governor-General from the multitude of petty and local business which besets him in such a town in the midst of such a population, and which may with great advantage be left to the local governor.

Denying, then, that Calcutta has any *primâ facie* claim, we must consider it on its merits, and let us see how far it fulfils the required conditions. It will be found that it is singularly ill-adapted to meet them.

Examination of actual fitness of Calcutta.

First, then, it certainly is not central, and, moreover, it is farther from England than any other important place, and the postal communication is considerably longer. We may assume (for argument) that, coming round the Cape, we commenced our empire at Calcutta, but on that very account it is an extremity, and, the route of communication being now reversed, it is actually the farthest extremity.

Continual absence of Governor-General;

Secondly, experience has proved that Calcutta is not, and is never likely to be, the place of permanent and uninterrupted residence of the Governor-General and Commander-in-Chief. Error may arise from the argument in favour of Calcutta which has been drawn just at present from the Burmese war, and the fact that the Governor-General has been called down to Calcutta to superintend that operation. But I maintain that a Burmese war is the exception, and not the rule; and that the Governor-General has merely been temporarily called from affairs of more permanent importance to look to a local accident. Wherever he is located, such necessities may arise, and, residing at head-quarters as the rule, he may without inconvenience make such temporary expeditions as the exception. Once in twenty or thirty years you may go to war with the Burmese, or Bornese, or Madagascarese, and send troops over the seas to promote your commercial interests and vindicate the honour of the national flag, but you would not in the last-supposed case (of war with Madagascar), because the Governor-General goes to Bombay to superintend the despatch of an expedition, on that account fix the Supreme Government permanently at Bombay. The Burmese war is not necessary or vital. Since the last war there has been no apprehension of danger to India, or to any part of it, from the Burmese. The mountainous country between Bengal and Burmah is a sufficient natural boundary. The Burmese have nothing to do with India, and no connection with Indians. You cannot even find a land route to march troops against them, and if you *will* go to war with them it must be by the aid of your ships. Neither have any non-maritime rulers of India attempted to conquer Burmah, nor are the Burmese really formidable or dangerous to India. Bengal is really quite secure from serious invasion from the east.

It is very different on the real frontier of India. From the north-west frontier conquering hordes have many times issued and many times conquered the country. All great movements in Asia have led to the entrance into India, from that quarter, of nations or armies. Its politics are of vital and constant importance. The north of India, the Hindostan of the natives, has always been inhabited by dominant and warlike peoples; *there* has always been the seat of former empire—*there* is now the nursery of our armies and the seat of our military strength. Calcutta is the point most remote from the frontier—far distant from Hindostan, and isolated from the body of our troops and the centres of our military power. It is not even conveniently situated for the political supervision of the chief native states within India. What follows? Whenever there is anything anxious in the state of frontier, or even internal, politics—whenever there is war or prospect of war (other than maritime and voluntary war)—and whenever there is any important business connected with the army—on all these occasions the Governor-General has been, and always will be, absent from Calcutta—not on occasional cold-weather trips, but habitually, and for years together. He has been in the habit of spending the cold weather in camp, the hot weather at Simla. The Commander-in-Chief has gone further; he has entirely ceased to make any pretence of ever going near Calcutta. I believe that, except to take the oath on his arrival, he has literally never sat in council for the last fourteen or fifteen years. Those then who advocate making Calcutta the head-quarters of the government must distinctly make up their minds whether they are also prepared either to fix the Commander-in-Chief and his staff permanently there apart from the army, or permanently to dissever the head-quarters of civil and military government. That dilemma is inevitable, and is to my mind alone fatal to the *possibility* of making Calcutta the permanent seat of government in the present condition of the empire and position of the army.

and permanent absence of Commander-in-Chief and staff.

We now come to the question of fortification and protection. It is undoubtedly quite necessary that the seat of government should be secured against accidents, and it is very undesirable that it should be placed so near the frontier that the first battle with invaders should be fought under its walls, and the capital be the first trophy of their success. But we are not on this account to go to the other extreme, and to fix the capital, not in the heart, but in the remotest extremity of the empire. If, commencing with a fishing village, we have acquired a great empire, it is an excess of prudence to look forward to the time when, the tide having not only turned, but completely ebbed, we are again reduced to the point where we commenced. When we lose our empire, and are reduced to a corner of a province, it will then be time enough

Question of fortification and protection.

to return to our provincial capital; and when our armies are finally beaten in the field—when even our fortified positions are insecure—when it is necessary to abandon the heart of the country, and our thoughts are turned to our ships, our name and dignity will not stand so high as to suffer much further from the necessity of transferring the remnant of our power from the imperial capital to the fort at Calcutta. I admit that we must render it impossible that any sudden *émeute* or any temporary and reparable reverse of our arms should make the seat of government no longer tenable; but I deny that it is necessary in the plenitude of our power, and in spite of every inconvenience, to keep the seat of government at that spot which, when reduced to the very lowest extremity, we shall in the very last gasp and article of our power the last abandon. We should be in the centre and present stronghold of our strength.

Calcutta is certainly far enough from external invasion. Denuded of troops as is Bengal, it is at least as liable to the approach of sudden internal disturbers as any other of our great cities; and I am not strategist enough to know whether the vicinity of the fort would necessarily save the city from plunder. But granting this to be the case, we merely admit that one necessary condition is fulfilled by Calcutta—not that it alone can fulfil that condition.

Naval protection.

But it is said that we are a maritime people, and therefore we should have a maritime capital; and here lies the fallacy which has had such force. It is true that England is a maritime nation, and that India is protected from the seabord side by the marine of England. But our empire in India is not naval. It is, on the contrary, essentially military. The very fact of the naval superiority of England makes the Indian marine of comparatively little consequence. We shall never (it is to be hoped) be attacked in India by sea; but many powers have looked to attack us by land, and it is to our army that we must trust. It is true that, if we are ever reduced to the fort at Calcutta, a fleet might throw in supplies there, and enable us to hold out the longer; but I have already argued that our last point of possession and defence in adversity is not necessarily the capital of our prosperity. You would not fix the capital of Britain in Scotland, because when Louis Napoleon conquers England you may hold out in Scotland.

But it is still argued, "the supplies of our army come from the sea." So they do; and that is a reason for keeping carefully and securely our seaports, not for fixing the government at the chief port. Calcutta is merely a place *en route*, and the Governor-General does not personally count muskets or weigh powder. As long as you have a fortified station to command the river and a commissary of stores at Calcutta, the seat of your government and the head-quarters of your army may be determined by other considerations than the superintendence of the transshipment of your supplies.

I say then that our maritime power is no sufficient reason for keeping our civil and military commanders in India immediately under the guns of our ships. When a child is a child he remains attached to his mother's apron-string; but when he becomes a man, if he hope to get on in the world, he goes abroad by himself, and does not remain for ever with his natural protectors, because possibly, in the event of his being sick and like to die, he may some day wish to return to them. If our Indian empire is good for anything, it is now fit to defend itself. It may be possible to have a sufficiently fortified seat of government elsewhere than at Calcutta, and in a more appropriate military situation.

In regard to climate, I need merely here say that the climate of Calcutta is tropical, and very unfavourable to European health—that at no place where it would be proposed to fix the government is there a worse climate. It remains to be seen whether we cannot find the other necessary conditions under a more favourable sky. No European remains at Calcutta longer than he can help; and the place is not, and never can be, a colony. It is to Europeans no more than an encampment.

Climate.

The scheme of administration prevailing in Bengal was formed when our knowledge was imperfect, and under great disadvantages—the result is not a favourable model. The Bengalese are an effeminate race, incapable of defending themselves—never found in our armies—unfit auxiliaries to a military power—and not the class whom we should most care to attach to us as our most immediate subjects—as the surrounders and supporters of our empire.

Government and people.

In one respect, and one respect only, is it an object to retain Calcutta as the seat of government. It would cost something to establish the Government elsewhere, and the question resolves itself into the degree of expense, and the comparative value of the advantages to be obtained by a transfer to any other place fixed on as the best. In regard to the buildings and offices of Government, I imagine that the Government-house would be almost the only loss, and that only in so far as it is larger than (it is perhaps double) such as would have been an appropriate Government-house for Bengal alone. I believe that most of the offices of the various departments of Government are merely rented; and if the Governor of Bengal occupied one side of Government house, and established his secretariat and some other offices in the other, the Government property would

Expense.

be sufficiently occupied, and it would be in the end as cheap to build offices for the departments of the Supreme Government elsewhere as to rent them in Calcutta.

Private house-property in Calcutta, of a particular description, might, no doubt, be for a time somewhat depreciated; but this, of course, cannot be considered as material in a great public question; and it is to be hoped that, in so great a commercial mart, increasing prosperity and private demand would soon fill up the gap left by Government servants and offices.

I am, however, very willing to admit that, in almost any place on the continent of India which might be selected as the seat of the Supreme Government (I except Bombay, as not on the continent), prudence would require the expenditure of more or less money in fortification, since the great native forts of former days may be little suited to modern warfare, and we have at present few fortifications of our own construction in the interior of the country. But I believe both that the best modern fortification (mud) is, in a country where manual labour is so low-priced, extremely cheap, and that money so expended would be, on general grounds, by no means thrown away. Continually advancing as we have been, it may have been prudent to abstain from sinking money in permanent works of this kind; but now that we have reached the natural limits of the empire and may hope to be more stationary, I very much doubt whether, as a foreign nation occupying a subject country, we can wisely neglect all fortification. An army in the field encamps in the open plain; but all precedents, ancient and modern, teach us that an army of permanent occupation derives great advantage from the possession of fortified *points d'appui*, in case of sudden disturbance or temporary reverse. I should say, then,

Necessity of fortifications elsewhere.

that a fortified post, in the most advantageous and central position and the head-quarters of the Government and of the army, would be, on many grounds, most desirable. When we come to name particular places, we shall consider the degree of expense and the amount of collateral advantages.

Conclusion in regard to Calcutta.

I conclude, then, that Calcutta, as the seat of government, presents several most important and fatal disadvantages, and no advantage except the saving of the expense involved in the change. I believe that in fact the Supreme Government of India will never be efficiently carried on at that place; that it is merely a question of time; that sooner or later a change will inevitably take place; and that the time is now come when the sooner we make up our minds to the change the better. What is the use of a nominal government at Calcutta when every Governor-General finds some reason to leave it as soon as possible, taking with him the whole power of the state? The strongest argument against nominally fixing the government in Calcutta is, that you never will succeed in really doing so, and that it is therefore better to give it up with a good grace, and avoid all the manifold and fatal evils of a constant division of the government into two inefficient parts.

Let us see, then, what better places can be found, and whether the expense involved is so great as to induce us farther to postpone a measure so essential to the interests and good government of the empire.

Examination of fitness of different quarters of India.

Before mentioning places, we may look to the quarter of India in which it is most desirable to fix the capital. The outline map prefixed to these pages shows the great provinces into which the country is now politically, and in some degree geographically, divided.

It will be seen that there are six principal divisions. A large space in the centre is occupied by a circle of the principal native states, which lie contiguous to one another in this quarter—Gwalior, Rajpootana, Hyderabad, Nagpore, &c. &c. Round this native quarter and contiguous to it (except on one side, where the desert interposes) lie the five great divisions of our territory—Bengal, Madras, Bombay, Hindostan proper (called by us the North-West Provinces), and the plain of the Indus. In which of these great divisions should the government be fixed?

The central quarter, being possessed almost exclusively by native states, would not be selected; and we must therefore give up the idea of finding a suitable place *quite* central to *every* part of India.

The Punjab is the frontier and outlying division, and, in some degree, isolated. The first campaign of an invading army would be there fought, and it would not be prudent nor reasonable to push so far forward our head-quarters.

Madras, though the most maritime of our territories, has not been proposed, and it is perhaps unnecessary to particularize the reasons against the selection of that province for our head-quarters.

In discussing the disadvantages of Calcutta, we have shown those of Bengal generally.

Bombay.

There remain, then, Bombay and Hindostan. Bombay is much the nearest to England, and the increased facilities of overland communication will soon give this fact great additional importance. With a railway across the desert, and screw-vessels in the Red Sea, the ancient line of communication may regain its former importance, and be generally used for the passage of men, stores, and valuable goods. The insular position of the town of Bombay gives it all the advantage of fortification; it is also nearer to and within shorter communication with the frontier than Calcutta, and is conveniently situated with respect to the principal native states. It is in tolerably easy communication with our territories in Hindostan, Madras, and on the Indus; and a railway from Bombay to Agra would be shorter, cheaper, and at least as useful, as one from Calcutta to Agra, and would more completely unite the empire. On the other hand, the Bombay territories are the least important and prosperous, or, at any rate, the least paying, of our possessions. They are not the seats of any of our most important civil and military interests; and the experience and example of administration afforded to the members of the Supreme Government would not be satisfactory. The Governor-General would be more frequently at Bombay than he is at Calcutta, but he would have very many occasions to be absent with the army in Hindostan and on other duties. A principal objection is this—that Bombay itself is in no degree less tropical or more healthy than Calcutta; and Poonah, or some such place more healthily situated on the continent, would cost as much in fortification, &c., as other places possessing greater intrinsic advantages. On the whole, then, I should prefer Bombay to Calcutta, but think that to *it* too great and material disadvantages attach.

Hindostan.

There remains Hindostan, the ancient seat of all the empires and dominant peoples who have ever ruled India; the most valuable possession in the prosperity, and the last seat of strength in the decline, of all great governments—in fact, the historical, and we may almost say natural, empress province of India, to the whole of which it has, in European parlance, even given its name. Since Hindostan has come into our possession, it has been the scene of all our most important political transactions, the basis of all great military operations. The Governor-General, in spite of the theoretical location of the government at Calcutta, has spent most of his time in these territories, and there exercised all the powers of the government; there the Commander-in-Chief, the head-quarters of the army, and the mass of our troops seem to be permanently located. *Primâ facie*, then, this province appears to be the natural and permanent seat of government. Let us see whether in detail it fulfils the required conditions.

To begin with, it lies unquestionably more central to all India than any other province in our immediate possession. It is the centre of the three great provinces (Bengal, Hindostan, and the Punjab), forming an unbroken line of the most valuable territory, now grouped together, and administered and guarded by the same service and troops. It is very conveniently situated to the principal native states, and is in easy communication with Bombay. Even from Madras, in a direct line, it is not very much farther than Calcutta. In short, we have only to look at a map to see at a glance why Akbar selected Agra as the capital of India.

Hindostan is not so near to England as Bombay, but it must be observed that it is much nearer than Bengal, and the postal communication with England is several days shorter than at Calcutta. I have already alluded to the probability of a railroad between Bombay and Agra. The Bombay line is the most advanced of Indian railroads; it will soon run over the Ghauts, and, before long, will probably reach Malwa; it cannot be then much longer before a central Indian rail crosses the dry and comparatively level country between Malwa and Agra, connecting the great countries of the west and centre with those of the north and east. Men and goods, despatched from London *viâ* Bombay, may then reach Agra within the month, and the old route by the Cape and Calcutta will be much less important.

Its fitness for seat of government.

Hindostan, while free from the weakness and peril of a frontier province, is as near the frontier as the capital can safely be; and, in fact, all frontier operations, political and military, have been from hence directed. The best proof that we could here depend on the continued presence of the Governor-General and Commander-in-Chief is in the fact that there has been hitherto no keeping them away. Here alone can we hope to retain a *united* government; and in a permanent and united government is our only chance of *good* government.

Hindostan is, and always must be, the centre of our military power. It is protected by a large outlying territory; and supposing (what is improbable) that an enemy should force the frontier passes, now watched and guarded by us, and should actually invade India, the first struggle would be in the Punjab. If we should perchance be defeated there, we may yet make a stand in Hindostan. But in Hindostan we shall fight no provincial battle; there we must rally all the forces of the empire; there we shall stake everything; there must a Governor-General and a Commander-in-Chief be present to direct a struggle of life and death; there they must concentrate their resources; and there a fortified civil and military centre will be of the utmost importance. Defeated there, we shall find no safety till we reach our ships; we must stand there, or give up India; and when we have given up India, and lost our military power, then, and not till then, we may make the most of our maritime resources, and retain the fort at Calcutta and some commercial guns to protect the commercial depôt of a commercial people trading to India. We shall have nothing more.

The climate of Hindostan is much the best in India, and it contains within its limits, places temperate, healthy, and pleasant; where we may not only advantageously locate both the European and native servants of Government, and form a capital worthy of us, but may also attain that very great desideratum as a centre and resting-place of our power—a colony.

Moreover, Hindostan forms, beyond all question and doubt, the best, and I think I may say the most important, of the subordinate governments. More matured experience, a better native system, a finer people, a more uniform language, some gifted individuals bestowed by fortune, the more immediate presence and interest of the heads of the government, and, it may be added, the superior energy and efficiency in Europeans and natives due to the superior climate, have all combined to make this province the model and success of our system. Here alone could the members of the Supreme Government learn a system worthy of generalisation. Upon the people of Hindostan we chiefly rely for our service and support, and them especially must it be our object particularly to attach to us. Most of the opium is produced in Hindostan * which is merely sold in Calcutta as an entrepôt, and there credited; and, setting aside this item, we shall find that in the chief local sources of revenue (especially land revenue) it is superior, and, even including the sea customs and other imperial incomes levied at Calcutta, is little inferior in total revenue to Bengal. Altogether, and in every way, we have a greater interest in the internal administration of Hindostan than of any other province.

I have then, I think, gone through the various conditions, and upon any general ground whatever I confess

* One opium-producing division, "Bahar," though a province of Hindostan, belongs to the Bengal government.

that I can scarcely conceive a doubt as to the propriety of fixing the central government of India in Hindostan.

Question of particular locality in Hindostan.

We have yet to consider the particular place in that province which presents the greatest advantages. Delhi and Agra boast an ancient, and Simla a sort of modern prescription. As between Delhi and Agra there can be no doubt that Agra is much preferable, and we may therefore dismiss Delhi from the question.

With respect to Agra, I think it may be asserted that it is not now to so great an extent a native, social, or political capital as to give it any very great claim on that ground alone. Agra has been only within the last few years made the seat of the government of the North-West Provinces, and it has not been found by any means necessary that the Lieutenant-Governor should continually reside there. The local business has no particular importance. The city is one of several of the most important towns within the limits of the government; but as I have before said, neither this nor any other place is at the present day intrinsically the native capital either of India or of Hindostan. The fact, then, is, that as concerns the natives we are free to select for our capital whatever place may best suit us, provided only that it be conveniently situated for their access, settlement, and residence. If in these respects there is no obstacle, they will soon flock in sufficient numbers round the permanent seat of our government and government establishments, and probably before long form a native city, as important as any which now exists, and which will in course of time become much more so. It is wonderful how soon on the site of the bazaars of a mere military encampment a city springs up.

This being the case, we may fairly, without detriment to the natives, consider also the interests of the Europeans, and of the European government, as involved in those of its servants and European subjects.

Importance of climate in the consideration

To them the possession of a temperate climate is of the very utmost consequence. I fear that, in the investigations of Parliament, due consideration has not been given to the vast importance of climate, not for the mere personal comfort of individuals, but as in fact and actual practice and experience most important, I may say essential, to the organization, working, and success of a government which must consist of Europeans, and in which an unfavourable climate causes a succession of absences, divisions, and changes altogether fatal to good government, destroys bodily and mental energy, and renders necessary much enhanced remuneration for much inferior service. This disadvantage may be inevitable to some countries, but, if in India we can choose between a good and a bad climate, why should we prefer the bad? In that country prudent men send their very dogs of European birth and breeding to the hills in the hot weather. Are not then our governors and councillors more precious than greyhounds? But there has been too great apprehension of the imputation of personal motives. Most of those who have given their evidence to the committees of Parliament have been, or hope to be, members of the government; and although nearly all have in practice been driven by public duty to the hills, none will bring prominently forward mere personal health and vigour as the valid arguments in determining the seat of government which they really are. It is not any private consideration which should weigh, but the health and efficiency of the government individually and collectively. The sanitary condition of his most valuable servants is of very considerable importance to the master.

—of a seat of government;

And it is not only to the immediate members of the Government that the climate of the capital is of such consequence. The general body of the European servants of Government, and those connected with them, form a vast and most important class. To them the permanent head-quarters of government and of the army, if favourably situated and in a good climate, will form, and it is highly desirable that they should form, a social capital of India (which Calcutta is not), where they will congregate for business, health, and pleasure, where they will become known to the heads of the government and to one another, and where there may be some interchange of ideas. The hard-worked government servant, who has a short leave from his solitary home in the jungles, will there not only fallow his mind by idleness, but will improve it by communications and acquire civilised associations. Especial advantage will be derived from the existence of a common ground on which official and professional men from all different parts of India will meet and learn to share with one another their varied mass of information; and not less will be the gain from the meeting and intercommunication of English and Indian servants, of head-quarter men and provincials, and of official men in general, with the non-official European residents in the country, who will doubtless frequent a European capital. All these advantages are lost if the capital be fixed in a bad and tropical climate, which has no attraction to non-residents, and is avoided by all as much as possible.

—of a European social capital;

I have also alluded to the possibility of combining a colony with a capital. This is not the place to discuss the whole question of the mode and degree in which we may with advantage attempt to colonise in India, and to amalgamate with

— of a colony.

the natives; but it may be generally asserted (with reference to the true and often repeated fact that we are yet but encamped in the country) that it would be a great additional strength, and afford many incidental advantages, if we could make our capital something of the nature of a colony—a centre of a resident European and mixed population—a home and an asylum for natives who may have adopted or approached our manners, our society, or our religion, or have intermixed with our blood—a nucleus of European education, arts, and manufactures—and a rest whereon to place the lever with which we may gradually move the whole mass of India.

Experience has proved that in ordinary private business unaided Europeans cannot to a great extent compete with natives, and that little private colonization takes place. But the fixed centre of a European government, the service of that government, the supply of its demands and of those of a European capital and large European residence, would at once furnish the necessary attraction for European and mixed labour; and if we can find a place combining some natural capabilities with a temperate climate, the classes referred to will undoubtedly colonise. It is, as has been said, essential that the place should not be unfitted for natives; but if we can combine the two conditions, a very great object will be attained. All things then considered, we may compare the different places which present themselves.

Objections to Agra;

Agra is admirably well situated for the seat of government in many respects. But though the climate is much better than Calcutta, it is yet very hot indeed in the summer. It is a tropical climate, and the difference between it and that of Calcutta is not radical, but only one of degree. It is on this account quite unsuited for a European capital. Moreover, the fort of Agra, though large, and in good preservation, is probably not a good place of modern defence; and, situated as Agra is, it might be necessary to expend a very considerable sum in fortification, in order to render both the offices and treasury of government and the native city fully defensible against any *coup de main*.

Simla, again, is in a fine climate, and a very pretty and pleasant place, but is in other respects very inconveniently situated. It is too far to the north, and is so far in the interior of the hills as to be very difficult of access. It is deficient in labour and supplies; altogether unsuited for a native, and most inconvenient for a European capital; and with no capabilities for a colony. I think that the objections to making Simla the permanent seat of government are insurmountable.

and to Simla.

But there is another place not yet brought into importance by the residence of members of the Government, but already as a place of private residence more frequented, and infinitely more accessible, cheap, and convenient than Simla. Mussoorie is not so well clothed and pretty as Simla, but it is in as agreeable and cool a climate, and decidedly more healthy. And it possesses the great advantage indispensable to a permanent capital, that it immediately overlooks the plains of Hindostan; and within five miles as the road now winds down the hill, or a much shorter distance in a straight line, is a very large fertile valley, exceedingly well suited both for native residence and resort and for European colonization, and abounding in labour and supplies. The hills of Mussoorie afford space enough for any number of European houses, a portion of which might be built close together in European style, while detached residences would extend beyond the limits of

Proposed site at Mussoorie-Deyrah.

the present station. Such a post could be impregnably fortified at a very small expense of money, and defended by a very small number of men. But one of the greatest advantages remains to be told. The valley or plain immediately under the hill-station—the spot in which would be the native capital, and which is already much desiderated and partially colonized by European and native Christian settlers—is walled in, as it were, from the great plain of Hindostan by the lower or Sewalic chain of hills—a sort of segment of a circle which surrounds the valley, and on either side closes into the great mountain range. This wall is low and comparatively narrow, but one mass of ravines and gullies, and in a natural state impracticable. Roads can, however, be made through it, such that it becomes no obstacle whatever to the easiest communication; and yet, except by these defensible passes or gates, it cannot be entered. It is the best of natural fortifications.

In short, the spot to which I allude, immediately overlooking the whole plain of Hindostan at the point where its great rivers issue from the hills, and in every way conveniently situated, seems as if it had been expressly formed by nature to fulfil the almost incompatible conditions required by us for a perfectly convenient seat of the European government of an Indian empire. The valley is the Deyrah Dhoon, and the position of the places referred to will be seen from the accompanying sketch.

Its situation and advantages.

Mussoorie, instead of being remote and isolated like Simla, is perched on the outer range of hills immediately north of Agra and Delhi, with which places it communicates by the best road in India through our most fertile and flourishing territory. It is at a point where the outer Himmalayas rise unusually high; on an impregnable clump of hills rising abruptly from

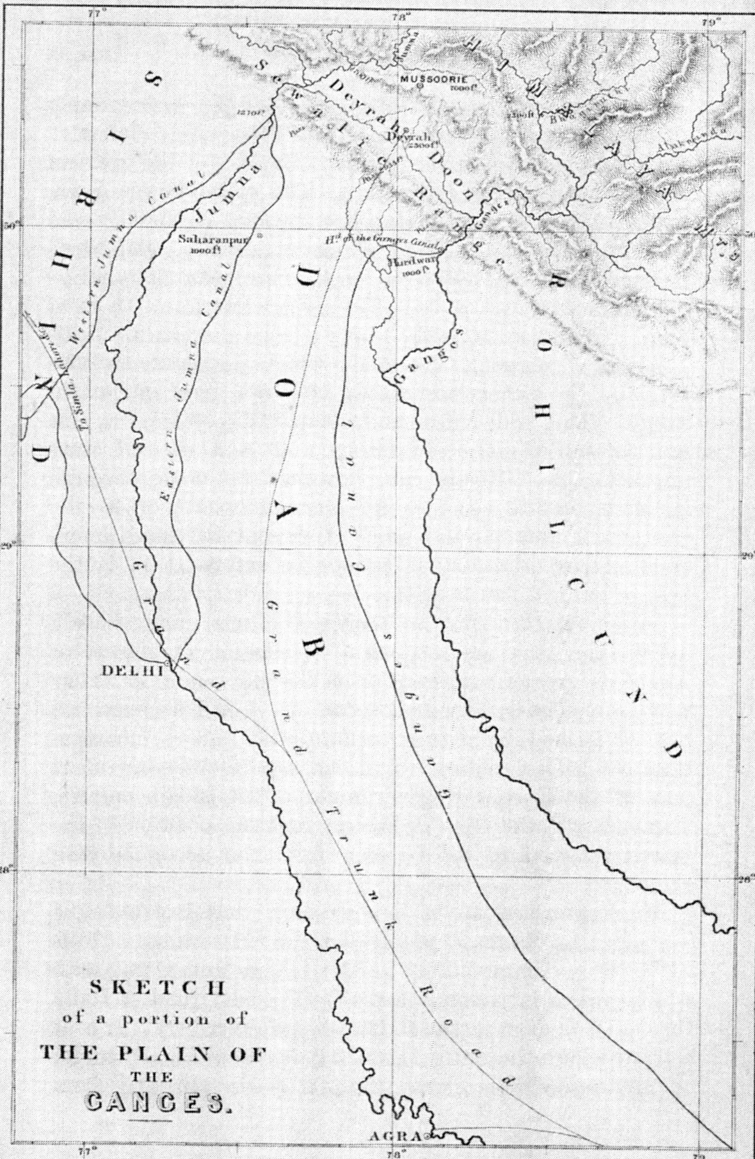

Published by John Murray, Albemarle Street, London 1853.

the plain, and flanked on either side by the Ganges and Jumna, which, here rushing deep and impetuous from the mountains, and cutting narrow chasms in the Sewalic range, may be seen from Mussoorie winding their way far into the plains. Immediately below is the head of the great Ganges Canal, along the bank of which a railway may be run from Allahabad to Deyrah for the mere cost of the iron rails, and without involving an additional brick or spade of earth. The present station of Mussoorie is on an average about 7000 feet above the sea; contains a very large number of detached houses; and there is still a considerable range of unoccupied hill rising even higher. The climate is altogether temperate, and unquestionably the best and most healthy yet discovered in India. Everything is as cheap and plentiful as in the most favoured spots of the plain country.

Deyrah is a particularly beautiful place, in a country which is quite a garden abounding in water and vegetation such as natives delight in, and a favourite resort of Europeans except when the heats of summer drive them for a time to the overhanging heights. The passes through the Sewalic range are even now practicable to all kinds of wheeled carriages, and at a very small expense the road might be made one of the best in the country. Immediately beyond the Sewalic range lies a broad and populous territory, abounding in productions of every kind, and watered by those two riches-bestowing rivers not inaptly deified by the Hindoos. Between them is the great Doab, the pride of Hindostan, and it is flanked by the fertile and famous provinces of Rohilcund and Sirhind.

Mussoorie-Deyrah, in fact, combines almost all the advantages of Agra and Simla, with several others besides. It is within such easy reach of the former place that it is little inferior in the advantage of a central position and speedy communication with all parts of India and with England, and it is admirably placed for the superintendence of frontier politics and military matters. Mussoorie is a better residence and capital for Europeans than Simla, and Deyrah for natives than Agra.

Fortifications of.

To make Mussoorie altogether impregnable would cost, I imagine, next to nothing; and it is difficult to conceive a place better suited for the head-quarters of an army acting on the defensive, or for the refuge, trysting, and recruiting place of a beaten or inferior force, than the Deyrah Dhoon, that pleasant valley flowing with water, abounding in corn and oil, defended by two most difficult rivers and the most perfect natural fortification which can be imagined, and surmounted by an impregnable citadel. If still further security be desired, the nature of the country would make it very easy, by the aid of the natural ravines and other assistance, to form on the side of the valley sloping down from the foot of the Mussoorie precipices a semicircular line of fortifications somewhat as shown in the annexed diagram, which should make the native capital defensible in case our outer defences were forced, and would enable us to retain to the utmost extremity our last hold of Hindostan. I do not anticipate that matters will soon come to this point, but it is merely conceding to those who argue the necessity of a very secure capital that I point out the treble security of the proposed site.

The expense of a Government-house would not be a great consideration in so important a matter; it would be as cheap to build offices at Mussoorie and Deyrah as to rent them in Calcutta; and the servants of Government would build for themselves.

Here then at last we might have a stable and energetic government. Neither health nor constantly recurring political and military business would carry away

PROPOSED SITE OF THE CAPITAL OF INDIA.

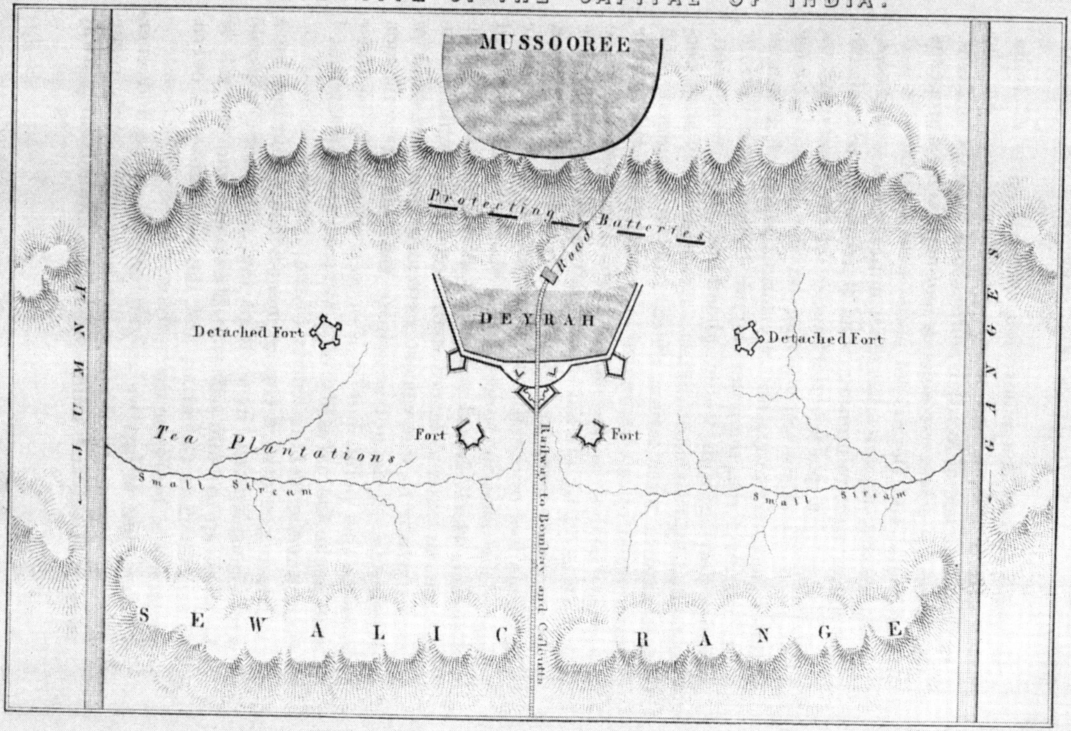

Published by John Murray, Albemarle Street, London 1853.

the Governor-General, the Commander-in-Chief, or the other members of the Government. They would never be absent except on short cold-weather tours, or on very extraordinary occasions. Here we might concentrate the whole of our European energies; here we should retain the services of men of whom we are now deprived by the climate; and here we might found an imperial system worthy of the reputation of the rulers and the greatness of the country ruled.

Proposed arrangements.

I would propose, then, permanently to fix at Mussoorie-Deyrah both the Supreme Government and that of Hindostan, and the head-quarters of the army, with all their offices and establishments. I would have at Mussoorie a European Government-house, the English offices, and the residence of the European officers; at the foot of the hill a native durbar-hall, the public sittings of the chief courts of justice, the principal educational establishments for the natives, the head-quarters of the ordnance and commissariat, the body-guard and personal escort, and other native establishments. The Governor-General and other European officers might come down for a few hours any day that native business was to be done, and in the cold weather would probably spend some time in the valley among the natives.

Around Deyrah might probably be formed a cantonment of native troops drawn from the neighbouring stations to form a head-quarter force; and the European regiments and artillerymen would be perched on the surrounding hills in the hot season, and descend to the valley for exercise in the cold weather. By a new road and fixed steam-engines the communication between the hill and the valley might be reduced to the smallest expenditure of labour and time.

The valley would become a colony of European

mixed, and native settlers and followers of our power.

and results.

And those natives who for us or for the truth's sake sacrifice their own social position would find themselves no longer outcasts.

There tea, and sugar, and hops, and oats, and many European products would be largely grown, and there we should have schools of art, and model cotton-mills and iron-foundries, and many other things besides.

In short, the settlement would be in every way the suitable centre and nucleus of our peculiarly situated power—would supply many deficiencies and secure many hitherto unattainable advantages—the government would be carried on as it ought to be—the Indian service of England would be no longer a penance and a pain—and we should have a connecting link between natives and Europeans. A more pleasant, beautiful, and interesting spot would not exist. The Indian capital would become a fashionable winter resort. Instead of going to Brighton, people would take out through-tickets in November from London Bridge to Deyrah, and spend an Indian "season" at an Indian capital. The great Asiatic possession of England would acquire the interest and importance which is its due, and from one point, thoroughly our own, our religion, science, and civilization might at last be in reality diffused throughout India.

In so great an imperial undertaking we should not be niggard of reasonable expense. The country well

Necessary expenditure.

managed can afford the funds for so necessary an expenditure. Yet, in the first instance, I would not propose anything at all proportionate to what is expended in this or any other country on the seats of the national Government: witness, for instance, our new Houses of Parliament.

Say that 1,000,000*l.* sterling were allowed to found an Indian capital; 500,000*l.* for public buildings, &c.,

and 500,000*l.* for fortifications and outworks, would be, I should think, in the first instance, amply sufficient. In future, all money expended for useful purposes would go infinitely farther than much larger sums unsystematically disbursed for similar objects in different places throughout India.

Future considerations.

I have dwelt so long on this subject because, hoping, as I do, that our empire in India will be lasting, it is of the greatest importance that we should possess a suitable capital and colony, and the question should now be permanently settled. It is a great pity in any way to postpone it. At the same time we must not decide a matter of this kind on any mere temporary considerations. We must have a capital which may be still a capital a hundred years hence. For instance, no one can doubt that the great lines of railway will eventually be completed. It is only a question of a few years sooner or later; and I think that in discussing the merits of Bombay, Agra, or Mussoorie, I am fully justified in assuming that there will be a railroad between those places, and that the traffic between Northern India and England will take the most direct route to the western coast. It is quite certain that as soon as we have a system of railways, and goods and passengers are carried by rail instead of by river, Bombay will be almost exclusively the port of Northern and Central India, and Calcutta only that of Bengal, Bahar, and perhaps Benares. We have but to look to the map to be sure of this fact, the more so as Bombay is an infinitely more convenient and cheaper harbour than Calcutta. The latter is situated a long way up a most uncertain river, which involves much risk and expense, and a freak of the Ganges may any day make it an inland town. Indeed, the tendency of the river is quite in that direction, for, where British fleets once manœuvred, the navigation is now confined to flat river-boats. We may, therefore, reckon without our host if we fix on Calcutta as a continuing city.

No one doubts the evils which have resulted from the division of the government. But some people say, "Oh, it is very true that the Governor-General is often obliged to leave Calcutta, but that would do no harm if he only took his counsellors with him." This I believe to be altogether a mistake. It is not only for want of advice that the Government absent from head-quarters is inefficient for great and deliberate undertakings, but also on account of its separation from its offices, records, and establishments—from its accustomed ways, and habits, and channels of reference—from its roots and branches, as it were. The Governor-General may at a considerable expense carry about with him his counsellors, but it is quite impossible that he should carry about with him all the vast establishments and machines subordinate to him. For local and personal duties temporary tours through the country are most useful, and not inconsistent with the conduct of the ordinary and most necessary current affairs of the empire; but for general review and superintendence, for the undertaking and digestion of great measures, I maintain that a permanent head-quarters and a united government are absolutely indispensable. The Governor-General at Simla and the Council at Calcutta are each quite inefficient for such purposes. Every executive officer in charge of a district feels the same thing. He goes into camp in the cold weather, and marches through his district, but all his most serious and important business is done when he is at his head-quarters with his full office establishment, and following a regular course of life and business. It is just the same with the Government. You may as well expect a tree transplanted every six months to bear

Alternative if plan rejected.

fruit, as a government which has no permanent abiding-place. In no executive office in India can you or ought you to depend on permanent residence in the cold weather. That is the season for movement, and at that time business tours should be not only permitted, but encouraged and ordered. It is, therefore, in the summer that the most regular and deliberate business is done. It is also in the summer that there is temptation to seek a good climate; and if you fix your seat of government in a bad climate, and permit the members of the Government to be habitually absent in the hot season for the sake of health, or on other grounds, all hope of efficiency is gone. You must, therefore, either determine for reasons already urged to fix the government in a good climate, or you must positively prohibit the Governor-General from going to the hills without permission—must subject him and the other members of the Government to exactly the same rules and restrictions as other European servants; and when health fails, you must appoint a new man, just as you would to any other office. I say that there is no medium between these two principles of action at all consistent with efficiency, and that you must adopt one or the other.

If Calcutta is to be the seat of government, let us choose the less of two evils. It is better that our governors should be hot and frequently changed than that the whole government should be inefficient. Calcutta, therefore, let it be, in earnest and not in name. Absolutely restrict business tours to the cold weather months — intrust the politics of the frontier without reserve to the local governor—bring down to Calcutta the Commander-in-Chief and head-quarter staff—and let all future absences be confined by precise leave-rules.

We have yet to consider the great executive divisions into which, under the Supreme Government, India must be portioned out. I think that the six principal provinces enumerated at page 118 will be the most natural divisions, and most nearly coinciding with previous arrangements.

Local governments.

It might be possible to unite the Punjab *cis* the Indus with the government of the North-West Provinces, making over Benares to Bengal, leaving Scinde with Bombay, and putting the strip of territory and political duties beyond the Indus under a separate frontier political agent. But, first, it is by no means an object to unite inconveniently large territories under one executive government, since personal gubernatorial supervision has been much wanting in India; and second, it would be highly inconvenient to divide between three separate authorities the plain of the Indus, the whole of which is the outwork of India, and has so recently fallen into our possession. Politically and socially there is much that is common to the whole line of the Indus, and to the whole of that large territory, between Sirhind and the trans-Indus hills, which has been, till recently, more constantly and exclusively a Mahommedan possession, and latterly the seat of that independent Sikh monarchy which rolled back the Mahommedan power on the one hand, and threatened Hindostan on the other. Both as being contiguous and intimately connected countries, and in order to promote the Indus route of communication, navigation, and commerce, I think it especially desirable to unite Scinde with the Punjab, instead of drawing across a particular point on the river a division line between two governments and armies far distant from and communicating but little with one another.

The plain of the Indus a fifth government.

I would therefore make the plain of the Indus a separate and fifth local government, a character to which its position and importance give it every claim.

Chief Political Commissioner of Central India.

The sixth great division is the aggregation of native states in Central India. It would be highly inconvenient that these should be parcelled out to the separate management of separate governments; still more so that each should be left to the varied views, character, and colouring of individual political agents. In no department is there so great an absence of any general, fixed, or recorded rules of conduct, and in none are individual servants of the Government so liable to be blinded or prejudiced, as the residents at native courts, isolated as they are in an atmosphere of native intrigue. They are apt to take up strongly particular views, and, having once adopted them, are often urged by the inimitable native talent for colouring, exaggerating, and telling one-sided stories, into honest but violent partisanship.* The Supreme Government cannot possibly look with sufficient closeness into all the details of every native state great and small, and therefore I think it would be well to profit by the fact of the great mass of these states lying contiguous in the centre of the country, and to adopt Sir John Malcolm's plan of a Chief Political Commissioner for Central India, immediately under the Supreme Government, who, free from the exclusive bias of particular Residents, might superintend all these central states,† and introduce some uniformity and system in their management.

The local chieftains isolated in the midst of our territories might be included in the local governments, while the Residents in Nepal and Oude (till the latter country is administered by us) would report direct to the Supreme Government.

* Outram Blue Book again.

† Including Hyderabad, Nagpore, Gwalior, Baroda, Rajpootana, &c.

Of our own territories there would then be five local governments—

Bengal,

Madras,

Bombay,

Hindostan—(the term North-West Provinces having become inappropriate)—and

The Indus territories.

First, of the personal constitution of these governments.

An important question arises on the threshold. Shall the Governor-General be a member of the local government of the province where the Supreme Government is located, and, if so, in what position? It is admitted on all hands that the greatest inconvenience has resulted from the present practice of making the Governor-General Governor of Bengal, with the mere power of delegating his duties temporarily from time to time to a member of council, in practice the senior for the time being. It is unnecessary to dwell on the manifold practical evils which have resulted from this system. But two arguments are urged on the other side—that the local government is the only opportunity afforded to the Governor-General of acquiring knowledge and practice of inferior details, and that the patronage attached thereto is necessary to his consequence and dignity.

Position of the Governor-General in a local government.

The first of these arguments may be a very good reason for not appointing a Governor-General destitute of experience of Indian affairs, but can be none for loading him with duties which he cannot by possibility properly perform. If it is necessary that he should have experience of inferior duties, it must be acquired before and not after his appointment as Governor-General. A man cannot perform at the same time two incompatible tasks. We may hope that, under such a system as I have proposed, we should have a class of superior statesmen not altogether destitute of Indian experience; but if a new man must be appointed as Governor-General, the only remedy is to let him remain long enough to acquire, and make use of, the experience of his own office. I would give him every facility for seeing and understanding the subordinate duties, but would not sacrifice the interest and welfare of our greatest provinces in order that, by now and then dividing with local duties the time which is fully required for the Supreme Government, he may gain some experience of the one to the neglect of the other.

The practical, working, local government of the presidency in which the Supreme Government is located must then (if the management of all India is to be intrusted to a Governor-General) be the duty of a separate and permanent Governor; but both for the benefit of the Governor-General, and because the local governor on the spot can be more minutely supervised than other governors, I would make him an officer of somewhat inferior rank, and in more direct subordination to the Governor-General,—would put him, in fact, on much the same footing as the present Lieutenant-Governor of the North-West Provinces. There would be no objection to make the Governor-General the nominal Governor—to give to him individually a full control over the proceedings of his Lieutenant (as he now has), and the right to know, advise regarding, and in some measure, when he so pleases, direct, all that is going on, besides exercising such share of the patronage as he sees fit. But the Lieutenant must still be a permanent, responsible Governor. The Governor-General will be individually his counsellor and officially his superior, but will not necessarily relieve him of any part of his duties, and will only interfere exceptionally when he thinks it expedient so to do. The reasons for relieving the Governor-General of the local details of a subordinate government apply equally to the Non-Regulation Provinces, which must all be included in the local governments; and it is on this account that some definite arrangement regarding the Punjab is absolutely necessary.

I think that the patronage of the appointments connected with the Supreme Government, the discretionary power over the patronage of the local lieutenant-governor, and the reserve of some control over the higher appointments in all the local governments under a special and separate rule, would amply provide the Governor-General with patronage. Too much small patronage is the very opposite of an advantage.

Governors.

For the other four provinces I would have Governors, as there now are at Madras and Bombay, but over whom a more immediate direction would be exercised than has hitherto been the case.

Counsellors hitherto existing.

The objection to idle counsellors in the Supreme Government applies with much greater force to Madras and Bombay. At these presidencies one counsellor is nominally chief of the principal court of justice in each; and at Madras the other holds the same position in the Board of Revenue. It may have been intended as an extremely rational arrangement merely, without additional expense, to enable and require the Governor to call into council the heads of departments; but if, as I understand it, the counsellors are in fact additional appointments, mere nominal, or at any rate supernumerary members of the courts and board, and to whom, on the other hand, the Governor has no power of delegating any portion of his own duties, in this character they seem to be unnecessary, if not worse. One objection which has been urged to a change is, that, there being at Madras and Bombay separate armies, and consequent military business, counsellors are thereby rendered necessary. But I confess that I am quite unable to see how the addition to the Government of two civil members of council can make it in any way more competent to deal with military matters. I would make the Commanders-in-Chief at Madras and Bombay (if the armies remain separate) *ex-officio* counsellors in military matters; and they would find it at least as easy to deal with one civilian as with three. The army of Bengal would remain as at present, under the Supreme Government. Another argument is, that, as the Supreme Government appointments have hitherto been for the most part given to Bengal servants, it would be unfair to those of Madras and Bombay not to leave council appointments in their own presidencies, to reward their services. This I answer, first, by again saying that public appointments must be made with reference not to past but to present work; and second, by referring to my former proposal, that all the appointments of the Supreme Government should be given to the most eligible men from all the presidencies without distinction.

In fact, it seems to me to be clear that an efficient local governor, being not so much a deliberative as an executive officer, would be much more effective wielding single and active power in his own person than with a council; and it must be particularly observed that he has in fact in each presidency regularly constituted boards and heads of departments, civil and military, his responsible and legitimate advisers, and is in this respect much more favourably situated than the Governor-General. Still, this much may be admitted, that if, as at present, English governors, totally unacquainted with India, are sometimes sent to the subordinate presidencies, there would be inconvenience in the want of any immediate responsible adviser. And I should also say that, where there are large commercial cities and European communities (as Calcutta, Bombay, and Madras), an unaided governor cannot well perform all his local duties, and at the same time have it in his power to make tours in the interior, and exercise the necessary personal supervision. On general grounds it would be in future highly desirable to abstain from the appointment of inexperienced men as local executive governors. But it is so great an object to keep open a school for future Governors-General, that I would not exclude by rule unprofessional persons. I would, however, propose a plan to obviate the difficulties which I have noticed, by the following scheme.

Proposed deputy-governors.

Instead of councils, each of the governors of Bengal, Madras, and Bombay, to have a deputy-governor, to whom he shall be authorised to delegate, from time to time, any portion of his duties, and who shall be also his counsellor and responsible adviser, on the same footing as the present counsellors. In every presidency at least one member of the government shall be a servant of ten years' service in India, appointed by the Governor-General.

The plan of a deputy or joint-governor is exactly that which works well in all the executive departments. A magistrate and collector in charge of a district has a joint-magistrate, capable of exercising any portion of his own powers, but subordinate to him. The deputy-governor, instead of being a mere idle adviser, will take a share of the work, particular business or departments for which he is most fitted being intrusted to him by the governor; and he will either take charge of the head-quarter office and local business while the governor is absent, or may be sent on tours of inspection while the governor remains stationary. The Governor of the Indus territory, and the Lieutenant-Governor of Hindostan, having comparatively little local business, will not need assistance till Mussoorie-Deyrah becomes a great city, and then, when the Lieutenant-Governor is absent on tours of inspection, and the Governor-General has not time to spare, the minister of the interior might take temporary local charge.

Appointment to these posts.

The rule in regard to the persons to be nominated will leave it optional to appoint to places in the government a limited number of persons without professional qualifications; but unless the deputy-governor be professionally qualified, an unprofessional person cannot be appointed governor, and *vice versâ.* The Lieutenant-Governor of Agra, and Governor of the Indus territory, being alone, must be professional men.

I would give to the Senate power to appoint from England to every vacancy for which a non-professional man is eligible persons in or out of the service; and to all other vacancies (or failing an appointment by the Senate) the Governor-General would nominate from the service in India, a veto being reserved to the Senate. All these appointments would be for five years, and the holders re-eligible; on the same footing as the superior officers of the Supreme Government.

The secretaries to the local governments will not be in the same position as the ministers of the Supreme Government, because the boards and other heads of departments fill the corresponding situations; and the secretary is (or ought to be if the governor is efficient) merely the ministerial organ of communication. A secretary in each presidency, with two deputies in

Bengal and Madras, and one in Hindostan, Bombay, and the Indus territory, will be amply sufficient.

The local governments, then, will stand thus, with the annual salaries affixed:—

Expense.

	£.	£.
Bengal—		
Governor	12,000	
Deputy	7,000	
Secretaries	6,000	
		25,000
Madras—		
Governor, deputy, and secretaries, as above .	25,000	
Commander-in-Chief, in addition to military pay	2,000	
		27,000
Bombay—		
Governor	10,000	
Deputy	6,000	
Commander-in-Chief	2,000	
Secretaries	5,000	
		23,000
Hindostan—		
Governor-General *ex officio* Governor.		
Lieutenant-Governor	10,000	
Secretaries	4,000	
		14,000
Indus Territory—		
Governor	12,000	
Secretaries	4,000	
		16,000
Grand total		£105,000

Powers, &c.

The position of the local governments, in subordination to the Supreme Government, has been generally noticed in explaining the proposed powers and duties of the latter. The provincial governments would be in every respect subject to its orders, and would transmit information of their proceedings in such form as may be directed. But I have suggested that, under a constitutional code, the Supreme Government should delegate to its subordinates certain powers of local legislation, &c.

The plan of submitting for approval at the commencement of each year a sort of provincial budget, embodying the proposed financial arrangements, seems a very good one. It might be left to the subordinate governments to arrange details within the limits of the budget, and subject to such interference as might be deemed necessary. For all excess beyond a limited margin special sanction would be necessary. The idea of permitting any government to spend money at its discretion, while it is under no sort of obligation to find funds to meet the expenditure, is altogether absurd.

In the disposal of patronage, it might be a good plan to require the concurrence of the Supreme Government in the highest class of appointments, and to leave the rest to the local governors, as is now the case in the North-West Provinces.

I would have the local governors absolute in their own duties, subject only to the obligation of taking advice where there are advisers. The deputy-governors in all things, and the Commander-in-Chief in all military matters, should be made cognizant of all proceedings, and should record their opinions; after which, the governor may act on his own responsibility, in case of essential difference reporting the proceedings to the Supreme Government.

Location.

The places at which the subordinate governments shall be fixed must depend so much on local circumstances that I shall not pretend a precise opinion in regard to all of them; but I would still bear in mind the public advantage of a good climate; would, as far as possible, consult the health and comfort of the officers of government; and would keep in view the principles referred to in discussing the seat of the Supreme Government.

There is no doubt that Calcutta must remain the

seat of the government of Bengal. I have already proposed Mussoorie-Deyrah for that of Hindostan. Lahore, having ceased to be the capital of the Sikh monarchy, and not being the old capital of the Sikh nation and religion, is not necessarily a seat of government. The Indus government might perhaps be advantageously and securely fixed on the outer range of hills overlooking the central Punjab—say near the issue of the Jhelum, which is the most navigable of the Punjab rivers.

I do not know whether it would be possible to remove the Madras government to Bangalore; but if not, the governor or deputy might now and then be permitted to spend the hot weather on the hills in the western portion of the presidency, and at the same time recruit his vigour and overlook the business of the districts in that direction.

The Bombay government seems to have established a migratory system. Perhaps the government and chief courts, &c., might be fixed at Poonah, which is in easy communication with Bombay, and shortly will be more so. But the insular position and commercial importance of Bombay itself may render the expediency of such a step doubtful. It will never do, however, that the governor, spending the hot weather and rains at Mahableshwar and Poonah, should have only the cold weather to visit his head-quarters, and no time whatever to make *bonâ fide* tours in his provinces. He must either fix his permanent residence at Bombay or move it elsewhere.

The chief political commissioner of Central India might have his head-quarters in the Saugor territory, which is our own. Hoshungabad, on the Nerbudda, would be perhaps a good place.

It only remains to provide for the contingency of its being deemed inexpedient to render the Supreme

Government, by a change of constitution, duties, and place, equal to the efficient superintendence of all India. In that case, I see nothing for it but to transfer the central power to England (great as would be the disadvantages of such a step), and to put the minor governments ordinarily under the direction, not of the Governor-General, but of the Senate at home. One governor of superior dignity should, in this case, have a power of control in emergencies; and it is desirable that the political power of dealing with native states should be concentrated in one hand. But for this purpose it would not be necessary to have a separate Supreme Government. For the same reasons urged in fixing the site of the Supreme Government, I would give this controlling power to the Governor or Governor-General of Hindostan, and would include in that province the Indus territory and Central India. Under the Governor-General of Hindostan I would have a deputy-governor of Hindostan Proper, on the same footing as the deputy-governors of other presidencies, and, when not charged with separate duties, he should act as minister of the interior, both for Hindostan and for emergent interferences in other governments. The Indus territory I would intrust to a lieutenant-governor, subject to the Governor-General, on exactly the same footing as the present lieutenant-governor North-West Provinces. The chief political commissioner of Central India would be like a lieutenant-governor under the Governor-General, who should also have a responsible political minister. The Commander-in-Chief would be, *ex officio*, counsellor in military matters, and the deputy-governor, political minister, and Commander-in-Chief would form, collectively, a consultative council.

Arrangements if no central government in India.

In case of the absence of the Governor-General on political duties, the deputy-governor, fully conversant with all details, would at once become the efficient Governor of Hindostan, under the control of the Governor-General.

Bengal, Bombay, and Madras would take their ordinary instructions from the Senate direct, and would refer to the Senate their legislation and finance.

CHAPTER III.

OUR POLITICAL RELATIONS.

External relations; the eastern frontier; the western frontier; internal political relations; necessity of revised system; contingents and native troops; political stipends; policy of upholding states and privileges; policy and opportunities of acquiring territory; the rules of succession.

External relations.

I HAVE referred to those natural boundaries of India which we have already reached, and to which I would adhere. Happily the country is so well fenced in by nature that our external relations may be confined within a narrow space.

We possess a compact, peaceable, and nearly isolated empire; and while so great a field lies before us within that empire, it will indeed be a misfortune if, deserting our natural limits, we plunge into the centre of another continent, and enter on another warlike and expensive career, to promote an inconsiderable commerce, to impose upon barbarians the diplomacy of civilized nations, or to gratify our warlike propensities.

The eastern frontier.

The possession of Burmah is, as regards India, quite unnecessary, and the advantage of acquiring that country must be altogether judged *per se*. I have no sufficient information to enable me to form a decided opinion in regard to such a step; but before committing ourselves we should well ascertain several things:—First, who the people of Burmah in fact are—whether they are a race patient of political subjection, or impatient of a foreign yoke? If the latter, the country will never pay. Second, whether the revenue is large enough to support our expensive government and expensive military establishment without aid from India? Third, who will be our neighbours—what is the country to the east of Burmah—shall we be free from troublesome hill tribes, and from the necessity of farther advance? Unless these questions are satisfactorily answered, the prudence of advancing our frontier may well be doubted. India having already a sufficient eastern boundary, being in no way threatened in that quarter, and even in so great security that it has been found unnecessary to keep any considerable number of troops in the east of Bengal, there can be no reason whatever that it should pay for keeping Burmah, if Burmah does not pay the whole of its own charges, direct and indirect. The great facilities for navigation afforded by the Irawaddy render the country so accessible that we have (it is to be hoped), under any circumstances, little reason to fear another Affghan disaster—but then it must be remembered that no one dreamt of occupying Affghanistan for its own sake. We sought but to make it a barrier against more distant and more powerful nations. Burmah subserves no such purpose; and therefore, even if we can hold it more cheaply and securely than Affghanistan, we have not the same grounds for doing so, and ought not to go to *any* expense with that view. Even if the Burmese cannot pay the expenses of the war, we need not farther punish ourselves for their barbarity. We need not throw good money after bad. If Burmah will not pay, let us beat the Burmese, vindicate our honour, obtain for the British merchant the 90*l*. of which the imperfect administration of justice in the Burmese territories has deprived him, and sail away home again.

It is not even necessary to have any diplomatic relations with the Burmese. Trade, after all, had better be left to the natural effect of mutual interests, and it is even better not to trade with the Burmese than to force our goods on them at the point of the bayonet. As to the Americans, I am not aware that they have ever threatened to occupy Burmah, and, if they do, we must treat or fight with the Americans, not with the Burmese. We may object to the occupation of Burmah by the Americans, just as the Americans would object to the occupation of Mexico by us.

To adopt the half-measure of annexing the lower part of the valley of the Irawaddy and leaving the upper part, seems to me to be the worst policy of all; for we thus voluntarily abandon a natural boundary to establish a political boundary where there is no natural division whatever, and with the certainty of being in close and undivided neighbourhood with a bitterly hostile state. In short, such an arrangement would render another war at no distant period quite inevitable, and we should in the end be obliged to advance at a great additional expense.*

The western frontier.

Our western frontier is a more difficult question. If we could occupy Affghanistan as securely as Burmah, it would be well worth our while to do so; but unfortunately there is not in Affghanistan a river navigable to our fleets, and we have learnt by experience that the Affghans are not a race

* While this passes through the press the annexation of Pegu has been declared, and we are fairly launched on lasting difficulties and expenses. The Burmese war seems altogether a most unfortunate affair, entered into with far less cause than any war in which we have ever been engaged, and of which it is now impossible to see the end. This is no *absorption* of a native state, but a *foreign* war of external conquest (we have annexed a country not yet conquered), into which we have been led by what I cannot help thinking a misapplication of European principles of diplomacy. Alas! I fear that it may long postpone many projects of improvement. We have no sooner gained our natural boundary on one side than we abandon it on the other. From Pegu we must go to Ava, and when we get to Ava our only chance of an eventual profitable result is to go on to Pekin.

fitted for subjection. Already we are sorely encumbered by the sovereignty over, and vicinity to, a few petty border tribes of Affghan race.

The worst result of our unfortunate Affghan war is the difficulty of now establishing friendly relations in that country. The conduct of the Affghans in the Sikh war was the extremity of folly. They showed enmity—committed, in an irregular way, overt acts of hostility—yet did not materially assist the Sikhs. I do not know whether Dost Mahommed avows the acts of his followers, but the consequence has been the absence of political relations with him. Another circumstance also tends to make our position in regard to the Affghans unpleasant, viz. that we have succeeded the Sikhs in the possession of territory beyond the Indus, recently conquered by the latter, and which the Affghans consider as their patrimony in the possession of an enemy.

To occupy Affghanistan is at present out of the question. It is enough that we guard the passes, and that we can at any time, from a basis now near and strong, take military possession of Cabul if the politics of Central Asia become threatening. We must, beyond a doubt, be fully prepared to prevent the occupation of Affghanistan by any other power; and it would be in the highest degree desirable if we could, without loss of dignity, re-establish friendly relations with the Affghans. The Dost might yet be permitted to disavow his sons' and subjects' hostilities in 1849, and to assure us that they are to be construed in a "Pickwickian" sense. The only settlement of our frontier relations upon which any dependence could be placed, and which seems at all feasible, is to get rid of two difficulties at the same time, by bestowing upon the Affghan chief, or some other person or persons of sufficient influence, in some kind of feudal tenure conditional on good behaviour, the most unpleasant and unprofitable of our trans-Indus possessions. The Dost might extract something from the tribes in his own way, and we should be relieved from the civil charge of a tract which we can only manage by a very large military expenditure, by compromises incompatible with our dignity, or by severities inconsistent with our creed. We should still retain possession of the military posts necessary for the security of India. The Affghans would become, in some measure, dependent on us—we should exact from them an obligation to admit no foreign power into Affghanistan—we should pledge ourselves to support them against foreign enemies—the chiefs and the people would look up to us and court our influence—and we might be in some degree arbiters in their more serious quarrels by throwing the weight of our influence in favour of those in the right, and against those in the wrong. The Ameers claim no dignity inconsistent with a feudal inferiority; and if we could establish such a system—fully convince them that having had enough of their territory we no longer desire it—and, in some degree, wipe out the memory of former injuries, Affghanistan might then be in every way that for which nature has designed it—the barrier of India—and closed against all foreign powers.

Whether we deal with Dost Mahommed or with the chiefs of the tribes of the Khyber, there can be no doubt of the principle that the only way of obtaining a hold over mountaineers is to give them a stake in the plains; and that, by gaining such a hold over the possessors of the passes, and keeping your troops in readiness to act on emergencies, you secure the frontier against the entrance of foreign powers at a much less expense than by permanently occupying the mountain country.

Our relations with Persia must be merely diplomatic, and our diplomacy under present circumstances must be solely directed to secure Affghanistan from attack. If diplomacy fails, a naval demonstration would probably suffice to prevent any future attempts on the Affghan territory. What might be our course in the event of Russia attempting to swallow up Persia is a wider question, upon which I shall not at present enter.

We need have no other external relations than those which I have mentioned. Impenetrable mountains and an undisputed ocean render us independent of the best diplomacy.

Internal political relations.

Now, as to our *internal* political relations. I have already noticed the extreme necessity of putting the native states on a systematic feudatory footing. A regular classification and a code of political management is urgently required. The fact is, that the practice which has grown up into prescription is scarcely borne out by the letter of old stipulations. It is hard to point out in treaties how some of the most petty states became otherwise than independent sovereignties; but, in fact, they are not, and cannot, be so. We must now add to former stipulations, first, this prescription in fact; second, the imperial superiority of the Moguls to which we have succeeded, and which, in the Royal name, we shall now avowedly assume; and third, fresh stipulations for mutual advantage and convenience. In reality, our practice has been founded on our succession to the Mogul dominion, and it is the want of the avowed imperial title which has caused the discrepancy between theory and fact. A distinguished legal authority gravely tells the Committee of Parliament that, according to the law of nations, as settled by jurists, it is ILLEGAL for a native state to empower our Government to make laws applicable to its territories, and that therefore our laws for the suppression of thuggee and

Necessity of revision of system and imperial organisation.

dacoity, though specially supported by treaty, are *illegal.* Even granting the right of European jurists, in their cabinets, to make laws for Asiatic nations, we must put an end to such theories. No state except Nepal should be recognised as in any degree an independent sovereignty. Even Nepal has come under such obligations that it is not really politically independent; and in regard to it, too, we are no way bound to adopt the European law of nations, but may make such stipulations as we can. I have noticed in 'Modern India' (pp. 160 to 171) the general circumstances and some of the most pressing requirements of our political system.

It is quite out of the question that, while we maintain a native government by our military support, we should altogether abstain from internal interference, but the nature of that interference should be properly defined and limited—should be regulated by systematic rules, and not left in that uncertainty which must give rise to all kinds of intrigue, and weakens to an undue extent the existing government. It should not rest solely with individual residents and governors irregularly to interfere or not to interfere in behalf of injured old ladies. We should have some fixed principles to which we can refer as real substantial rules practically observed. At present there are certain rules, no doubt, but they are such that we refer to them when we wish to keep them, and say nothing about them when we are necessitated to break them. It is so, because the nominal terms of our political relations and the theoretical position of native states are great anachronisms impossible in practice and inconsistent with fact.

I would divide all native states into classes with reference to the degree of independent power to be exercised by each, and would provide that they may be from time to time raised or degraded, according as they govern well or ill. I would assume the imperial power to make imperial laws for all India in certain matters;—for instance, I would abolish suttee, and regulate the levy of customs on the great lines of traffic, not by separate treaties, but by imperial decrees.

Revision of political service.

I would conduct the political administration of the British Imperial Government through a regular and systematic political service, which is far from being the case at present. Everything now depends on individuals. Some of these are good officers, others are rewarded by political appointments for services of a totally different nature, or are put into such situations by an exercise of patronage, and have no particular qualifications whatever. The personnel of this service should then be remodelled at the same time with the whole political system. Things have much changed in the department since the present arrangements were made, and the distribution of offices is by no means what it should be. I believe that considerable reductions and improvements might be effected. Many of the political appointments should be revised, altered, and consolidated; and under the chief Commissioner of Central India I hope that a great portion of the political administration would be much systematised.

Contingents.

The whole of the system of contingents should be revised; and I should say that every state might reasonably be called on to contribute to the imperial military defences, either in money or in efficient troops. Military aid all are bound to furnish, but in very few cases are the native troops at all efficient. Some states furnish regular contingents; in some the obligation has become a dead letter. I would revive it in all, and would exact from all either a payment towards our army proportioned to the revenue of each state, or troops which would be, with some exceptions, under the direction of European officers, and should be entirely available for our service. The better contingents are already of this description. It may be a question whether they should not be mobilised and united with the regular army; but in regard to this arrangement the same military questions must be considered which affect the separation of the different British armies in India, and which are foreign to my present subject. There are doubtless some advantages to the governing power in the possession of distinct forces which have not everything in common.

We should also at the same time avow a distinct right to control the whole of the private military arrangements of our feudatories, whether in regard to some troops which may become formidable from their discipline, or to others which may become dangerous or troublesome from want of discipline; or again in respect to fortifications. In some instances it will be inexpedient to allow native states to establish too strong citadels; in others it may be expedient to encourage them to construct forts, provided that we make it (as we should do in every case) a condition that they are at any time available for our service. I would now and then exercise the right of entering such forts, just to test the allegiance of the feudatory, it being understood that any hesitation would involve instant forfeiture of territory. For instance, the Raja of Patteealah has been spending a great deal of money on a very fine modern fort. We have nothing to fear from him, for he has a fine territory in a plain country, which we should be happy to seize on the least provocation, and, in the event of an invasion of India, Patteealah is the very spot where a strong fort would be most useful to us. But then of course it would not do to leave the Raja's fidelity untested till a crisis actually arrives.

In regard to the only state which at present maintains

forces of its own such as may give serious ground of apprehension to us, something should certainly be arranged. We have nothing to fear from small regular forces, but the Nizam's large establishment of irregulars might some day be exceedingly troublesome. They seem to be professional and hereditary soldiers of the most warlike tribes in Asia—Arabs, Rohillas, and Sikhs—the very men who might maintain a considerable guerilla war if we became embarrassed with the Nizam's territories—if we had occasion to use force towards them—or if they had any special opportunity. It is extremely desirable to get rid of so turbulent and formidable a force existing in the heart of our empire. To suppress them suddenly, without in some way providing for them, might involve the very evil which we would avoid. I would by no means render them desperate, but would prevent the accession of fresh recruits (especially Arabs), and arrange for the gradual extinction of the last native military force, or for its transfer to our service.

The Nizam's troops.

The political stipends should be gradually reduced as lives fall in. A pension voluntarily granted to a fallen potentate is in most instances by no means a contract in perpetuity, and it is every way fitting that, as the shadows of former power become more indistinct, the country should be relieved from these very exorbitant payments.

Political stipends.

We must also, in future, be less excessively liberal in similar arrangements. It is our duty to be just before we are generous, and we have no right, in a spirit of magnificence, to burden the country which we hold in trust with unnecessarily large payments. There are a great many things necessary for the good of the people yet undone, and which should be done before we are liberal to excess to privileged individuals.

The Bombay presidency seems quite incorrigible in its liberality with other people's money, and it is too bad that it should be permitted to draw on Bengal. We have heard enough of the Sattara question. No one supposed that in that matter the Company had sold its conscience for nought. The late Sattara Raja had a territory in the heart of our dominions close to Bombay, and a revenue which enabled him to keep up a large establishment, including a considerable body of native troops, and I believe to save money besides. If ever there was an acquisition in which profit seemed to be secure, here it was. Yet would it be credible on any other than official authority that the following is the balance-sheet (of the mere civil expenses, without paying for a single soldier), resulting from the way in which they manage matters at Bombay?—

Result of annexation of Sattara.

		Rupees.
Annual revenue of Sattara		20,52,400
Annual charges:—		
Political stipends	3,60,850	
General charges	3,85,400	
Judicial charges	5,00,000	
Revenue charges, including 9¾ lacs allowances to zemeendars, grants to mosques, &c.	11,57,260	
		24,06,230
Deficit		3,53,830!!!

If all these obligations were left to us by the Raja, how on earth did *he* manage, and who furnished him with funds to pay his troops? It seems as if the Bombay government were bent on taking revenge for not being allowed an unlimited credit in all things, by making away with the Sattara revenue before it reaches the general treasury. No wonder that there is no money to make roads. This sort of management must most assuredly be reformed.

By such reformation and the general contribution to our army the imperial finances may be considerably relieved.

While regulating the mode of government, we must also make clear the tenure on which each state is held. Most of the larger states are undoubtedly evils both to the people who have the misfortune to be misgoverned, and to the imperial Government charged with the whole expense of the empire from which they subtract a large portion of the revenue. In these cases we should take every opportunity, consistent with good faith, of acquiring the direct rule of the territory—there is no consideration of policy in maintaining such states. But it is otherwise in other cases. There are many states the maintenance of which is a matter of policy on several grounds, and in such cases it is desirable not to leave the matter in uncertainty, but to declare our intentions, with such reservations as may be necessary.

Tenure of native states.

Policy in upholding.

The general rule seems to be that the large states are the most obnoxious to objection, and would be the most profitable acquisitions; the small states both by far the best managed and the most answering the purposes of our policy. Some of the small states are really very well governed, but, of course, it depends on the individual ruler: a year hence the best of them may be in confusion. The political objects to be kept in view by us are as follows:—

1. It is expedient to leave a refuge and asylum to those natives who dislike or have not become accustomed to our system.

2. Where there is not a single ruler, but a dominant tribe, to rule or pension whom in European form would be difficult and expensive, it is every way desirable to uphold the native system. This is the case in the

Rajpoot states; they are great clans; and whoever may be chief, it is our policy, as it was that of the Mahommedans, to maintain the clan.*

3. In tracts where the country is so peculiar, sterile, and unprofitable that it would not pay us, and may be more cheaply administered through native feudatories, it is better thus to manage it. This would have been the case in the greater part of Scinde and of the trans-Indus portion of the Punjab, and it is so as regards the possessions of wild hill tribes.

These considerations would induce us to maintain, under all circumstances, many of the smaller states, and I would classify them accordingly, making provision for the exercise of the necessary degree of interference. The reserving a refuge for the discontented is necessary in the first instance, but gradually becomes less so,† and only applies to the maintenance of small states where large ones formerly existed. Rampore has served this purpose admirably as regards the Patans; the small Mahratta states in the south have probably the same use with respect to the Mahrattas; and if the Sikhs had not entered our service a similar arrangement might have been expedient in regard to them. Perhaps small principalities in Scinde might with advantage be given to one or two of the old Sikh chiefs of the Manjha: there is now hardly a representative of that class who has any political position. I am afraid that to give them jagheers about Peshawar would involve too continual warfare with the Affghans.

* This principle would still more strongly apply if there are any states where the Government is *really* native—where the rulers are actually identical with the great body of the ruled. But this is seldom the case. In such states as Oude and Gwalior the rulers and the ruled have nothing whatever in common.

† The more we elevate the natives in our service, the less will be the necessity for maintaining native states.

It would be a great advantage of a good political system, that, while guarding against abuse, we should be better able to make *use* of a discreet feudatory policy. The abuse, mismanagement, and misconception of the system have created in some quarters a prejudice, perhaps excessive, against any arrangement which leaves a remnant of native political power. Now both I think that *small* native states, properly controlled and systematically managed, may be in some cases very useful members of the empire, and, while I deprecate the lavish way in which the greater part of the revenue of newly acquired territory is sacrificed by the Bombay Government in favour of what are called political claims, it seems to me that under a good political code we might for political purposes assign small political privileges, and save money by the arrangement. A moderate revenue in this form may be left to those who have really substantial claims, at a very much less cost to us than by assigning large money stipends payable from the treasury (as is now generally the fashion), to the much greater contentment of the recipients and their followers, and to the better fulfilment of our political policy.

For instance, a feudal chief has what is called a jagheer, that is, the government rights in the land of one or more villages, in which he lives with his retainers. If the jagheer is one which ought to be resumed, by all means resume it; but if the whole or any part is to be upheld, it is one thing to leave the accustomed management in the hands of the jagheerdar, and another to pay over to him the annual proceeds. The latter system he detests. To enable him to manage his barony we might find it necessary to give him, not the powers of an independent sovereign, but a certain moderate jurisdiction defined by law, and subject to appeal to the European district officer.

The rights of the zemeendars would be defined, and they would still be much better off than they were before. But it is the too common practice of the present day to consider the jagheerdar as a matter of course a tyrant, to take the management of the village at a considerable cost and trouble to Government, but to pay over to him the whole proceeds in money, thus giving him the means of mischief without contenting him. I think that this has been too much the case with regard to the Sikhs. During the Sikh rule they were of course absolute masters of the zemeendars; but now the tables are turned; the zemeendars, a large and united body, bully the Sikh jagheerdars in every way, deprive them of their just dues, and even reclaim land which the Sikhs have themselves cultivated for very many years. We do not attempt to give a reasonable support to the jagheerdar, but, at once pronouncing him a tyrant, assume the whole management. Every claim to political privileges of any kind is treated with very great jealousy, every claim to pecuniary allowance with very great liberality. This sounds very well, but is extremely expensive to Government; and the habits and feelings of natives of the classes lately dominant are such, that they can in no way appreciate mere stipends. I believe that a Sikh had rather exercise a reasonable control over one village than receive the revenue of a dozen, and, as the case now stands, I must say that I think the Sikhs have been let down rather suddenly. I should see no objection to the retention for a time of petty personal jurisdictions, something like that of an English country gentleman who is a justice of the peace. On a reference from Government I once submitted a proposal for making some of the larger jagheerdars of the cis-Sutlej states hereditary deputy magistrates; but I believe that they are still unprivileged subjects.

Whether the privileges of native chiefs be political or

civil, they must form part of our system, not breaks and blots in it. Our political difficulties and inconsistencies have principally arisen from our recognising in theory nothing intermediate between independent states and simple subjects.

Policy in acquiring.

These objects provided for, we come to those states of which the lapse is desirable. They may revert to the imperial power—first, when our stipulations with them admit of our assuming the direct management of the territory; second, when heirs fail; third, when through disorder and mismanagement they become nuisances to the empire, and must be occupied in self-defence. I would add that when the misgovernment and wretchedness of their subjects reaches an extreme pitch we are under a moral obligation to rescue the people; but some persons may question that doctrine, considering respect to the assumed rights of princes more binding than our duty to the peasants over whom we have acquired an imperial dominion, and whose fate is in our hands.

On the first-mentioned ground we have it in our power to take possession of much-misgoverned Oude; it is one of the richest countries in India and the most conveniently situated, and is already in our military possession. It would be a very great addition to our finances (always supposing that it is not managed in Bombay fashion, and that most absurdly extravagant pensions are not assigned to everybody); while the people would benefit immensely, and would be delighted by the change. I cannot conceive upon what ground we hesitate to take this step. A jagheer might, without detriment, be left in the hands of a considerable and meritorious person as an asylum for discontented Mahommedans.

Gwalior might have already lapsed for want of heirs, and the measure would have been most profitable and beneficial, but it has been re-established under arrangements which, by the way, expire this year. I suppose that we must now continue them, and wait the chance of another failure of heirs. In the diagram of India (see title-page) I have shown by a dotted line the position of the Gwalior territory.

The Nizam's territory might be occupied on the third ground, being seriously dangerous to the peace of the empire, but probably would not be profitable in the first instance, as we must entertain his disorderly troops. We might, however, thus more effectually take measures for reducing them, or rendering them effective regulars in our service. I do not know enough of the territory to judge whether we could assume the direct civil management with financial safety. Mysore, established by us, reverted into our hands on account of mismanagement, and, since it is administered by us, it is useless and absurd longer to keep up the name and the expense of the raja; it should be finally incorporated in our territory.

Connected with failure of heirs is the old question of adoption. There is no LAW whatever applicable to this case, and that which it was attempted to apply to it was simply the law relating to private and personal property. Wills seem to have been unknown to the Hindoos,* but they have the power, in default of natural heirs (whom they cannot deprive), of adopting during their lives heirs to their property, and that is, in fact, their mode of making a will. We might as well argue that an English sovereign can, by will, leave his crown as a legacy, as apply this law of private property to the succession to native principalities, which is in no other respect regulated by the laws of property. The same principle would lead to the equal division of inheritances. In regard to most

The rules of succession.

* The word for a *will* in Hindostanee is now borrowed from the Arabic.

native states no regular system of succession has been established, because for a long time past might had always made right, and the great majority of these states are of too recent origin to have established any practice in the more regular times of the Mahommedan empire. The Mahommedan emperors in their day retained to themselves the right of granting investiture to feudatory princes, and none had a valid title without that imperial sanction; but as they only maintained Hindoo states as matter of policy, although the direct line of the chief might fail the policy remained, and another member of a clan doubtless frequently received investiture. We must act on the same principles as they, and assert the imperial right to regulate successions. Lineal hereditary succession has been generally recognized, but even this rule is not uniform; an unfit eldest son is often set aside. After late decisions it cannot again be contended that any feudatory of the empire has a right to adopt an heir without the imperial sanction; but when heirs fail in those states which it is our policy to maintain, we shall not the less grant investiture to a new chief, approved by the clan and by ourselves.

In future the question will be, not "is there a right to adopt or not?" but, "is the state one to be maintained or not?" "has it been hitherto respected merely to keep faith with a single individual or family, or is it a really native and clannish government, and a territory which it is not desirable that we should directly possess?" In the one case, we shall take advantage of lapses; in the other, we shall grant new investitures. By profitable lapses our finances will be much benefited,—the loss entailed by unprofitable ones we shall avoid.

As heirs of entail to all lapsed estates we shall admit no power of the former possessors to mortgage the public revenue for their debts.

CHAPTER IV.

THE CIVIL ADMINISTRATION.

Present state; necessary amendments; relation of government to its subjects; necessity of codification and systematization; agrarian code and policy; duties of new Law Commission; penal code; criminal procedure and police; civil procedure; the civil law; commercial code; abolition of local and personal distinctions; judicial establishments; proposed College of Justice; separation of executive and judicial functions; heads of executive departments; local district executive; union of executive power in same hands; size, establishment, &c., of districts; municipalities and proposed octroi; location of stations; language of business; mode of centralisation; relation of the government to its servants; personnel of the service; real nature of question covenanted or uncovenanted; necessity of a line between European and native offices; employment of natives; European service, comparative cheapness and advantage of; question of profession or no profession; the uncovenanted European servants; proposed opening of important offices to persons not in the service; civil employment of military officers.

I HAD intended separately to notice the measures which I believe to be required in each of the great departments of the civil administration; but I find that neither time nor space will permit of my now doing so—and perhaps detailed professional schemes may with advantage be postponed till the form of the future government is determined, the more as we shall shortly have additional evidence and information on these subjects.

I shall content myself then with generally indicating the objects to which it seems to me that the labours of Government must be directed, and the nature of the machinery required, reserving further details and plans for a more convenient season. It may, however, be necessary to discuss at some length the personnel of the government service, as involving questions which must now be determined by law.

Present state.

The Indian civil administration is in some respects excellent. The efficiency of the executive is considerable, and very superior to much of what we see under free institutions. The purity of its higher departments is admirable, and in comparison to any indigenous administration in any country, and under any form of government in the world, most striking. Nowhere are the acts of the Government and of its superior servants determined, or are the offices of government filled, with so small an intermixture of personal or class influence, or so honestly and sincerely with a view to the good of the people governed. This, then, is an advantage which we must not at any time forget, or in any way risk.

Great purity.

But still the executive is not in all things, positively speaking, *so* efficient as it ought to be and might be under a government which combines the advantages, usually almost incompatible, of a concentration of absolute power on the one hand and purity on the other. The checks, inconsequences, and want of sufficient centralisation, properly incident only to popular elective and federal governments, have been in some degree suffered to interfere with the action of a vigorous absolutism. The English rulers of the East seem to be hampered with a sort of arrière pensée—a feeling that they are not quite free to act according to their own good judgment—that they are bound to some degree of English conservatism, and responsible to the outcry of individuals in measures for the benefit of the mass. Our position as foreigners ruling a country in all things so strange to us has also very much interfered with our efficiency. The great division of authority—some very important

Drawbacks to efficiency.

defects in the machine of government—some peculiarities in the constitution of the services—the want of permanence in individual officers—their imperfect comprehension of native manners and of indigenous institutions—and their want of confidence of support in attempting improvement and innovation—all these causes have prevented the executive from attaining the highest degree of efficiency. Generally speaking, then, I say that the executive is in some respects good, but not *so* good as it might be. It is principally wanting in progressiveness and generalization.

Of that part of the duties of government which may be generally classed as judicial, including the whole system of laws and determination of rights, it is impossible to give so favourable an account. We are sadly deficient of a good judicial system, and it is much to be feared that, with the very best intentions, by an obstinate perseverance in ideas and rules injurious to any country, but especially so to India, we have counterbalanced much of the good derived from the pure and tolerably efficient executive. In an over-anxious and mistaken desire to secure the rights of individuals by principles of law, some of which have grown out of the misuse and perversion of the institutions fitted to bygone days, while others were solely designed to protect the political privileges of free Englishmen during that transition state when the liberties of other countries were overthrown—principles which the natives do not appreciate for good, but of which they are most prone to avail themselves for evil—we have done much injury to the mass of the community; and not only have we, in some things, followed wrong principles, but we have been sadly wanting in any systematisation of our laws and policy. These evils have been much aggravated by the want of trained jurists. No lawyers are so bad as unprofessional lawyers. It is urgently necessary that our laws should be amended and our judicial system reconstructed. We want both good laws and good lawyers.

We may also do much to remedy the imperfections of the executive, and it is every way to be desired that we should take measures to that end, provided always we take care that in so doing we in no way risk that honesty and purity which is our greatest boast. It would indeed be an irreparable loss if, in aiming at efficiency, we lost a virtue which is indispensable to efficiency.

Necessary amendments.

I have already proposed improvements in the constitution of the Government. Arrangements may also be made by which the present exceptions to the general personal efficiency of the services may be obviated and a greater power of advance secured. The frequency of change may be much mitigated, and the efficient services of valuable men secured for longer periods in the same departments. The results of experience may be collected and collated till we really understand India. By making more intelligible the honest working of an honest system, our English public may become less accessible to misrepresentation, and our public men more confident and bold in acting in the right. The revolution in English opinion on legal subjects will render comparatively easy a change in our judicial system, and judicial or quasi-judicial conduct and policy; and an improved government and instruments of government may use all these opportunities immensely to improve the general administration without permitting the growth of other evils.

Doubtless in all our arrangements, executive and judicial, we shall, in accordance with natural reason, and with the ancient native and the modern English opinion, study simplicity and common sense rather than complicity and technicality. We shall rather bring the executive of our older provinces to a system more nearly approaching that followed in the "Non-Regulation districts," and our courts to the model which all now desire to introduce in England, than follow the elder examples of Indian or English law. And fortunately we can effect these reforms unhampered by the mass of prescription in fact and conservatism in principle which has made English reform so slow and difficult.

Relation of Government to its subjects.

The government conducted in the name of the Crown may be, and it is desirable that it should be, more avowedly imperial and absolute than at present. Government will always be government in theory as well as in practice, and in no way on a level with its subjects; but in its conduct it will be not only as fair and equitable, but also as mild and paternal as ever.

We shall doubtless continue to the natives that great degree of personal freedom which is so peculiar to our system in the rule of a conquered country—which goes so far to secure contentment and to compensate for the absence of political freedom. We shall at the same time show them that, while European subjects are freely admitted to the country, we cannot and will not continue to any class exclusive privileges of exemption from the law. It may be necessary to put in form such rules as are required to protect the Government and the general public from aggressions to which they have been hitherto too much exposed—for instance, to enact a good law of libel, making in some degree penal wilful misrepresentation of the acts of Government or of individuals, as also the betrayal of state secrets, and the use of language regarding the Government inconsistent with its character and position in such a country, and calculated to bring it into contempt. But all such laws should be little severe in theory and should be rendered very mild in practice.

If by improvements in the conduct of official business we succeed in bringing useful official knowledge into reasonable compass and available form, it will be as easy as it is desirable to publish such things as may with advantage be made public, and in laying open to the organs of public information the opportunities of learning the truth we shall take away their best excuse for fiction.

Necessity of codifying our laws and systematizing our policy.

The great measure which is most pressingly and primarily necessary as a preliminary to systematic good government is the codification of our laws designed by Parliament twenty years ago, and the failure of which I have already noticed. The legislation of an absolute government in some respects differs from that of a free people, but it is not the less important that the rules which shall determine the relations of Government to its subjects, and of those subjects to one another, should be put upon a fixed and rational basis, and that they should be made patent to all—simple, clear, and intelligible. We must not longer remain in an uncertain and transition state. We have now had a large experience, and we have it in our power to enact laws which shall be no longer the varying and often inconsistent efforts of an imperfect and divided policy, but the systematic, permanent, and respected landmarks, which shall remain when the surface is vastly altered—which shall determine the form and the manner of a future imperial civilization, such as we may hope to make both great and lasting. Hitherto we have been but encamped in confusion and disorder. It is now our duty to mark out the lines on which a great city is to be reared; and we have all the advantage of those who undertake such a task where a great conflagration has levelled all old buildings before it—all the old native systems which preceded us. We may make our streets broad and clear—our buildings regular and wholesome. But if we now neglect system, there is springing up, without order, a mass of narrow, devious, and unhealthy lanes and structures, which we shall bitterly repent, and which much time and labour will not enable us to remove.

Good laws then we should have, and have quickly, and they must be not only just, practicable, and expedient, but also in such convenient form that they may be readily accessible both to the officers and to the subjects of Government. Codification is most necessary in India, both on account of the imperfections of that which we have and the importance of that which we have not.

We want the following codes:—

Necessary codes.

1. An administrative code, defining the constitution, powers, and relative position and duties, both of the Supreme and subordinate governments, and of all the services and servants of Government, from the highest to the lowest — the division of authority and the modes of exercising power —the rules of appointment, promotion, leave, removal, &c. &c.—in short, everything connected with the Government and its servants.

2. The political feudatory code already alluded to.

3. A revenue code, including, as its principal element, an agrarian code.

4. A penal code.

5. A code of criminal procedure.

6. A code of civil procedure.

7. A code of commerce, in anticipation of

8. A general civil code.

Of these codes, Nos. 1, 2, and 3 will be separately

drawn up, and only shortly referred to the law commission, to be technically scrutinized by them before being promulgated. The remaining codes will be the task of the law commission, aided by such special assistance as may be, from time to time, supplied to them by Government.

The time has now come when the great questions of landed rights and interests, so long disputed, and regarding which so many opposite systems at this moment prevail, should be deliberately determined and set at rest. The position and rights both of Government and of the several classes of its subjects interested in the land should be clearly defined and adequately protected by a good agrarian code.

Agrarian code and policy.

This will form the most pressing and important duty in the department of the minister of agrarian affairs; and it may probably be necessary that he should be assisted by a special commission principally composed of natives.

The greatness of this subject is not easily realised by English minds, to which the single relation of landlord and tenant seems so simple, but it is one which in India we have only learned in some degree to understand by very long and dearly-bought experience. To the great mass of the inhabitants of India it is by far more important than anything else—I may almost say than all other subjects of legislation put together. Great injury has been inflicted on great classes by many of our experiments, and in some parts of the country the present state of things is extremely unsatisfactory. But at last it may fairly be said that every system has had an amply sufficient trial, and we owe it to the people to make an effort to combine our experience and to put these all-important interests on a secure and advantageous footing.

The same principles and rules are exactly applicable

throughout all India, but there is a considerable difference in the facts to which those principles are to be applied, and we have pledged ourselves in particular provinces to some measures which cannot now be altogether obliterated.

I can here only make general allusion to the main principles by which it seems to me that we should be guided.

It is certain that Government must always principally depend upon the land-rent for its revenue, and it is desirable that it should be so, because the greater part of this rent is simply property reserved for public uses, and for so much of our expenditure as is not supplied in this way we must resort to actual taxes. That share of interest in the land which does not belong to the State is the property of the cultivator. We must both arrange for the collection of the Government rent, and leave so large and valuable an interest in the soil in the hands of individuals as may suffice to secure its improvement, the extension of cultivation, and the performance of those functions which a great Government cannot itself directly undertake. Setting aside minor differences, there are three main systems on which the Government has proceeded :—

1. By dealing direct with each cultivator.
2. By dealing with corporate bodies of cultivators on a principle of joint responsibility.
3. By placing middlemen between Government and the cultivator.

Now not only is it theoretically clear that it must be absolutely impossible for a great Government directly to deal in an efficient manner with very many millions of the smallest and poorest class of cultivators, numbering as many as 170,000 in a single district, but it is certain that in practice all such experiments have failed of success. It is found that such single cultivators are quite unable to take leases, or in any way to fulfil the most acknowledged conditions of successful tenantry. Government is equally unable to perform the duties of a landlord towards them. The mode in which it has attempted to do so has been this—to fix certain rates on the cultivated land, to ascertain as far as possible the cultivation of each year and to charge accordingly, to make remissions in favour of those who cannot pay, and to collect the rest. Such a system on such a scale leads to immense confusion and abuse; it militates against every principle of political economy and practical experience, and is injurious both to the Government revenue and to the interests of the people. The more one hears of it the more one is convinced that it is absolutely impracticable. None of its defenders have ever pretended that it *has* succeeded. The most sanguine only argue that it would succeed under various modified systems proposed by them; yet it has had a long trial, and if it were to succeed should have succeeded ere this. The greater part of Southern India is still by this system condemned to fiscal confusion, and to many agrarian evils which contrast strongly with the state of things in other parts of the country. There is little substantial landed property, no permanence of cultivation, and no security for the Government revenue. It is indisputable then that the introduction of some practicable system into those territories is urgently required.

The corporate agricultural body is a most remarkable native institution, and, wherever we can avail ourselves of it, it answers all purposes admirably. In this shape the united cultivators are strong and self-supporting; they take long and large leases; with them Government can well deal. The rights of the body and of individuals are preserved, and the greatest possible share of the produce of the land is secured both to Government and to the cultivator, since no portion goes to any middleman, and nothing is wasted in the impossible attempt to deal separately with each single cultivator. But unfortunately these corporations, though everywhere traceable, do not now everywhere exist in perfection. Under the Ryotwar system they have been altogether (so far as our present purpose is concerned) dissolved; it is doubtful how far they can be reconstructed; they will only succeed with good cultivators; perhaps only when there is already some clannish bond between those cultivators. If we can reconstruct them, it is in all respects most desirable to do so. But where we cannot I think that there is every possible reason to prefer to dealing with individual cultivators, the judicious interposition of a good class of middlemen, under a system which has been proved by an ample experience to be both practicable and successful. I would neither establish gigantic zemeendars of whole districts, little more able and much less willing than the Government to deal properly with the cultivators, nor would I make over those cultivators to mere grasping farmers whose interests are altogether temporary; but in small and manageable estates I would establish intermediate proprietors of limited rights from among those middle classes most likely to do justice to such a trust. I would register and fully secure all the previous rights of the cultivators, but would give the new proprietary farmers a certain share of the rights of Government, and a hereditary and transferable interest in those rights. Each village would be an estate; a certain price or premium would be taken (as a security against neglect) from the new proprietor, and he would be bound to certain conditions. These estates, coming from time to time into the market, would draw capital to the land as an investment; capitalists would turn the cultivators and the land to the best account for their own interests, and would perform those duties which Government cannot perform. They will thus be enabled both to make a profit for themselves, and to pay to Government a larger revenue than would otherwise be realised, while the rights of the cultivators will be fully protected and their condition improved by the capital and assistance of a landlord of limited rights. This is practically what has been done, and these results have followed in a large proportion of the villages of the North-West Provinces. The system is not at first so satisfactory as that of good corporate villages, but is most assuredly infinitely preferable to the Ryotwar practice, and is that into which it is perhaps inevitable that the corporate system should eventually merge.

Proposed arrangements.

What I would propose, then, is that in all the Ryotwar territories the cultivators of each village should have the option of uniting, if they can, on the principle of joint management* and responsibility—taking long leases—and so dealing direct with Government. If they cannot or will not thus arrange, each village should be marked out as an estate, the rights of the existing cultivators should be well defined, and then, a rent being fixed calculated to leave a considerable profit, a long lease and the rights of a "village zemeendar" should be given or sold to a fit and *resident* person, who would make the most of the village, both by arrangements with the existing cultivators and by bringing into cultivation the waste land.

Something approaching to this system was once before, for a short time, attempted in the south, but

* In describing these tenures on a former occasion I have fully explained that there is no joint cultivation or intermixture of private affairs.

it never had a fair trial.* The condition essential to its success is the existence of a considerable amount of capital in the country. When we obtained the territory, after a long course of most destructive wars, capital was altogether wanting, and this alone was a fatal objection to such a system as I have proposed. Under our peaceable rule capitalists have had immense advantages, and there has been undoubtedly a great accumulation of capital. For that capital the land is the great subject of employment, and I at least know that in Northern India landed investments are much sought after, and that there is a fully sufficient supply of capital for the working of the system which I have described. Considering that under our Indian Government capitalists are nearly wholly untaxed (the indirect taxes fall almost exclusively on the millions), the mismanagement of Southern India must be greater than I can suppose if there is not yet capital enough to admit of the introduction of landed proprietors possessed of a little money. Much will depend on a good definition of the tenant-rights of the cultivators. The possessors of tenant-rights should be empowered to claim leases from the landlord; and, in case of dispute, the collector should have judicial power to determine rent-rates, either in money or in a proportion of the grain, which, in favour of permanent cultivators, should be fixed at a percentage below the market value. Provision should also be made that the tenant, so long as he occupies the land and pays those rates as fixed from time to time, should not be liable to additional rent on account of capital invested by him. For instance, if he has built a well during his lease; the

* It is certain that the system was precipitately changed in spite of the remonstrances of the most competent persons. I recommend the recent native petition from Madras as giving the best account which I have seen of the history of the Madras land-revenue management.

general rent of land in the country may have risen 10 per cent., and in taking a new lease his rent is raised in this proportion; but nothing is added for the increased value derived from the well. I would give no right of reimbursement to outgoing tenants, but would make tenant rights transferable by voluntary sale. By these arrangements, and by the periodical re-adjustment of rent-rates (on the expiry of leases) according to the state of the rent-market, many evils will be remedied. The continual changing from one field to another, the abandonment of cultivated land to take up new ground at lower rates, which is so much complained of in the Madras and Bombay presidencies, would be put a stop to. It seems quite certain that nothing can be worse than the present state of things in the south. The neglect of petty works of irrigation and such matters, attributed to the Madras Government (so far as really borne out by facts), is probably due not so much to want of will as to the impossibility of the government's performing the duties of a landlord.

In Bengal it is now, perhaps, impossible to make any considerable change. The old social fabric of the agricultural classes has been altogether swept away, and another has been substituted, of which we must make the most we can. We neglected and sacrificed the ancient rights of the cultivators, and we gave rights to the wrong people, but they have now become investments of capital, and must be maintained. The definition of boundaries and registration of rights should be fully carried out: we should, in the course of doing so, regain all that has been lost through fraud *since* the permanent settlement; the tenant-rights which may now be found to exist should be fully secured, and every facility should be given for the creation and preservation of new tenant rights.

Some regulations are also necessary regarding the

corporate cultivating bodies which are still so common in the north of India, and may perhaps be reconstructed elsewhere. It is urged by Ryotwar collectors that the *theory* in the north is not altogether different from theirs, because any proprietory cultivator may by law claim to have his share divided off and altogether separated from the rest. And so, in fact, according to the regulations, he can. In practice, however, there are obstacles, and the right has not been generally claimed in democratic villages—but the existence of the right, together with the unrestricted sale of individual shares in corporate properties, must undoubtedly tend to their dissolution. I am not sanguine enough to suppose that it is possible in a more highly artificial state of civilization, by an unlimited law of entail to maintain with advantage for ever the indivisibility of these corporations; but I do think that it is in every way most undesirable, pernicious, and unfair to facilitate their premature dismemberment by laws altogether inconsistent with their previous constitution and rights. I would not give to every individual, however small his share, a power to break up the community, or by sale to introduce a strange element: and I would so provide that, when in course of time they are dissolved, they should resolve themselves not into a Ryotwar state of things, but into zemeendaree tenures. My plan is this. In a perfect and numerous community I would in the first instance refuse to separate small shares, and would permit the transfer of such shares only among those already members of the community, or to other persons with the consent of the majority, or of the collector as representative of the superior lord. The right of separation and of unlimited sale I would give only to holders of say not less than one-fourth of an estate, and provided that they pay to Government on their share not less than 200 rupees per annum. It would follow that, so long as the community remains tolerably perfect and uniform, a forced dissolution would be prevented; but when in peaceable and prosperous times inequalities gradually arise—when the more prosperous shareholders begin to absorb the less prosperous—the former, becoming possessed of large shares, will acquire, if they desire it, separate rights, unrestrictedly transferable — will become, in fact, village zemeendars; while their less prosperous brethren will gradually sink into tenants, labourers, or servants, or seek other professions. In this way, not rashly and suddenly, but in due fulness of time, we shall leave behind us the pleasant institutions of a former age, and naturally and gradually merge into that state of things which must accompany the accumulation of capital and the modernization of manners.

Law of primogeniture.

Much has been said in the Bombay and Madras presidencies of the evil resulting from the division of inheritances. I do not understand how this can be so greatly felt where there is avowedly so much waste land, unless it be that, owing to the inequality of the assessments, the low assessed fields are subdivided, and the others left uncultivated. In the north I do not think that this evil is much complained of among the mere cultivating classes. They somehow suit themselves and their occupations to circumstances; and if there are too many, some go elsewhere, and farther extend the cultivation of the country. I doubt whether it would be possible to carry out a law of primogeniture in regard to these small holdings—it would be so much opposed to the unwritten but all-powerful law of the country. But I *do* think that, in that non-cultivating zemeendaree tenure *created* in fact by our government, the evil of too great subdivision is enormous, and we have a perfect right to arrest it. It is already much felt; and if the family of an original zemeendar of a village be allowed to subdivide *ad infinitum*, we may soon be in a worse state than if the village were Ryotwar, for we may have a whole tribe of small zemeendars dominant over another tribe of small cultivators. They will eat up the Government revenue, and we shall have to deal with an infinity of small estates. The system also gives rise to extreme uncertainty as to the real ownership of such estates, and to much fraud and litigation. I would, therefore, propose a rule, the converse of that suggested, in regard to the separation of corporate villages. I would have it that no zemeendaree tenure should be divided beyond a certain point, unless the proprietors become a joint cultivating community.

I would make a law of inheritance which should not prevent a man possessed of *several* villages or estates from dividing them among his sons (for resident village proprietors are every way desirable), but which would render indivisible every existing zemeendaree holding, from a village downwards, the major part of which is not actually cultivated by the zemeendars themselves. It should go to one heir only, to the eldest son, or to another by will, and the rest of the family must seek a livelihood elsewhere, or become tenant-cultivators. The Government would thus be protected from the growth of an immense class of idlers by which they are threatened, and against which some protection is absolutely necessary. If the zemeendars are *bonâ fide* cultivators, and sufficiently numerous, the collector will have it in his power to constitute them a cultivating corporation.

Assessment.

It is unnecessary here to dwell on the advantage of an equable and reasonable assessment; but I think I may say that, even supposing our information to be sufficiently perfect (which it has never yet been), it is neither necessary nor desirable to make permanent settlements. Very long leases, and a principle of assessment under which capital, beneficially invested in the land, shall not be taxed, will be sufficient for all good purposes; while it is fair that Government should, at certain intervals, have the benefit of the increased value resulting from the general progress and wealth of the country, and an opportunity of rectifying inequalities. No landlord would think of making a permanent settlement with his tenants. They would have all the gain of good bargains, and *he* all the loss of bad ones. On the occurrence of balance every effort should be made to avoid the extreme measure of sale or forfeiture; but when proprietors are incorrigible their rights must be sold or forfeited. I would give to Government the option of declaring an estate to be forfeited by non-payment of revenue, instead of selling it, so that future arrangements may be discretionary. When the proprietors cultivate, their proprietary rights must be distinguished from tenant-rights, and the latter will remain with them even when they lose the former. In the case of extreme bad cultivators I would adjudicate tenant-rights to be forfeited in satisfaction of balances, to the Government or to the intermediate proprietors, so that the holders, being ejected, may be reduced to the condition of labourers, and better men put in their place.

Judicial determination of agrarian rights.

One more measure is very necessary to the welfare of the agriculturalists,—that the judicial determination of their rights, and of the privileges accorded to them by Government, should rest with those who are qualified for the duty, and who have the means of performing it without giving rise to endless and harassing litigation, and affording opportunity to all kinds of legal chicanery.

Indian landed tenures form an important science, and

one which much depends on the possession of a mass of records. A great proportion of the existing landed rights have been created, and all have been altered, regulated, and determined, by us. This science is acquired and practised by the revenue officers—these records are formed and kept by those officers—these rights have been in the first instance ascertained and registered by those officers. The Civil Courts, on the other hand, have none of these facilities. They have no laws which can sufficiently guide them in determining rights which have not heretofore existed in their present form, and they know nothing about revenue matters. Yet because the landed interests are considered to be *property*, the judicial determination of landed rights is referred to those Civil Courts, either in the first instance or in appeal from the decisions of the much better qualified Revenue Courts. The consequences are most distressing—ruinous litigation, great injustice, and an uncertainty of tenure which, after all that Government has done to render it certain, is a monstrous and crying hardship.

Most questions of this kind can be well decided in the Revenue Courts and from the revenue records. Still they may also involve questions which more properly belong to the Civil Courts, and to permit the revenue officers to decide such points might create legal discrepancies.

The plan which I would propose is this—that all such cases should be first heard in the Revenue Courts; and if the records and evidence possessed by or available to those courts are sufficient to decide the whole or any part of the matter in dispute, that it should be decided accordingly, without appeal to the Civil Courts, but only to the superior Revenue Courts. If there remain issues of law other than revenue law, or issues of fact which the collector does not think himself competent to decide, and regarding which there seems to be reasonable ground for seeking a judicial decision, then he is to state the issue, and to give a warrant authorising the trial of that issue in the Civil Court. Every decision of such issues should be subsequently attested by the collector as practicable, and not inconsistent with revenue law, and then executed by him. The collector would not, under this system, acquire any arbitrary power, as the appeal from his decisions to the higher Revenue Courts, and, eventually, to Government, would be an amply sufficient security. Under the provisions regarding the transfer of small shares, the holdings of petty proprietary cultivators could not be sold by auction in satisfaction of civil claims without the consent of the representative of Government; and I think it by no means desirable that tenant-rights of any kind should be compulsorily sold, except in special cases with the consent of the Government, which has the chief valuable interest in the soil. But it is an essential part of the scheme that the rights of the proprietary middlemen should be in every way freely transferable.

There remain the more properly legal codes, for which we shall look to the committee of justice.

Duties of the Law Commission.

Hitherto the Law Commission has certainly signally failed. It is quite melancholy to read the story how the first commissioner made a penal code—how, for the next eleven years, it was bandied about without any result—how the commissioners meantime, instead of making the urgently required code of civil procedure, waited to see the fate of the penal code—how, at the end of the eleven years, the Government of India was ordered to revise and adopt it—how the next head of the commission pronounced it *unphilosophical*, drew his pen through it, and made another code—how the rival codes were referred by the Government of India to the Court of Directors, and by the Court of Directors to the Government of India—and how, at this day, we are just where we were. But still this by no means proves that an efficient department of the Government, charged with similar functions, might not succeed. As to the past, at the worst we have, after all, only the fact that Mr. Macaulay, in a comparatively short time, made a penal code, which did not meet with universal approbation, but regarding which we have arrived at no decision whether it is good or bad. That nothing has been done since 1837 is the personal fault of some person or persons, but no proof that something might not have been done, since no one has tried to do anything. I believe that a man of strong will and resolute hand, uninfluenced by prejudices, bent on achieving the object in view in the best way, whether by creating, borrowing, or adapting—looking to use and not to the most perfect philosophy—preferring to rescue India from the lowest juridical state, and to raise it to the level of the best of the imperfect systems yet discovered, rather than vainly imagining to make it more perfect than all the world beside—I believe that such a man, devoting himself uninterruptedly to the subject, and well supported by Government, might have and would have long ago effected all that is most urgently required; and I think that it is well worth our while to make another attempt, and to determine that it *shall* succeed. If the Indian Government, being itself efficient, wills it, and goes the right way about it, we may at least succeed in obtaining, with very little delay, the codes most pressingly required—a code of civil procedure and a penal code. The penal code, having been so long in hand, being by far the most simple, and being immediately required in order to subject all classes to a uniform law, may be first finished, but one member of the committee of justice should at once take in hand a code of civil procedure. The other codes would follow, and, in the mean time, a special commission might be issued to digest the materials for the great work of a civil code.

Everything will, of course, depend on the men selected for the task. Shall I venture to say that, if we could obtain the services of a good foreign jurist, he might be not the least useful member of the committee of justice?

I shall here merely glance at the nature of the codes and of the policy which I would propose.

We have not, in most parts of India, coped with crime with sufficient success. Something may be done by improving the executive; but we also especially require an improvement of our laws. Good criminal codes, both of crimes and punishments, and of criminal procedure, are much wanted.

Penal code.

A mere penal code (as distinguished from criminal procedure) may be very much the same all over the world; and Mr. Macaulay's code seems just as applicable to France or England as to India. We have already in India more and better laws in this department of justice than in any other; but we have no foundation for our patchwork legislation. Our classification of crimes is altogether imperfect; and there are great defects in our punishments, especially as regards the property and civil rights of criminals, which are often more dear to them than a few years' liberty.

Mr. Macaulay's code is certainly constructed on a refined plan not very intelligible to the multitude, and in very hard language. These are evils: are they inevitable? Let us look at the French penal code. The French are a highly civilised nation; they seem content with their penal code. Is it so complex in structure and language? It seems to me that it is by no means so. It follows our preconceived ideas of the arrangement of crime, and is in very simple language. Macaulay, while following it in some things, seems to have exceedingly refined upon it in others. Here is the definition of theft and robbery (*vol*), which the French find good enough for them :—" Quiconque a soustrait frauduleusement une chose qui ne lui appartient pas est coupable de vol." Mr. Macaulay makes it :—" Whoever, intending to take fraudulently anything which is property, and which is not attached to the earth, out of the possession of any person without that person's consent, moves that thing in order to such taking, is said to commit theft;" to which there follow seven explanations and twenty-six illustrations; and robbery is separately defined.

Again, in the French code, all the aggravated forms of theft and robbery are classed under that head, with their punishments, very much as is now the case in India; while in Macaulay's code you have to analyse and *cumulate* punishments.

In fact, if we omit offences against the state, the French penal code seems simple enough. As Macaulay's code would do for France, so the French code might do for India. Suppose we make a present of our code to the French, and borrow theirs? That is my plan. I should think that the French code adapted might suit us admirably well. We should strike out many of the offences against the state, and insert some particular provisions peculiar to India. The code would be very easily translated; and within six months we might have it in full operation.

I do especially protest against the omission from the Indian penal code of several crimes recognised as such by all native laws (and hitherto by British Indian law), because those acts are not penal in England. I would instance crimes relating to the chastity of women—adultery and seduction. The natives have the strongest feelings on these points. Unhappily their manners are such that they do not trust to female honour, but to actual and legal restraint. They look on the seduction of their women as the most aggravated form of robbery; and nothing so outrages their feelings as the legalising such acts. Yet do we look on those acts as more justifiable than they do? And because our manners are different, and our restraints and punishments are social rather than legal, is it not the height of intolerance to force our principles upon them? I hope that the social position of their women may some day be so raised as to stand in need of no bars and legal defences; but till then we must protect their dearest property, or we risk their allegiance. We must both restore a runaway wife to her legitimate owner and punish the man who stole her. The law commissioners argue that the higher classes will not resort to our courts in such cases. I am not at all clear that it would be so under a proper system; and even if it were, are the laws made only for the higher classes?

Criminal procedure.

In criminal procedure, more than anything—if we wish to succeed—we must especially avoid following English or American models or ideas. The laws to determine the relative rights of man and man may be the same in the purest democracy and the purest despotism; but criminal law is a law between the Government and the individual subject. The laws of criminal procedure, designed to protect freedom, and not unsafe where a free public takes an active part against crime, are inapplicable to a despotism, and in India may lead to the triumph of crime. Our criminal laws must be formed rather on a continental than on an English model. A new code of criminal procedure would open many questions on which there might be great difference of opinion; and as we are already to a certain extent provided with the most necessary rules, I would be content to leave the complete performance of this task till more pressing wants are supplied. But there are several amendments which might be meantime made; and it is quite necessary that the hands of Government should be materially strengthened in dealing with crime, since experience shows it to be at present far too weak in this respect.

The principal change which I would recommend is one of those which may not altogether accord with English ideas, but which I believe to be in India highly just and expedient, and necessary to enable us efficiently to cope with crime. I would put the judicial administration of the penal code into the hands of those who are at the same time responsible for the police and peace of the country, and who have the best means of judging of the real facts of the case; would separate it altogether from the judicial establishments of the civil courts; and would unite the whole criminal administration in one department. It would still fall within the province of the minister of justice; but I would put the whole of the criminal duties (executive and judicial) in each local government under a separate criminal board, charged with the detection and suppression of crime. The immediate superintendence of the magistrates acting in their judicial capacity, the hearing of appeals, and the trial of the more serious cases, should no longer rest with the civil judge of each district—often a nervous old gentleman, and always one who knows nothing of the parties—who is in no way concerned in the suppression of crime—who has no jury to bear the responsibility of a conviction *—and in whose view it is the *safe* side to take

* I believe that this is really one of the principal causes of the difficulty of

the course—reasonable or unreasonable—most favourable to the prisoner. I would vest these powers in a really superior officer, exercising an appellate and superintending power over several districts, and one who must consider two things—justice to the prisoner and justice to the public. In short, I would transfer the powers alluded to from the civil judges to the commissioners of divisions, who have now a good deal of time to spare, and who would thus unite the whole criminal superintendence.

I have alluded to the necessary distinction between the criminal rules of a free and a despotic country. In this country the public take an active part against crime. Although many guilty may escape, there is not the fear of crime eventually getting altogether the better of justice. A suspected criminal might even be unfairly run down by popular enthusiasm. A judge is a moderator and arbitrator between the public and the criminal; and the decision of fact lies with a jury taken from the injured public. You must also guard against the use of the criminal law for political purposes; and on that account you cannot trust its administration to the executive. But in India the public does *not* take an active part—if the judge is merely an umpire, it is a one-sided arbitration—there is very great fear that crime may get the better of justice, and throw the country into confusion—and no political check is required. We must therefore have criminal judges who are charged with the suppression of crime, and who feel that they are condemned if the guilty escape; in fact, connected with the executive; and they should be permitted

obtaining convictions, so much complained of in India. An English jury sympathise not only with the prisoner but also with the injured party and the endangered public; they divide the responsibility with the judge and among themselves, and convict many cases which a single Indian judge would acquit.

to avail themselves of *every* kind of evidence. In this case justice would be fairly done, and the public might be sufficiently protected; while a reasonable provision for appeal would guard against any indiscreet use of power.

In India a jury, properly so called, is unfortunately in most cases impracticable as an instrument for the substantial decision of criminal accusations. The natives are very ready to decide causes between one man and another, but they will not take the responsibility of deciding between individuals and Government, or, if they did, they might be influenced by various feelings. Assessors are, however, very useful in the most serious cases, as some relief to the judge. It is a very severe task for a single man to decide alone most difficult questions of fact, involving, it may be, the life of a fellow-creature; and native assessors, if they relieve him of little real responsibility, seem to lighten his mind, and may sometimes be really very useful. Their use should be by all means promoted; and there are some cases in which the actual decision may be with advantage left to a jury or panchayet.

It is in every way desirable to obtain popular assistance in the criminal administration. We must therefore, as much as possible, encourage the people to take an active part against crime; and this is chiefly to be done by making criminal justice easy to them, which it at present is very far from being. I would give small judicial powers for the decision of petty criminal cases to the native revenue collectors and other respectable persons, so that such cases might be summarily decided on the spot. When more serious cases have been judicially investigated by the magistrate, I would dispense with the great and useless hardship to the parties and witnesses of a second trial, except when it is substantially necessary. The European magistrate can at least be depended upon not to send false and fraudulent records of the trial. When the case is clear, when the prisoner confesses, and the evidence is so overwhelming that commitment is a mere matter of form, I would send the papers to the commissioner, and authorise him to pass sentence after perusing them and weighing the opinion and recommendation of the magistrate. If, on the other hand, the case is a doubtful one, and he thinks it necessary to examine the parties and the witnesses, they must be sent, and a second trial must take place. Similar arrangements to those which I have just proposed have been tried in some of the Non-Regulation districts with great success.

Police.

Great efforts must be made to render the police as good as possible; but this, after all, depends more on the general efficiency of the executive services than on any principles of action that can be laid down, and I shall not here attempt to go into separate details in regard to the discipline of the police.

I think that a general detective police, within proper limits and restrictions, should be established; and that the responsibility of the landholders, and discipline of the village police, should be more fully enforced. As regards the ordinary preventive police establishment, the general system adopted in Northern India is good; and it seems only necessary to render it more effective in its execution and details. Even with improved laws and a good system we shall not cope successfully with crime without good agents and an efficient police service.

Civil procedure.

Still more pressing than the criminal system, as regards the necessity for change, and affording at the same time much less scope for difference of opinion, or for collision with English ideas, is the procedure of the civil courts. Here we ask only that reform which has now been to a great extent granted to England; but we claim it more urgently because—while in England the old system has in a manner grown up with the old institutions of the country, has been from time to time in many respects adapted to its peculiar habits, and has been so long borne only as a time-honoured load which had descended from our ancestors—in India no such prescription or adaptation has in any degree lightened the burden; it has been imposed in modern times by perverse foreigners, and its ill effects have developed themselves with such startling rapidity and intensity, that, if we delay much longer, they may be beyond our power to remedy. On this account a good code of civil procedure is our most crying want.

To prevent misconception, I may as well say that the present procedure, originated by the Cornwallis regulations, is not properly English—it is rather parallel than similar. It seems to have adopted many of the bad parts of our system, the technicalities and expense and the most intense special pleading, without the good parts—the brevity of the record—the clearness of the issue—the promptness and vigour of the trial and verdict when a case *does* come on at Nisi Prius. The system of rambling written pleadings filed in court seems more to resemble the Scotch or the Chancery procedure; and, if you suppose that a case goes through the difficulties and expenses of English law in its worst days, till the time for trial arrives, and then discover that we have no intelligible issue, but a mass of elaborately concocted written contradictions of fact and of law upon all sorts of points, which are then formally supported by strings of marshalled witnesses, beyond whom the judge cannot look—that the native judge of the first instance understands the habits of the country and, it may be, the subjects brought in dispute, but has no good or well-established legal system to guide him—that a succession of appellate judges have neither law nor juridical science, nor properly understand the subjects in dispute, having been, through all their previous service, otherwise employed—and that judges and parties of every degree invariably prefer technicalities to facts;—if you imagine all this, you will then have some idea of a trial before the Indian civil courts.

The grand evil of this system results from the proneness of the natives to adopt it, and the consequent vast growth of most unscrupulous and noxious litigation, amounting to an internecine war among all classes, carried on with technical weapons charged with fraud, perjury, and forgery.

The courts are now quite sufficient in numbers and strength to administer this justice, such as it is; but it is the quality of the material which must be altered. The growth of perjury and forgery is the most alarming symptom. While I very much doubt the extreme difficulty of discovering the truth from natives *as we find them*, I am too well convinced of the difficulty of extracting the truth from the worst evidence, taken in the worst way, from the worst native witnesses, *as we make them*. We put a systematic premium on perjury, and when, in lapse of years, perjury springs up, we complain of the perjurers. A man tells his story in writing first—supports it by witnesses afterwards. The judge's business is not to seek out the truth, but to determine between the two opposite sets of witnesses; he may count them or he may weigh them, but in either case witnesses, and skilled witnesses, are most valuable.* A villain who is encou-

* It seems to me that both in India and in this country witnesses are too apt to divide themselves into two classes—unwilling witnesses and too willing witnesses. People are either dragged into court against their will, and without sufficient remuneration, or they are paid not only their expenses but a sort of premium on their evidence. The way in which in this country professional

raged by our legal system to go to law will not let his case fall to the ground for want of evidence; the demand creates a supply, and a supply there is. But I believe that, if judges ceased to consider themselves mere judicial machines—if the facts were properly sifted—if the character and antecedents of witnesses were ascertained—it is not so difficult to get at the truth as is popularly believed, and that *uncrammed* natives are not such bad witnesses after all.

A reformed code of civil procedure, and judges who are not sham but real lawyers, we must then quickly have; and the new procedure must be principally directed to the object of enabling the judge to search out the truth in every possible way from the best and most independent sources of information, and to get rid of technicalities and special pleading,* and of everything which tends to make litigation a game of skill. We must engraft on our system some provisions of the nature of *equitable* remedies; and stringent rules must be enacted to prevent fraudulent evasions and ensure the due execution of decrees. The public registration or attestation of deeds must also be facilitated and carried much farther than at present. When we have a sufficient code of law

witnesses are retained as advocates is most scandalous. I understand that large fees are habitually and openly offered to and accepted by them as the price of their evidence. Having received these fees, they come into the witness-box, and under the name of evidence make partizan speeches. This evidence-giving is by far the most profitable branch of the profession of science. The allowances to witnesses should be so arranged that, so far as possible, they should not lose by coming to give evidence, but certainly they should not *gain*; and I would make it highly penal to pay them anything beyond the taxed allowance.

* The Hindoo lawgiver seems to hit on the happy medium in regard to technical inaccuracies. "If," he says, "there be small irregularities in the proceedings, the party shall not on that account lose his cause, but the magistrate shall fine him." The power of amending now given to the judges in this country is a great improvement, but some penalty should be imposed to prevent carelessness, which may sometimes involve serious inconvenience.

it may be a question whether, in the more important class of cases, the issues of law and of fact might not be with advantage distinguished and separately tried.

Trial by jury in civil cases.

I would promote to the very utmost—indeed I would, at the discretion of the judge, enforce—the use of juries (after native fashion) to decide issues of fact in civil cases; and, till we have our civil code, it may even be necessary to trust to juries issues of native law, or rather the facts of law—the custom of inheritance, for instance. As between one man and another, juries are a most admirable indigenous institution, and we should avail ourselves of them to the utmost, under proper regulations. When the case is clear and simple, it saves much expense and inconvenience if it can be at once decided by the judge; but when there are serious and doubtful issues, a well-directed trial by a jury will generally be much more satisfactory. The jury can judge of the witnesses infinitely better than the judge, and a systematic reference to such a tribunal is in itself the best check to perjury. The regulations admit voluntary references to arbitration, but of course the professional followers of the law are always opposed to such a course, and they generally find their clients willing enough to carry on the game of litigation. A general system of trial by native juries will then be one of the most important parts of the new civil procedure.

While the encouragement now afforded to litigious and dishonest proceedings is remedied, and the decision of cases affording real ground for litigation is rendered more trustworthy, it will be every way desirable greatly to increase the facility of using the courts as the instrument for enforcing undisputed claims; and especially it will be an object to provide for the summary decision of trifling matters. With this view, the introduction into the lowest class of courts of a very summary procedure will be most advantageous.

By far the most difficult task of all is to codify the civil law. It is so complex, so varied, so personal, and so local, that to do so is a most serious undertaking. Happily its immediate urgency is not so great. If we have a good procedure, we may get on for a time with the indigenous lights to native law, till more necessary things are disposed of. But the eventual philosophical classification, compilation, and, when necessary, amendment of the civil laws, and the establishment of a *lex loci** of the country, are most desirable and most incumbent on us.

Codification of the civil law.

There is one part of this subject which must not be delayed. We much want a commercial code. Class-laws are all very well in classes, but, where different classes meet, different laws must clash; and a commercial *lex loci* is indispensable. Europeans and other foreigners complain much of the difficulties of the civil law. A commercial and an agrarian code, with a good system of procedure, would meet most of their requirements. I would at once issue a competent commission to prepare a commercial code, which the committee of justice would revise; and I have already suggested that, while more pressing and simple codes are being prepared, a civil law commission should be collecting materials for the great work of a

Commercial code.

* A *lex loci* is very much required for those classes who have no ascertainable law of their own, but the difficulty is *what* law to adopt for this purpose. The English law would be quite inappropriate: first, on account of its peculiar and municipal character; second, because it is nowhere codified in accessible form. Probably the Roman law might answer best, as the most universal, and the foundation of most modern codes. I do not know what laws generally prevail among the Christian population of Western Asia, but it is not improbable that the Roman law may be well applied to the Armenians and such classes in India now said to be without any law.

civil code. We shall find natives admirably fitted to render great assistance in these duties.

The Crown courts.

Mistaken as is the procedure and injurious the practice of the civil courts, there is yet one little point of view in which they appear favourably. Compared to Her Majesty's courts in India, they are white and pure. They at least understand something of the country, the language, and the people, and their machinery has been in some respects adapted to the most urgent necessities. Bad as is the evidence before them, they are not absolutely bound to believe it.

The utter inadaptation of the procedure and practice of the Crown Courts has been in no way mitigated, but on the contrary has been aggravated to the utmost possible extent, to the profit of a large legal profession, exclusively European, who thrive on costs and charges monstrously disproportioned to the extent of the jurisdiction, and to the value of money in the country. I do not now speak so much of the usurped jurisdiction (assumed partly for the benefit of lawyers, and partly in consequence of the facilities afforded by the court to dishonest and litigious persons) which has rendered the Supreme Court a name of terror (to which the Spanish Inquisition only can be compared) to the higher classes of the native population of the interior, whom the law has expressly exempted from its jurisdiction. The Government of India has already the power to legislate on this subject; and it is very necessary to put a final end to the many *dodges* of constructive residence and constructive amenability which have been made the instruments of most abominable tyranny, and have subjected natives of rank to indignities the most galling and injustice the most flagrant. But I now more particularly allude to the legitimate jurisdiction of the Crown Courts, and the calamity thereby inflicted on the inhabitants of the presidency towns.

The whole machinery of unreformed English law has been transplanted into a country where it is utterly and absurdly inapplicable. We have Common Law courts, and Chancery, and Admiralty, and Ecclesiastical courts, and all the paraphernalia thereto appertaining. The judges are utterly ignorant of the language and strange to the people; so much swearing is so much evidence; and processes are issued on affidavits infinitely more valueless than that most worthless form of evidence in this country. The facilities for fraudulent and artificial litigation thus afforded to a people most prone to such arts are quite terrible, and probably nowhere in this world is litigation carried to so great an extent. The perjury and fraud of the Mofussil courts are trifling compared to the state of things prevailing in the presidency towns. To the judicial system may be in a principal degree attributed the demoralisation which is so remarkable in those towns. The European lawyers, who maintain an exclusive monopoly of the profession,* and the European officers of the court, being paid (as the price of European labour in India) many times more highly than in England, in a country where money is many times more valuable, the proportionate cost of litigation is probably ten or twelve times greater than it ever was in England, and nothing has so much tended to impoverish the people and interfere with the accumulation of capital.

Abolition of local and personal distinctions.

The abolition of local and personal distinctions and jurisdictions will then be of course an essential part of the scheme of codification. The distinction between Regulation and Non-Regulation Provinces will no longer remain, except in the case of such very recent conquests as are actually

* It has been lately seen that admission to practise as an attorney is strictly refused to every native.

under martial or political law. The expensive * Crown Courts existing at Calcutta, Madras, and Bombay will be abolished, and reasonable local tribunals will be substituted in their place. It is therefore unnecessary longer to dwell on the many evils and abuses of those courts—their inconsistency with the present state of things, and the disproportion of their great establishments to the jurisdiction. Europeans and natives will be put on the same footing (with a few exceptions) in the eye of the law.

Judicial establishments.

Supposing the necessary improvements in the system of procedure to be effected, the general arrangement of the ordinary judicial establishments seems good—with this exception, that it is absolutely necessary that there should be in Bengal and Agra, as in Madras and Bombay, a class of European sub or assistant judges, so that European judicial officers may acquire some experience before being promoted to the office of judge. In creating the class of sub-judges we may diminish the number of district judges.

The greatest part of the judicial business is already conducted by native judges, and will continue to be so. The superintendence of judicial districts I do not think that you can yet intrust to them; but I would certainly have one or two natives as judges in the chief court of each presidency, and in the Supreme Court for all India—receiving of course a lower salary than the more expensive foreign judges.

It has been proposed to unite the Crown and Sudder Courts. But any such union on terms of equality—much

* With reference to the expense of the Crown Courts, I may remark that the sum charged in the Indian accounts is not the gross but the *net* cost. The fees in the Company's courts are credited to Government in the shape of stamp-revenue, and the gross cost is charged; but in the Crown Courts the numerous officers of the court receive large fees from the suitors which are not brought to account.

more if precedence be given to an English judge—would be most unfair, because it would be elevating the present Crown Courts from local tribunals into a supreme jurisdiction over the whole country exercised in conjunction with some Indian judges, but in which with their usual assumption of superiority they would probably attempt to absorb the chief share. I should see no objection to the introduction into each chief court (till we obtain a regular judicial service) of one European jurist, appointed by the Indian Government, both as a juridical adviser and a judge in cases between Europeans. While we have no *lex loci*, it is necessary to administer English law to Englishmen. But I would on no account admit of a larger introduction of a very unsafe and undesirable element, and had much rather leave the Crown Court unmolested in a jurisdiction of its own in Calcutta than give it a general joint jurisdiction from Calcutta to Peshawar. No person should be appointed from this country to any judicial or other office in India, except by the Senate.

As soon as we have a regular system, the present jurisdiction of the Privy Council in Indian cases must cease. Not only is that tribunal necessarily ignorant of Indian matters, but it is a monstrous and ruinous hardship that the appeal should lie to a court in a strange country, so many thousand miles off, and it is an odd inconsistency that we should give the legislative power to the Indian Government, and keep the judicial power at home—so that the Governor-General makes laws, and her Majesty interprets them. This judicial duty would be transferred to a Supreme Court in connection with the Supreme Government, and composed of the best Indian lawyers, European and native. I would permit the Governor-General in Council to receive special appeals from the decisions of this court when it appears to the Government that the court are misconstruing its laws; and the legislative government should be authorized to issue authoritative interpretations of the law.

Position of the Government in courts.

I would make the position of the Government in the civil courts very much that of her Majesty in this country. A suit against the Government should only be tried on production of the warrant of a great executive officer. A man who has a claim against the Government should first bring it forward by petition in the revenue courts, and, if there defeated, should apply for a warrant for the trial of certain issues in the civil court, which, if there is reasonable ground, should be granted.

Provision for obtaining good lawyers.

The best of laws, ill administered, will become bad, and law in its best form is too great a science to be properly administered by other than professional jurists. I have proposed to separate from the proper judicial department the judicial duties connected with revenue and criminal law. But the civil law will afford scope to great lawyers, and will be an amply sufficient field for a judicial service. I shall explain, in connection with the civil service, the mode in which I propose to secure due qualifications in the European judges. It is still more important to make the natives good lawyers, and they are eminently capable of becoming so.

Proposed College of Justice.

My plan is to establish a great central college of justice in connection with the Supreme Court and the judicial department of Government; and I may here remark that I should look to this establishment for much of the assistance necessary to the committee of justice in carrying out the required codes. I would give the natives a thorough juridical education, and shall afterwards propose to bring the European judicial servants into connection with the college for a time. I would here collect the best expounders of the different native laws; and would give the college a very high status, not only as a place of education, but as a sort of public and privileged association of jurists and great juridical university. The details and farther uses of this plan I cannot here enter upon.

Separation of executive and judicial functions.

I would draw a broad and permanent line between the executive and judicial departments. The criminal administration of an absolute government is the performance, by the executive, of a corrective duty for the protection of the public; but Government is not directly concerned in a private suit between man and man; and it is no doubt quite necessary in an advanced state of society that it should delegate the duty of deciding the civil rights of individuals to professional judges other than the ordinary executive officers. Bad systems of procedure and bad laws have brought law and lawyers into disrepute, not good laws well administered. Laws as they ought to be are but for rendering natural justice and equity more certain, clear, and attainable, and for determining, arbitrarily but certainly, those things where equity may be wanting; and it is certain that an artificial state of society and the accumulation of property engender questions of civil right which can only be solved by lawyers. Lawyers, then, we must have; but the great object is, that they should be professional and good lawyers. It is here that the Indian service is chiefly wanting. Yet the members of the service are not to blame, but the system, which makes no man a lawyer by profession, and yet comparatively late in life calls upon him to perform the duties of a full-blown lawyer. All this must be changed. Let us have a service of professional lawyers; let men of talent be set apart to that profession from their youth, and duly trained up to it. I doubt not that Indian servants will then become as remarkable for judicial as for executive efficiency. At present a civil servant has no legal training whatever till he is made a Zillah judge, a situation in which he is called on alone to perform more difficult legal duties than fall to any single judge in Westminster Hall. To qualify himself for such duties he must devote himself solely and exclusively to them; and it is on this ground that I especially insist on finally and permanently dividing, by an absolute line of demarcation, the judicial from the executive service of Government.

The bar.

An indispensable requisite to a good judicial system is a good bar. The greatest of judges could hardly, with confidence, decide difficult legal questions without the assistance of an able and honourable bar; and that is one of the most important of the many difficulties under which Indian judges have laboured. It will be a good beginning of a bar of a higher character if the European judicial servants acquire their first experience as advocates of Government; and we must strive to obtain a respectable native bar. Talent is not wanting; but we must try to add legal education, and the character and honour of gentlemen.

In the moral and material improvement of the country and people an immense field on which we have yet but little entered lies before us and demands all the efforts of the Government, but such efforts must depend on the possession of funds, and I must therefore leave these subjects till I have separately noticed our military and financial position, which I have also excluded from this chapter.

We must now look to the machinery subordinate to the executive government.

The system by which, in each presidency, heads of departments—boards and superintendents—are intrusted with the management of the details of their respective charges, is good and necessary. While the Government directs, the departmental heads secure a sufficiently minute supervision and a uniform management throughout the territories of each local government. It is by a similar arrangement in connexion with the Central Government that all India may be united and efficiently administered. Connected with this subject is the question of the relative advantages of a plural board and of a single superintendent. In unity and energy of action the latter has great advantages; but where a very great mass of detailed business is to be transacted, and where uniformity is urgently required, a plural board is necessary. It is to secure uniformity and due consideration that the chief courts of justice are, and must be, plural. I think that the quantity of minute business in the revenue department of the local governments is also so great, it is so necessary to maintain a uniform system, and so much of the business is of a quasi-judicial character, that the boards of revenue must be continued. Under this system the continuity of action and usage is not broken on each change of an individual officer. The two revenue commissioners at Bombay might be with advantage united in a board; and, when the Indus territories are put under a governor, part of the present Punjab board may form a board of revenue.

Heads of executive departments.

Revenue.

I have proposed to unite in one department the whole criminal administration — the prevention, detection, trial, and punishment of crime. The police stands much in need of a more general superintendence; so do our criminal courts and the discipline of our jails. All these duties I would intrust to

Criminal.

the criminal boards (one under each local government) which I have already suggested. The members of the board may well arrange among themselves to divide the duties, while they unite in conclave on important subjects.

Education.

I fear that the great variety of opinion on educational subjects entertained by amateur members of the councils of education has done much to paralyse the educational efforts of Government, and it seems to me that they will only be effectual when the supervision of the whole educational system of each presidency is intrusted either to a paid professional board of limited numbers, or to one executive superintendent, with no other duties, and under the immediate orders of the governor, who will again receive instructions from the central ministry of the interior. Under the general superintendent we should have local superintendents of divisions.

Public works.

In the department of public works great change is also necessary. If considerable works for the improvement of the country are to be carried on, it is absurd, and in the ordinary construction and repair of public buildings it is inconvenient in the last degree, to intrust the supervision of every brick and every broken pane of glass in the civil department to the military board far away and already overburdened with duties of their own, which, as they are situated, they cannot possibly perform. If a pane of glass is broken in the cutcherry of the collector of Delhi, the bill for replacing it, after passing through various official grades, must be referred to the military board at Calcutta, who, if upon consideration they approve of the expense of a new pane, are, I believe, actually allowed to sanction so small an item without troubling the Government. But if the expense exceed a certain very limited sum the matter is much more serious, and farther reference and correspondence is necessary. On the other hand, the civil executive officers are naturally averse to such a system, and, having in their hands some small local funds for local improvements, they go to the other extreme in respect to the administration of the latter. Each magistrate does nearly what he likes with his road and ferry and other local funds, and has no professional assistance whatever.

Now both it is to be hoped that Government will in future be enabled to spend money more generally on public works other than military, and it is desirable that there should be some system in the direction of local funds. It is quite necessary then that the local government should have immediately under its orders a civil engineer's department, and that the military board should be relieved of the superintendence of civil works. I would have a superintending engineer at the head-quarters of each government, and under him an executive engineer of each civil division.

Accounts, &c.

I should say that the offices of accountant-general, civil auditor, and treasurer in each government (except perhaps Bengal) might very well be united in one superintendent of finances, with a couple of assistants and a suitable office establishment.

I need not say that there must of course be as now a postmaster-general for each government, and it may be matter for consideration whether there should be a postmaster-general for all India, or whether the minister of the interior can perform that duty.

Legal.

I would have in each government an advocate or procurator-general and establishment of government advocates, the legal advisers of government and of its executive officers, charged with the maintenance of the interests of government in all courts, and with the prosecution in the superior courts, at the instance of the executive officers, of criminals, revenue defaulters, and persons on whom the government has claims of any kind.

A division (I use the word in its technical sense) comprises about half a dozen districts. The divisional commissioners of revenue and police are not at present very onerously burdened; but I think that some such officer will be necessary for the supervision of district establishments, standing between the government and the actual local executive; and I propose to give him additional work, by making him the superior criminal judge. He will have the general executive charge of his division; will be a censor of the acts, characters, and qualifications of the district officers, and charged with such local arrangements as government may intrust to him. He will hear appeals in all the executive departments, and will try the most serious criminal charges. He will be the connecting link of different departments, and insure *bonâ fide* and active co-operation. The civil engineer, the educational superintendent of the division, and the government advocate, will be under his orders; and he will be in communication with the General commanding the military division, and with the commissariat officer. He will actively direct the combined operation of the police. I would make this class of officers then uniform throughout India.

Commissioners of divisions.

In regard to the local executive, I think that there can be no doubt whatever of the advantage of uniting in the hands of the same local officers the whole of the ordinary executive duties—the whole executive representation of government—according to the system which is for the most part followed in every part of India except Bengal Proper. The habits of the country, the nature of our government, and every con-

District executive.

sideration of unity, energy, convenience, and economy, all clearly urge such a course, and it is in fact impossible to obtain executive efficiency in any other way.

Union of executive power in same hands.

The usual practice is this—that one experienced officer has executive charge of, and is responsible for, a district, being at the same time provided with certain assistants, European and native, with whom he may divide the work at his discretion, according to their respective capabilities, but over all of whom he exercises a control. Under him then all the ordinary current business is conducted, but special duties requiring exclusive attention are intrusted to special officers. Thus, when a *settlement* of a district is to be made—that is, when the land revenue is to be fixed for a long term, and landed rights are to be accurately defined—a special settlement officer, selected for his skill in that particular department, is sent to make the settlement, and having made it he then leaves it to the ordinary management of the local executive. Customs, canals, salt, opium, the thuggee police, &c., are separately and specially managed.

The criminal administration being separated from the judicial department as an executive duty, the question of union or disunion here principally arises with respect to the union of criminal and agrarian functions, especially of the offices of magistrate and collector, or superintendent of lands, as the latter should rather be called. The prejudice which has been in some quarters entertained against this system seems to arise from confounding the position of the collector with that of an English tax-gatherer, than which no two things can be more distinct. The collection of the land revenue is merely an incident of the management, and, except when a discretion is to be used as to remissions (which is not the proper business of a tax-gatherer), is one of the least difficult of

P 2

a collector's duties. The lord-lieutenant of a county is not expected to collect the taxes, but the owner of a large estate intrusts the general management and the collection of the rents to the same agent, because the one duty depends upon the other. In India then, while the magistrate in his criminal character sees the worst side of the people, and is seen by them only as a corrector of the wrong, bearing the rod of justice, as collector he is their feudal superior, their protector, and their friend, and exercises an influence essential to the successful performance of his harsher functions. The two characters act and react on one another; the collector tempers the severity of the magistrate, the magistrate gives dignity and weight to the collector, and the two united form a local governor such as the natives can appreciate and respect, love and fear, and who can carry his useful functions considerably beyond the strict limit of either of the two offices which constitute his nominal title. I admit that, if we have reason to apprehend that the collector would unjustly extort money, his power as magistrate would much aid his designs, and that, if the magistrate be bent on getting up a false charge, his influence as collector might avail to secure false evidence. But this argument is reduced to the simple question, Is there really any such ground of apprehension? Is it really necessary to make a most inconvenient division of authority to secure the natives from extortion and injustice? I am speaking of the European grades of the services, and in those grades it most certainly is not. Their purity is undoubted. There may be occasional indiscretion and over-zeal, but even in those cases, under a Government which is cautious of offence to an extreme, the unlimited right of appeal, so freely exercised, is a more than sufficient security. Nowadays a Government officer has much more to fear from the result of over-zeal than of under-zeal. (Will not every man in the service bear me out in saying so?) Every person who disputes the dues of the collector has the benefit of every possible doubt, and it is a lamentable fact that the criminals are a great deal too many for the magistrate. *He* needs strengthening, and not they. The interests of the people then certainly do not require a disunion, the evil effects of which they are the first to feel.

The question remains, whether the knowledge required is so great, and the duties to be performed are so overpowering, that the same officers cannot efficiently manage both departments. I believe that it is not so by any means. In personal and local knowledge there can be no doubt that the business of one department assists the other. There is only question regarding professional knowledge. Now, is the legal knowledge necessary to a magistrate so great as to make it requisite for a man of reasonable talent and industry to devote his whole life to that duty exclusively? I should say, certainly not. The criminal law indispensable to a magistrate may be put into such simple form that it may readily be acquired. Some juridical knowledge is certainly needed, but a moderate amount will suffice. It is chiefly knowledge of character and persons, and practice in dealing with the people, that are most necessary. You want something more than an unpractised country gentleman to make a good magistrate, but not the best consulting lawyer in Westminster Hall. Even in this country of complicated laws and unskilled magistrates it is remarkable how seldom (comparatively speaking) points of law arise on criminal trials—the cumbersome law of evidence excepted. It is generally a mere question of fact. A theft is a theft; and the only question is, did A steal B's pocket-handkerchief, or did he not? I fully admit that at present legal difficulties are more common in criminal proceedings in India; but this arises from the want of a clear code of law, and the consequent wider field for difference of opinion. Let us but have a simple code, and require universal personal efficiency in the servants of Government—they will then have no difficulty in mastering sufficient criminal law, and yet retain in their heads room enough for some revenue law. It is not the criminal but the civil law that requires thorough professional lawyers.

Assuming, then, that a magistrate need not be *exclusively* a criminal lawyer; must a collector be *exclusively* devoted to revenue law? Here, again, I say no. A collector undoubtedly requires an immense deal of practical and professional knowledge; but it is for the most part precisely the same local knowledge which is most necessary to a magistrate. No man can be a good Indian magistrate who does not understand the peculiar village institutions, relations, and situations of his district. I have supposed the detailed surveys, settlements, and adjustment of rights to have been performed by a separate officer; and after this I say that a collector principally requires personal knowledge of the people, their institutions, and their manners, and an acquaintance with revenue law, and with a summary judicial procedure, such as are quite compatible with a respectable knowledge of criminal law.

The union of power and responsibility is most necessary; but if the chief feels himself strongest in police, and thinks that one of his assistants has a greater turn for revenue, he intrusts a larger share of revenue duties to the latter, and *vice versâ*. The government, of course, arranges the posting of officers with a view to particular qualifications or defects. Altogether, I believe that a tolerably good man, commencing as assistant to a magistrate and collector, may well, by the time his turn comes to take charge of a district, be every way qualified for the superintendence and control of both departments; and if it is so, it is impossible to gainsay the advantage of uniting the duties.

Evils of the opposite system.

In Bengal the practice is different, and the separation of offices is attended with the worst results. The magistrate is the youngest and least experienced officer in the district. Upon him, unguided and unaided, fall the most onerous and difficult duties. He is merely a police magistrate, and is supported by none of the influence of a landlord or a local governor. Can we be surprised that he fails — that crime is rampant, and dacoits are triumphant? By the time that he has become experienced he ceases to be a magistrate. He is made a collector, and his salary is doubled. This arrangement is especially absurd, since in Bengal onerous collectorate duties cannot be pleaded as a reason for entirely relieving him of the police. The revenue of this province being settled in perpetuity, and the collector's power of interference in landed affairs being very much limited, he has, in fact, a remarkably easy post. The greater part of his duties are such as an uncovenanted deputy on a very much smaller salary usually performs in other parts of the country.

I would then unite the offices of magistrate and collector in Bengal, and make the practice uniform with that in every other province. If, on the other hand, it be considered that, in the circumstances of Bengal, the collector should be merely a tax-gatherer, take his salary from him; give it to the magistrate: make the latter as efficient as may be; invest him with the general representation of government; and charge him with the maintenance of the boundaries of estates, and such necessary duties. Let the collector be merely a treasury officer on a small salary, under the orders of the superintendent of finances sitting at the receipt of money, and selling rights and interests by auction if the money does not come. His judicial duties might in that case be turned over to the judicial department.

In all the other provinces (and probably in Bengal too) the only object will be to render complete and uniform in particulars the system of union of executive powers which has hitherto answered so well. Everything that can be well performed by the ordinary executive should be intrusted to it.

The local educational establishments should be managed by the district officer, subject to the concurrent supervision and report of the divisional superintendent of education. It is only by the exertions of the local officers that village schools can be rendered efficient. Colleges, again, of a more general character will be under professional superintendents.

On a similar principle, local and petty public works will be executed by the magistrate with the advice and assistance of the civil engineer; while greater works will be made over to the execution and responsibility of the latter; and he will be aided by the former in many things essential to his work. The engineer will keep canals in order, and superintend the supply of water; but its distribution, the collection of dues, and imposition of various necessary fines, will most properly be left to the district officer.

Inferior grades.

My observations as to the union of departments under the same executive officers apply to the European grades of the service. I have not yet noticed the arrangement to be pursued in the inferior grades—the native establishments subordinate to the district officers. Here, again, there is a question. In Northern India the native police and revenue establishments have been kept separate: in Madras and Bombay they are united.

Some of the arguments in favour of unity of action apply in these grades also; but then the same purity on the part of the officials cannot be claimed, and it may be in some degree dangerous to trust exclusive power to one native officer. It is also found that among the natives the duties of an actual *operative* police officer—of the man who should in person trace out and apprehend offenders—are in some degree incompatible with those of the local superintendent of the landed interests and collector of land revenue. It is necessary to have men of a different character, exclusively devoted to the duty, and in charge of smaller districts. It does not appear that the police administration of Madras and Bombay is by any means successful.

As the native collectors are respectable and highly paid men, I have little doubt that the best plan is to give them certain judicial powers, in both the criminal and revenue departments, and to make them generally the representatives of the executive head of the district in matters of education, public works, &c., but to retain separate officers and establishments of the active police under the immediate orders of the magistrate. Both classes of servants will be within the range of the personal knowledge and supervision of the chief of the district.

Size, establishment, &c., of districts.

Districts vary much in size, population, revenue, &c., and it must necessarily, in some degree, be so in consequence of the varying nature of the country, people, &c., but it would be well to equalise them on the same general principle as far as can conveniently be done. An area of about 3000 square miles, a population of about 800,000, a land-revenue of about 150,000*l*., and a radius of 30 or 40 miles round the district station, seem about the best average and model of an executive district. This size and population nearly correspond to the counties of Kent and Sussex united. The present Madras districts I should take to be inconveniently large, especially with so minute a revenue system. In each district there would be as now, besides the chief, one European deputy, and one or two native deputies. There would also be under the orders of the chief a district engineer, a revenue surveyor, a surgeon, a superintendent of village schools, and perhaps a superintendent of detective police—all natives; while in subdivisions there would be the native general and police establishments already referred to.* I do not think that the cost of the present district establishments need be very materially increased, or at any rate the additional cost would not be more than might be saved in other ways.

Municipalities.

The last and lowest administrative unit is the corporate village, whose officers would be maintained, not as overpaid hereditary drones performing duties by deputy, or not performing them at all (like the present Bombay village officers, or English ecclesiastical abuse-holders), but as working responsible agents of government, paid only for the duties performed by them. It is a pity that, while the village constitutions are so perfect, the large towns should be so wanting in municipal machinery. I am not at all sure that very useful municipalities might not be formed and worked with due supervision if it

* There are about half a dozen native collectors in each district. The whole executive administration will then stand thus:—

Under twenty-five senators, one Governor-General.

Under the Governor-General, half a dozen governors.

Under each governor, half a dozen commissioners.

Under each commissioner, half a dozen European district officers.

Under each European district officer half a dozen native officers.

Under each native officer about 250 villages, a land-rent of 25,000*l.*, and a population of 120,000 to 150,000.

were not for the want of funds. The large towns have no corporate property, and direct taxation the natives cannot endure. We shall never have in Indian towns the most ordinary comforts and conveniences of civilisation if we trust to direct taxation. The small house-tax for watchmen has cost more trouble and lost us more allegiance than all the sum collected would recompense. But there is one indirect local tax, common and ancient, not only in India, but also in Europe—the octroi of towns; and I am not clear that, in the abolition of the obnoxious internal transit-duties, we may not have unwisely swept away a local tax which would have been paid without resistance or hardship, which might have been collected without much abuse, and which would have supplied the funds so much needed in all Indian towns. The fact is, that in India the inhabitants of towns pay to the state almost no taxes whatever (the salt-duty and the external customs alone affect them in a very slight degree), and a moderate taxation for their own benefit can be no hardship to them. It is simply a question between direct and indirect taxation. They abhor and resist the one;—are there insuperable objections to the other? I am not clear that there are. It is by an octroi that Paris is made so magnificent a city—the London coal-dues are in fact an octroi—and the other day I saw on the outskirts of the good city of Perth a little sentry-box, where the municipality collects a regular octroi on all kinds of articles of consumption. There is a great distinction between an inland transit-duty levied on commerce from strangers (who may suffer extortion rather than discontinue their route) and an octroi levied simply on articles entering a town for consumption, and levied from people resident in the town or neighbourhood, who have every opportunity of exposing abuses. In this way the octroi is simply an

Proposed octroi.

indirect tax on the inhabitants of the town, just as our sea customs are indirect taxes on the inhabitants of this island, and it is the fairer as it is levied exclusively on articles not produced within the town. Produce in transit remains in caravanserais without the octroi line, and articles of commerce are distinguished from those of consumption, and are exempt from the tax. It may seem unpleasant to an Englishman that a gendarme should go through the form of looking into his carriage at the barriers of Paris, but after all it is matter of taste. All taxes are disagreeable. Some people like to be hit directly, some indirectly; but if we are to have the benefit of taxation, we must elect between the two. In India I should say that the indirect form would be preferred, and that in the large towns, at any rate in those which are the head-quarters of a district, an octroi might be raised without hardship or inconvenience by an arrangement between the magistrate and the heads of the market, and that it would supply the means of municipal management and substantial improvement, to the great benefit of the inhabitants. We should then have paving and draining, and trees for shade. A supply of water would be the greatest of blessings, and vegetable oil-gas might be furnished wonderfully cheap in a country where you get two or three gallons of vegetable oil for a shilling. All these things are now wanting, and must remain wanting till we devise some means of raising money.

Location of stations.

In fixing the head-quarter stations of districts and divisions I would be guided by the same principles as those which I have urged in regard to the seats of government, combining as much as possible native and European considerations.

In districts it will seldom be possible to be largely influenced by the convenience of the European officers.

Local executive work depends for the most part on local circumstances. But wherever it is possible to choose, we must select a healthy situation. If the European officers are continually falling ill and consequently changed, a district cannot be well administered. The work of commissioners of divisions, on the other hand, is less local; and at the head-quarters of a division in the executive, judicial, educational, engineering, and other departments there will generally be a large European staff whose welfare may well be considered. In very many instances it is possible, without inconvenience, to place the head-quarters of a division in a good climate.

Language of business.

With respect to the languages to be used in the transaction of business, it is not necessary to say very much, since the present practice is for the most part reasonable and good.

In the executive administration the practice is this—that everything under executive heads of districts and other local offices is conducted in the vernacular language of the province, and everything from those functionaries upwards in English. The higher parts of the executive must always be essentially European, and English must therefore be the *general* executive language. There is then, in this respect, no need of any general native language, and in the performance of local executive functions a perfect knowledge and constant use of the local dialect are alone necessary. It only remains to enforce more strictly this already recognised principle—to require of all European functionaries a complete knowledge and use of the vernacular, and to prevent the excessive intermixture of Persian, to which both Europeans and the higher classes of natives are too prone, and by which they contrive to evade the orders of Government, and, in fact, to use a language quite different from that of the people.

Hindostanee is a lingua franca all over India, of which all foreigners pick up more or less, and it is the knowledge thus acquired which interferes with the use of the proper vernacular dialects. A man thrown among the natives *must* communicate with them somehow; but if he finds that his Hindostanee suffices for servants, Government officers, &c., they interpret between him and the people, and he may get on in an inefficient way without learning the real vernacular. In the executive of Bengal, and other provinces where Hindostanee is not the proper vernacular, you must *prohibit* the use of that language for local executive business.

But in the judicial department matters will be somewhat different. In the local administration of justice, and especially in recording evidence, a strict use of the vernacular is quite as necessary as in the executive. But when you go higher, in order to insure uniformity and certainty, so much depends on a precise use of words, that it is quite necessary to have some general language in which laws, legal rules, and legal terms may be promulgated, which may be referred to as the standard, and in which important judgments may be eventually recorded. It is of essential importance that the judges generally should be acquainted with this language. The large share of the judicial department which is and will be in the hands of natives renders it impossible to make English the general judicial language. But Hindostanee, being, as I have said, a lingua franca throughout India, is common to all the higher, and I may say to all the ambulatory classes (servants, sepoys, &c.), to all Mahommedans, and to all European residents; and it has a peculiar principle of adaptation to a degree far beyond any other language of which I have ever heard. If a word cannot be easily and exactly translated into Hindostanee, no periphrasis is attempted—it is at once adopted, be it Persian, Arabic, Portuguese, or English; and it is wonderful how convenient and useful the practice is. We can use Hindostanee for anything. Hindostanee, then, must be the general judicial language; and all important decrees, appellate proceedings, &c., must be recorded in that language.

Mode of centralization.

Throughout the whole official chain, from the Governor-General down to the lowest servant, I would revise and improve our system of centralization, so that, while the central wires may thoroughly command the whole, the working of the active local executive may not be impeded or checked. I have, I think, already alluded to a principle propounded by the new emperor, Louis Napoleon, on the organisation of his internal government—"One can govern from afar; one can only administer from near." And on this principle I would proceed.

Personal responsibility and subordination.

I would keep a firm hold on the responsibility of individuals, not a check on their acts. Each official grade should be thoroughly subordinate and responsible to its superior, and should furnish the clearest information of all that is going on, in the most tangible form: but having secured efficient men as executive officers, holding them most strictly responsible that they act in accordance not only with the letter but with the spirit and understood wishes of the Government and of their immediate superiors—making their promotion, and every advantage and indulgence, to depend on a *bonâ fide* and discreet fulfilment of their duties and exercise of their powers; with all these guarantees, I would then in some degree put trust in them, give them some latitude of action, and support them honestly, till you have substantial grounds for believing them to be wrong. It is in this way that unity of government and energy of administration may be combined. Servants of Government must understand that they have no right to act on individual opinions which are not strictly in accordance with those of their superiors. They may explain and advocate their views—they must in good faith act on those which are sanctioned by legitimate authority. But it being understood that neither inefficiency nor perverseness will be tolerated, when you *have* a man sincerely and well doing your work, you must relieve him as much as possible from petty restrictions on and jealousies of his conduct. On the spot he can best judge of the means; and you must not watch and guard him, and tie him down by severe official bonds, in a way which can only be justified by the presumption of such gross inefficiency, indiscretion, wrong-headedness, or corruption, as would be good reason for turning him out altogether. You must give him head a little — must not oppress him with too constant an exaction of too detailed official reports about petty matters—must not reverse his acts without very cogent and unavoidable reasons; and you must treat him personally as well as you can. If he betrays your trust, then be severe to a degree which will be a warning to others; and if he is unfit for it, turn him out. It has perhaps arisen from the want of sufficient personal responsibility—from the general feeling that mere indiscretion, or stupidity, or mistaken though honest views, and such reasons, are sufficient to screen the person who acts while the acts are reversed—that everything is so hampered by strict rules and prohibitions, and so jealously sifted in search of the shadow or suspicion of a flaw in a multitude of successive appeals. If you insist that your men shall be good, honest, and discreet, on pain of degradation, and believe them to be so, many of these checks may be removed, to the great advantage of the administration.

You must make all departments work together for a common object; and you must not allow strength to be wasted in a mistaken or unauthorised direction, or neutralised by different men working in different directions. You must chalk out the work to be done, and then set your men to do it, giving them sufficient freedom of action, but maintaining a strict personal discipline in all departments. Great inconvenience and loss have resulted from the separation, and even antagonism, of different departments of the same government, and you must insist that all shall work together for a common object—shall play into one another's hands as it were.

Relation of Government to its servants.

We must always maintain the proper relation between an absolute government and its servants. We must guard against too much independence, and must not carry too far the principle of vested rights. Government must have that large power over all its servants which is necessary to enforce the personal responsibility and system of personal centralisation which I advocate. It is necessary to limit its choice, but within those limits it should exercise a wide discretion. At present the Government has the most complete hold over its superior servants, as regards their purity, uprightness, and honourable conduct, but comparatively little beyond this. If a man does anything amounting to the smallest delinquency, he is ruined; but, short of actual delinquency, he may be to a considerable degree indiscreet, careless, and inefficient, and the Government has little power to make him feel its displeasure. This should be remedied. The tenure of office must be on condition of good behaviour and continued fitness, and at the discretion of Government. A man should not be, without reason, turned out merely to make room for another, but should have no right to office if the

Government finds it convenient, for reason assigned, to dispense with his services.*

While Government has the power and the will to punish, degrade, and dispense with the services of the bad, it should both promote and reward, and, so far as is compatible with the public service, indulge the good. Great consideration is necessary towards Europeans serving in a tropical climate, and there can be no greater mistake than to suppose that you at all make up for the deficiencies of the unwilling by overworking the willing, and that you compensate for the abuse of general rules by restricting the use of fair and necessary privileges. I fear that the Government acts too much on these mistaken principles. There is too great equality not only of rewards but also of punishments. It is to be hoped that a greater personal control will remedy both evils, and that the Government, while it sets itself against abuses, will be liberal and politic (for it is the best policy to take care of a valuable slave) in its general rules regarding, and conduct towards, its servants.

Personnel of the service.

I now come to the means by which efficient servants are to be secured. Certain rules regarding the exercise of patronage, and in particular the mode in which selection shall be made of that portion of the servants of the Indian Government who are specially entertained and imported from this country, must doubtless be prescribed by the British Legislature. A line must be drawn by law between contract and pa-

* The system in regard to the tenure of public office followed in this country seems inconsistent with efficiency, and gives rise to great abuses. No public principle seems to be deemed possible. A man either holds office during pleasure, and is liable to be turned out without any reason whatever, or he has a "*freehold*" right (offices are actually legal freeholds), and cannot be turned out, however unfit he may be, or however unnecessary his office. We must avoid both of these extremes. All private employers go on the principle which I have suggested, and are on this account in this country so much better served than the Government.

tronage. The further regulation of the services will be included in the proposed administrative code.

It is more necessary that the law, in order to prevent abuse, should determine what persons shall *not* be employed, than that it should give extended rights of employment to particular individuals. We must look, then, to the distinction between different classes of servants.

Much has been said of the distinction between covenanted and uncovenanted servants, which, in fact, is not a question of the privileges of individuals, but simply of the relative advantages to the state of specially hiring persons in England for the Indian service, or of entertaining such persons as may be found in India to fill each office as vacancies occur.

Nature of distinction between covenanted and uncovenanted servants.

This question again resolves itself into two entirely separate and distinct subjects—first, the extent to which we can with advantage employ Europeans and natives respectively; and second, the mode in which the European service shall be supplied—how far, with what tests, or on what conditions, persons shall be sent out by the Home Government for employment—and how far the Indian Government shall be allowed to entertain European servants. These two questions do not run into one another, because India is in no degree a colony. There is no question between mother-country men and colonists of similar blood, manners, and qualifications. Hardly any pure Europeans are domiciled (properly speaking) in the country. The persons of mixed blood are in every way Asiatic, and may properly be classed as natives.

It is very desirable to draw a distinct line between the European and native services. In the latter we have the immense advantage of freedom from personal connection and personal influence in the distribution of appoint-

Line between European and native offices.

ments, and there arises no question of mere *patronage*. If we admit Europeans and natives to the same appointments, there is every probability that patronage will be brought into play in favour of the former. It is, in fact, in every way proper and convenient that a division of appointments should be made, for no principle is more incumbent on us strictly to observe than this, that all appointments which natives are capable of filling should be filled by natives. It is not only just to the natives that it should be so, but, European labour in India being ten or fifteen times more expensive than native labour, it is a duty of the Government to avail itself as far as possible of the infinitely cheaper material. Of native material there is available an unlimited supply, and Government should therefore be bound to fill with natives every appointment the duties of which are not such as to render European qualifications and a European education indispensable; and from time to time, as the standard of native qualifications is raised, the line of demarcation may be also raised. That standard is not yet so high as to give ground to apprehension that the line will include in the native share of office so much as to interfere with our political supremacy; and we may, with advantage, exclude Europeans by rule from native appointments, lest, by an exercise of patronage, a dearer and inferior article should be hired, when the place might have been supplied from among the natives.

On the other hand, there is a large class of appointments to which, in the present stage of our government, European character and European education are indispensable; and in this grade of the service business is carried on in a European fashion, in a European language, with European feelings and European manners. These latter facts must not be under-estimated, for they are of the utmost practical importance. Business is conducted by English gentleman dealing with English gentleman, and there is much in the chain of communication and of official conduct and discipline which essentially depends on this social medium. In fact, the whole habits and modes of European and native business and feeling are totally different, and the official and personal aptitude and qualifications of Europeans and natives are as it were incommensurate things. They cannot be estimated by the same standard. If a certain class of offices are to be filled by natives, we must adapt all the arrangements to a native standard and a native system—and if by Europeans, to a European standard and system. There are very few duties which can be equally well performed, and in the same way, by a European and by a native. In some things natives excel, in some things Europeans; but they work differently, and we must make our election.

The fact is *not* that any one is debarred from any appointment by reason of birth, colour, or religion, but that the natives are not yet qualified for European duties and European modes of conducting business. The real *native* natives are admirable and excellent servants in their own way, but I confess that I have not much faith in the Europeanised natives of the presidency towns. If we can suppose a talented native to have come over to this country—to have become so completely Europeanised as to be really and practically on the footing and imbued with the character of an English highly educated gentleman—to have completely ridded himself of all native weaknesses and failings, moral and physical—and, I may add, to have thoroughly dissevered himself from native connections, friendships, and enmities—then, and not till then, such a person might well be appointed to an office hitherto exclusively held by Europeans. But there are not yet such instances, and, till there are, expensive as is European agency, to that agency we must continue to intrust a considerable portion of the duties of our government. For the reasons then which I have urged, I would not leave it to each individual governor, in each individual instance, to determine whether a European or a native shall fill an appointment, and whether the business shall be conducted in European or in native form. I would from time to time define the classes of appointments which are to be filled by the two classes of servants respectively—not to give a monopoly to Europeans, but to secure to natives *exclusively* all the appointments for which they are fitted.

The only difficulty is in a sort of marginal neutral ground, caused by the acquisition, first, by natives—half-castes and others—of a sort of semi-European qualification for certain duties which might have been classed as European—for instance, such duties as require only a knowledge of the English language and system of accounts, but nothing more of the European; and second, by Europeans long resident in the country, of such native knowledge as may in some degree qualify them for native duties.

I would include this neutral territory in the share of the natives on the grounds of justice to them, cheapness to Government, and protection from the risk of abuse, and would assign to them all such appointments (without any exception) as may be well filled from the native or mixed population. If a few competent Europeans are thereby excluded, there is no great harm done, because they have all the world before them in which to exercise their talents; and, moreover, there is in India a great field for private European enterprise, and so small a supply of private European talent and respectability, that it is anything but desirable that Government should monopolise that small supply. The situation of the Christian population, native to or domiciled in the country, is, on the other hand, particularly hard. They can claim no other country, yet are without social position in India, and depend principally on the service of Government. Despised as they are, I believe that they must be the nucleus of the social reformation of the country, and that, properly encouraged, and raised from their humiliating position, they may be eminently useful servants of the state. I would, therefore, on every ground of justice and expediency, employ them as much as possible, and in all offices which can be equally well filled by them or by Europeans would give them the preference.

Persons of whatever lineage, born and brought up to manhood in India exclusively, and domiciled there, must be considered natives; and I would permit the special naturalization of persons who in good faith settle in the country, and acquire property or other permanent ties, as well as native knowledge, language, and manners.

Employment of natives.

While I distrust any progress which we have yet made in the Europeanization of the natives, I exceedingly admire, and would in every way promote, that indigenous native talent, character, and education, which is now becoming moulded and adapted to the requirements of our service, and which we find so useful. We must avail ourselves of this material to the utmost possible extent.

I believe that the natives exceedingly well fill the offices which are now open to them, and that their employment in those capacities is an immense improvement in our administration. But I am not prepared generally to say that they could at once, and *per saltum*, be with advantage very far advanced beyond their present position, or that the present supply of high native qualification, suited to our service, far outruns the demand. The degree to which a present demand is over-supplied is the best test of room for farther advance, and I think it will be found that the Government of India is not censurably backward in availing itself of native qualification. There is now, generally speaking, sufficient opportunity for adequately employing in due season thoroughly qualified and deserving persons; the supply of qualifications of the very highest class is *not* disproportioned to the demand, and for the present there is no very pressing claim to a very sudden general extension of the field of native employment. Their position will doubtless from time to time be raised, and in the mean time it will be very desirable if a few of the higher appointments in particular departments can be assigned to natives, in order to give to Government an opportunity of rewarding and promoting the best of the present native servants, and availing itself of their talents. For judicial duties they are extremely well fitted, and in touching on the judicial arrangements I have suggested that they may eventually fill some of the very highest judicial offices. In the executive department I think that neither are the natives yet fitted by energy, character, disinterestedness, and other qualifications, for the superior charge and control of districts managed on our European system, and especially for the exercise of the patronage thereto attached; nor is it politically desirable that such duties should be intrusted to them. On the other hand, under the direction of an efficient European district officer, I believe that much of the most important, and all the inferior work, may be performed by natives, and that the chief should only have a limited European assistance, of which he may avail himself in some matters, and which may serve as a school for the younger

European service. I do not think that one European can yet, unaided, do, at all times, in the whole executive management of a large district, all things in which European vigour, education, and honesty are requisite. He must have one well-qualified deputy. But either of these two officers may very well temporarily do all that is required during the absence or sickness of the other, and they may from time to time divide the duties of the district according to their respective tastes and qualifications. An inexperienced European assistant is of comparatively little use, but may sometimes be brought into play, and it is necessary that every man should pass through this grade before he attains the higher offices. With these exceptions natives may well fill all the offices of the ordinary district executive, and similarly in special departments they may be intrusted with everything except the general superintendence. Although I would not intrust executive superintendence to single natives, I think that in all *plural* offices, boards, &c., it is quite possible, and desirable, to have native members. A native member of the board of revenue, for instance, might be most useful, and modern Toder Mulls might arise. I would strongly recommend this plan. In the departments of medicine, engineering, education, accounts, and in all the useful arts, natives only require to be taught to attain the highest perfection; and there is no political objection whatever, but everything in favour of their promotion to the highest grades for which they may become fitted. Their success in the medical department may be followed up in many ways, and the offices to which they are eligible must be from time to time regulated by Government in accordance with their progress. It will be well to introduce in all departments preliminary tests of fitness, such as precede all native judicial appointments.

Particulars regarding the inferior native offices are connected with the detail of the different departments.

Discipline, &c., of native services.

I need here only refer generally to the discipline and system of promotion of all the inferior grades, upon which more than anything else depends their efficiency. Judicial education we alone can give, but in the inferior executive we have a large supply of educated native talent, and it is on its selection, construction, and management, that the result of our work entirely depends. We are but the superior officers — the soldiers of our civil force are exclusively native: the difficulty is to protect them on the one hand from the caprices, ignorances, and prejudices of individual superiors, continually changed from day to day, and to ensure due reward proportionate to merit; and on the other hand to avoid hampering the efficiency of the executive officers by depriving them of power, rendering their subordinates too independent, and taking into the hands of the superior departments of Government duties which they cannot properly perform. At present both these evils are felt. The European service is so continually changing, and so imperfectly disciplined, that it is not surprising that there is a want of discipline and system in the employment and promotion of the native subordinates, than which no evil can be greater or more damaging to our administration. Government had good reason to interfere; but in merely putting great checks on ejectment from office, without any provision for systematising employment and promotion, it perhaps only makes matters worse.

The subject is an extremely difficult one, and it is impossible to propound in few words any plan which will at once remedy the evil. But much will be effected by improving the discipline of the higher grades, and rendering them much more permanent, more responsible, and more universally discreet and efficient. Government must gradually and carefully introduce a great system of regular discipline throughout all grades, and the soldier cannot be properly disciplined till the discipline of the officers is complete. Some standards of qualification and merit must be established; over-praise (in written characters, &c.) must be treated as an official fault, just as much as disregard of real merits; native servants must not be followers of individual Europeans, but the servants of the state, known and appreciated by all who may be set over them; and on the other hand, the European officers must have ample power of promptly recognising, recording, and promoting merit, and of punishing and ejecting demerit. Carefully and laboriously these objects may be in the end more or less fully effected, and in this will be found the great secret of executive efficiency.

The Government is now quite inclined to be liberal in the payment of its native servants, and, considering the cheapness of labour, I do not think that there is, generally speaking, much ground of complaint in this respect. There are, however, considerable discrepancies and inequalities which should be remedied, and in certain departments some increase of allowances may be necessary.

Upon these principles, then, I would employ the natives, and would only, in so far as is absolutely indispensable, call in the expensive European agency. I hope that that necessity will every day diminish—that the proportion of natives holding important offices will every day increase.

It must be particularly impressed on all European servants that it is their duty to do nothing themselves which they can get any one else to do for them. Their duties are on far too large a scale to leave it possible that they should themselves do the work, and nothing is so destructive of efficiency as a jealousy of trusting to subordinates to a discreet and legitimate extent. The efficient superintending officer is not he who does most work himself, but he who gets most out of others; and many zealous Indian officers make a mistake in this respect. It is only by a good system of distribution and division of labour that our administration can be rendered efficient. It strikes me that the labour of the superior officers might be much abridged, and their efficiency increased, by delegating the responsible performance of many duties to ministerial or inferior officers. The latter do in fact perform such duties, but generally in the name and on the direct responsibility of the superior, who signs his name to everything, and who is distracted from more important matters by details. I should be inclined to give to native officers of each court or office larger powers of acting in their own name (subject, of course, to the control of the superior), so that there should be less room for the imputation of indirect and irresponsible influence. An English judge, who is entirely relieved of details, and comes into court with his mind free to grapple without reserve with essential arguments, has a great advantage.

We now come to that European service, which, although we have proposed to limit it as much as possible, must still be of considerable numbers and of vast importance.

European service—comparative cheapness and advantage of.

And here I may remark that it is a great mistake to suppose that our civil administration in general, or the European portion of it in particular, oppresses the country by its expense. Of course a perfectly pure and impartial native administration would be cheaper, but *that* the country has not known and may never know (few countries indeed have that fortune); and as we must estimate everything *comparatively*, I say that so far as the civil administration is concerned the country *never was so cheaply governed.* More especially the higher appointments were never so cheaply filled as by European officers. The fact is, that the system of native governments is totally different from ours. They have not the same moral ties and social hold over their servants, and to be well served they are constrained to have recourse to great rewards and great punishments. The successful and efficient superior servant of a native government receives directly or indirectly, but always at the expense of the country, immense rewards; the unsuccessful or disgraced servant is treated with unscrupulous severity and stripped of everything. Trust is placed neither on a man's honour, nor in an official system; but rewards are fully apportioned to the magnitude of the trust, and it is made worth a man's while efficiently to perform his duty. In this way native states may be sometimes exceedingly well served, but only in this way. No native government would ever think of intrusting a native servant with a province or a district, and attempting to prevent his enriching himself in a way which they consider in fact legitimate. They do not attempt to muzzle the oxen that tread out the corn; and I repeat that under no native government whatever have superior offices been so cheaply filled as under our present system. It would be for instance quite out of the question that any native under the best native government, holding an office of power and trust equal either to the governor of a presidency, or to the magistrate and collector of a district, should not make a vast deal more money than the European officer.

Our system then is quite different. We trust in a great measure to official discipline and personal honour, and our rewards are not so great. We cannot as yet fully combine the incompatible advantages of cheap native labour and a cheap European official system. In proportion as you introduce your system among the natives and adapt them to it, by all means employ them; but so long as they are not sufficiently adapted to your new European system, and sufficiently bound by European sanctions, to be trusted with the highest offices, it is infinitely cheaper as well as infinitely better to give European prices for European labour than to revert to native system and native rewards. I say all this not to detract from the claim of the natives to employment. I would admit it to the utmost possible extent, and would give them the benefit of every doubt; but I argue that our European civil officers, judged by any standard which has been known in India, are by no means expensive, and that, in so far as they are actually required, there is no hardship to the country in their employment. In truth, the country can very well afford the expense of our civil system. When we come to military establishments and finance we shall see wherein lies the real expense of our government, which I fully admit to be very great. The European civil servants will be comparatively few, but it becomes every day more and more necessary that those few should be exceedingly good. Let us look then to the mode of securing good Europeans.

Question of profession or no profession.

It is in regard to this class of servants that the question of covenanted or uncovenanted really arises; and we must be careful to keep it separate from that of native or European. The real question is profession or no profession. The newspaper cry about the exclusion of uncovenanted servants is for the most part raised by the comparatively few uncovenanted Europeans who are or wish to be in the service of Government, but they put forward native claims as the pretext for making all persons eligible to all appointments. The question, in fact, is simply this: "In filling the class of appointments held by Europeans, shall the Indian governors be restricted to a limited profession of persons engaged for the service in England, tested, stamped, and guaranteed as sufficient and genuine? or shall they have it in their power to appoint at their discretion such persons as they see fit?" The opening to the uncovenanted of appointments hitherto covenanted would amount simply and solely to this latter alternative—to a transfer of patronage from the Home to the Indian Government. The uncovenanted are merely persons entertained by the Indian governors, without the intervention of the Home Government. As I have before observed, there is no European colony in India, and the European candidates are in either case equally natives of these islands.

We have to look, then, to the comparative advantage of hiring a produce of Britain for service in India, in England or in India; that is, whether we shall order what we want in the native English market, and send it out express, or trust to the articles which by private means may happen to find their way to India. Certainly, considering the very large and regular supply which is required, all reason, experience, and analogy seem in favour of the former course, as better, cheaper, and surer in every way. It is better to have a thing made according to our own directions, purchased at the cheapest rate in the wholesale market, and sent out in the required quantities, than to trust to precarious and expensive supplies of a variously-fashioned article of doubtful quality. We send out supplies of muskets, and European soldiers, and even of paper, pens, and ink, rather than trust to such articles as we may pick up in the Indian bazaars; and we know that, if due care be taken in the selection of these articles, the small proportion which may turn out bad is more than compensated by the superior quality and cheapness of the remainder. One would say, then (even if we carry the argument no farther), that the same rule will hold good in regard to European civil servants; and that to send out stamped and tested supplies from Europe is infinitely better than to pick up unstamped adventurers in India.

As a question of patronage the reasons for adopting such a course are even more irresistible. That is the only subject in which we can place no reliance on the public virtue of public men, when needy relations, connections, and partisans can be served by its exercise. The Governor-General is but a man of the same country and class as the dispensers of government patronage in this country, with as numerous personal and political connections; and if he were to be freed from the limits of a profession and permitted to appoint at his discretion to all Indian offices, he would be at once surrounded by a host of dependents, and there would be an end to all hope of an efficient Indian service. Hitherto the Governors have had very little, I may say no opportunity of serving, in a considerable way, even their nearest and dearest friends; but once let them have patronage which should be an object to English gentlemen of no profession, and abuses would be inevitable.

But, on the other hand, the plan by which the patronage is divided, by which the Home Government, under strict rules and tests, appoints young men to the profession, stamps them as eligible for Indian employ—while the nomination to particular office in India is left solely and exclusively to the unfettered discretion of the Indian Government—this plan, I say, has undoubtedly worked in the most admirable way. It is one advantage of the prescription in favour of seniority, which to a certain extent prevails, that it is a check on any disposition to job; but allowing for this, it is still wonderful how fairly patronage is distributed in the civil service. I do not say that it is in proportion to merit, but that it is free from personal influences to a most remarkable extent. This is an advantage which we, perhaps, hardly sufficiently appreciate. I attribute it entirely to the peculiar system of limiting the governor's choice to a qualified profession, the members of which are all judged by the same standard, and which would be united in opposition to an abuse of patronage. We shall do well to bear in mind this most important advantage of the system, when it is proposed to break down the barriers of the profession.

I think, then, I may assume that there are very good and sound reasons for the system which has been hitherto followed, of sending young men from this country for the Indian civil service. Still there are some offices which may be otherwise filled; and some Europeans not members of the regular service are now in the employ of Government. Previously to 1833 hardly any Europeans beyond the pale of the profession were employed in civil appointments. The uncovenanted appointments of that day were intended for natives *exclusively*. The inferior judges, for instance, were expressly designated "native judges." The Act of 1833 provided that "no person shall, by reason only of his religion, place of birth, descent, or colour, be disabled from holding any office, place, or employment." As regards the natives, there never was any such exclusion. I believe that there was not even any test of religion, birth, descent, or colour on appointment to the civil service, any more than there is now; but Europeans could not be appointed as "native judges." The result of the enactment was, then, neither to

The uncovenanted European servants.

open anything to the natives which would not have been opened to them quite independent of that provision, nor in any way to open covenanted appointments to European uncovenanted persons, but only to open native appointments to uncovenanted Europeans. The following provision of the Indian legislature is literally all that has been found necessary to give effect to the provision:—

Act XXIV. of 1836.

"I. It is hereby enacted that the officers who, in the "regulations of the presidency of Fort St. George, are "designated as native judges and native criminal judges, "shall, from the 1st day of November, 1836, be desig- "nated as principal sudder ameens.

"II. A similar provision with respect to Bombay.

"III. And it is hereby enacted that, from the said 1st "day of November, 1836, no person whatever shall, by "reason of birth, or by reason of descent, be incapable of "being a principal sudder ameen, sudder ameen, or "moonsiff, within the territories subject to the presi- "dencies of Fort St. George and Bombay."

During the last twenty years the general field of uncovenanted employment has been largely extended; and it has followed that a considerable number of Europeans have found their way into the service of Government, not as holding any appointments in common with the professional or covenanted European servants (whose appointments remain, for the good reasons to which I have alluded, as distinct as ever), but as sharing with the natives the uncovenanted appointments, being eligible to everything to which natives are eligible, and to that only. Hitherto these appointments have been of comparatively little value on the European scale of remuneration; but some men, very good, useful, and fit in their degree, have been entertained. So far the result is not, generally speaking, to be objected to; but there being no test of qualification, abuses* may take place greater than anything which could have occurred in the civil service. Young Europeans, quite unfit for the duty, may be put as a small provision into appointments which might have been excellently well filled by natives; and there can be no doubt that, if the uncovenanted service were considerably advanced, without making any distinction between Europeans and natives, very great abuses might and would take place. Indeed, this would be the principal objection to opening certain appointments to the natives under the present system. For instance, if we were to throw open a proportion of the higher appointments, what would prevent a governor from appointing his second cousin, or a troublesome editor, a member of the Board of Revenue, instead of a native? We must therefore limit the employment of uncovenanted Europeans.

As regards the higher appointments, you cannot have incompatible advantages; you cannot have the security of an educated and tested profession and the advantage of subsequent unlimited competition; you cannot both have a civil service and leave it to governors to appoint to offices whomsoever they choose. The exclusion is not a greater hardship than that a person not a barrister or a priest cannot be made Lord Chancellor or Archbishop of Canterbury, however well qualified he may consider himself. Moreover, notwithstanding all that has been said, the truth is, that the best and most experienced Europeans are not to be had for small salaries. They would not be a bit cheaper than the professional servants. As regards the inferior appointments, clever, good men are worth more money in their private capacity; and it

* I *have* heard of such an instance.

is only either when they are quite inexperienced, or after they have broken down in some other profession, that they seek the service of Government. Admitting as I do that Government has thus obtained the services of some very useful and efficient persons, I also say that many of the uncovenanted European servants are of one of two classes,—those performing duties which might be as well, or better, performed by natives, and those holding inferior European appointments, which might be as well and cheaply filled by the indifferent bargains of the civil service.

It may be desirable to keep some of these latter appointments—such as require little talent, but some European education, honour, and honesty—as a provision for those exceptional individuals of the professional European service who, in spite of every precaution, may turn out to be deficient either in intellect or in bodily vigour, who are unfit for promotion, yet not utterly useless nor deserving of being thrown helpless on the world. Under any system a few such persons must creep in, or persons once fit for higher duties must become unfit when it is too late to get rid of them. It is cheaper and fairer to employ them on small salaries in those inferior duties for which they are sufficiently qualified, than to promote them to offices for which they are not fit. The charge of treasuries, some of the duties in the offices of accounts, customs, &c., some ministerial offices of the superior courts of justice, and such like places, might be turned to this use.

But there may be exceptional cases in all departments in which it is desirable that the strict professional rule should be relaxed. There are undoubtedly certain European appointments in which we may sometimes with advantage go beyond the limits of the profession. First, there are some inferior appointments in which European energy rather than European education of a high order is required. For these I would provide by permitting the governors, with the sanction of the Governor-General, to fill at discretion these inferior European appointments (which have been first properly defined) on salaries not exceeding 1000*l.* per annum, merely sending home, for the sanction of the Senate, a quarterly statement, with full particulars regarding the persons so employed. Secondly, there are certain superior appointments to which the regular course and education of the civil service does not necessarily lead, some of which might possibly sometimes be filled by persons of private experience in India, while to others persons officially educated in England or home servants of the Indian Government might be with advantage specially appointed. I would define this class of appointments, and would make them in future open to all persons either in or out of the regular service, but would provide that persons not members of the service should be appointed only by previous special concurrence of the Governor-General and Senate, in the same way as I have proposed to appoint the unprofessional ministers. Either the Governor-General or the Senate would be at liberty to make a proposal to the other in anticipation or on occurrence of a vacancy. The reference would only occupy two months, and, in the event of final disagreement, the place would be filled up from the professional service. I think that this plan would be very useful, and would at the same time prevent abuse. I do not think that you could intrust a more extended power either to the Home or to the Indian Government separately.

Proposed appointment to important offices of persons not in the service.

The following strike me as appointments to which this rule might be applied:—

Appointments in the salt, opium, and customs department:
The post-office:

One seat in the Supreme Court of Justice (only till our judicial system becomes more perfect):

Most of the local offices of the presidency towns, and those which will come under the direction of Government when the present Crown Courts are abolished:

Offices in the department of accounts and audit.

Still it must be remembered that, although the course of the professional career of the civil service does not directly lead to these appointments, they require great business qualifications, and are places of immense trust, patronage, and responsibility. They have been on that account held by civil servants on high salaries, and, as regards purity of conduct, the Government has a hold over the present and future prospects of a civil servant which has rendered that service the purest in the world. Now, if these appointments are held by other persons, you must insure sufficient qualifications; you must have thorough gentlemen; and you must retain a sufficient hold on their future conduct. I will even say that an absolute Indian Government could not, and should not, tolerate that amount of jobbing of which almost every official man possessed of patronage in this country, and subject to all the checks of public opinion, is guilty. Removed from the checks of public opinion, we have seen the scandalous abuses of office and actual frauds perpetrated in India by men supposed to be gentlemen, but not in the regular service and not under the immediate control of Government. I confess I think it would not only be necessary to prohibit the holders of office from any private business, but that I would very much hesitate before intrusting some offices to men who have been in business and who have formed private connections. If we have an efficient civil service, most of the offices alluded to can generally be better filled from the profession than from any other body not possessed of any very special qualifications; and I would make appointments to superior offices of persons not in the service altogether exceptional.

Before coming to the regular civil service there is another question to be disposed of, viz. the employment of military officers in civil duties. A considerable number of this class of servants are now so employed in certain of our territories and in the political department; and Lord Ellenborough has proposed that persons in unlimited numbers and eligible to every office should be drawn from the army in India at the discretion of the Governor-General and Governors, and permanently placed on the civil establishment; an arrangement which would be in fact equivalent to dispensing with a separate civil service altogether, for it would be useless to send out a civil service if governors may dispense with it in favour of their own nominees. I would not altogether object to discriminating in some degree in England between such of the persons who receive Indian nominations as are most fitted for the civil service and such as are most fitted for the army; but to the plan of selecting civil servants from the army in India I think that there are most insuperable objections, and that it is so whether we contemplate the use or the abuse of the system. These objections I divide as follows:—

Employment of military officers in civil duties.

1. The misplacement of patronage;
2. The want of a civil education;
3. The injustice to the army involved in the plan.

As regards the patronage the proposed plan would again amount to giving to the Governor-General and Governors the greater portion of that share in the patronage of the civil service which is now possessed by the Home Government, without the possibility of imposing the same tests and checks, and in addition to the ample share of patronage already possessed by the

Indian governments in the distribution of all appointments. Any person who can get a cadetship, and is possessed of the extremely slender qualification necessary to that appointment, might then be at any time pitchforked into the civil service, and appointed to any office by the Governor-General as a mere matter of patronage and favour; an arrangement which would give to that functionary an excessive, most dangerous, and undesirable degree of patronage, and which would altogether upset the principle on which it has been hitherto so successfully partitioned. It is said that we shall thus have a selection of the cleverest among a greater number of men. But I ask, if you cannot make such a selection in England, how is it to be expected that you can make it in India? By all means let the civil service be picked men; but if you find it difficult, with all the checks, and tests, and means of supervision which you possess at home, to effect this object, how is it probable or possible that you can in any way effect it in India? First, how are you to bind the Governors to give away so very valuable patronage without favour or affection? and second, how are the Governors themselves to find out the best men? You can have no such efficient tests as in England—no uniform standard by which to measure the capability, for duties of which they have no experience, of many thousand officers scattered over the whole continent of India; and a Governor-General cannot personally know enough of the candidates to enable him to form a personal opinion in one case in a hundred. In most instances he must either proceed by favour or he must trust to the various recommendations of various persons, judging by various standards, and nine-tenths of whom consider over-praise the whitest of white lies. Would this be an improvement on the best system of selection in England which can be devised?

The small experience of this kind of thing which we have yet had is not a measure of what it would be on a larger scale, but already objection may in some degree be made to it. As long as the political or civil employ of a military man is merely a very exceptional case on very special grounds there is little room for abuse: on the contrary, the services of some most brilliant and useful men have been thus obtained by Government, and I should be far from wishing to prohibit such exceptional cases. But when considerable numbers are drawn from the army for civil employ—for instance, on the occasion of a large extension of territory—what is the result? Why, this; that, as the opportunities for exhibiting fitness for civil duties afforded to officers serving with their regiments are necessarily most rare, the supply of men *known* to be fit is extremely small. The Governor-General, whether he will or no, is therefore obliged to take men at haphazard who may be capable of becoming fit, or *may* be grossly unfit. And so it is the fact that nothing is more purely a piece of patronage; there is nothing in which a Governor-General can so well serve a friend (or, what is more common, some one else's friend) as by transferring him from the army to civil employ. The system, even in its present limited form, may be, and sometimes is, abused; while some first-rate men are really selected by Government, some men are also appointed as a matter of patronage who, even under the present mild system, would have been plucked at the door of the civil service.

All that I have said refers to the abuse of the system,—now let us look to its use. Suppose, for a moment, that you can select the best men in the army, I have no doubt that, picked from such a body, they would be a set of very clever fellows. But for a comparison you must suppose a *selection* to be also made (as it ought to be made) in England—and then, what do you compare?—why, an educated set of clever fellows with an uneducated set of the same—a service trained with the best available training for duties which are most certainly well worthy the professional education and labour of a life, with a set of men sent out to India as boys, and whose duties have since consisted in learning and teaching the rudiments of drill. *Can* we compare the two systems? If you had a divining rod, and could draw out the cleverest men in the British army, you might as appropriately appoint them judges in Westminster Hall, on the ground of selecting from a larger body than the limited number of successful barristers.

And this brings me to the last objection, and not the least serious. Supposing that you *do* get the best of the several thousand officers in the army, and transfer them to the civil service (and it is only on this supposition that the plan has any recommendation whatever), can one conceive anything more unjust and fatal to the army? What! does the army require no share of talent? I admit that the first duties of a young officer are not of the most intellectual kind; but does the command of a regiment require no talent?—are we sure that we shall never want generals?—and are the duties of a general such as any fool can perform? If any man thinks so, I recommend to him an immediate study of M. Thiers or Mr. Disraeli. Let him consider that striking passage, the appropriation of which is almost pardonable. He will then be convinced that in truth a great general is no ordinary man. He must combine intellect, discretion, and moral firmness, with mere military knowledge and military courage. Generals of the second class may be altogether unfit for statesmen (we have had some recent instances), and the greatest statesman may be utterly unfit for a general; but I believe it to be incontrovertible that no man can be a truly great general who does not also possess statesmanlike qualities. It is not in the nature of things that it should be so. A Peel might not have made a Wellington; but a Cæsar, a Napoleon, a Cromwell, or a Wellington must ever be capable of making a Peel, or greater than Peel. We may some day want a great general, and we every day want good commanding officers. Are we then so overflowing with military brilliancy in the higher grades, that we can afford to weed out our most talented men (our future Wellingtons, if Wellingtons there be), and turn them into judges and collectors? I suspect that the fact is far otherwise, and that it is much more desirable to bring forward and encourage to the utmost military talent in the military service, in its own sphere, than to draft it off elsewhere. Under the proposed scheme (*if* successfully carried out) the cream would go to the civil service, and the army would be composed of the sky-blue milk left behind. What would have become of us (some one, I think, has asked) if Wellington, instead of commanding at Waterloo, had been a member of the Board of Revenue at Madras, as he certainly would have been under such a system?

It is a great mistake to suppose that new territory in India is necessarily or usually administered under martial law and on a military system. It is generally by no means so. The natives of the plains are accustomed to be conquered and understand our system. Great battles are not succeeded by popular bush-fighting. As soon as we have beaten the native government, and acquired a plain territory, the people acquiesce as a matter of course —are as quiet as if they had been our subjects for a hundred years—and no martial severity is necessary. For instance, the Punjab was never for a day under a government in the very least degree military. In fact, in the territories where military men are usually employed, their military qualifications are in no respect brought into play —they merely perform the duties of civilians. The Scinde Government is the only military administration which has existed in India for many years; and there it was rendered necessary (*if* necessary) not by the inhabitants of Scinde, but by the foreign robber tribes.

In regard to the energy and activity necessary for the establishment of a new government, people may also be misled by confounding the character and duties of Indian civilians with those of mere official men of the pen in this country. In truth they are quite different. Most civil servants have quite as much occasion for physical qualities as military men, and a much greater habit of acting energetically on their own responsibility. In their private capacities also they are, perhaps, more generally accustomed to ride, and to shoot, and to move about the country. I think, then, I may venture to say that civilians have not been found wanting in any of the qualities most necessary to govern difficult territories. Such men as Mr. John Lawrence will not suffer by any comparison civil or military.

Still, so much advantage to the civil and political administration has accrued from employment in exceptional cases of brilliant military men, that I would by no means deprive the Governor-General of the power of making such special exceptions.

New territory, really subjected to a military government, may well be left to military men, to whom civilians might be called in merely in aid; but in regard to all territories which have been, or are fit to be, brought under a civil form of administration (including the whole of our present Non-Regulation provinces), and also all political appointments, I would make a separate and distinct provision. New and good codes of law would be as applicable to Non-Regulation as to Regulation provinces. But I would, by a minute of the Supreme Government, sanctioned by the Senate, from time to time define the places and appointments to which military men should be eligible in common with civil servants. I would leave to the Governor-General the power to employ any military man on these duties, for special and recorded reasons to be transmitted to the Senate; but he should be most distinctly prohibited from appointing any military officer to a political or civil situation without such reasons. In ordinary cases, if a man is good for anything, there is ample field in the military service; and if he is good for nothing, he is of no advantage to any service. In either case he should not be sent off to a residency without special reason. Those so-called *political* appointments, of which the army has had of late nearly a monopoly, are in no way an object to the civil service (which has already quite enough to do), but they are a considerable disadvantage to the army; and if they cannot be much reduced, it would be well to have civilians enough to be able to spare some for this department.

I would provide that military men, posted to civil duties, should, within a certain time, pass an examination of the same kind as that to which civil servants should be subjected; and if they pass, the places in their regiments should be filled up, and they should be borne as supernumeraries.

All those at present employed should be also examined. The regimental places of those who have displayed special aptitude for civil duties should be supplied; and if any have displayed nothing of the kind, they should be sent back to their regiments.

CHAPTER V.

THE CIVIL SERVICE.

Present state and defects ; necessity of enhanced standard ; nature of proposed remedies ; question of limit to numbers ; tests, positive or relative ; objections to relative test ; positive test by a single examination ; by a series of tests combined with education ; Haileybury, its state and defects ; proposed remedy by transfer of education and tests to an Indian College at Cambridge ; Cambridge University Commission Report, and argument derived therefrom ; education of executive students ; separation and training of judicial students ; selection of a college ; alternative of amendments at Haileybury ; appointments ; distribution of service in India ; farther training of judicial servants ; abolition of "college" system ; training of executive servants ; promotion ; tenure of office ; salaries ; leave of absence ; pensions ; proposed rules.

Present state.

I HOLD that the civil service, as a body, is exceedingly efficient ; that it is a wonderful instance of the effects of systematic official education acting on a material naturally little above par. But I also hold that there are important exceptions to that efficiency ; that we want a still higher general standard ; and that the favourable result of an official training, acting on an average material and a moderate education, far from being an argument in favour of letting things alone, is a proof that a higher education, acting on a superior material, would lead to higher results,—that we are in the right path, and need only follow it with greater vigour to attain all that has been hitherto wanting.

A member of the Committee of the late House of Commons on Indian affairs has pointed out, in a recent pamphlet,* the fact that very considerable imperfections

* A Letter to T. Baring, Esq., M.P., on the Indian Civil Service, by Sir E. Colebrooke, Bart. London, 1852.

do exist in the civil service. Those imperfections call very urgently for attention. They are much more felt now than they were thirty years ago. This is not because the service has retrograded—by no means; but I say advisedly that the general standard of qualification for admission to the service has not been raised one whit during the last thirty years; and, on the other hand, the scale of the duties required of the service in India has been very much raised—the large class of comparatively unintellectual appointments formerly existing has been swept away; our machine of government has been vastly enlarged and complicated, and the work to be done by it has become much more onerous. The duties of the same or a smaller number of European officers have been extended over a much larger surface, and consequently the general importance and difficulty of the duties falling to each individual have been much enhanced, and will be more so every day. I therefore say that the same class of men, the same service which well performed the duties assigned to it twenty years ago, will be quite unequal to those which will fall to it twenty years hence; and that it is altogether wrong that the standard of qualification is not much enhanced. I altogether deny that there has been any such enhancement of late years, as will be seen when I come to particulars; and I say that there is very little *selection* in appointments to the civil service. The question very seriously affects the value of patronage, but it should not be slurred over.

Necessity of enhanced standard of qualification.

With regard to the exceptions to the general efficiency, I maintain that, notwithstanding the general respectability of the material, a few men, whose intellects and qualifications are very much below par, always have been, and now are, sent out in the civil service—the Company's bad bargains, as they are called. I farther say that these men were known and ascertained to be fools before they left England—before they were appointed to the service; that they might and ought to have been stopped. The injury to India was comparatively small when such men could be shelved in comfortable sinecures; but now-a-days hardly a single sinecure is held by the civil service (always excepting the seats in Council), and an inefficient man not only draws a salary for which he does not return competent labour, but he does inconceivable injury by mismanaging important offices, and perhaps deranges not only his own duties but those of others. The official chain is so connected, that if a single link be rotten and bad the whole becomes useless. If one man be inefficient, he completely neutralizes the efficiency of all under him and of all over him, so far as his sphere extends. Hence it is in the highest degree necessary that no man who is not tolerably capable should be employed.

Not only we must get rid of the exceptions, but the *general* standard must be also raised. It may seem inconsistent to admit great general efficiency, and yet to say that more is required. It must, however, be remembered that the duties exacted are no common duties; but, on the contrary, such as demand and give scope to the very highest intellect, energy, and accomplishment: the more so as they are performed in a foreign country, and under very great disadvantages. They are not such as any man with a moderate education can perform. It requires great qualifications to keep right when surrounded on every side by manners which are altogether strange to us, and by persons over whom we have no social control. I may particularly instance the judicial branch of the service, in which especially the duties which ought to be performed have been much raised of

Nature of duties to be performed.

late years. If our Indian judges have failed, it is not that any common men would have succeeded. I believe that a more arduous task than to perform well the duties of an Indian judge does not exist in this world: without law, without lawyers, without an established system, and yet bound to be guided by law; in a foreign country; without juries to relieve the judge of the facts; without separate officers to relieve him of details; to create order out of chaos, is a feat of which any man or body of men might well be proud. The duty of a judge, sitting in a regular court, under an established system, aided in points of law by numerous colleagues, and altogether relieved by juries of the responsibility of facts, is mere child's play compared to such an undertaking. Yet you pitchfork a middle-aged gentleman, without a regular judicial education, into these duties, and you are surprised that he does not succeed. The duties of the executive are quite as important, and require a union of qualities such that those who sufficiently fill great posts must be very rare and first-rate men indeed.

Remedies for present deficiencies.

I am of opinion, therefore, that the civil service now requires an enhancement both of talent and of education. I by no means argue that you should have a service exclusively composed of geniuses—such a body would probably in practice work far from efficiently—but *all* should be men of superior qualifications. You should commence at a point of natural capability considerably above the average as a *minimum*, and go from that point *upwards*; in short, you must, to a certain extent, *select*. You should admit of no single exception to this rule, so far as can be insured by the strictest and most honestly-administered tests. You should educate the men selected to the highest possible point.

All my arguments have tended to show that the professional civil service is already, for the regular duties of the civil administration, infinitely preferable to anything which we are likely to get elsewhere, and, in its improved condition, I would not only not contract but would extend its sphere: not to enhance the privileges of a privileged class, but to put the profession on a broader basis, to give a wider field for selection. I would so arrange that all should not draw prizes; and as, in spite of every test, there will be in the end very various degrees of efficiency, I would provide employment for each individual only in proportion to the qualifications which he ultimately exhibits. It is with this view that (while the natives must fill all the appointments for which they are fitted) I would retain, for the employment of the inferior* members of the European professional service, some of the less arduous appointments now held by uncovenanted Europeans: such as require little talent, but involve considerable trust and responsibility.

A good system of promotion and reward must be established concurrently with the enhancement of the standard of qualification. While some men undoubtedly get on much better than others; while the service is by no means a dead level; it is clearly the fact that the inequalities are not so great as they would be in what I may call a *natural* state of things. I mean that, while men of average, or below average, qualifications get on better than in any other profession, the best men, for a much more severe and less agreeable life, are not (taking climate, &c., into consideration) so well rewarded

* I do not allude to exceptions to the general high efficiency as in future likely to arise from the first exercise of patronage, but to such as may—and, to a certain extent, will—*afterwards* occur, in spite of every precaution. Flaws will eventually be found in the use of a few of the very best selected articles; and subsequent changes, especially the effect of ill health in such a climate, cannot be altogether averted in any body of men.

as the best men of other professions. For instance, I believe that the number of *practising* barristers at the English bar is not so great as that of the Indian civil service. Both professions comprise all grades of intellect and education. I have no doubt that the generality of men in the civil service make a much better thing of it than the generality of those who hardly pick up a living at the bar; but there can be as little doubt, not only that the very highest prizes of the latter profession are (to Englishmen) much more numerous, valuable, and agreeable than those which the Indian civil service affords, but also that any decidedly successful man—any barrister in large practice—is much better off than a correspondingly successful man in the civil service. Take an English judge—or a barrister at the age of forty-five, in a silk gown and a leading practice, making four or five thousand a year, with perhaps a seat in Parliament, and everything farther yet before him. Even in the present state of the law there are a number of such men. Can you compare a man in such a situation with the corresponding man in India, who may possibly have risen to be a sudder judge, but whose constitution is already sorely tried by five-and-twenty years' Indian service in exile? If the Indian servant be an iron man, he may have it in his power to struggle on for a few years more; or he may choose or may be forced to retire with an annuity of about 750*l.* per annum, and with savings yielding an income of a few hundreds more, but with no occupation or profession to fall back upon. The situation is altogether inferior, and the consequence is, that, if you attempted to impose any very severe tests on entering the civil service, without in some degree changing the mode of promotion and reward—if you measured young men by the standard of others following professions in this country—you would find that appointments which would be gladly accepted by moderate men would not tempt the very best men, and you would get rid not only of the fools, but also of the geniuses. This is the objection (and, I have no doubt, a sound one) taken by some competent persons to the plan of testing by a high Cambridge standard.

The correction, then, of the imperfections of the service arising in appointment and after appointment must be made simultaneously: first, by imposing much more severe tests on appointment and educating more highly; second, by making the appointment a claim only to the lowest grade of office and emolument, and all further promotion to depend on efficiency alone; third, by promoting, adequately rewarding, and treating well and indulgently good men when you get them; fourth, by a provision for pensioning off, on reasonable terms, men who, at any period of their service, become unfit for duty.

Before going into particulars of the tests to be applied, I must observe that you may regulate the supply to the profession in two ways: you may either impose your test, and permit men who have passed that test to go out in any numbers to seek service in India, leaving the demand to regulate the supply; or you may send out a certain limited number, such as you require. The former plan is that for the most part corresponding to civil professions in Europe, and has many advantages in a country where the members of the profession are native, where those who do not succeed can turn to other avocations, and are merged in the community, and where advancement does not depend on patronage, but on private demand for marketable services. But men who go out to India to seek Government service would have no other mode of employing themselves. The essential principle of the Government service in that country is freedom from private occupa-

Question of limit to number.

tion and connections. If, then, you do not give a man a moderate salary from the beginning, no one who has not some private fortune can attempt the profession, and the best of those who have private fortune would not be likely to attempt it. A man who has not some means, and is not successful in obtaining employment, must starve. You would have then in India not the best men to be found in England, but a *very* limited class, either of men who, having private means, are yet willing to try their fortune in India, or of very desperate men who go to live or to die. It is, therefore, under the peculiar circumstances, necessary that every man admitted to the profession should be, to some extent, paid by Government; and Government, of course, will not consent to pay an unlimited number of candidates. Moreover, if the numbers who go out be unlimited, we again throw into the hands of the Governor-General too great a share of patronage. Men would go out who have previous assurance of employment. There would be no real free trade, and you would merely transfer the selection from the Senate to the Indian Governors. I think, then, that you must limit the number admitted to the profession; but my object is to gain some of the advantages of an unlimited profession by extending that limit, by providing more fit employment for mediocrity, and ensuring a larger field of selection for superior offices.

The effect of the extension of native employment will of course be to diminish the number of civil servants required by the Government in any given territory; but, at the same time, it may be presumed that the extent of territory directly administered by us will be occasionally increased, and the territorial sphere of the civil service will be consequently from time to time extended. The result of these mutually compensating prospective changes might be to balance one another, or to admit of some diminution of numbers while we require enhanced qualifications; but the addition of some inferior European appointments, and of many of those now held by military men, would again render necessary some numerical increase, with a view to the broader basis which I have proposed.

Under the arrangements suggested in the previous chapter, the following offices will be filled from the civil service.

To be filled from the civil service exclusively—all European appointments in the regular line of the civil administration not expressly excepted, and descending a good deal lower in the scale of European employment than at present:

To be open to the civil service in common with civilians not belonging to the profession—certain civil appointments to be specially named:

To be open to the civil service in common with military officers—certain civil and all political appointments.

The number of the civil service at present somewhat exceeds 800. It is less than it was 20 years ago. Till within the last few years the extension of native employment enabled the Government to reduce it, but, owing to recent extension of territory, the service is not now equal to the whole of the civil duties, and it has been necessary to supply the non-regulation and political appointments from the army. Civil servants can only be made available for these duties, and the requisite weeding of the holders of superior appointments can only be effected, by promoting natives, and so releasing some of the European servants from their present duties. I hope that this may be done to a considerable extent, but still, to carry out my plan and to admit of sufficient selection, I should say that the number of the service must be rather increased than diminished. It will be, however, remembered that many of these servants will be less highly paid than at present, and the cost to the state will not be increased. The higher appointments will be filled by men *selected* from a large body of select persons.

Tests—positive or relative.

The number then being limited, we come to the tests of admission. Tests may be either positive or relative. You may either fix a standard, and say that no one shall be nominated who does not come up to that standard—*e. g.* that no one shall be nominated who is not six feet high—or, putting patronage altogether aside, you may choose relatively from among all candidates, *e. g.* the tallest men who present themselves shall be nominated. An attempt was made by the last Act to find a middle course between these two systems. It was provided that four times the number of persons required should be nominated, and that the best should be selected. Now this would have been very proper, if, simply from the persons on whom the patrons would have wished to bestow their patronage, the best could have been selected; but a farther consequence was overlooked, viz. this—that no one would be sent up for examination who did not hope to be among the elected: the great mass of fools and moderate men would be eliminated, not by, but before, the examination; they would not go up merely to subject themselves to the ignominy of being rejected, nor would the Director so sacrifice his right of nomination. In short, none but very first-rate, or very bold and confident men would be nominated in the first instance, and from them you would elect one in four. It would not be the *crême*, but the *crême de la crême*. In fact, in the end it must have amounted to unlimited competition. For this Government was not prepared, and therefore the scheme was abandoned. In truth, it seems clear that, if we once admit relative competition, and altogether reject the greater number of candidates, the result must be such as I have described. You cannot put a limit to it; in any form it will practically end in something very near unlimited competition. It is in this light then that we must consider it.

Objections to relative test.

The principle of selecting the best men, whoever they are, is at first sight captivating, but there are several objections. I have already subscribed to the proposition that you do not want a service composed exclusively of men of very brilliant and forward genius. There would be no managing them. You want a good intellect and superior education as indispensable to all, and among these the natural proportion of genius in a few. Intellect and education of the very highest grade do not form the sole qualification for every office. In many appointments, an honest, willing, discreet man, of reasonably good abilities, will be a more useful servant of Government than a more brilliant person; and therefore I believe that unlimited competition would not be the best way of securing the greatest practical efficiency in the service. Moreover, the result of such competition is, that, putting up the appointments to auction in the market, you get its extreme marketable value in talent. You bestow no gift, you simply make the best possible bargain. Now, while I in every way desire to see appointments to the civil service assume much more than at present the nature of a contract, I think that there is great danger in exacting the utmost limit of value, in altogether sweeping away the marginal difference which is the field for patronage. It seems to me that in responsible civil offices in all countries men are and ought to be paid something more than the barest market value of their services,—for this reason, that you ought to have some hold upon them; they should have something to lose, their appointments should be in some degree valuable to them. They should not be like mere monthly servants engaged on the lowest possible wages, and without any feeling of favour or obligation on either side. Your confidential and responsible servants must have places which they considerably prefer to private occupations and earnings. I therefore think that there is on this ground the greatest objection to the auction by public competition, even when payment is made in talent. And still greater is the objection when payment is made in money.

Plan of general nominations to Indian service, and relative selection.

The only relative test which I can conceive at all practicable is that which has been suggested of making all nominations to the Indian service the same, and leaving it to all who so choose to go to the Civil College and become candidates for the civil service; the best to be selected to the required number, and the remainder to go out in the army. This plan is free from many of the objections to a selection of the civil service from the army in India, and I confess that, as regards the civil service only, I should think it an extremely good plan, and the best and simplest way of securing efficient men; in fact, I would have no hesitation whatever in adopting it. But as concerns the army, there is still the fatal objection that you would draw away the greater part of the talent of a service which requires much talent. Civil appointments are so much more prized, that there can be no doubt that nine-tenths of the young men likely to be successful would be candidates for that service, and the army would be a body deprived of its salt, its savour, and its essence. I think that this would be an insuperable objection to the entire adoption of the plan.

So much only of the suggestion I would adopt, as to permit a portion of the limited number of candidates nominated for the civil service, who may prove unfit for that duty, and yet be considered fit for the army, to be sent out in the latter service. There is not the same objection to a limited selection as to an unlimited competition of the whole body of nominees—to the subjection of the whole army supply to a demasculating process. Although you must not take all or the larger proportion of the talent from the army, there is no doubt in that service room for a larger number of men of very moderate intellect, but good thighs and sinews. From a comparatively small portion of the army nominations, the best are taken for the Engineers (a corps which is an admirable instance of the advantage of selecting), and the inferior cadets are sent out in the infantry, without rendering the whole of the latter branch destitute of talent. If the civil service test be severe, some selection will no doubt be made by the patrons in sending up only those of the patronised who are tolerably likely to succeed; and of these, some who do not succeed (not forming a very numerous body), if sufficiently fit for the army, may be lost in so large a mass without very perceptibly diminishing its general talent. In fact, an arrangement of this kind does at present almost invariably take place: when, in rare instances, a young man does not pass for the civil service, he is withdrawn and renominated to the army. I would only, by rendering this course regular and avowed, take away the pretext for unwillingness to pluck on the ground of the hardship of "utterly ruining a young man." If the said young man is not fit for important civil duties, and, being fit for the army, is assigned to that service, there will not be the slightest ground for compunction.

While I am against a general relative test, I would have a positive test so high as to render necessary a strict selection, and to debar from the civil service all but very superior men. The grand difficulty in any positive test is, to secure a sufficient degree of severity. The fact is, that patronage and selection are, so far as each goes, incompatible things. You cannot both have exactly the men you would most wish to patronise, and at the same time secure a superior average degree of natural talent. You may educate the men of your *election*, but you cannot put brains into them. Brains are only to be found by selection. It is then but to be expected, that, while there is an honest and praiseworthy desire to educate, and even to exclude those who *will* not be educated, there is much greater tenderness in regard to natural intellect. I believe that of late years the standard of education may possibly have been in a very slight degree raised; the standard of intellect not one iota, but the contrary. And apart from other information, I need ground my assertion solely on this fact, that the number of plucked and rejected is not only not increased, but has positively diminished. I deny that there is any sufficient test of intellect and accomplishment, and repeat that fools may still go out in the civil service of the East India Company. I do not for one moment pretend that the test can be enhanced without trenching on patronage. As you enhance the test, you *pro tanto* diminish the patronage. I think that, without altogether obliterating the latter, you should much enhance the former. I would not only require of the patron to educate his nominee to the utmost, but I would insist that he should select persons possessed of more than average brains. At present, with respect to any person who can get a civil appointment, the *rule* is that he passes; it is only the exception if he is deterred or plucked. I would just reverse this, and make passing the exception. For instance, say that a

The positive test.

Present state of.

Director has half a dozen connections to whom he would be willing to give civil appointments. At present, perhaps, one who is both stupid and idle is either deterred from accepting the nomination, or, accepting it, and being very reckless, is plucked ; five pass and go out in the civil service. I would have it, that four should be deterred or plucked, and two should go out. These two would be superior men, but all would not necessarily or probably be geniuses. I ask whether it is possible to deny that under the present arrangements, if a man can get a civil appointment for his son, he does not generally with due precaution and cramming get him through; whether an ultimate failure is not looked on as a peculiar misfortune and exception, and the result of intense recklessness in the young man. Does it not then necessarily follow that the average material can be little above par? This must be changed. Let us look then to our tests.

The positive test may be imposed in two ways,—either by leaving candidates to private education, and subjecting them to one great examination; or in connection with a course of special education provided, or prescribed and supervised, by the Government, in the course of which they are subjected to a long series of tests.

Objection to test by a single examination.

I do not think it in any way possible that the object desired can be sufficiently effected by any single examination. Every such examination is made the subject of a system of professional cramming and coaching to such a degree that it is quite impossible to trust to it alone. If you make the examination so severe as to be beyond the reach of cramming alone, you shut out many of the best candidates, who do not add intense cram to natural talent and liberal education; and if you make it less severe, it is open to cram without talent or real education of a high order. The fact is, that our ordinary

English education is by no means of the most practical or useful description. I very much doubt whether an education of the kind necessary to Indian civil servants is to be sufficiently obtained at any place of public education in this country as at present conducted. Candidates must therefore resort to private cramming. This cramming system of education for a particular examination is most noxious, and every way to be discouraged. Nothing whatever is taught beyond the mere answers to particular questions which are likely to be put by the examiners. This little is generally taught in the worst way, under the most unfavourable circumstances, and involves a complete stoppage of all regular systematic education, and of all that cultivation, beyond mere book-learning, which a boy gets at a good school. The object should be to ascertain that a boy of good intellect has been generally well educated, not that he has been artificially coached for a particular exhibition. It is totally impossible, in utter ignorance of the boys who are brought up to the post—of their characters, circumstances, and antecedents—to determine by one examination, with any approach to accuracy, which are likely to make the best servants of Government. Such a test is very well as a preliminary, but can be nothing more.

The examination at the India House, before admittance to Haileybury, answers this purpose tolerably well; but it is not, and never can be, alone sufficient as a test of fitness for the service. The subjects and style of examination are very good, and the papers seem very hard; but it does not at all follow that they are fully answered, and such answers as are given are very deceptive; because the crammers, by long practice, seem to know pretty nearly what will be asked, and get up their pupils accordingly. The consequence is, that what may seem a severe examination (and to unprepared people would certainly be so) is passed by boys of every degree, with or without intellect, and often with a very moderate education indeed. Some few are generally plucked, but they come up again and again, and, in the end, very few indeed are really finally rejected. Very little *selection*, then, eventually results from this examination. For the reasons to which I have alluded I would not attempt very materially to enhance it. It may be made a little more strict, to meet the improvement of the science of cramming, and the higher character which I would give to the college, but I would not essentially alter its character. It is conducted by examiners appointed by, and under the immediate direction of, the Board of Control, and, so far as it goes, is honestly carried out.

Necessity of professional education, and a series of tests.

But you must farther specially and professionally educate the candidates for the service, and, in connection with this education, you can impose much better, surer, and more severe tests, extending to a later age. If you discover a fool any time before he goes to India, he should be stopped while there is yet opportunity for doing so. This professional education and these essential tests can be best obtained by a specially-selected place and course of education, where all may alike have the benefit of the best and most appropriate instruction, and where all may be judged by the same standard.

Haileybury, its present advantages and disadvantages.

This, then, is the object of Haileybury; and, in some respects, that institution has very many good qualities compared to ordinary places of education in this country. Far from dispensing with the system of special education, I would carry it very much farther, and I think that the future efficiency of the profession very much depends on it. I likewise consider it anything but undesirable that the men who are in future to carry on the same duties in all the different parts of India should be brought together in, and started from, the same professional workshop; should drink of the same well of knowledge; should imbibe a certain *esprit de corps*; should form some personal acquaintance with one another; and should in future be united by some common souvenirs. Haileybury is even now the only point of union of a widely-dispersed service, and, imperfect as it is, I believe that there results from it a beneficial common feeling and good understanding, which would be wanting in men picked up from different quarters and sent to India without any intercourse or acquaintance with one another. These advantages Haileybury possesses, and I should be very sorry to see it abolished without a sufficient substitute. But I object to it as too little interfering with patronage; as not fulfilling the main purpose for which it was intended. In all other superior places of education learning is voluntary. Of Haileybury you expect more—it should be the instrument of selection, of discriminating the capable from the incapable, and of giving to the capable, not only the opportunities of voluntary education, but a very high degree of acquirement as indispensable to entering a privileged service. Haileybury was, as has been said, a compromise with the patrons formerly possessed of an unlimited patronage, and on that very account a strict selection ought to be there carried out. But, in fact, this duty is almost altogether evaded; and of the young men who are admitted to Haileybury, after passing the very uncertain preliminary test, very few are now finally rejected. Rejections are only rare exceptions, in case of extreme idleness and misconduct, and the great mass are sent out to India with no selection or elimination whatever. I stated in 'Modern India,' p. 265, that, in my time, of the students at Haileybury some fifteen or twenty per cent. were plucked, and went out in the army. In this I have, to a certain extent, inadvertently misstated. The number who finally lost or gave up their appointments was never so great. About the proportion mentioned were probably, on an average, plucked each term, but many of these eventually passed, and say from five to ten per cent. were finally eliminated. Things have been now somewhat changed under a new régime. We are given to understand that a higher standard of education has been introduced, and that the students are all "highly distinguished." But what is the fact? Why, this,—that there is very much less *selection* than formerly; that where a dozen were plucked before, not more than three or four are now turned back for a term, and hardly any eventually lose their appointments, except in one or two cases of gross misconduct. In short, through the admirable Principal this pleasant and satisfactory arrangement has been effected, equally agreeable to all parties (the governed excepted), that the public is gratified by the announcement of an enhanced standard; the patrons cannot grumble, for their nominees are not rejected, and their patronage is intact; and all the friends and relations of each and every student are delighted, for the boy, hitherto supposed to be a booby, is represented as "highly distinguished." If these facts be doubted, let us at once have the statistics of Haileybury for say the last three years, and figures will bring the matter to an issue. Let us have the number plucked and the number finally rejected in each term, the number of those sent to India each term who were reported "highly distinguished" and "passed with great credit," and the number who were not thus honoured. I rest simply on those facts. I confess that I place no faith in enhanced standards which are not proved by the statistics of rejection. Haileybury does not do its duty in respect to selection; but, on the contrary, I repeat, altogether evades it, and the matter very much wants looking into.

Fate has, unfortunately at this time, deprived us of one equally respected and loved, and who was perhaps better qualified than any other man to give a fair account of the real working of Haileybury, and the character of the young men sent out in the civil service.

Twenty years ago Mr. Empson thus testified:—

Q. "Is there anything in the present system which makes it obligatory on the professors to send out young men who are not qualified to go?"

A. "I should say there certainly has been felt to be in the college a moral obligation of that description."

* * * * * *

Q. "Do you mean to say that the general opinion and feeling of persons connected with the present Indian system are such that the professors cannot effectually exercise that power of selection which, by theory, you possess?"

A. "I certainly say so. Their experience, unfortunately, convinces them of it."

The facts are still the same, but I do not attribute them to the causes which might, perhaps, be inferred from this evidence. I am well convinced that no direct influence from without is really exercised, and I principally attribute the blame to the professors themselves, in not with sufficient firmness performing their duty. A single professor of a European subject has it not in his power to raise the standard, because his subject may be altogether neglected without loss of appointment; but the body of the professors, acting together according to their duty, have it fully in their power to raise it. Yet at the present day, notwithstanding greater pretension, the results of the college, from whatever cause, are just the same as those described by the late Mr. Empson.

Suppose a general to write,—"We have had a desperate engagement with the enemy: balls flew about thick as hail for three days, but, owing to the indomitable courage of my troops, I rejoice to state that nobody was killed, and only one man wounded. I have the honour to append a list of those who particularly distinguished themselves, containing, I am happy to say, the name of every individual in the army. I claim for my noble soldiers the reward of their devoted bravery." We should certainly think that more credit was due to the dispositions of the general than to the courage of the soldiers. Yet this is exactly the counterpart of a Haileybury report of the present day. It is all very well for the satisfaction of anxious relations, but, so far as the public service and public duty are concerned—it may be very vulgar to say so, but I must relieve my mind of the opinion that—it is all "humbug." In truth, there are very good opportunities of education for those who like to learn, but no tests of intellect whatever, and the smallest possible test of education. The very small amount of compulsory education is, for the most part, confined to the Oriental languages. Although opportunities of learning the useful moral sciences are provided, perhaps better than anywhere else in the kingdom, a young man may, if he chooses, go out utterly innocent of the very first rudiments of jurisprudence and political economy. I do not believe that those honourable men, the Directors of the Company, in any way promote, or desire to connive at, this state of things. But the professors are appointed by the same persons who nominate the young men; they are, as it were, socially connected with them and with the patrons; the rejection of a student is always looked on by his friends as a very hard thing;

the individual professors who would more strictly perform their duty cannot alone do so; and, altogether, it happens that the necessary union of all in the performance of an apparently harsh duty is not obtained. The students are educated as well as circumstances will permit, but no selection is made.

Even in regard to those students at Haileybury who really work, I think that the *professional* education is not carried nearly far enough, especially in the case of those who are to perform judicial duties. The greater part of the time is frittered away in obtaining a very slight smattering of the Oriental languages (and especially that absurd Sanscrit), which are either of little use, or which may be learnt in India in one-tenth part of the time.

Several of the defects of Haileybury (and especially the mal-arrangement which makes Sanscrit so prominent and indispensable) are generally admitted. Yet from year to year no alteration takes place. It has been a question whether the Court of Directors or the Board of Control is responsible for this mismanagement; and in truth it seems, in a great degree, to result from the division of authority. It is shown that by law the direction of the mode of education rests with the Board of Control; but then the Directors appoint the professors, nominate the students, and conduct the whole executive management of the college, and the Board of Control really knows nothing at all about it. The Directors cannot order the professors to relax the present tests, and they may consider themselves exonerated from the duty of enhancing them, while the continually-changing President of the Board is utterly ignorant of the details of the examinations, and never thinks of interfering. But I have no doubt whatever that, if any plan of improvement and enhancement of tests were digested and submitted to the Board, it would be readily sanctioned; and when the responsibility is thrown on the Board, I ask, has the Board ever negatived any good plan? has any plan of improvement been proposed to it? If not, I say that the responsibility still rests directly with the principal and professors. The objectionable parts of the system are merely maintained because no one takes the initiative to alter them.

I am sure that the subsequent year, usually spent in doing nothing but all manner of mischief in Calcutta, would be much more profitably devoted to an additional year of really professional study in this country. The Orientals abated, three years properly bestowed would suffice for an excellent professional education. And a young man thoroughly grounded in all that can be well learnt in England, including the alphabet and earliest rudiments of Hindostanee, going out to India at the age of twenty or twenty-one, and immediately sent to a station in the interior, would very soon acquire that practical knowledge of the vernacular tongue which is necessary to give effect to his education.

Many of the disadvantages of Haileybury arise from its isolation. I doubt whether in any isolated place you can be sure of a severe test in the absence of any independent standard with which to compare it. You cannot say "We wish our men to be equal to such another class of men," for there are no means of comparison; and when the Principal reports that nineteen out of twenty young men are "highly distinguished," it is difficult to say "Can't help that—you must pluck more."

The repugnance to pluck is greatly enhanced by the circumstance of a young man being already altogether set apart for a particular profession, and having abandoned the routes leading to other professions, so that to reject him seems to be ruining him for life,—not denying him admittance into a profession, but turning him out of one. The fact that practically he goes out in the army seems to me to take away all excuse from the authorities at Haileybury for failing in their duty; but theoretically a young man is turned on the world. If he were still in the route to other professions there would be much less difficulty about it.

It is also certain that the peculiar isolation and circumstances of Haileybury cause a great deficiency of tone and character. It is something between a school and a college. Schoolboys are growing into men, and are suddenly freed from all the restraints of school, yet are not brought within the moral and intellectual influences of a university. They have nothing to induce self-respect, and no sufficient field for competition, or for comparing themselves with those entering other professions.

I have already expressed the opinion that some such college as Haileybury cannot be dispensed with—that you must have a place of education where the candidates for the civil service shall be educated and tested together. The question is, whether you can at the same time preserve this principle, improve the practice, and enforce a substantial system of selection.

Proposed transfer to an Indian College at Cambridge.

I have much considered this subject, and have lately made some inquiries with a view to a project which I had long entertained. Everything has induced me to form the strongest opinion that all the disadvantages of Haileybury might be at once obviated, and very many additional advantages secured to the service, by transferring Haileybury to Cambridge, instituting an Indian College in connection with the university, and there combining a certain special education with the general tone, system, and character of the university, and the opportunity of comparison with an independent and enlarged standard there afforded.

The present university education would not yet be alone sufficient for our purpose, nor would an ordinary university degree be by any means an adequate test; but Cambridge and Haileybury combined would, I think, answer admirably.

The principles of education at Cambridge have lately very much tended towards the recognition and encouragement of those sciences which (as forming part of a public education in this country) were at one time almost peculiar to Haileybury. Jurisprudence, political economy, and other *moral* sciences are now much regarded; and although they have not attained the important position which is their due, and the facilities of instruction are not so great as could be wished, the rules are such that it would not in the first instance be necessary altogether to separate the Indian professional education from the general education of the university, but only to direct the studies of the young men destined for India into one of the several channels which the university already recognises and patronises; and then to add some more purely professional knowledge, just as in the case of those who are destined to the professions of divinity, law, or physic. A man can now without mathematical or classical honours go up for honours in the "moral sciences" tripos.

If then we could arrange to transfer our students, and so much as is necessary of our special establishment, to a College at Cambridge, and to require of *all* nominees to the civil service an ordinary degree, certain "moral science" honours, and a special certificate or degree of the Indian College, we could lose nothing of the present education, and we should gain that which is now wanting; we should still have our special college for special purposes, but all the defects of tone and conduct resulting from the isolation of Haileybury would be removed. Merged in the university, we should have the university tone.

There would no longer be any difficulty in imposing sufficient severity in the tests, because we should have an independent standard; and it would be easy to fix exactly the grade of men whom you would admit to the service. You might say, We must have men equal to those who take a certain class of honours, or to those who obtain fellowships in such a college; and we might insist on such a standard.

Under the present university system a young man need not, and under the rules which we should prescribe he could not, give himself up to classics and mathematics, but he would still have a sufficiently wide range of recognised and important subjects in which he could legitimately and usefully measure his strength with those who are to follow other professions. The object will be, perhaps, best and most simply effected by requiring so much in particular subjects that the honours of other departments will be impossible, rather than by a prohibitory rule; or if it be found necessary, we might at once prohibit competition in those subjects which would be of least practical use.

While the tone and education acquired by the members of the civil service would be much improved, they would also be more known and appreciated by the English public. An English lawyer of eminence may now treat with contempt the rough proceedings of a rough and unsatisfactory judicial system; and an English statesman may not fully appreciate a mere Indian administrator. They know nothing of the personal qualities of the Indian judge or the Indian commissioner. But if they knew that these men had been their rivals and equals at the university, they would regard them with infinitely greater respect.

A good man reading for three years at the university, and taking honours there, would go out to India a really accomplished English gentleman. And on the other hand, I should think it one of the greatest advantages that those who do not take the prescribed honours and pass the prescribed tests will be no worse off than before; they will still have followed the regular course of education leading to all other professions, and may still apply such talents, tastes, or accomplishments as they may possess in any way that they see fit. If a man who cannot pass for India is also thereby forewarned that he need hardly take the trouble of trying the law of England, he may still, for instance, go into the church. His university career would not be lost.

I have before alluded to the apprehension that the *best* men, having measured themselves with others, might prefer to go into other professions; but then, as I have also said, I would at the same time so constitute the service that it should be a sufficient temptation to the *best* as well as to moderately good men.

Abstractedly, then, it seems to me impossible to doubt the advantage of a change such as I have suggested. But we must now look to the expense and to the particular mode in which it may be carried out. Of course something must be lost on the building at Haileybury, but it need not be altogether sacrificed. Even if the Indian Government can find no use for it as a military college, or a school of practical art for natives coming over from India, and mechanical Europeans about to be sent out there, it is so near London that it might doubtless be sold for a school, or a mad-house, or a convent, or something of that kind. Say it cost 100,000*l.*, it might perhaps be sold for 50,000*l.*, and 50,000*l.* would be lost—no very overwhelming sum in the finances of India.

Expense, &c., of transfer.

Well, suppose we sell Haileybury for 50,000*l*., we have that sum in hand to begin with. I think that, instead of founding a separate college at Cambridge, it might be for several reasons better, if possible, to form a union with one of the existing colleges. An arrangement of this kind would be cheaper and easier; we should more readily fall into a recognised place, and it is, I think, desirable that the college should not be *exclusively* limited to avowed candidates for the Indian service. I would look out, then, for one of the less well-endowed and prosperous colleges, possessed of room for building and extensions. Its members would, without doubt, be delighted to rise into importance by the support of the Indian Government; the legislature would remove any legal difficulties; a mixed college constitution and rules of government would be formed; and abuses would be well provided against. The Indian Government would supply the funds for an increase of accommodation, making the college capable of holding perhaps double the number required for the Indian service. Suppose that this costs (to do it handsomely) 100,000*l*.,—that is 50,000*l*. in addition to the proceeds of Haileybury,—the college would in return undertake to give a preferable title to admission to a sufficient number of persons nominated by the Indian Senate, and we should trust to the general educational attractions (with which we would invest it) to fill up the remaining places. The library and other furnishings of Haileybury would be transferred to this college.

Suggested arrangements.

Arrangements might be made with the university by which the Indian Government should supply anything that may be wanting to a complete university course of political economy, history, and jurisprudence; of all those subjects, in fact, which, while especially necessary to the Indian service, have also been recognised as branches of university education. Some additional professorships (of which the Indian Senate would be patron) might be supplied from Haileybury with great benefit to the university. Considering also the importance of India as a portion of the British empire, the university might be willing to admit certain Indian professional subjects as university studies to be tested and weighed in the same way as other professional subjects for professional degrees. Perhaps we might found professorships of Indian law (when we get our codes) and of the Indian system of administration, or at any rate we should have lectures on these subjects in our own college, and the knowledge acquired would either go to form the total of a high university honour, or be a separate test in *addition* to a moderate honour. With all the additional establishment of tutors, professors, &c., supplied to the college and university, the future annual expense would not exceed that now incurred at Haileybury, so that the 50,000*l.* lost at Haileybury and re-expended at Cambridge would really be once and for all the whole expense.

Cambridge Commission Report, and argument derived therefrom.

I had written thus far when I obtained the long-expected Cambridge Report, and I have now looked into it. I am thereby more than ever convinced that the proposed arrangement would be most beneficial, not only to India, but also to Cambridge and to Enlgand, and that we are most fortunate in having to arrange for our Indian education at the very time when the universities are in course of review and reform. I cannot pretend to give details of a considered scheme in this place, but the general nature of certain arrangements may be alluded to. It seems to me that by adding Haileybury to Cambridge we should, while securing our own objects, at the same time give to the university the very things of which she stands in need, and that we should be received with open arms by that body.

The university especially desires to encourage the moral sciences, but she is cramped for want of means. There is a professor of political economy, but he receives no salary; his average earnings are 62*l.* 10*s.* per annum, and the study has not made the progress which it deserves. The handsome salary and distinguished abilities of the Haileybury professor of political economy would be an immense gain to the university. There is a professor of civil law, whose salary is stated to be inadequate, and an Indian ex-councillor is Downing professor of the laws of England. But the commissioners are of opinion that it is very desirable to give a much wider basis and more extended facilities to legal studies. How welcome, then, would have been the accomplished jurists who have held office at Haileybury! There is a reader of Arabic, who seems to profess Oriental languages generally, and receives annually 40*l.* 10*s.*, but the commissioners remark, with special reference to our Eastern possessions, on the inadequate provision for this branch of education, and the importance of encouraging it if the means can anywhere be found. A Haileybury professor of Oriental languages would be exactly what is wanted. On the other hand, we find at Cambridge, as professors of moral philosophy and modern history, the great names of Dr. Whewell and Sir James Stephen. In fact, by a singular coincidence, Cambridge and Haileybury seem each to supply precisely what is most wanting to the other.

The commissioners further remark on the want of a provision for civil engineering and for modern languages, and propose to remedy the want. There is the same want at Haileybury. There is nothing more advantageous, I may say necessary, to the executive branch of the civil service than a little engineering knowledge, and at present every man is forced to pick up something of the kind in India in an unscientific way, and principally from intelligent but imperfectly educated natives. A very little science as a basis would immensely extend his practical usefulness. A knowledge of French would also be most desirable; and especially to the judicial branch of the service an acquaintance with the juridical literature, to which French is the key, will be almost indispensable. The Indian Government, then, might well assist the university to endow professorships of civil engineering and modern languages.

Religious tests.

An objection to the university might occur to some persons in regard to religious tests; but at Cambridge no religious test is required for the educational course. It is only at the end of the course a condition to the actual granting of a degree that the graduate should subscribe a test which the great majority of the classes usually appointed to the civil service have no difficulty in swallowing, but to which a few would object, and to which they should not be subjected. If this test were to be retained, there would probably be no difficulty in securing in these cases a test of knowledge without a degree. But the religious test will no doubt be speedily abolished in accordance with repeated recommendations. Whatever argument there may be in regard to "internal discipline," "religious ordinances," and "religious peace," at Oxford, as a purely Church-of-England establishment; at Cambridge, where people of all religious persuasions are admitted to the whole collegiate course, to refuse them degrees and honours is a simple piece of antiquated absurdity and injustice, which rests on no better foundation than a verbal direction of the orthodox King James I., on the occasion of a visit to Newmarket, and which must of course cease. At Haileybury the students all attend muster in a Church-of-England chapel without any objection, and I believe that in this respect it in no way differs from Cambridge, so that the ordinary university discipline could be no objection.

The present term of residence at Cambridge is three years and one term. This the commissioners propose at once to reduce to three years, which would be just the right time for Indian students.

Residence, examinations, &c.

The present limits in regard to the age of admission to Haileybury (17 to 21) would be unobjectionable. The preliminary India House examinations would still be necessary, because there is no sufficient test on admission to Cambridge, and it is indispensable that the students should have so much preliminary acquirement in the way of general education that they may afterwards devote themselves more exclusively to special subjects. The half-way examination, or "little go," at Cambridge is merely a mitigated and reduced form of our India House examination, and therefore, for our purposes, would go for nothing. The final examination for the ordinary degree of B.A. is now so arranged that it does not necessarily involve considerable mathematical or classical acquirements, and can be no insuperable bar to a separate study of special subjects. The commissioners, however, propose a great improvement, viz. that the "little go" should be slightly enhanced, and that, after passing this midway examination, students should be altogether freed from the farther necessity of reading classics or mathematics at all, and enabled to devote themselves exclusively to special or professional studies. An honour in any tripos, or a professional qualification, would then (coupled with the previous examination) entitle to a degree at the end of the course. This is exactly what would suit the Indian College.

The "little go" as enhanced would still be hardly beyond our preliminary examination, and it would be necessary to have at the same time a private examination of the Indian students as a farther test, and with a view to a report and discrimination of persons destined for different branches. A knowledge of modern history, moral philosophy, the first principles of jurisprudence and political economy, and of French, should at this time be required.

A special college committee would be charged with the supervision, under the instructions of the Minister of Indian Affairs, of the characters and qualifications of the Indian candidates. At this point—that is, at the end of one year and a half, immediately after the little go—I would have a report from the committee, specifying which students seem most fitted for and most desire the judicial branch of the service—which the executive branch—which seem fitted for neither, but may be well fitted for the army—and which are not fitted for India at all; and I would distinguish the students accordingly. The studies of those destined for the judicial branch of the service would henceforth be more properly juridical. Those reported fit for the army should forthwith have the option of qualifying themselves for that service. Those whose intellects, health, or other reasons would make them bad bargains for Indian service, might immediately turn their attention in some other direction. The remaining students would continue their studies till the end of the usual university period.

Distribution of students according to qualifications.

Of the young men who pass the "little go," those assigned to the executive department (the large majority) would still prosecute the moral sciences,* a moderate acquaintance with all of which will throughout their whole career be most useful and necessary to them. To these studies would now be added the elements of civil engineering

Education of the executive students.

* Jurisprudence, political economy, moral philosophy, modern history.

and of the mechanical arts, and a little Hindostanee; and an opportunity might be taken to explain the most successful methods of popular education.

In the department of executive jurisprudence I would especially require attention to the principles of criminal law and the science of punishments, and the general Indian administrative system should be thoroughly mastered. Those who have a scientific turn would have an opportunity of learning the elements of geology, chemistry, and botany; and it would be extremely desirable if we could institute a reader of practical agriculture, than which nothing would be more useful to Indian executive officers. It is most desirable that men who are to superintend the executive of large districts should acquire in England a little knowledge of a variety of European practical sciences, which they will have so many future occasions of extending by experience; and it will be a great advantage to India if particular members of the service acquire a taste for, and subsequent more perfect knowledge of, particular sciences.

Final test.

I would require at the final examination a fixed university honour in the moral sciences tripos, which under the proposed new system would also entitle to an ordinary degree. At the same time we should have a college examination in Indian history, the Indian administrative system, the elements of Hindostanee, and one physical science selected by the student. Any additional qualifications in any other practical science would be recognised and taken into consideration in the relative classification of rank and merit. The particular university honour to be required, and the severity of the private test, of course cannot be exactly defined here; but they must be so high as to insure the weeding out of fools, and the best education of men of good and superior intellect.

Even those who may differ in opinion as to the advantage of a transfer to the university, under the system which has hitherto prevailed there, must admit that the scheme proposed by the Cambridge Commissioners would meet all our requirements, and render the arrangement in every way feasible. I have said that there are even at present very great opportunities of education at Haileybury;—but if by relieving the students from the incubus of Oriental languages; extending by one year their term of education; placing them at the university; enhancing the tests, and weeding out inferior men—if by these means we send out men of a better average of natural intellect, much more accomplished, the fruit produced in India will be much better, and the exceptions to efficiency will be greatly fewer.

At the same time it is by no means desirable that the executive officers should go out at an advanced age.

Age on appointment.

We only sow the seed in this country, which must grow up to practical efficiency in India; and it is of the utmost importance that young men should be naturalised, as it were, in the East, before their ideas and habits are completely formed. They must become to a certain extent Asiatic, to administer properly an Asiatic government; and too great delay exceedingly interferes with this object. I would by all means encourage the sending students to Cambridge at 17 or 18, so that those destined for the executive may go to India at 20 or 21. To India then they should be sent as soon as they have passed.

Reasons for distinguishing judicial students.

I think it necessary to distinguish the students destined for the judicial department early in their career; because, if we are to have a separate judicial department, it is, as I have urged, absolutely necessary that the European judicial officers should be educated and professional jurists; and to get good jurists for India, you must specially educate men to the profession. Suitable articles are not to be found in the market. I have already alluded to the extreme difficulty of an Indian judge's duties, and the importance of his situation as the head and superintendent of a large judicial establishment. To qualify men for such duties, you must have the highest education added to great talent, and it is indispensable that the education should commence in England. I therefore propose, at the half-way point in the university course, to separate a certain number of students, and to educate them as professional jurists. The first four or five terms will give a sufficient insight into tastes, talents, and character, and I would select accordingly, and from this point would render altogether distinct the judicial and executive services.

I believe that higher general talent and acquirements are necessary in the judicial than in the executive department, for this reason—that, while our political situation will always make it necessary to keep in the hands of Europeans the greater part of the executive direction, and duties which afford scope to many grades of talent and acquirement, the natives are very well fitted for, and have a much larger share of, judicial duties, and I propose to give them a regular legal education. The Europeans only hold high, and for the most part appellate and superintending offices, and they will be of no use whatever, unless they are men of very superior qualifications, capable of properly directing most acute native judges. In the executive, one man orders, another executes; but in a good judicial system there will be an inevitable comparative admeasurement of intellect, black or white, covenanted or uncovenanted. The number of European judicial officers will then be small, but they must all be first-rate men,

And for requiring greater qualifications.

whom a moderate experience will render capable of holding high office. There will be almost no places for second-rate men. I would not, however, by any means select *all* the best men for the judicial branch. As good, or, perhaps, more *brilliant* men are necessary in the first ranks of the executive; but the latter department can employ a larger proportion of *second-rate* men. In the case of those selected as best fitted for legal duties, I would, therefore, exact a more severe test of the *minimum* of talent and acquirement.

College education of judicial students.

From the time, then, of the half-way examination and consequent separation, the judicial students would devote all their energies to professional subjects. They would study the science of jurisprudence, the comparative features of different European codes, the history and first principles of Hindoo, Mahomedan, and Anglo-Indian law; and it may be expected that at the end of their college career they will be possessed of a knowledge of the theory of law which will be a sufficient foundation for a superstructure of good legal practice. I would require then, at the final examination of judicial students, a very high certificate of the "Board of Legal Studies" (proposed by the University Commissioners), and likewise a good knowledge of French and the rudiments of Hindostanee. The other practical sciences would not be necessary to them, but such as can spare time and talent might, as in the other department, acquire accomplishments worthy of being weighed in the classification of merit.

And practical education.

If we had in India a sufficient working legal system into which a young man would enter on his arrival, his education might here end, and he would be sent to commence the practice of law in India. But in India we want practice as much as theory. We have not only to supply lawyers, but to create a system, and I therefore think that some practical education in Europe is of very great importance. It is not so necessary as in the executive department that a judicial officer should be early naturalised : there are fewer duties for young men, and there would be no objection (but rather every inducement) to send them out at a somewhat later age. I would therefore strongly recommend that on leaving the university they should for a time be brought into contact with the practical working of some European legal system.

I do not think that it would be at all desirable that our system should be founded exclusively on English principles, but would rather try to combine a knowledge of different systems through individuals educated in the same theory of jurisprudence, sent out for a time to see different practical systems, and then united in the body which is to found a new practice. My plan therefore is, that after leaving college, students should be permitted to select a place of practical study, where they should devote one year to acquiring a certain qualification in the legal practice of that place.

The present rules of the inns of court in regard to calling to the bar are these :—terms must be kept for three years, of which two years are kept by dinners alone, and during the third the student must attend a course of legal lectures ending in an examination and a certificate of a moderate qualification. Members of the university are permitted to keep the dinner terms by dining three times in each term, which involves an absence from college of but two days. I would propose, then, that judicial students should be permitted to keep terms while in college, and that those who select English practice should afterwards complete the remainder of the legal course, pass the examination, and qualify for the bar. I would also require a certain attendance in the courts of justice, and would make the students transmit notes of the proceedings in their own handwriting to an examiner. The general legal atmosphere of the courts and inns would be useful, and in every way I think that much good would result from the acquisition of this practical qualification by a proportion of the judicial nominees. The spirit of the age is now diametrically opposed to the old "technicalities of English law;" and nothing more tends to disabuse a man of the popular mis-notions concerning law (which have much misled our Indian judges) than an attention to and comprehension of the proceedings and changes of the Westminster Hall of this modern day. I may add that there are some parts of the peculiar English mode of trial, which practically work remarkably well, and may with advantage be copied. The clear way in which an issue is joined, and the promptness and dash with which a case once in court is tried and brought to a verdict (right or wrong), is doubtless worthy of all commendation.

Again: the Scotch law is founded on the civil law common to continental Europe; many of the Indian servants are Scotch, and a proportion of the students might well study the Scotch practice. The rules of qualification for the Scotch bar are these:—

First, an examination in the civil law.

Second, another examination, after an interval of one year, in Scotch law.

I would make this qualification, with a similar attendance in the Scotch courts, an equivalent for the English qualification.

It would be very desirable that some students should go to Paris; and in the absence of the same inducements which London and Edinburgh would afford to Englishmen and Scotchmen, it might be desirable to hold out some premium in favour of those who do so. I am not at present sufficiently acquainted with the rules of the *Ecoles du Droit*, but would exact a reasonable French qualification. If any men were found conversant with the German language, a German qualification would also be very useful.

Thus, then, the judicial students would spend the year or year and a half after getting out of college, and, having attained a practical qualification in some legal system, they would be sent out to India about the age of twenty-two or twenty-three.

My plan does not at all approximate to another of which I have heard, viz. that Indian judicial officers should be selected from the English bar by the judges in this country; inasmuch as, first, my Indian nominees would be subjected to a very high test, independent of the qualification for the bar; second, while in favour of a slight knowledge of the practice of the courts of different countries, I think that to become professionally attached and wedded to English law would be injurious, as involving many principles and views quite inapplicable to India; third, even supposing the judges to exercise the very best discretion in the selection, they could not be supposed to know enough of a man till he has been six or eight years at the bar, and if sent out at that time he would be nearly useless for several years more—he must commence his Indian education, just the same as a younger man (it would not be proposed, for instance, to put him on the bench till he is familiar with the languages), and he would enter upon actual business much too late in life; fourth, all the best men, all who are likely to get on at the bar, after being there long enough to prove themselves, would not accept the appointments, or not without extravagant salaries. For many reasons, then, this plan could not in any way succeed; we must have a separate judicial establishment.

Selection of a college at Cambridge.

If the university scheme be accepted, it will then be time enough to determine regarding a particular college. I think I may assume that there is no part of the *university* discipline of Cambridge which will be any obstacle to young men destined for India. But the question of founding a separate college or joining another must principally depend on the degree to which a sufficient control and unobjectionable system of collegiate discipline can be secured by the articles of union. I think that all the Indian students must be in the same college; but I also think it of great importance that it should not be confined to them exclusively, but that others desirous of particularly attending to those most useful branches of liberal knowledge which form so large a portion of the Indian qualification should be admitted and attracted, in order to give the institution a less exclusive character and to encourage intercourse, comparison, and competition. We principally wish to give to civil servants, before leaving Europe, the most useful parts of European education, while we superadd the foundations of professional acquirement; but the greater part of their more strictly professional knowledge they will acquire in India. It is, therefore, by no means desirable altogether to segregate them from the rest of the world sooner than is necessary. Either, then, in founding a new college, or in a union with another, I would provide for a proportion of general students.

If a union be in any case practicable, I should say, judging from the University Report, that Downing College is exactly what we want. It is a recent college, unembarrassed by ancient statutes and rules; it has a large endowment, but the funds were miscalculated; and a Chancery suit put everything wrong. The college was commenced on a great scale, which was not carried out, and it seems to be unfinished and almost stranded, notwithstanding a large expenditure of money and a considerable income. Here has been introduced the system of incorporating with a college professorships of modern sciences (recognised by the university), which is exactly that which we should find most convenient in the Indian College. If, then, Downing be willing to form a union, it will suit us exceedingly well, and we might, at a moderate cost, make it one of the largest and most important colleges, with provision for, say, 150 Indian candidates and 150 general students.

If difficulties be found to exist in the way of a union with an existing college, I would still found a separate Indian college in connection with the university, and imagine that there could be no obstacle to such a measure. We might still admit a certain number of non-professional students, and might show England the way to an improved system of education, more practical than that which has hitherto prevailed.

I should say that chaplains, civil engineers, schoolmasters, and other persons destined for the Indian service, might, with great advantage, be educated in the college patronized and provided with Oriental facilities by the Indian government; and eventually it may become the fountain-head of our Indian educational and polytechnic establishments.

If scheme rejected, proposed amendments at Haileybury.

If, on the other hand, for reasons which are not, I confess, at present intelligible to me, it be considered desirable to keep Haileybury in its present situation, I need only say that many of my suggestions will still be applicable. I would still diminish the study of Oriental languages, and would increase that of the practical sciences. I would impose a series of examinations, which should be sufficient tests of intellect and of substantial acquirement, and would take measures to enforce a due administration of those tests. I would distinguish the judicial servants at an early period, and would give them some considerable juridical education before sending them to India. I would provide that, regarding every student passed for service in India, the college council should not only certify to certain arbitrary educational marks, but should also furnish to the Government the following declaration :—

"We hereby declare, upon honour, that, from our sufficient knowledge and experience of A. B., we fully believe him to be a person of good intellect and attainments, likely to become fitted to fill highly arduous, important, and responsible offices."

I would no longer leave it in the power of the professors to say that, while theoretically bound to send out fit men, they consider themselves under a "moral obligation" to send out unfit men. I aver that some young men are now sent out of whom the professors could not sign a certificate in the form which I have proposed; and I submit whether any person should be entertained of whom so much cannot be predicated. I believe that the minimum test for entrance into the service is even now higher than that required for entrance into any other profession; but then we must bear in mind the exclusive nature of a service limited in numbers; the difficulty and importance of the duties; the peculiar circumstances which render it impossible to employ innocuously any unfit men, and the consequent extreme necessity of guarding to the utmost against any individual exceptions to general efficiency. I therefore do most strongly urge that the test of minimum capacity should be raised.

I have thought it almost waste of argument to dwell on the manifold reasons for dispensing with the excessive proportion of the Oriental languages in the education exacted at Haileybury. Every one is agreed on that subject. I believe that there is no law requiring that the students' time and attention should be sacrificed to a tyrannical imposition of Sanscrit (that hardest of languages). No student can make any practical use of Sanscrit, and not one in a hundred prosecutes it as a literary accomplishment one hour after he closes his books at Haileybury. I would therefore at once abolish it. In regard to the practical languages, I would go simply on this principle—that so much as can be learnt in England as well, or nearly as well, as in India, should be learnt in England; but that everything which may be learnt with much greater facility in India should be left to be learnt in India. I would especially insist on this arrangement, because there is a great deal more that is worthy of being learnt in England, and which there is no opportunity of learning in India, than the student is at all likely to accomplish in the prescribed time. I think that the Oriental alphabets and something of the grammar and very earliest rudiments of the language may be learnt in England nearly as well as in India, and so far I would go, but not one step farther. With this foundation the civil servant will pick up a much better practical knowledge of the vernacular tongue in India, without expending one-tenth of the time and labour wasted in England. In India, of course, an application to, and sufficient knowledge of, the language must be rigorously exacted; but that the time at Haileybury should be wasted in acquiring what is in practice a mere infinitesimal knowledge is monstrous and absurd.

Study of Oriental languages in England.

In sending men to India in the executive branch of the service, due regard must be paid to physical fitness. It is but entailing a burden on the Government to send out, in any capacity, any man whose health is not equal to a

Necessity of physical qualifications.

very hard service. The fact (to which I have before alluded) must be particularly remembered, that an executive civil servant is by no means a mere man of red tape and official routine. It is, in this respect, a peculiar and a sort of semi-military service. A man must be as ready to ride as to write; to head an armed party as to count rupees; he must discipline his police, be prepared for all emergencies, and never apply to the military except in such extreme cases as very seldom occur. We must therefore have men who can not only write but act.

Appointment and distribution of civil servants.

The English education of the candidates for the civil service being successfully completed, and the tests surmounted, they will be appointed and sent out to India. You will have for service in that country a body of men of not less than moderately good intellect and of very high education.

The first question which here arises is, whether there shall be, as at present, several distinct services for different parts of India, Bengal, Madras, and Bombay; or whether all shall be sent out for general service, leaving it to the Supreme Government to distribute them according to the requirements of each locality. The latter practice now, in fact, prevails in the Bengal service, comprising upwards of three-fifths of the whole number, who, after arrival in India, are distributed to Bengal, Agra, and the Punjab by the Supreme Government. There are many strong arguments in favour of this course, and I have previously alluded to the especial desirableness of establishing some intercommunication between the services.

Still the difference of language and other reasons make it quite necessary that there should be local divisions of the service; that particular officers should be *ordinarily* employed in particular provinces; and in the executive branch it is of essential importance that the practical education should be at once commenced in the province for which each servant is designed. The young servant's first year will be employed in learning the vernacular language, and in this everything depends on locality. It would be useless to send him to the seat of the Supreme Government, to be thence immediately sent elsewhere. I would therefore send the executive nominees of each year to the different local governments, according to a scale of distribution to be furnished by the Governor-General; but I would not constitute altogether separate services.

The judicial servants on arrival in India.

In regard to the judicial department, I would propose another arrangement. I should not consider the legal education of the judicial servants complete when they sail for India, and would not plunge them immediately into judicial duties. I have alluded to the circumstance that we must have a general native judicial language for all India, in which laws, precedents, and final appeals may be authoritatively promulgated to the natives, and which language must, without doubt, be Hindostanee. A critical knowledge of legal Hindostanee will be therefore essential to all judicial officers; and a moderate time spent in acquiring it will not be in any case lost to them. They should also have opportunities of studying the higher branches of Indian law and observing the Indian practice. The number of European judicial students will not be large enough to form several separate colleges; and I would therefore, in the first instance, send them all to the head-quarters of the Supreme Government, where they would be attached as "novices" to the college of justice, in contact with the supreme court of justice and with the central establishment for the juridical education of the natives. They would there obtain a knowledge of Hindostanee, and of Indian law, Indian courts, and Indian judicial officers; and I would try to arrange that they should practise for a time as advocates before the head-quarter courts. When sufficiently qualified, they would be distributed to the local governments for practical service, and they would then be required further to qualify themselves in the local language. Their first employment would be as Government advocates; from this they would be promoted to be sub-judges, thence to be zillah judges, and so on, according to their qualifications.

I think that the existing service should be at once divided into executive and judicial branches

Transfers from one branch to another.

I have supposed the judicial line to be entirely separated from the executive; but n a few exceptional cases of entire misconception of a man's talents, or loss of his physical vigour, it may be necessary to transfer him under a special rule, rather than sacrifice him altogether. I would permit such transfers only with the sanction of the Governor-General, after a special report of the local governor, and the circumstance should be immediately reported to the Senate. The person proposed for transfer would be sent to the college of justice, or as assistant to the head of a district (according as he is about to enter the judicial or executive department), and would be required to learn his new duties from the beginning, and to pass a very strict examination before being employed in any important office. He would then take his place at the bottom of his new department.

Ordinary local distribution and extraordinary interchange.

Although I would distribute all the civil servants, I am decidedly for breaking down the present impassable line between Bengal, Madras, and Bombay. I would have, as of right, but one service; would, in practice, ordinarily distribute, but would permit extraordinary interchange: in short, would put the whole service on exactly the same relative footing as that on which the different divisions of the Bengal service now are in reference to one another.

My principle would be to make service ordinarily much *more* local than at present; but in extraordinary cases, and especially in the highest grades, less completely and exclusively so. It is, I think, of the greatest importance to have more regard to localities as the ordinary rule. In a service of foreigners we have little occasion to fear the ill effect of local connections; but, on the other hand, infinite evil results from the way in which, to suit the strict rule of promotion and other personal objects, men are continually transferred from one extremity of a presidency to the other, without the smallest regard to local considerations, and especially to language. In Hindostan, Hindostanee is the one universal language which every one, sooner or later, acquires, and a want of knowledge of the language is a deficiency hardly ever attributed to any civil officer of considerable standing in that province. But even in Bengal Proper, ignorance of Bengalee is a most serious practical evil; and I understand that in the Madras presidency the variety of languages and consequent ignorance is much felt. Even where language is no insuperable bar, for many other reasons an officer is infinitely more efficient in a locality with which he is acquainted than in one of which he is totally ignorant. I would make it, then, the rule that men should not only be distributed to different local governments, but that each local governor should, for ordinary service, distribute them to particular provinces, where they might acquire a thorough familiarity with the vernacular language, and other local information. Beyond certain local limits there should be no claim to promotion or change as a *rule*. I would give to local governors the power of transferring within their own limits exceptionally, and on recorded grounds; and to the Governor-General a similar power of transferring from one government to another on very special grounds, to be reported to the Senate.

I have already stated that the offices of the Supreme Government would be filled at discretion from the whole service; and I would especially forbid the gradual formation of any separate bureaucratic service, to which there might, perhaps, be some tendency. Local experience and practice would be the only proper qualification for employment in the offices of the general government.

As it would produce inconvenience if all the best men should go to a favourite local division, it will be better to make the distribution to different governments matter of patronage, as at present. The power of local distribution within a government, and the exceptional transfers, you must trust to the governors and Governor-General, subject to review by the Senate. It will, of course, be desirable so to settle pay and other matters as to make service in different localities as nearly equal in advantages as possible, and to leave as little scope for mere patronage as may be.

Abolition of "college" system in India.

In proposing the third year of English education at Cambridge, I have already absorbed the year now wasted, and frequently much worse than wasted, "in college," as it is called at the presidency towns.*

In 'Modern India' (p. 268) I have explained the Calcutta "College" system. Anything more useless to the very good, and more noxious to all who, for the

* When I say a year, I mean to take an average (perhaps under the fact), as the stay in college really varies from two months to two or three years, according to the idleness, extravagances, and love of a town-life of the individual.

first time let loose in life, are not perfectly steady and under complete self-command (the great majority), it is quite impossible to conceive. There is, in reality, no college or discipline of any kind, but a mere premium on commencing the service by a protracted course of injurious idleness and extravagance. During the whole of this time a young man receives the pay of government, and he does not learn one-half so much as he *must* have picked up in a couple of months in any magistrate's office. He lives just as he pleases, but is required eventually to pass a mild examination in the most unpractical parts of two languages. Beyond his books he hardly learns a word of any language. In spite of all the disadvantages of such a place, he may easily (even if he have no turn for languages) learn enough to pass the examination, such as it is, in, say four months: everything beyond this is sheer idleness. When he is passed as "qualified for the public service," he can neither speak, nor read manuscript, nor do anything else necessary to his duties, and is quite as useless to government as the day he landed; while, on the other hand, he has generally got into debt, and done much to injure himself. Till lately, if he expended the utmost limit of time, he was always passed in the end; and the theoretical rule for sending home again those who failed to pass had fallen for many years into total desuetude; but I am bound here to state that, the practice of remaining "in college" and doing nothing becoming worse and worse, one or two examples have actually been made. One young man has undoubtedly been sent home from Madras, and it is said that two others are to come from Calcutta. But even supposing that the examination is *bonâ fide* passed at the end of a couple of years (*plus* time on medical certificate), very little is gained, and the evils remain nearly as great as ever. When Lord Wellesley founded a college, it was merely because he wished to supply in India an education which has been since provided in England; and now that the Indian College has ceased to exist, he would never have dreamt of the ridiculous farce of keeping young men in the presidency towns to pass in the languages.

A few individuals defend the present system on one solitary ground, viz. that it is desirable that young men should see something of society and the world, and become known to the heads of the government. Most assuredly they are at that age infinitely better away from the society and world of such a place as Calcutta, and their longer stay in England and at the university will fully supply any real desideratum of this kind. It might be well that the principal men of the local government should know something of their future subordinates; but of the good men who pass quickly and go away they know little, and their knowledge of the others is of the most unfavourable description. Even this argument does not in any degree apply to men destined for Upper India now kept in Calcutta; and in all cases the object would be much better effected by afterwards encouraging and promoting the occasional temporary visits to the seat of each government of the men employed under it. I would propose, then, utterly to put an end to the "college" system in India, so far as concerns the executive department. The judicial students would be older and more usefully employed, and I hope that they would not fall into mischief.

Executive department. First apprenticeship of a young civilian.

I would at once send a young executive servant as apprentice to a good magistrate and collector, where he should remain *in statu pupillari*, on a moderate allowance, till really qualified for small duties. A native teacher should be assigned to him; and, as soon as he knows enough of the language, he should translate the ordinary petitions, &c., of the court.

Before noticing particular examinations, I may here say that, as young men should be sufficiently tested both in intellect and character before leaving home, I think it very undesirable and unfair that, after putting them in the way of temptation, and allowing them an exorbitant time to learn a smattering of the languages, you should then, if they do not pass, send them home upon their friends utterly ruined, and too old to begin any other profession. I would rather use discipline towards the refractory. They should be permitted no more than a reasonable time at a good station, and on a tolerable allowance. If a man does not pass, he should be at once banished to the most disagreeable and solitary station to be found, put on the smallest subsistence allowance, and kept there, all leave and indulgence of every kind being absolutely refused (except in case of extreme illness), till he passes. If he does not pass, I would employ him as an English copying clerk, and pay him by the piece.

First examination.

I would require, first, that he should obtain a sufficient colloquial knowledge of the vernacular to understand and make himself understood; second, that he should be acquainted with the most ordinary rules and practice of office. This first, and comparatively slight examination, should be conducted by a committee under the commissioner of the division, who must certify upon honour. As soon as it has been passed, the young man would enter the lowest official grade as an assistant, and would be employed in those minor duties for which he may be fitted, and which are most likely to give him practical knowledge.

Appointment as assistant.

The government of Bengal has the merit of having lately instituted an excellent system of farther examinations.* The first examination will prove nothing beyond the mere rudiments of knowledge. But it is most important that a man should not be farther promoted till he has the knowledge necessary to form a really efficient officer, so far as can be ascertained by examination. Till lately there was no such test in any presidency, and I believed it to be now confined to Bengal proper, but have lately seen a statement that there is something of the kind at Bombay. There can be no doubt that it should be universally enforced, that a high degree of knowledge should be required, and that no man should have any claim whatever to promotion beyond the grade of assistant till it is passed, but, on the contrary, should be altogether debarred from advancement. Those who never attain this qualification must remain throughout their service in the inferior situations for which only they are fitted.

Second examination in official duties.

For so important and severe a test, it is necessary above all things to secure uniformity, and a strict enforcement of the wishes of government. I think, therefore, that we could not trust it to separate divisional committees; and *now* it would be every way advantageous that those who have reached this stage should become known to the heads of the government: I would, therefore, have an examination committee only at the head-quarters of each local government, and the examinations should be annual. All assistants who are duly

* I learn that the Bengal examinations are carried out with great firmness and honesty, and that most of the assistants are successfully puzzled. I would only remark that I would not lay too much stress on a *critical* and polished knowledge of the languages. If a man can familiarly talk and understand, that is quite enough; to require more would be giving an advantage to men of mere philological tastes and talents which would be no way desirable.

prepared would come up to head-quarters for a series of examinations. I would require a complete knowledge of official duties, a familiar acquaintance with the language, and a certificate of temper, energy, and conduct fitting the assistant for higher duties. I would place *relatively* all who pass in each year; and seniority, as a claim to future promotion, should be reckoned from the date of passing this examination. The government, having, at the same time, the opportunity of personally seeing and judging of the passed assistants, would be the better able to determine regarding their future employment.

For whatever department of the executive a man is destined, I think that up to this point all should alike be trained in the ordinary duties of a district, but some distinctions may be henceforth made. Particular men may be set apart for special duties. Some, who have shown aptitude for revenue details, would be employed in settlement duties, some in the special police, some, perhaps, in the departments of salt, opium, and accounts, or in the political department. It is very important that in all departments, of which the superior superintendence is in the hands of the civil service, one or two juniors of that class should also be employed and trained for future promotion. It is absurd to appoint a man suddenly as head of a peculiar department of which he knows nothing; yet this practice is too common in all offices out of the regular executive line (and in none more than the judicial department). If civil servants are to manage the manufacture and sale of salt, opium, &c., they should have some opportunities of acquiring experience.

Subsequent distribution.

The point which we have now reached must be, I should say, the limit of examinations. We cannot carry farther any fixed rule of promotion. We know that without a certain knowledge no man can be efficient; but the *measure* of subsequent efficiency is by no means to be altogether tested by an examination—very far from it. Efficiency may depend on many other qualities than those which can be thus ascertained. Henceforward, then, we come to the more difficult question of discretionary promotion.

Promotion.

I am far from supposing that you can altogether dispense with a limited system of seniority in a service so constituted. It is, in fact, unavoidable; and it must always be remembered that the prescription in favour of seniority is a great guarantee against jobbing or personal favouritism in the distribution of patronage, and is exceedingly effective to that end. Not every governor has nerve to break through the prescription in cases which would fully justify his doing so; but no governor dares to do so when he has not most decided and unquestionable grounds. Every man is well known, and the attempt to promote over the heads of seniors from mere private favour would never be quietly submitted to. If we once admit a very nice weighing of not very remarkable merits, without regard to seniority, in the ordinary routine of office (in which we want good, but not necessarily the best men), we open a wide door for the influence of other feelings.

But, on the other hand, the rule of seniority must be confined within very moderate limits. No unfit man must be appointed to any office, however old his standing; it must merely be a question of the *order* of promotion among the fit, and the highest appointments must be altogether excluded from the seniority system. In the superior offices you must have not only good, but the best men; and in regard to these, the opinion of the service and the public is found to be a sufficient guarantee against jobbing.

I have proposed that seniority for promotion should count from the date of passing, and in the order of passing, the final examination. With this basis, added to a little more support to the governor in excluding from promotion unfit men, and the separation of departments and localities, I think that the order of promotion now obtaining in the North-Western Provinces would become in the main satisfactory, and that it would hardly be prudent to interfere to a very much greater extent with the rule of seniority; nor indeed would there be very great scope for farther change. An assistant, passed as qualified for promotion, will be appointed in his turn (unless there be any special disqualification) deputy to the head of an office; in this position his capacity will be very fully tested, and, if he appear unfit for an independent and important office, it will be the bounden duty of the governor to promote him no farther. In particular instances of a man's proving decidedly unfit for the duties already intrusted to him, I would put it in the power of the government to turn him back to some such inferior duty, on the pay of an assistant or uncovenanted deputy-collector.

But these cases would be, I hope, the exception, and among the fit I should not be disposed to make the order of promotion to the head of an office altogether discretionary. Due regard must be had to special and local circumstances; but otherwise, with the limitations already mentioned, I would let seniority be still the general rule in regard to this particular step of promotion. The best juniors might be employed with the least efficient seniors: they would have their reward afterwards; for beyond the grade of head of a district, or departmental office, I would, I repeat, absolutely repudiate any rule of seniority, as is now, in fact, for the most part the case in the North-West Provinces. I cannot suppose that it would often be desirable to promote a man to a superior appointment till he becomes, by the rule of limited seniority, head of an office ; but that grade attained, he will be immediately eligible for any further promotion, especially if (as is often the case) he has, as deputy, already done the greater part of the work of a district.

I confess that at this stage one effect of my scheme did at first sight somewhat appal me. I could not help reflecting on the unhappy fate of some districts if it had not been in the power of the governor to kick the magistrate and collector upstairs into a judgeship ; and the cessation of that resource, however beneficial to the judicial department, seemed full of danger to the executive. But the power of dispensing with the services of men who become inefficient must be an essential part of the system ; and if you must get rid of the head of an executive office, you must make him retire on a pension, instead of promoting him to be a judge. A fit and tried man, promoted to the head of an office, is not likely, under ordinary circumstances, to become unfit before he is entitled to his regular annuity, and, when he is so entitled, Government must have the fullest power to cease to employ him.

Commissioners of divisions, members of the revenue and criminal boards, chief secretaries to Government ministers, and other superior officers, will then be selected from the best of those who have attained the grade of head of a local office, without any farther regard to seniority beyond the fair preference to the senior as between two *equally* fit men, to which no one will object.

I have referred to the present course of promotion in the executive department of the North-Western Provinces; but when we are assured that promotion no longer goes by seniority, it must not be supposed that the infringements on the strictness of that rule, ventured by Mr. Thomason, are general. I do not know the exact practice in Madras and Bombay; but this I can say, that no assertion regarding the abolition of seniority in any degree applies to Bengal proper. Seniority there holds to a most noxious and improper extent, and is even extended to the higher appointments. Nothing can be more monstrous than the system by which a man, in due course of a seniority service, is made successively—first magistrate, then collector, then district judge, then opium agent, then commissioner of revenue, then judge of the chief court. Seniority is here a great and crying evil, and a change is absolutely necessary. It can only be effected by appointing a permanent and efficient governor, and thoroughly supporting him in a course which will require in the first instance much firmness and much support.

Hardly less important than the rules of appointment to office are those regarding the tenure of office. Till a man is entitled to his regular retiring annuity, deprivation of office or degradation to an inferior appointment must be a special proceeding, on special grounds; but it is a duty which the local governors should be required firmly to perform when necessary; a right of appeal to the Supreme Government being reserved to the deprived individuals.* I would empower the governors either themselves to act as judges in these cases, or to intrust to a sort of jury of peers the duty of giving a verdict regarding either specific offences or alleged inefficiency. They should take into con-

Tenure of office.

* At present these appeals lie to the Home Government direct, which is generally neither competent to judge of the facts nearly so well as the Supreme Indian Government, nor sufficiently firm and free from personal and external influences. No such case should come home till the Governor-General has pronounced upon it.

sideration anything and everything in any way affecting a man's practical efficiency, his ability, conduct, character, private affairs, private habits, and everything else. One provision, however, is absolutely required by every consideration of justice and expediency, and is, in fact, quite necessary to insure the strict enforcement of the principles proposed. I mean a moderate pension for persons shelved without their consent, for reasons other than gross culpability, before they are entitled to the retiring annuity. At present there is no sufficient provision of this kind, and I maintain that without it you cannot get rid of inefficient men, who, holding appointments, not only do not earn their pay, but do infinite harm. You cannot turn a man on the world to starve, if he has been guilty of no crime; yet some men must, from various causes, become inefficient. Men unfit for *any* appointment must be put on a pension-list without scruple. We want something corresponding to the military invalid establishment.

When the period of service necessary to entitle a servant to the regular retiring annuity is completed, I would be by no means so scrupulous as hitherto. The end of the annuity fund should be answered not only for the benefit of individuals but for that of the public service. A man should not only be deprived for special fault or utter incompetency; but it should be open to Government simply to say, "We do not farther desire your services." I should be very far from wishing to discourage the retention of good men; on the contrary, I would hold out every inducement to them to stay; but, when an indifferent man is entitled to the annuity, an annuity should be assigned to him. If a man is not then particularly efficient, he most assuredly never will be so, and it is infinitely better that he should avail himself of a sufficient provision and give place to better men rather than go on till he declines into senility. If he is passed over in the promotion to superior appointments, discontent will infinitely aggravate his defects. Debt, far from being a ground for permitting a man to remain, would be an excellent reason for getting rid of him. I would propose, then, that as each man becomes entitled to his annuity, if he does not intimate his intention of taking it, the local governor should give an opinion regarding his efficiency, say whether it is desirable to retain his services, and submit the case for the orders of the Governor-General. If the decision be in his favour, he should be requested to remain; if not so requested, he would be put upon the annuity as a matter of course. After this period, a man who continues to serve in India is always very liable to break down; and I would therefore farther provide that every man entitled to an annuity, but requested to remain, shall hold his appointment for five years only, at the end of which time he will be re-eligible, but must be specially re-appointed in the same way as the ministers and governors. The Government will thus have an opportunity of periodically reviewing a man's capability, without directly condemning men who were once efficient.

In treating, in the previous chapter, of the civil administration, and of the relation of Government to its servants in general, I have alluded to several principles of discipline and treatment which particularly apply to the civil service. (See especially p. 223, on the subject of personal responsibility and subordination, and the inconvenience of too great independence.)

Salaries.

I have, on a former occasion, stated the rate of salaries received by the different grades of the civil service, and have also compared these salaries with other standards of official remuneration.*

* Modern India, pp. 283-285.

I think it will be found that, considering all the circumstances, I have by no means taken an excessive rate in calulating the market price of European labour in India to be three times as high as the same labour in this country. Few men receiving a fixed income in England would be tempted to go to India for less than three times the amount. Inquire whether in the private labour market European labour is not paid three times more highly in India than in this country. Not only is Indian service infinitely less agreeable, but an appointment in which a man becomes exhausted in a few years is very different from one which he holds for a long life. I have before said that it is by no means desirable to pay too high in proportion to work; but you must pay sufficiently with reference to the duties and responsibility, and especially you must do so if you exact high qualifications and a very large measure of work performed under very rigid conditions.

In this view, and calculating at the rate which I have assumed, I think it must be conceded that most Indian civil offices (supposing them to be efficiently filled) are by no means too highly paid; and those who have had the best opportunities of judging seem to be of this opinion.

It might be well to give a young man as small an allowance as possible till he has passed the first examination and commenced actual service; but when he begins to work, the pay of an assistant is not much more than enough to maintain him in the necessary position, and hardly sufficient to provide against sickness and such contingencies. The final examination passed, and the passed man promoted, and employed on most important duties, he receives on an average the equivalent of about 350*l*. per annum in England, no very exorbitant remuneration. It is not till he becomes, after a long service, head of an office that he is at all highly paid, and then I am sure that, if he is in the least degree fit for the whole charge of a great district or a large judicial establishment, he is anything but over-paid by a salary equivalent to from 700*l.* to 1000*l.* per annum.

In some cases the remuneration may be higher than is absolutely necessary (*e. g.* some political, and perhaps some salt and opium, appointments); but shall I venture to say that in any case it is too little? A proposition to raise salaries is apt to be received with little favour; but if my comparative rate of calculation be admitted (and I see not how it can be controverted), I cannot help suggesting that, in the present state of the service and of promotion, some labour of the highest class is hardly sufficiently remunerated. It is all very well to comment on the fact that some men would never have otherwise earned the salaries which they receive; but there are also many men whose offices could not elsewhere be so well supplied for double the money. In fact, I believe that it is only through the system of entertaining men of all degrees at a fixed tariff, as it were, that Government gets so many good men. It is like contracting with a fisherman to buy all the fish he catches, great and small, at a certain price for each fish; we get many little ones not worth the money, and some large ones worth much more than the money. I have from the first urged that we should substitute natives wherever we can, and should employ the very expensive European agency as little as possible; but when we must and do employ it, we must pay sufficient value for the best articles. If you would insist on a high standard—if you would have, for instance, as judges in your highest Indian courts, men in any degree equal to judges in England (and ought you not to have such men?),—can you hope to get and to keep them if you pay them less for service in India than is paid for service in England? If you said to the fisherman, I will take none of your fish under 10 lbs. weight, he would of course reply, Then you must raise your price for the large fishes. I confess, then, it seems to me that, to secure for a continuance that high talent and efficiency which are indispensable to the highest offices of a great empire, you must make up your mind to put sufficient premiums on the highest prizes. As the service now stands, the first men by no means accumulate fortunes; their services lead to nothing in their native country, and altogether they are inadequately rewarded. The smallness of the reward resulting from the highest Indian service is notorious and patent to all, and the evidence recorded on the subject is incontestable. Considerable salaries are drawn in high offices in India, but they are also attended with large expenses, and they are only reached late in the service, and held for short periods; so that, in fact, men come home after spending the whole of the vigorous portion of their lives in the service, and attaining the highest posts, with but a very moderate provision, and no opportunity of subsequent employment or emolument. Compare this with the reward of practical and successful labour in this country—public or private—lay or professional. I have instanced legal prizes, and we may also take directors of joint-stock companies or managers of mercantile houses. The conduct of important interests is always highly paid—practical talent and labour always bear their value in this country. Much will be gained by rendering the promotion of the best men more rapid, and by opening a field for Indian service and distinction in the home Government; but we must still calculate salaries with reference to the nature of the labour required.

Not only is European labour more high priced in India than in England, but I may also say that from really working men a much more complete, devoted, and unrelaxed labour is exacted than in the vast majority of English or colonial appointments. A civil servant is interdicted from all private business of every kind; and many men are devoted body and mind, in office and out of office, to their official duties, in a way of which most quiet holders of quiet offices in this country have little idea. In fact, the work done by some men in many of the most important offices I believe to be in amount of labour far beyond *anything* known in this country—it is so constant and unbroken. In England a man of office or business has his hours in office and his hours out of office, his holidays, his vacations, and his relaxations, his changes from writing to speaking and from town to country, his trips up the Rhine, and his visits to Scotland. But in India, in most instances, he has nothing of the kind, unless he throws up work altogether, and takes long sick-leave. Day after day, it may be night after night, month after month, and year after year, he goes round and round in the same eternal mill, and, well or ill, any indulgence must be purchased by a large sacrifice of salary; a fact which must be a material consideration in estimating the rate of payment. I do not at present refer to the lax system of leave on medical certificate, which I shall shortly propose to alter; it is only by the abuse of some rules that the harshness of others is mitigated. Referring to the present leave rules,* it will be seen that the only indulgence without sacrifice of salary permitted to working servants is one month's leave in the year, if it is convenient to Government to give that leave, and to the servant to take it, and provided that no loss is incurred by Government. Since, owing to the slowness of travelling and difficulties of moving in India, most men are not in a situation to avail themselves of a

* Modern India, p. 279.

single month, it was formerly permitted (and it was no more than reasonable and just) to accumulate the leave of three successive years, and then to take three months at one time; but Lord Ellenborough was pleased, in that amicable spirit towards the civil service which distinguished him, to revoke the latter part of the privilege, and to restrict absence to a single month, at intervals of a complete year. The consequence is, that three-fourths of the officers of Government cannot and do not take the month, and practically, on an average, a man has not this month's leave more than once in several years.

London is not after all so hot or disagreeable a place as an Indian station; but I ask how would a member of the ministry, or a salaried officer of Government, or a judge, like to be so rigorously confined to his office as only to have a month's leave of absence once in three or four years, no railways to go out of town by, and no leave to go anywhere, unless he submit to have his pay cut. How would a county court judge, or a bankruptcy commissioner, receiving 1200*l*., 1500*l*., or 1800*l*. per annum for running down by rail to his jurisdiction to sit a moderate number of times in the year, and prohibited from giving himself more than three months' leave at a time—how would he like to be subjected to our Indian rules, and kept close to his work? It is a sort of thing that people don't understand in this country. I do not compare with ancient abuses, but with modern offices considered to be hard worked on the English scale; and it seems to me that the aforesaid county court judges (said to be under paid) and bankruptcy commissioners hold as *valuable* appointments as the highest of the working officers under our Indian Government, without doing one-half of the work, and without the necessity of qualifications of nearly so high an order; and that this is a fair comparison of payments and duties.

We must consider the union of mental and physical qualities required in an Indian servant. Mere men of action may be obtained at a comparatively cheap price, mere men of the pen are sometimes not very highly remunerated; but a combination of these qualities is much more valuable, and must be taken into account in estimating the rate of salary. I believe that there are many men who fill with great credit important civil offices in this country who would entirely fail in Indian duties.

I would then, I repeat, go on the principle of paying inferior men in inferior appointments no more than they are worth, but sufficiently remunerating the efficient holders of the most important offices, bearing in mind what I have before asserted—that our civil administration and superior civil officers are the cheapest ever known in the country, that India can afford to pay for being efficiently governed, and that the cost of the civil service is, after all, small compared to the army, and the proportion of European officers infinitely less. Even while requiring increased qualifications, I would not increase the average remuneration of each individual. I think that, in regard to a good many appointments and a good many persons, money might be saved, but that it may be eventually necessary again to expend it in providing sufficient rewards for the highest appointments and the most efficient persons.

Leave of absence.

I must also here touch on the important question of the rules regarding leave of absence, which must now be considered and decided. The present rules are on all hands admitted to be obsolete and inapplicable to the present day, and several attempts have been made fundamentally to alter them; but it is one of the most remarkable instances of the evil resulting from the imperfections of, and division of power in, the Home Government, that a change on the necessity of which all are agreed has been from time to time delayed, and eventually postponed to await the result of the legislation for India which now approaches.

Three main defects are evident and undeniable in the present rules,—first, that there is an inconvenient and detrimental laxity in permitting leave, on sick certificate, for long terms within the geographical limits of the East India Company's charter; second, that there is the most unfair and injurious obstacle to all leave to Europe for however short a term; and third, that there is a want of sufficient temporary indulgences to working men.

There is no medium between no work and excessive work. A man is permitted to go on sick leave to the Cape, Australia, Syria, &c., for two years at a time, drawing a great portion of his allowances, retaining his appointment, and the time being counted as residence in India. He may (and some do) repeat this several times, so that seven or eight years of his Indian service may in some cases be thus spent in idleness, without any compensating advantage whatever, such as might accrue from the mental cultivation of a visit to Europe, and men who work throughout their whole term are on exactly the same footing as those who have done nothing of the kind. Medical certificates may be somewhat lightly granted, but by far the greatest abuse is on the part of men who are without doubt fully disqualified for service, but who take advantage of this rule to spin out their salaries for a couple of additional years, during which they deprive those who really do the work of the appointment and the pay, while they themselves cannot and never expect really to resume their duties for any length of time. It has become quite a fashion for men holding the highest appointments to take leave to the very last day which the rules will permit, then merely to rejoin for a few weeks or months in the cold weather, and resign before the disagreeable season comes round again. This is most assuredly an abuse. It is every way an object to give every possible indulgence to working men in order to get more work out of them, but most certainly not to permit the retention of appointments of which the possessors cannot or will not do the work.

On the other hand, the case of a man who prefers to come to Europe is very different. He sacrifices his appointment, he may or may not be entitled to a small furlough allowance, the time does not count, on his return he may be knocked about till he is a beggar before he again falls into a good appointment; and altogether the disadvantages are so great as to amount almost to a prohibition of leave to Europe for a short or moderate period to every man holding a superior appointment. It is certain that it is infinitely better that he should come to Europe than go to the Cape, and he can now get to the former in a shorter time than he can to the latter. The disparity is therefore an absurd anomaly which ought long ago to have been rectified. It seems that a law prohibits the receipt of any portion of Indian allowances beyond certain limits, and that there are difficulties in the way of the Indian Government's sufficiently legislating on the subject. It cannot be doubted that Parliament will be willing to remove these difficulties. All that is wanted is to remove the geographical line of demarcation, which had its origin in an entirely different state of things, and to permit the government of India to make good and equitable rules applicable to all places alike.

The great difficulty and principal object to be kept in view is to combine a fair degree of indulgence and consideration towards the working servants of government, with a sufficient regard to the permanency of incumbents and to the great evils resulting from frequent change of administration. I have all along dwelt on this latter object as most essential. But at the same time we must remember that it is quite impossible to bind down exotic servants in a tropical climate by the rules which you might (but do not) apply to men serving in their own country and climate. In fact, the holders of *permanent* offices in this country seem to forfeit office by no length of absence or degree of incompetence; but the question is put in the committee—Would you permit a secretary of state to be absent for two years and then to resume his appointment? Now, even waiving the temporary nature of the latter appointment, you cannot argue that, because you would not permit a man holding such an office in this country to absent himself for a long period, you therefore would not in some necessary cases permit certain absences from Indian appointments. The cases are not parallel. It is hardly possible that a European devoted to the harder services of the Indian government can go on for a protracted period without some indulgence, and you bring about the very evil against which you would guard if, on every such occasion, you absolutely sever from his appointment the man of the greatest experience and fitness. A temporary absence may be much less injurious than a frequent entire transfer into new hands, especially if the rules regarding acting appointments be changed in a way which I shall presently propose. I think it will be found that the interests of a district are not incompatible with a fair indulgence to individual officers, but rather that the efficient administration of the one depends on a fair treatment of the other. So far as the personal interests of the service are concerned, it comes to the same thing whether appointments are retained or vacated during leave, because after all the same appointments are distributed among the same body, and in either case what is gained in one way is lost in another; if appointments are vacated there is quicker promotion;

if not, they are later attained and longer held. But it makes a great difference if we attach to leave to Europe the penalty of loss of appointment, and other prohibitory sacrifices, none of which appertain to leave to any part of Asia, Africa, or Australia; and if we at all desire that civil servants should visit Europe, we must put the rules on a more equitable footing in this respect. As regards the period of leave to be permitted without sacrifice of appointment, it is merely a question of degree. No one would think it desirable absolutely to vacate the appointment every time that a very short leave is granted. We must consider, then, where is the point at which the evil of absence begins to exceed the evil of change of the permanent incumbent. I think that, as an ordinary rule, the present term of two years on sick certificate is too long. It is in most cases decidedly injurious to permit a man to absent himself for so long a time, and then reclaim his appointment; and as at present some take leave within the prescribed limits keeping their appointments, some go to England sacrificing their appointments, we must in future, if we would avoid an increased number of acting appointments, adopt some middle course. In abolishing geographical limits, I would therefore, first, diminish the period of privileged absence; second, diminish the absentee allowance now received; and, third, remedy the present inconvenient and unjust rules regarding acting appointments.

It seems to me that one year is the proper limit to absence without loss of appointment. It will only cause injury if you refuse a good man, who has been many years doing good service, a moderate leave, such as may enable him to recruit his health, see his friends, and attend to his private affairs. If you permit this moderate term of absence, the duties may in the mean time be very well managed by a good deputy, after the fashion prescribed by the principal; and the term of absence completed, you will again have the permanent incumbent thoroughly acquainted with the locality and the duties. I believe that nothing more tends to prevent men from becoming at all local or acquiring local knowledge, than the necessity of giving up an appointment if it be necessary to visit Europe for ever so short a time. After such a visit, it is at present a hundred to one that a man is employed in a totally different place, different appointment, and different duties from those which he relinquished. This then must be borne in mind if we are inclined to carry too far our horror of acting appointments. But on the other hand, we must not permit leave to extend beyond necessary limits, and I should say that a year is sufficient for the purposes to which I have alluded. If a man is so shattered in health as to require a long residence in Europe, or for other reasons desires a long leave, it is every way proper that he should give up his appointment; and I would only enjoin on the Indian government to take the earliest opportunity of employing him on his return.

There is considerable ground for debate as to the extent to which it is desirable to encourage a resort to Europe. There can be no doubt of the great advantage in many ways of such a change of scene, and the service at present suffers much from the obstacles to such intercourse. But it is also argued, and not without reason, that a too prolonged residence in England is not always beneficial to the personal efficiency of an ordinary Indian servant. He may be apt to acquire too much of English habits and English tastes for future rough service and for contentment with his lot in India. I should therefore say that, while it is by no means undesirable that a man who has any intellectual tastes should *once* take a long furlough, and supply what has been wanting to his English education, long leave should not be too much encouraged, or repeated too often. In this view it seems to me that the desirable limit very much coincides with that which I have fixed on other grounds. Nothing does a man so much good as a run home during a single year. Change of climate, scene, &c., everything is beneficial to him physically and mentally: he sees and learns much—his body is invigorated—his mind refreshed—while, on the other hand, he has not time to settle into English habits and luxuries, or to forget his work and become idle. Such occasional trips after a course of hard service I would by all means encourage, and would restore a man to his appointment on his return.

I would not propose to give Indian allowances in Europe. I have already assumed that a man is paid for service in India three times as high as in England—I would give him then, during these absences, one-third of his allowances. But Government should not profit by the illness or absence of its servants, as under Lord Ellenborough's rules it does. All that is cut from absentees ought to be received by those who act; I would provide that Government should not be a loser, and no more.

Acting rules.

At present, when a man takes leave for ever so short a time, his whole official power and responsibility pass absolutely from him. This seems quite unnecessary, and in many ways injurious. Whenever it is in any way possible to do so, I would invariably appoint a subordinate to act for a superior during the limited terms of absence which I would permit; and I see not why, if the principal be within reach, he should not communicate to his acting deputy such instructions as he may very well give without being on the spot. The general system and tone of the district would thus be preserved, and every acting appointment would be no longer, as at present, a complete change of management. For instance, when the head of an office has a few months' leave from his hot district station to the neighbouring hills, and his deputy acts for him, why should he not in some degree supervise the proceedings of the latter? and even if he go for a somewhat longer time, and on a more distant journey, he might leave notes of his proceedings and mode of management to which his *locum tenens* should be bound to conform. I would make it distinctly the rule, that, in all acting appointments, it should be the duty of the *locum tenens* to act not exclusively on his own ideas, but to carry out *bonâ fide* and earnestly the principles and practice of the permanent incumbent, unless he obtain the sanction of higher authority for altering them on sufficient grounds. Future favour and promotion should very largely depend on an honest fulfilment of these views, so that we might not have so much of that misdirected energy and constant undoing by one man of the doings of another, which is too common in India. If a man is fit for his appointment there can be no harm in carrying on his duties when he is absent as he would have carried them on if he had been present; and if he is unfit, the sooner he is shown up the better. But two men may be each very good officers, yet differ in their modes and ideas; and it is most objectionable that the whole system of a district or an office should be altered during temporary absences. On such occasions I would encourage, as much as possible, private arrangements, and would attend to personal wishes, in regard to acting appointments. Thus A, in applying for leave, might say that B is willing to conduct his duties, and that he would have confidence in B, and requests that Government will make that arrangement.*

* A county court judge when he absents himself (within prescribed

By these provisions, and by the proposed decrease of privileged absence from two years to one, I think that much of the evil of acting appointments would be obviated, and that there would be much less objection to short and temporary absences involving no change of system or cessation of responsibility.

I have several times referred to the mistaken system of working a willing man to death, by way of making up for those who don't work. When a man has been long slaving in the public service and has brought his duties to a state which will admit of a temporary absence, I see not why Government should grudge to give him a moderate leave: he will do all the more work when he comes back. There is a great deal too much indulgence to men who go on from medical certificate to medical certificate, and a great deal too harsh measure to those who devote themselves to their work and do not go on the sick list till absolutely compelled to do so. Two months' leave in a year (when the public service will permit of such indulgence) is not considered an exorbitant allowance in any public office in this country, and might enable men in India to obtain a change which they cannot effect in one month; and if a man has been at work for years without a day's leave, he may fairly be allowed to accumulate a few months' leave. It would be, of course, in the discretion of Government to be guided by circumstances; but it can tend to no man's efficiency to go on for many years together without break or variety in the hard duties of a hot station in the plains, and, if once in three or four years, with or without medical certificate, he can have a short leave to the hills, while his duties are carried

periods) is allowed to appoint his own deputy at his discretion. This would be going a little too far; but the wishes of the permanent incumbent should receive due consideration at the hands of government.

on by his deputy under his direction, it will infinitely tend to improve his efficiency and prolong his service, to the great advantage of the public. I would therefore strongly urge a reasonable bestowal of this kind of indulgence, so far as is consistent with the discharge of public duties. The system must not be carried too far—a resort to the hills, whether of a Governor-General or a district magistrate, must not be habitual but exceptional. There can be no more injurious error than to confound the use with the abuse of indulgences; and Lord Ellenborough made no greater mistake than when, because he found one or two idle red-faced fellows on medical certificate in the hills, he thought fit to abridge the already scanty privileges of working men. I would have as little as possible to depend on medical certificates, but would have no foolish jealousy of indulging, as far as conveniently may be, those who deserve it, be they at the moment sick or well. It is easier to preserve health than to restore it when lost.

Computation of term of service.

At present all leave within the Indian limits counts towards the prescribed period of Indian residence; all leave beyond those limits does not count. As both must clearly be put on the same footing, we must settle some middle rule as to computing the period of residence. It will be found that hitherto out of twenty-two years' nominal residence an average aggregate of several years has been spent on sick leave, and it would be manifestly unjust to cut off the privilege of computation without giving some compensation in counting the time of service. I should say that the fairest arrangement will be to take the average absence on leave within Indian limits during the term of service, to deduct that time from the prescribed period of residence, and to provide that in future so much time spent on leave (without reference to geography), and no more, shall count as service. Not less than two years must be allowed on this ground, exclusive of short temporary leave. The real average of actual and effective service will be by no means diminished, but the term will henceforth be a measure of active employment, not of nominal service. It must also be remembered that civil servants will in future go out somewhat older than hitherto.

With reference to my former proposal to employ Indian servants under the Home Government, and the anticipated abolition of geographical distinctions, I would provide that, as regards pensions, &c., half the time of service under the Home Government should count as service in India.

Pensions.

I have already alluded to the necessity of pensioning men incapable of efficient service. To provide for unavoidable cases you must either have sinecures in India or pensions in England. The latter plan then is much the cheapest and best. At present there is no attempt at provision for a man who has not completed ten years' residence, and whose health compels him to retire from India; and after ten years' residence till completion of the full term, there is only a contingent provision from the surplus value of untaken annuities, if there happen to be any of the latter—a fund which has hitherto been available, but which will be in future altogether precarious. This is a most objectionable state of things, and one which goes far to excuse the retention of unfit men. It is undoubtedly the duty of the Government, after having entertained, with sufficient precaution, fit men, in some way to provide for such as become unfitted in its service; and I would therefore propose that a moderate invalid pension should be at once provided.

The retiring annuity after the full period of service is

most useful, but is not really as concerns the Government nearly so large a pension as is usually supposed. An excellent arrangement has been lately made, and one which puts the pension in its true light. It is no longer necessary, as heretofore, to make up half the value of the annuity in order to receive the full 1000*l.* per annum. A man may now (provided a certain annual number is not exceeded) claim the accumulated value of his contributions to the fund, *plus* an annuity of 500*l.* per annum, in part value for which the government receives all the contributions of men who die or retire without receiving the benefit of the annuity fund, or continue in the service till they have paid more than the half value. Government is, in fact, towards the service merely an insurance office for deferred annuities, granting more favourable terms than a private insurance office, and thus really contributing to the value of about 300*l.* per annum as a government pension. This is certainly no extravagant allowance for such service. As the object should be that all whose services the government do not desire to retain should retire when qualified for pensions, I do not see that there is any sufficient reason for limiting the annual number of retirements. The limited number of annuities allowed has been hitherto sufficient; but we are now getting into years (1828 to 1831) in which there will be an unusual number of men qualified for pension, and under the proposed system a larger proportion will retire. I would therefore abolish the limit of number, and merely give the fixed allowance to all who have served their time, just as it is in the army.

There is much to be said in favour of an increasing pension for increased length of service; but it would be a temptation to men to hang on in the service when they are not wanted, and would be, I think, on the whole, undesirable as a rule. But when particular individuals, at the special request of the Government, do good service beyond the usual period, they should certainly be rewarded with additional pension. I would leave it to the Home Government, acting on the recommendation of the Governor-General, to bestow special pensions for special services.

The pensions to widows and children are provided almost entirely by the contributions of the service, forming a fund which is, to a small extent, aided by, and is under the control of, the Home Government. Till lately these pensions, to which all contributed alike, were (by a most absurd rule) only available in the absence of private means, so that a careful man's family was no better off than that of the most improvident. This rule has been abrogated by the service within the last two or three years. I do not know whether the Court of Directors have yet sanctioned the proceeding, but there can be no doubt of its justice and necessity. It may, however, be expedient to diminish the incomes of the families of men who have been but a very short time in the service, and have contributed very little to the fund.

I here annex the rules regarding leave, acting, and pensions which I would propose:—

Proposed Civil Service Rules.

1. All geographical distinctions are abolished.
2. Two years' general leave (exclusive of temporary leave), and no more, to be reckoned in period of service.
3. Twenty-two years' service, including two years' general leave, to entitle to retiring pension.*

* Or if we make it as at present twenty-five years' service, including three years' furlough and two years' privileged general leave, it will come to the same thing. The only difference will be, that men who have not already taken furlough will do so (as they do now) at the end of service, and receive 500*l.* per annum as furlough allowance instead of pension.

4. Temporary leave may be granted by Government, if it be not inconvenient to the public service, for periods not exceeding two months of each year; and said leave may be accumulated for three years, and not more, and may then be granted at one time. Absentee to be subject to deduction only of such expense as Government may actually incur in consequence of his absence.

5. General leave, not exceeding one year, may be granted after seven years' continuous resident service, and may be repeated after similar terms of service. Appointment to be retained during absence, and absentee to draw one third of his salary. Active service for two years after return to be a condition of leave: failing which, whole salary received to be refunded.

6. Officers incapacited by sickness may anticipate the whole or any portion of the leave permitted by Rule 5: provided that no leave under this rule will be granted till after three years' continuous resident service; no second leave till after ten years' total service; and no person shall have the benefit of this rule more than twice.

7. After ten years' service furlough for three years may be granted on same terms as at present; but of whole absence on furlough and general leave no more than the two years prescribed above will count as service: provided also that no person who has taken leave under Rules 5 or 6 shall be entitled to furlough till after seven years' continuous service from the conclusion of the last leave, and that all future claim to leave under other rules shall be counted only from time of return from furlough.

8. Sick furlough on half-furlough allowance may be granted at any time, and may be repeated; but every person returning from sick-leave must be examined,

with a view to ascertain his fitness for farther efficient service, and, if not fit, shall be pensioned.

9. In all cases of absence without sacrifice of appointment, the immediate subordinate of, or person recommended by, the absentee shall, if possible, act for him.

Every officer acting for another shall be guided by the instructions and views of the absentee, unless the same be disapproved by Government.

10. An officer acting at his own station, for another absent on temporary leave, shall receive no acting allowance; and if at a different station, only his necessary expenses, at fixed rates, which shall be deducted from the absentee.

11. An officer acting for another absent on general leave shall receive the sum deducted from the absentee. But if he have another appointment of his own, he is to receive no more than the higher of the two salaries; and if another officer acts in his appointment, the same deductions shall be made from his salary as if he were himself on leave.* Surpluses to form a surplus fund, from which the Government to grant personal allowances to officers returned from furlough and without appointments, till they obtain permanent offices.

12. Any officer incapacitated (without culpability) from farther service in India, before having completed ten years' resident service, to be entitled to a pension of 150*l.* per annum, *plus* the value of his subscriptions to

* Thus, if A has 3000 rupees per mensem, B 1500, and C 600—A goes on leave, B acts for him, and C acts for B—C would receive 600 + 1000 (two-thirds of B's salary), but he may not draw more than the higher of the two salaries; he therefore has 1500, and 100 are credited to government. B has two-thirds of A's salary (2000) + one-third of his own (500) = 2500. A during his absence has 1000 rupees. But if B does both his own duty and A's, his salary would be 1500 + 2000 = 3500 (which exceeds the higher salary), and 500 would be credited to government. Considerable surpluses would accumulate in this way.

the annuity fund; after completion of ten years and before completion of full term, to 250*l.* per annum, *plus* value of subscriptions.

13. After completion of prescribed term every civil servant shall be entitled to a retiring annuity of 500*l.* per annum, *plus* value of his accumulated subscriptions. For farther services beyond prescribed term, Home Government to have power to grant special pensions in special cases.

14. Widows and children of men who have served less than ten years to receive from the civil fund per annum, widow 150*l.*, each child 50*l.*

Of men who have served more than ten years, widows 300*l.*, each child 100*l.* (as at present); in all cases without reference to private property.

CHAPTER VI.

MILITARY ESTABLISHMENTS.

Financial importance of the army; its statistics; distinction between regulars and troops commonly called irregular; cost of the army; comparative cost of different arms, of different elements, and of different presidencies; composition of the native army; comparison with former periods; necessity of European troops; regular sepoy army, its state, causes of its deficiencies; employment of natives in superior grades; proposed cavalry arrangements; proposed infantry arrangements; infusion of new blood into the native army; the commissariat, proposed change; supply of European officers to the army; naval establishments.

It is principally with reference to finance that I shall venture to touch on military subjects, and if I incidentally allude to some opinions on matters not purely financial, contracted during a service in which civilians are brought into very close contact with military affairs, I hope that I shall be excused.

Financial importance of the army.

The army is not only vastly important as the means of that security, without which the best government would be of little avail, but is also the overwhelming financial item, on the regulation of which our financial prosperity principally depends. It is our army which is really the expensive part of our government of India. While we owe to it our superiority over the native powers, we have at the same time obtained that superiority by a more lavish expenditure. Our armies have been less numerous than those against which they fought, but they have cost infinitely more; and it is in the cost of our army, not of our civil establishments, that the natives of the country pay for the advantages of our rule. The reason that we have smaller funds at our disposal for public works and public magnificence than the Mahommedan emperors, is simply that the money saved by our more economical civil administration is lost by the much larger military expenditure. We have incurred of late many extraordinary military expenses, but even supposing these to be abated, the annual cost of the army maintained on its present scale is still enormous. It amounts, in fact, to about two-thirds of the net revenues of the country—to twice as much as every other charge of every kind put together.

Our net revenue, as usually calculated, is in round numbers about twenty-one millions sterling; but of this sum about three millions go to payment of the interest of debt and stock, and of the remaining eighteen millions upwards of twelve millions is the cost of the army, and about six millions is the sum devoted to the whole of the civil, political, marine, and ecclesiastical expenses at home and abroad, judicial and police charges, public works, post-offices, outlying settlements (including Scinde), and everything else of every kind. It is clear, then, that the possibility of a moderately cheap government of India depends on our military system.

The peculiarity of our military situation is this,—that neither are the numbers of the army very excessive in proportion to the magnitude and population of the country, nor is the expense of each soldier very great when judged by European standards. But it is when we compare the expense with the revenues of the country and the price of labour that we find the great disproportion. We have not a larger army than France, while we have a much larger territory and population; but then our Indian army costs, I believe, nearly as much as that of France, notwithstanding a very much smaller revenue, and in a country where labour is vastly cheaper.

The Government has at its disposal, in round numbers, about 310,000 fully disciplined troops, of which about 22,000 are regular contingents under European officers paid by native states, and about 288,000 constitute the British Indian army. Of this latter force the numbers attached to each presidency are nearly as follows:— Its statistics.

Bengal (including Agra and the Punjab)	165,000
Madras	65,000
Bombay	58,000

The different arms of the service stand as follows:—

Infantry	234,000
Cavalry	35,000
Artillery and engineers	19,000

The army comprises—

Europeans, including European officers of Native troops	50,000
Natives	238,000

The Europeans are classed as follows:—

Her Majesty's troops	29,480
Company's men	14,579
Company's commissioned officers	6,297

And the different arms are thus composed:—

Cavalry—	
Europeans	3,700
Native regulars	10,200
Native irregulars	21,100
Infantry—	
European	32,500
Native, with European officers of companies	162,000
Native, with Native officers of companies (commonly called "irregular")	39,500
Artillery and engineers—	
Europeans	7,700
Natives, including gun Lascars and ordnance drivers	11,300

In classifying the different arms I have used a periphrasis in regard to the infantry usually designated as "irregular," because the term is not, properly speaking, in any way correct. The irregular infantry are just as regular soldiers as those called regulars. They are disciplined and equipped in exactly the same way. But the only European officers are a commandant, a second in command, and an adjutant. The officers of companies are exclusively native, and are efficient men, promoted on the ground of fitness, not of seniority. Some of these corps are also more or less local. The regulars, on the other hand, are supposed to be provided with European officers of companies, *besides* a peculiar class of native commissioned officers, and this is the sole distinction between the two branches of the infantry service. With this explanation, then, I shall use the conventional terms regular and irregular infantry. In the cavalry, on the other hand, the irregulars are on a totally different footing from the regulars. They are officered in the same way as the irregular infantry, and the men find their own horses, arms, and equipments, and dress, ride, and fight in purely native fashion.

Distinction between regulars and irregulars.

In regard to cost there is a discrepancy in this as in all other matters of account between my statements and those officially furnished to the parliamentary committees, resulting from the fashion which still obtains at the India House of turning the Company's rupees into the extinct Sicca rupees, and thence into pounds at 10 rupees per pound. I believe that 10 current Company's rupees per pound sterling is the most correct value,* and it is certainly the most con-

Cost of the army.

* There is more silver in a Company's rupee than in two shillings, but a smaller seignorage on silver is taken in India, so that, on an average, I believe that a rupee in India and two shillings in England will purchase, as nearly as may be, the same weight of silver.

venient rate of exchange; but I must correct the India House accounts by 6½ per cent. to bring them to the ordinary standard.

The annual expense of the army, according to the latest accounts, stands thus:—

	£.
Queen's troops in India	960,000
Company's cavalry	1,207,000
Artillery and engineers	652,000
Company's infantry	3,616,000
Staff	416,000
Medical	142,000
Ordnance	155,000
Commissariat	1,249,000
Buildings, works, stores, &c. &c. &c.	1,701,000
Total in India	10,098,000
Add 6½ per cent. difference between Sicca and Company's rupees	656,000
Total	10,754,000
Military charges defrayed at home	1,300,000
Grand total	£12,054,000
Or Company's rupees	12,05,40,000

Of the military expenses defrayed in India, the relative cost of each army is as follows:—

	£.
Bengal army	5,269,000
Madras ditto	2,536,000
Bombay ditto	2,293,000*

The ordinary military expenses defrayed at home are nearly as follows:—

* These accounts make the Bengal military expenses smaller, and those of Bombay larger, than the presidency accounts hitherto furnished. This must arise from Bombay having formerly debited Bengal with part of the cost of its army, on the ground of its being employed beyond its own strict limits; and we thus find that the Bombay deficiency was much greater than before supposed; and the only ground on which its financial state could be explained is taken away.

	£.
Payments on account of her Majesty's troops .	300,000
Military stores	250,000
Transport of troops and stores . . .	40,000
Retired pay, &c., of military officers . .	600,000 *
Military pensions	70,000 *
Recruiting charges	40,000
Total . .	£1,300,000

But many of these charges have been considerably exceeded in all the late years of war, and some are gradually increasing.

Comparative cost of different arms;

The numbers and expense of different branches of the army vary from year to year, but, as nearly as I can calculate, the following is about the average comparative annual cost of each soldier of each arm (including officers) as shown by the returns:—

	£.	s.	d.	
European cavalry	53	0	0	each man.
Regular Native cavalry . . .	47	0	0	,,
Irregular Native cavalry . .	37	0	0	,,
European infantry . . .	29	10	0	,,
Regular Native infantry . .	18	5	0	,
Irregular Native infantry . .	11	0	0	,

I shall not attempt to distribute the general military expenses, but to compare regular with irregular cavalry we must add the cost of horses, &c. &c., found for the former, and which the latter themselves find; and, to compare Europeans with natives, we must add the expenses in Europe, and for barrack accommodation, incurred on account of European soldiers and officers. These charges, as regards European soldiers, I take at 10*l.* per man per annum; and I find that the home charges on account of European officers of native troops cannot be calculated at less than at the rate of 3*l.* per

* These are continually increasing charges. I have made an allowance for marine pensions.

man. To get the true comparative annual cost of each description of force I have, therefore, made the following Table :—

Branch of Service.	Regimental charge.			Cost to Government of providing Horse and Cavalry Equipments.	English and other Expenses of European Soldiers and Officers.	True comparative Cost.			Proportional Cost of Cavalry and Infantry.	
Each man of—	£.	s.	d.	£. s. d.	£. s. d.	£.	s.	d.		
Dragoons	53	0	0	27 0 0	10 0 0	90	0	0	Cavalry.	5
Regular Native cavalry .	47	0	0	23 0 0	3 0 0	73	0	0		4
Irregular Native cavalry	37	0	0	. .	. .	37	0	0		2
European infantry . .	29	10	0	. .	10 0 0	39	10	0	Infantry.	3½
Regular Native infantry	18	5	0	. .	3 0 0	21	5	0		2
Irregular Native infantry	11	0	0	. .	. .	11	0	0		1

It thus appears that four dragoons cost as much as five regular native troopers, and two European foot soldiers as much as three and a half regular sepoys, or seven irregular sepoys. If we allow something additional for the indirect cost of European soldiers we may thus put it :—

Cost of 3 dragoons = 4 regular Native troopers.
,, 1 regular Native trooper = 2 irregulars.
,, 1 European foot soldier = 2 regular sepoys.
,, 1 regular sepoy = 2 irregular sepoys.

The regular cavalry is, it will be seen, a very expensive arm, but I find that my calculation very much corresponds with one which I remember to have heard from a very high authority, who made a regiment of dragoons to cost the state about 70,000*l.* per annum, and a regiment of regular native cavalry about 40,000*l.* A dragoon regiment in India averages 700 strong, and a native cavalry regiment 500 ; so that this would make the cost of the dragoon 100*l.*, of the native trooper 80*l.*, per annum, being a little higher, but in the same proportion as my calculation. The larger sum is, for the most part, accounted for by the difference of 6½ per cent., which must be added to my figures.

of different elements;

Taking the whole *personnel* as distinguished from the *matériel* of the army, I calculate that the European troops cost something more than one-fourth—about 28 per cent.—of the whole charge, which leaves 72 per cent. as the cost of the native army. In the regular native army I believe that the European officers cost about the same as the native men and officers. In the irregular force (in all, cavalry and infantry, about 60,000 men) the proportion of the European element is very much less, but then the large army staff, wholly European, makes up the difference; and, altogether, we may take the European officers of the native army at about half the whole cost. This calculation, then, gives for the whole army—

Cost of European troops	28 per cent.
„ European officers of Native troops .	36 „
„ Native soldiers and officers . .	36 „

and of different presidencies.

There is not a very great difference in the comparative cost of the soldiers of different presidencies; those of Bengal seem to be rather the cheapest. But there is a very singular discrepancy in the cost of the staff. With the exception of one year, 1848-9, in which the Bengal staff exhibits an extraordinary charge (probably caused by the war batta), the general average of ten years gives the proportion of staff-charges as follows:—Bengal, 14; Madras, 13; Bombay, 12—notwithstanding the great disproportion of the armies. The Madras staff-charge is regularly increasing, and in the last year stated we have—

Bengal staff	£149,217
Madras ditto	148,106

—although the armies are in the proportion of 165 to 65, and the Bengal staff includes that of the Commander-in-Chief in India. This is an example of the result of the separate governing establishments of the minor presidencies, and should be looked to. Madras officials may have grounds for complaining that they are not allowed money enough for useful purposes, but they should also look at home.

The Madras army consists entirely of regulars, those of Bengal and Bombay include a considerable proportion of irregulars.

Composition of the native army.

The Bengal regular infantry is composed for the most part of particular classes from a particular part of the country. The great majority of the sepoys come from Lower Hindostan, from Lucknow and Cawnpore down to Patna. The predominating castes are Rajpoots and Bramins of the cultivating classes. Men of low or doubtful castes are strictly excluded.

The Bombay army is a much more miscellaneous body; men of inferior height, caste, &c., are there admitted. Many Hindostanees serve in the Bombay army, the others are natives of the west of the peninsula of every class. I understand that there are even many Christians and Jews in the Bombay native army. I believe that a large proportion of the sepoys of the Madras army are Mahommedans, the remainder Hindoos of various classes; and that they are almost all natives of the south of India.

Of the cavalry, a majority are everywhere Mahommedans, and the irregular cavalry are generally a superior class of men. Patan horsemen, from the north of Hindostan, serve all over India.

The irregular infantry comprises a great variety of variously constituted regiments. Some include all classes, some are for the most part confined to men of particular localities, some to men of particular classes—Sikhs, Goorkhas, Mairs, Bheels, and Affghan borderers.

There is, I believe, a great difference in the discipline of the regular armies of Bengal and Bombay. In the former there is a much greater respect for Hindoo prejudices, a great preference for high-caste men, and a much less strict and less Europeanised discipline. Promotion goes for the most part by seniority, unless there are very strong reasons for passing a man over.

In the Bombay army a certain conformance to our European system seems to be a condition of service; all classes serve together, all are promoted in the order of merit, and a much more European style of discipline is enforced.

I have said that the number of the Indian army, in comparison to the magnitude and population of the country, does not seem excessive when judged by a European standard; but then we must consider the isolation of the country, the present freedom from formidable foreign enemies, and the enormous expense of our military system. We must admit that the army seems by no means to eat the bread of idleness,—that taken in detail it is generally shown that the sepoys have plenty to do. But before we fully yield to this argument we must compare with the numbers and duties of former periods. It is also to be observed that expensive regular troops are now employed on a variety of petty duties—escorts and guards of various kinds—which could be at least as well performed by the cheaper irregular force. And the advantage of railroads will not only be felt in rendering our troops more easily available where wanted, but the mere saving of escort duty will make a prodigious difference. I believe that a trunk line of railway through the country occupied by the Bengal army would relieve us of duties which fully occupy 50 regiments, or 50,000 men.

From the conclusion of the peaceful times of Lord William Bentinck the army for some years continually increased, and it reached its maximum about the time of the first Sikh war. The whole increase, therefore, took place before, and not after, the commencement of our conquests from the Sikhs. The numbers now remain about the point which they then reached. Our military expenses at home and abroad for the four successive years 1845-6 to 1848-9 averaged not very far short of 13 millions sterling; but in the last year of which we have accounts (being that from which I have taken my statements) the charge has come down to about 12 millions, as has been seen. Unfortunately, we have now another war upon our hands.

Comparison of the strength of the army with former periods.

In comparing the first with the last of the fifteen years from 1835 to 1850, we have 183,000 men in the former, against 288,000 in the latter; and an expense of about 8,050,000*l.* against 12,054,000*l.*, being an increase of 105,000 men and 4 millions sterling. Meantime our frontier has been advanced from Sirhind to the trans-Indus hills.

The number of troops now employed west of Delhi nearly corresponds with the increase of the army as thus shown:—

Division.	Men.
Sirhind	23,753
Jullunder	17,277
Cis-Jhelum	21,394
Trans-Jhelum	11,537
Sind Sagur	7,099
Scinde	15,425
Punjab local corps	7,756
Total	102,241

The Meerut division (to the east of that of Sirhind) comprises 21,708 men, and, taking the country from

Rohilcund to the Jhelum, we have concentrated in the territory within 150 miles on either side of Sirhind (or the "Head of India"), and within call of the proposed seat of the Supreme Government, an army of about 90,000 disciplined troops, of whom a very large proportion are Europeans.

Including the greater part of the Sirhind division, we may take it that about 95,000 men are now occupying stations in advance of their position in 1837. But I argue that we are thereby released from the necessity of keeping up a frontier force in our older territories, and that our military expenses within the desert ought in consequence to be reduced. I should be sorry to suppose that 100,000 men are required merely to keep down the inhabitants of our newly acquired territory in the plain of the Indus. If it were so, it would be, indeed, an expensive acquisition, and some change of system would be necessary. But if, as I believe, owing to the advance of our frontier and the more complete settlement of our internal system, we can draw, say 50,000 men, from our old territories to occupy advanced military posts, and add another 50,000 for the local duties of our new territories, paid from the revenues of those territories, we shall have a great frontier army without any additional cost as compared with the peaceful times previous to 1838. Everything, however, depends on peace. If we must send troops across the seas to conquer and to occupy Burmah, and must keep others to watch the Nizam's mutinous and unpaid force, an army of the present strength may be necessary; but if we get rid of such demands, surely great military reductions might be made in all our settled territories.

The strength of the army depends, however, on so many unforeseen contingencies, that I shall not presume to express an opinion of the feasibility of reduction. I content myself with pointing out the extreme desirableness of reducing, as much as possible, this gigantic abyss of our resources; and shall proceed to make a few observations with a view to saving money, independent of reduction of strength.

Necessity of European troops.

The European troops are in numbers between one-sixth and one-seventh of the army, and I certainly do not think it in any way expedient to reduce them by one man. It is certain that in all our late pitched battles we have mainly depended on the European soldiers to bear the brunt of the battle. This may in part be owing to defects of the native army which may be, and ought to be, remedied; but it is a fact which must not be forgotten. And still more important are the Europeans on *internal* grounds when we consider the very serious mutinous combinations which have taken place within a few years in our sepoy army. Even the cost of European compared to native troops is not so very disproportionate as might at first sight be supposed, since the matériel is just as expensive in one case as in the other, and European soldiers serve at less wages than European labourers, whereas the regular sepoy costs (officers included) five or six times as much as a native labourer.

As regards cavalry, I cannot conceive a comparison to be made between four European dragoons and five native regular troopers (the cost being the same). And for the more serious duties of the army, I confess that, when we meet such foes as the Sikhs, I should think our money better expended on one European soldier than on two of the present sepoys. I shall propose, then, rather to increase than to diminish the European branch of the army.

Of the native army much the greater proportion is composed of the regular sepoy regiments, under European officers. It has been till the present day the fashion (handed down from ancient times) to praise the "noble sepoy" under all circumstances, and I believe that he has very well deserved the character, and would now well deserve it under a better system. I should hardly dare to say anything against him, had not the subject been already broached, and were it not now pretty generally understood that the matter has become very serious. I am not at all clear that in recent battles we were ever so near being vanquished as is sometimes asserted. The fact is, that in all our late wars we have come into the field an immensely superior against a very inferior power—we have brought the empire of India against a province. But still I fear it must be considered as perfectly clear that, if only sepoys had been opposed to Sikhs, we should have trembled for our empire; and I do think that the system is very much to be deprecated under which our commanders, while praising all alike, *practically* place no faith in the sepoy troops, and fight great battles simply by hurling one European regiment after another at the batteries of the enemy, and triumphing at an immensely disproportionate cost of European life. I put it to any military man whether in late battles this has not been repeatedly the case? It is certain that native soldiers are not wanting in physical courage, and that they are capable of a very high degree of discipline. Something then must be wanting in our present system.

State of the regular sepoy army.

I admit that the sepoys perform equally well at a cheaper rate many duties which no one would think of imposing on Europeans, but I argue that, while the Europeans are cheaper troops in great battles, these secondary duties can be quite as well performed by the native regiments called irregular.

It is impossible to attach too great importance to the subject of sepoy mutinies. Shall I venture to say that the great combinations which occurred a few years ago were compromised rather than quelled? The system and discipline under which such things may any day occur must be anxiously looked to. Most serious mutinies have occurred in the early days of our army, but they were local and open outbreaks, and were quelled with the strong hand. General, silent, deep combinations, involving concession and compromise, are much more serious.

Causes of its deficiencies.

The following remarks I can apply only to the Bengal army, as I know nothing of those of the other presidencies, but the Bengal army is by far the largest and most important. I attribute the defects of the sepoy army—

1. To the system of discipline, and especially the mode of officering.

2. To the system under which the office of sepoy has become a sort of vested right, and certain exclusive classes entering our army rise according to a regular fixed system, having comparatively little to gain or to lose from the favour or disfavour of their superiors.

I shall dispose of the latter reason first. I have mentioned that the great majority of the sepoy army is composed of certain classes from a particular part of the country, and that all but very good caste men are strictly excluded. This gives an immense facility for combination, the more so as there is a large proportion of Bramins—always a wily, intriguing race, exercising more or less influence over their fellows. The regiments are generally recruited from the relations and friends of the sepoys already serving. Once entered as a sepoy the service is one of almost pure seniority. Particularly bad men are passed over, but a man who is not remarkable for good or for evil rises steadily till he becomes in his old age a subahdar, without any particular regard to his merits. A very false centralisation is attempted; no power over their men beyond the prescribed drill is permitted to commanding officers. The head-quarter office attempts a minute supervision which it is impossible that it can properly perform. Every sepoy who is not promoted, or who considers that he is deprived of any portion of his vested rights, may appeal to the Commander-in-Chief, and the commanding officer must produce in answer full and sufficient categorical reasons. I also think that the too general military system of indiscriminately praising everybody and everything is most noxious. Where, in all recent wars, has the smallest distinction been made between those of our native troops who fought and those who ran away? Praise, and sweetmeats, and batta, have been distributed to all alike. When the European troops have done the work, the sepoys have equally shared in the triumph. Why then should they fight?

It seems to me that soldiers will only fight for one of the following reasons: patriotism—partizanship—pugnacity — pride — pay — promotion* — discipline. The patriotism of patriot troops is often supplied in mercenaries by partizanship. Our sepoys were partizans in the early period of our career. But now they have ceased to be so, and are the servants of an established, rather than the partizans of a rising, power. They are a comparatively cold and calculating race, and have not so great natural pugnacity as Sikhs and Goorkhas. If they run away they keep one another in countenance, and their pride is saved by the lavish bepraisement of the Commander-in-Chief's despatches. Pay and promotion they get just the same whether they fight or leave that

* The alliteration is accidental.

duty to the Europeans, and their discipline is not so perfect as to make them fight at the mouth of Sikh cannon through discipline alone. I repeat, then, why should they fight? and, fully admitting that they have very many good qualities, that they are the material of very good soldiers, I do think that the vested rights of the sepoys of our army do not produce efficiency.

As to discipline, I will make bold to say that I believe too great respect to prejudices to be a very great mistake, and especially, I think that the preference for high caste, which is carried to such a pitch in the Bengal army, is the greatest possible error. We carry this prejudice very far beyond native governments—indeed, the latter almost invariably entertain low-caste men, and find them among their best and most trustworthy soldiers. It is all very well to have native gentlemen riding their own horses as irregular troopers, and in order to draw good officers from the ranks you must have a proportion of men of education and superior qualities; but, for a mere regular soldier, I believe that the lower your raw material the better.* There is nothing so elastic as the prejudices of high-caste men. Yield to them, and they will become narrow to a degree. Make it a condition of your service that they should yield to you, and they will expand to a wonderful extent. In the one case they will strain at a gnat, in the other they will swallow a camel. I believe that the high-caste men, understanding our weak point, parade their prejudices as a means of maintaining their monopoly.†

* It is said that no man makes so bad a regular soldier as a broken-down gentleman, and no man so bad a cavalry horseman as a groom.

† I confess to have once had rather a prejudice against Bramins, and I made it my principle that all who chose to serve me must serve alike, and that I would not make allowances for caste. But I did not in the least get rid of Bramins. Men of that caste voluntarily took places about me, and, by way of ensuring favour, volunteered to do all kinds of things usually supposed

I *do* think then that the Bengal army might in this respect with great advantage imitate the Bombay system.

The January number of the 'Edinburgh Review' has remarked, with great justice, on the defects of our system of officering our native regiments. There are no creatures in the world more *leadable* than the natives of India. The personal influence exercised over them by those who understand their feelings or command their respect is immense. All who have had to do with bodies of natives must have noticed how completely they seem to follow their leaders. Talk over the head men, or the self-elected spokesmen of a mob, and the others follow like sheep. On this account the officers are, perhaps, more important in a native Indian army than in any other in the world. If you have proper officers, and are sure of their fidelity and good conduct, you are sure of your army. In regard to officers, our sepoy regiments are singularly deficient. A system of double or dividing officering has been attempted, which has ended in having neither efficient native nor sufficient European officers. Let us look to the constitution of a sepoy company. The native officers are simply the oldest sepoys; they have neither sufficient influence over their men, nor sufficient motive to use such influence as they possess on behalf of Government. When the great mutinies took place, it was a regularly organized thing that the native officers and three senior sepoys (the next for promotion) of each company stepped forward and declared their rea-

to be utterly abhorrent to their prejudices, and in the end I found that several of my most immediate followers, and of my most useful and unscrupulous native officers, were Bramins—almost in spite of myself. This is not usually the case in the civil offices of the north as it is in the south. The Bramins are seldom so well educated as the Mahommedans, Kaits, and merchant classes; but the two best detective police officers I have ever had were both Bramins.

diness to go wherever Government might order them; the rank and file remained behind. No real native officers of a corps efficiently officered by natives would have dreamed of pretending for one moment that they could not influence their men. They would either have joined the mutiny, or brought over their men.

On the other hand, it is utterly absurd to suppose that the companies are properly officered by Europeans. Of an insufficient number of European officers, all who have any means of recommending themselves to superior authority get staff and other appointments. Those who remain behind are by no means always the worst officers; but it may be presumed that, if merit and energy in asking have *some* little effect in military patronage, they must be on the average below par. They are, at any rate, the most disappointed and least contented officers of the regiment, and it is hardly to be supposed that they have *very* great zeal and pride in their work. If there is one European officer to each company it is a fortunate corps, but the majority of these officers are young men, quite unfit to exercise any sufficient influence over the sepoys, barely understanding the most ordinary routine communications made to them in a sort of Anglicised regimental Hindostanee; and it very frequently (I may almost say ordinarily) happens that one officer has charge of two or three companies. There may still very generally be found one or two good, steady, old sepoy officers with each regiment, but they cannot perform the functions of officers of companies, and the race is becoming every day more rare. A very important fact, which vastly affects the efficiency of European sepoy officers, is the change in modern times in European habits in India. The officers used, to a great extent, to contract native habits; they became intimate with the language and with the men, and exercised a large influence over their soldiers; but there is nothing of the kind now-a-days. The habits of European officers are purely European, and they know little of their men.

The promotion of the European officers of the Company's army follows the most inflexible rule of seniority, without any exception whatever. The commanders of regiments are generally twenty years past their prime, and those only attain superior commands who far outlive the common term of humanity.

The system followed in the regiments called irregular differs much from that of the regular regiments. Vested rights have not yet grown up; commanding officers are permitted to exercise a larger discretion. Men are taken from classes not common in the regular army, but the lowest caste men are still excluded. Promotion does not go by seniority. The companies are officered by efficient native officers, and by natives alone. The European regimental commanders, if not selected strictly in proportion to efficiency, must be at least above the average, and have certainly this great advantage, that they are in the prime of life. The native regiments which have been most distinguished in late battles have been of this description (the Goorkhas for instance); for ordinary duties I believe them to be fully as efficient as the regulars at half the cost; and they have not mutinied. Their system of equipment, drill, and physical discipline is, as I have said, exactly the same (in the infantry) as in the regular regiments. The irregular infantry are, in fact, exactly the description of troops who gained for the sepoys, in former days, that excellent character which has always been attributed to them.

Proposed remedies.

We must, then, seek some remedies for the deficiencies of the army, and they must be at the same time economical remedies, for money we positively cannot afford. The most important question is the extent to which natives shall be employed as commissioned officers. While the natives have much progressed in all the civil departments, in the army they have not only not advanced, but have retrograded. All the higher grades have been almost exclusively filled by Europeans, at a great expense. Is there sufficient reason for such a course? Is it necessary, and is it politic? If so, it must either be on the ground of the incapacity of the natives, or of the impolicy of trusting them. I do not now speak of the command of regiments. I am not yet prepared to say that we should trust to natives the command of regiments, any more than the charge of districts; but as regards the command and officering of companies (duties which seem to me to correspond to the subordinate civil charges under European district officers, which are held exclusively by natives), I should say that the natives are exceedingly competent, and that the only question to be debated is the policy of trusting them. That question resolves itself into this: Have you the greatest hold over your native army through competent native officers, or without such officers? In the latter case you have not the benefit of the influence of officers in your favour, but you also do not run the risk of their influence against you. I have already argued that, if you have good officers faithful to you, you can depend on the men. Now, which are most likely to be in your interest—officers promoted by you, who owe everything to your service, who have much to gain by fidelity, and much to lose by misconduct—or the men who, with little to gain or to lose, combine on some petty question of pay? It seems to me that you would have every possible assurance of the good conduct of good officers under such circumstances, and that all our experience tends to the belief that it is so. I think, therefore, that, under the eye of a good commanding officer, proper native officers of companies would do the

Employment of natives in superior grades;

work with efficiency and safety, and I see not why the majority of our native regiments should not be so officered. In any case we must fully make up our minds to one of two things—either to increase the number of European officers, and thus fully to officer the corps, or to trust to good native officers. The double system is altogether a failure, and only involves a double expense with a much diminished efficiency. To supply the requisite number of efficient European officers would be so expensive that we cannot afford it; and if we could, I should very much doubt the policy of the measure.

I am, therefore, for adopting the other alternative, and for putting a majority of the native regiments on the footing of the present irregular corps, to the great pecuniary saving of the state, and, as I believe, to its greater safety and more efficient service.

and change from present system to that called irregular.

The following are the arrangements which I would propose:—

First, of the cavalry. I shall not enter into the comparative merits in the field of regular and irregular horse, but this I *will* say, that, if the regular troopers are of no use in the field, they are certainly of no use anywhere else. They are not like the infantry regiments, who perform many miscellaneous duties, and are employed on continual escorts. It seems to me that, with the exception of two individuals acting as orderlies to the General in command of a division, the regular cavalry, in times of peace, do nothing whatever; and therefore if, as their detractors allege, they run away in the day of battle, they must indeed be an unprofitable, as they are assuredly a most expensive, arm. The irregulars, on the other hand, whatever they may be in a pitched battle, are certainly a most useful set of fellows on ordinary occasions. They

Proposed cavalry arrangements.

are continually all over the country, on all sorts of duties; and there can be no doubt that, in any irregular guerilla war, or in pursuit of a beaten enemy, they would be the most effective of all troops.

After all that has been said against the regular cavalry, the most convincing argument is their enormous expense. It may be a surprise to find that their cost is in so large a proportion to that of European dragoons; it was so to me, and I might have doubted the accuracy of my calculation if I had not called to mind that of one of the best possible authorities which I have quoted in confirmation of mine. I say then that it is quite absurd to keep up five regular native troopers at a cost equal to that of four dragoons or ten irregular horsemen; and that you had much better dismount them forthwith, and supply their places by dragoons or irregulars. On the principle that in a cavalry regiment three-fourths of the expenses are just the same for Europeans as for natives, and that, therefore, it is comparatively cheaper in this arm than in the infantry to maintain a European force; and, considering that we should have in our army a due proportion of regular cavalry; I would substitute for the regular cavalry a large body of dragoons.

On the comparative scale which I have calculated, the total cost of our present cavalry is as follows:—

3,700 dragoons, at 90*l*.	£330,000	
10,200 regular troopers, at 73*l*.	744,000	
21,000 irregular troopers, at 37*l*.	777,000	
Total		1,851,100

I would have—

10,000 European dragoons, at 90*l*.	900,000	
21,000 irregulars, at 37*l*.	777,000	
Total		1,677,000
Saving to the state		£174,000

—besides being possessed of a far more efficient force.

Artillery.

I shall not attempt to discuss the artillery. The natives make capital artillerymen, but, as the material costs the same with native gunners, it may be sound policy to retain a majority of Europeans. The strength of the arm seems small in proportion to the army (and our six-pounders certainly proved of little use before the Sikh batteries), but I do not think that we can afford to increase it at present. If we keep plenty of guns and shot in our depôts we may increase our artillery to any extent while the Russians are marching from the Oxus. I imagine that, with a few practised artillerymen to lay the guns, the same very artificial discipline acquired by very long practice, that is indispensable to an infantry soldier, is by no means necessary to serve a battery; and that we might man our guns, on an emergency, just as they are manned in the navy every time that a ship is put into commission.*

I would keep the European infantry at its present strength (about 32,500). With the command of the cavalry and artillery, and a more judicious organization of the native infantry, I think that we should be safe for the present, without an increase which we can ill afford.

Proposed infantry arrangements.

Now as to the infantry. With regard to the native infantry we must not change our whole system too suddenly, and must deal cautiously with the vested rights of existing sepoys; but we might very soon bring about a change. I would not desire altogether to abolish the regular native regiments, especially as it will always be necessary to

* It has often struck me that for the defensive militia of a great city nothing would be so good as artillery. Suppose we had in London 1000 heavy guns, with an artilleryman to each, and served by volunteers or militiamen. If the French were to land at Brighton, we should harness the dray-horses, go out to the new Crystal Palace, draw up our guns in a line, and support an inadequate infantry with an enormous artillery. It would be just what we have felt in attacking the native Indian powers.

maintain a school for European officers, whence, after having thoroughly learnt their duty, good men may be drafted to the command of other corps. But, in those regiments which are to be officered by Europeans, I would increase the number of officers, keep them with their regiments, and make them really effective officers of companies.

I calculate the present personal cost of the native infantry, including officers' pensions paid at home, to be nearly as follows:—

	162,000 regulars (including veterans), at 21*l*. 5*s*.	£3,442,000	
	39,500 regulars at 11*l*.	434,000	
Total	201,500		3,876,000

I would have—

	50,000 regular native infantry with European officers, at 25*l*.	1,250,000	
	150,000 ditto with native officers, at 11*l*.	1,650,000	
Total	200,000 men		2,900,000
	Saving to the state		£976,000

I would admit men of all classes, and would introduce a strict system of discipline; men of the very lowest class of all might, if necessary, serve in separate regiments. I would make it a particular object to get new classes into the army, and especially the different military and pugnacious classes. I would enlist as many Sikhs and Goorkhas as possible. They fraternize with our European troops, respect and appreciate us, and are ready to drink grog and fight, eat whatever they can get, and cook however they can, with a most laudable absence of prejudice. Nothing can be a greater contrast to the immense paraphernalia of a sepoy regiment, and its innumerable cooking-pots, than Sikhs marching light and messing

Necessity of infusing new blood into the army.

together like Europeans. I have alluded to the unusually complete and entire deprivation of *all* political privileges which has overtaken the Sikhs. This can only be politically justified if we at the same time entirely draw all their political teeth by employing their men—and I am sure that those men will make the best soldiers in our army. But if they are employed beyond seas, or in distant countries, it is to be hoped that their health will be cared for. Being almost as much foreigners as Europeans, they must be sufficiently supplied with food. They cannot live on rice alone, for it is a food to which they are totally unaccustomed—and it seems a pity that a Sikh regiment should have been cantoned at Dacca, where all the men have been seized with fever, when the sepoy regiment which refused to go to Burmah had been much more appropriately sent there. I would make some arrangements with the Nizam to relieve him of his troops. He should pay us what they cost him, and we should take military charge of his territories, and, taking the Arabs and Sikhs into our infantry, and the Rohillas into our irregular cavalry, we should probably find them on regular pay capital servants, and some counterpoise to the present sepoys.

The seniority system of promotion must cease, and those men must be promoted who are likely to make good officers while they are yet in their prime and vigour. With the view of obtaining good officers, it will no doubt be desirable to use every effort to induce a proportion of men of education and influence to enter our service. In the first instance efficient men may at once receive commissions as officers; but in future it will be better that they should all first enter the ranks, and should thence be promoted, after the fashion which prevails in the Austrian service; the more as the rank which they can ultimately reach will not be very high. I do not think that cadets of families of rank or considerable pretensions would be at all useful to us; but the style of educated middle-class men, whom we find as officers in the troops of native states, and in our irregular cavalry, will answer our purpose admirably.

I am not sufficiently acquainted with military matters to venture an opinion on the expediency of uniting the different armies; but I have no doubt that there are certain advantages in the maintenance of a distinction between different native forces, since if all were on a uniform system the occurrence of differences between Government and its soldiers, on questions common to the whole army of India, might be very inconvenient. Perhaps the excessive staff charge at Madras and Bombay might be reduced, and our military arrangements might be centralised in some things while left distinct in others.

Union or separation of different armies.

I would as now keep a very large portion of the army near the site of the proposed capital, about Meerut, Sirhind, and Jullunder. The name "Head of India" (Sir-Hind) very well expresses the situation of that part of the country. Troops stationed there are alike available for frontier service and for our older provinces; and if anything were to occur in Central India, the head-quarter army, marching through Agra, would at once get into the centre of the native states. I would post most of the European regiments along the outer Himmalayas, from the borders of Oude to the Indus.

The union of the Commander-in-Chief, the military offices, and the military board, in one permanent capital, would be a very great advantage; and the military board, properly located and constituted, and relieved of civil duties, might become fitted for its many onerous tasks, and the fit advisers of the Governor-General and Commander-in-

Union of military offices in a permanent capital.

Chief. If the board, and the departments subordinate to it, become thoroughly efficient, a great saving may be effected in some of the largest items of our military expenditure.

The commissariat.

One of the most important of the departments under the military board is the commissariat, and, though I do not venture upon military details, civil servants have so much to do with the commissariat, and take so large a part in procuring supplies, that I must say a word upon it.

In speaking very disparagingly of the commissariat I am sure that I am only echoing the opinion of the whole service, military and civil. Whatever it may be as an instrument of distribution, it is certainly most grossly inefficient as an instrument of supply. Not a regiment can move except by the instrumentality of the civil authorities. So long as the duties of the commissariat merely consist in selecting among competing cantonment vendors and keeping the accounts, they manage their own affairs, but the moment anything is wanted, which is not voluntarily thrust upon them, they do not dream of making the smallest exertion to procure it, but, with the utmost indifference, send off an indent to the magistrate. When troops are to be moved, or real service commences, nothing whatever is to be got from the commissariat.*

The most crying evil connected with the department is

* The story goes that, when the Sikh army crossed the Sutlej and commenced the war, the Governor-General sent for the respectable head of the commissariat, and asked how soon he could move the troops. That functionary, having considered, replied that, looking to the emergency of the case, he thought that, with aid from the civil authorities, it might be done in six weeks. "You will do it in three days," replied the Governor-General, "or I will find some one else who will;" and he found some one else who did. The then political agent, whatever his other qualities, was a man of energy, and in three days the army was on its way to meet the Sikhs.

the total absence of any arrangements whatever for the supply of carriage for military movements. There is a great deal of carriage in particular parts of the country which private individuals have no difficulty in procuring for mercantile purposes, but the commissariat hardly ever procures a cart, and indents for carriage are simply handed over to the magistrate. On the other hand, that functionary has it not in his power to make proper arrangements for the voluntary supply of carriage. He has no funds whatever applicable to such a purpose; he can neither contract for a fixed supply to be drawn from other districts nor anticipate probable wants, nor insure the due payment and good treatment of the carriage which he supplies; he is not in a position in which he can deal on equal terms with individuals, nor is it his habit to do so; and it generally happens that the particular districts in which there is the largest military demand are those in which there is the smallest supply. When a magistrate receives an indent for carriage to be supplied within a very few days, he must get it in his own district as he can; and, when the demand is large and the supply small, he is constantly obliged to press all the carts he can lay his hands upon. The more this kind of thing goes on the less becomes the supply of carriage; the candle is burnt at both ends; and so, in poor districts, where large bodies of troops are quartered, and are continually passing, the evil becomes most frightful; no owner of a cart and cattle can call them his own, they are constantly seized, made over to the troops, and marched off at the mercy of the soldiers. In case of sudden emergency such evils may be inevitable, but it is too bad that they should habitually occur in times of peace, and they can only be remedied either by a trunk line of railroad or by a decently efficient commissariat, or, I should rather say, by both.

The supply of carriage.

While the commissariat falls so far short of its duties it is abundantly expensive. I do not assert that the European officers make money, or vouch for the truth of the popular belief of widely-extended corruption in the department; but it has an exceedingly bad name, and this much is certain, that matters are conducted in a loose and *native* style, which is not now known in any other department, and that commissariat officers seem to have a lofty disregard of all public financial considerations. As long as their accounts are regular, and they can make out bills in due form, they are quite indifferent to the amount.*

I believe that, being much pressed, and when a war is much protracted, the commissariat *does* sometimes do something in the way of getting up supplies of grain, but they do this only by putting unlimited trust in individual natives, who take the matter up as a speculation, make their own arrangements in native fashion, render their own accounts, and are paid on their own terms;

* A large camp was once passing through my district. On such occasions a constant source of strife between the villagers and camp followers is the destruction of peepul-trees, which are called sacred, and are really the ornament and shade of the villages, but of which elephants and camels are particularly fond. In this instance the complaints were unusually numerous and urgent. Bodies of camp-followers completely stripped of its branches every peepul-tree for miles on each side of the line of march; and at the same time I found that my supply of fodder for the camp-cattle was not taken off my hands. I went to the commissariat-officer: "Surely," I said, "there can be no necessity for robbing private property when I am ready to supply fodder at a reasonable price." "Oh," he replied, "I pay for fodder. There is no reason why they should cut peepul-trees." "But," I said, "your people don't buy fodder. Let us compare your bought account with my sold account." "Oh no, no," he said, "I can't go into these particulars. There is a fixed allowance of fodder for the cattle; and so long as that is not exceeded, and the cattle are kept in condition, I can't interfere. If you catch them cutting peepul-trees you must punish them. I have nothing to do with it." I could not catch an army with a few policeman; and if I had authorised the villagers to turn out and fight pitched battles in defence of their property there would have been a pretty return of killed and wounded.

and who are the real masters of the European commissariat officers.

I principally attribute the inefficiency of the commissariat to the absence of any regular commissariat service. Commissariat appointments are filled by regimental officers possessed of no particular qualifications, and changed from time to time. I will even, without periphrasis, express my belief that most of these officers are quite unfit for such duties. It seems to me that the commissariat ought to be a sort of mercantile establishment; and if it is necessary in the English army to make it a separate department, much more is it so in India, where everything is so strange to us. Nothing requires a more thorough knowledge, both of mercantile business and of native customs and manners, than commissariat dealings; and of all people in the world the least likely to acquire such knowledge are regimental officers. We shall not now establish a purely native commissariat as we might have done in the days of Clive. Let us make use of the natives by all means, but let us have efficient European officers to supervise them; and for so peculiar a service we must have men specially appointed to the department and who devote their lives to it.

Cause of inefficiency of commissariat, and proposed change.

It remains to notice the mode of supplying European officers to the army. Under the arrangements which I have proposed the numbers may be in future diminished, but a much larger proportion of men considerably above the average will be required. The efficiency of native regiments commanded by European officers will altogether depend on having good men to command them. Hitherto the appointment of officers of the army has been matter of pure patronage in the first instance, and

Mode of supplying European officers to native army.

of pure seniority afterwards; and but a very small proportion of the whole have received some military education at Addiscombe. I do not think that you can test efficiency in young officers by examinations to the same extent as in the case of young men intended for civil service, but some preliminary test is very advantageous, and a military education is most necessary. I believe that we are the only nation in Europe the body of whose officers, not promoted from the ranks, do not receive some military education in military schools before appointment to the commissioned grades, and hence the unscientific character of our army as compared, for instance, to that of France. But in the English army the peculiar discipline of a regiment acts as a sort of education to the young officer. In India, on the other hand, the system of a native regiment is not at all the same thing: the officers live apart from their men, and apart from one another; they are few in number; they get away from their regiments whenever they can; and I must venture to say that there is not the same discipline among the officers as in one of her Majesty's European regiments. A military education is, therefore, very necessary; and, instead of selling cadetships, it will be infinitely better to require the expenditure of the money in education and enhanced qualifications.

The Court of Directors, rightly considering it inexpedient that it should remain a matter of doubt whether their officers can read and write, and in correspondence with the lately instituted examinations in the Queen's service, have recently required of all cadets to pass a certain examination; but we must, I think, go a step farther. The arguments which I have used in favour of a particular selected place of education for civil servants apply with still greater force to the purely professional military education; and I would therefore have a great military polytechnic school, to which all cadets should be sent for at least two years, where all unfit persons should be eliminated, and all fit persons should acquire a certain military education and discipline before being sent out to India. Addiscombe is, I believe, an excellent institution; we only want such a place for *all* cadets.

Proposed military school;

On arrival in India I should say that a young officer might be with advantage attached for a year to a European regiment. He would then be posted to a native regiment officered by Europeans, and from these latter regiments good officers would be selected as commandants of the ordinary native regiments.

and proposed system in India.

It is of essential importance that officers withdrawn from their original regiments should cease to be borne on the regimental rolls, and that staff officers should be put on an unattached or staff list. It is also much to be desired that the inequality between the emoluments of staff and regimental officers should be diminished, and that there should be as few staff appointments open to regimental officers as possible. Officers should feel their regimental duties to be their profession, and not be continually seeking staff appointments. I should say that the quartermaster-general's department might be (like the commissariat) with great advantage separated from the general staff, for it is at present by no means efficient, and in all late campaigns the complaints regarding it have been loud and deep. For the adjutant-general's department, the military board, and some other duties, you must no doubt select good regimental officers, and pay them well; but petty staff appointments should be as rare as possible, and should not be made prizes by large allowances. I have already argued that it will be a great advantage to the army if it can be relieved from the temptation to covet civil and political appointments.

The public are now well aware of the evil of the system by which officers, when quite unfit for duty, are elevated into important commands, and it is unnecessary that I should dwell upon them. But the system remains the same. Even the Cabul lesson has had no effect, and God forbid that we should some day at length receive a sufficient lesson in some disaster of still more fatal magnitude and vital importance. Now-a-days wars will be concluded long before the chapter of accidents has produced a school of good generals. Shall we not, then, while there is yet time, devise some remedy?

Naval establishments.

One word on our Indian naval establishments. The Indian navy, after deducting certain receipts, costs on an average about 400,000*l.* net * per annum—not a very large sum compared to our military establishments, but still important in the present condition of our finances. The question is entirely one of degree. Although a squadron of the British navy protects the Indian Ocean, some local flotilla is no doubt necessary to an empire which has a great sea-coast. The Indian navy consists almost entirely of steamers and light vessels. There are eleven large steamers, some smaller river steamers, and a few sailing vessels. If this force is to be employed in Burmese and Chinese wars,

* The gross charges are about 545,000*l.*; the receipts from various sources about 145,000*l.* There is a discrepancy between the general statement of charges on account of the Indian navy given at p. 783 of the Report of the Commons' Committee and the detailed Indian and English accounts. Both the disbursements and receipts stated in the latter are larger. The Indian accounts give a charge exceeding 400,000*l.*, and receipts exceeding 90,000*l.*—net charge 310,000*l.* The home accounts—disbursements, including building stores, &c., about 140,000*l.*; receipt from her Majesty's Government for conveyance of mails 50,000*l.*—net charge 90,000*l.* It is then only by including this last-mentioned receipt of 50,000*l.* (which is said to be excluded) that the net charge is brought down to 400,000*l.*

or in the naval police of the Eastern Archipelago, it is probably not too large, and it is, I believe, efficient; but I should think that its duties might be with advantage confined within narrower limits, and in that case money might be saved. There has been a good deal of question with regard to the employment of the government steamers in the conveyance of mails and passengers. I have no doubt that the duty, taken alone, may be better performed by a private company; but if we are to pay for government steamers at any rate, I see no reason why, when they are idle, they should be debarred from such duties merely that one great private company may have a complete monopoly of the traffic. No one is constrained to go as a passenger by a government steamer; but it is perfectly natural and reasonable that Government should send some of its mails by its own unemployed steamers, instead of paying other people to do the same thing. The French and other Governments follow the same system. It is quite clear that the Peninsular and Oriental Company, while they have already so much to do, made such efforts to get possession of the comparatively petty Bombay line, not so much because it is in itself of great importance to them, but because it is the only little loophole through which a few persons escape the meshes of their monopoly.

CHAPTER VII.

FINANCE.

General financial position; necessity of improvement; how to create a surplus; review of items of receipt, and proposed measures in regard thereto; review of items of charge, and proposed reductions; home charges; general result; application of the surplus; finance of different local governments; financial treatment of Madras; Punjab finance; altered form of accounts; local finance and responsibility; plan of local budgets, and financial distribution; remittances by hypothecation.

ON a former occasion * I have made as clear as I can our financial circumstances. Another year's accounts do not render our prospects more promising.

General financial position.

The year 1849-50 turned out, indeed, more favourably than was estimated, and there was a surplus exceeding 300,000*l.*; but in the following year a very much smaller sum was realised from opium; the salt revenue also fell off; and the estimated deficit is upwards of 600,000*l.* The charges for these years must have included the remains of some war charges which we might have hoped subsequently to reduce had we not been again involved in another war. I understand, however, that the opium is selling well this year.

Taken altogether, it appears that our finances, while by no means in a desperate state, are certainly not in a prosperous condition. The comparative situation of our revenues and charges is not such as would justify a prudent government in remaining content with things as they are. We barely pay our expenses in time of peace; protracted war and extraordinary deficiencies must involve farther loans; and under the most favourable cir-

* Modern India, chap. x.

cumstances we have no permanent surplus to devote to the improvement of the country.

Necessity of improvement.

I think that in the exercise of proper prudence, now that we have completed the empire and cannot look for extraordinary extension of revenue, we should make a great effort to put the finances on such a healthy basis that we may not have occasion to get further into debt, and that our ordinary charges on our ordinary revenue may leave both that marginal surplus for extraordinary contingencies which is indispensable to all trustworthy finance, and a sufficient revenue available for public improvements. If the Indian Government has not been *very* extravagant—has not got recklessly into debt beyond its power of payment—it must also be admitted that the proportion of the revenue expended on public works and improvements has been excessively small. We are, no doubt, in a better position than states which have undertaken great works by a profuse expenditure of borrowed money; but while in peaceable possession of so great an empire, it is certainly our duty to do more than pay our current establishments. We ought to improve the country and promote the civilization and comfort of the inhabitants. My present end is to consider how the means for these objects can be obtained. I certainly would not borrow money for ordinary improvements. The noxious and dishonest modern practice of drawing bills on posterity, to obtain money for present expenditure, has been carried a great deal too far, and the faith of national creditors will, perhaps, only be shaken when these constantly-increasing, never-diminishing, loads of debt become too heavy to be supported, and recoil in great national bankruptcies and repudiations. I would only at present make an exception as to borrowing money for trunk lines of railroad in India, inasmuch as the immediate saving and facilities afforded thereby must more than repay Government as a mere government speculation, and Government alone can make railways in that country. But for everything else we must either find ready money for improvements, or the country must remain unimproved.

At present we have no money for such purposes. How are we to get it?

How can we create a surplus?

We can but look for slow and gradual increase of the income derived from our present revenues, and some of our taxes are such as we should certainly mitigate whenever we are in a condition to do so; while, on the other hand, I know no new tax which we could with advantage impose. It has been often remarked that, under our rule in India, capitalists, and all the superior classes unconnected with the land, do not contribute a fair share to the expenses of the state and in payment for their own protection,—in fact, that they are hardly taxed at all. It certainly is so, but neither can I suggest any mode of getting at them short of the arbitrary confiscations of native rulers, nor am I clear that the exemption of the capitalist is not in the end advantageous in a country where capital is not yet so abundant as we could wish, and where all classes depend very much on the capitalist for assistance. An income or property tax would never work in India, and, in truth, every cultivator, every weaver, and the Government itself, benefits by the increase of capital in each village, even though it is in the hands of others. I am not prepared then to recommend any plan for a great increase of taxation.

Inexpediency of increasing taxation.

Political means of improving our finance.

In the previous political and military chapters I have already indicated the quarters from which it seems to me that financial improvement is most likely to arrive. By a political management, less liberal in great things and more discreet in small things, I think that we might save money; and if we assume the management of Oude now, and of Gwalior on the first convenient opportunity, and manage them on prudent principles, we shall undoubtedly find great gain to our revenue.

Military savings.

By a redistribution of the army without materially reducing its numbers, and even increasing the main element of our strength, I have proposed to save annually 174,000*l.* + 976,000*l.* =	£1,150,000
To this I would add (supposing that we get rid of the Burmese war) reduction of expenses resulting from peace—from the cessation of war charges, and of the extraordinary expenses of a new territory for military buildings, &c. &c	700,000
Saving by improved management of the commissariat and other departments under the Military Board, and by reduction of staff, &c., of minor presidencies	500,000
Total immediate military saving	£2,350,000

And if we can reduce the strength of the army, that will be so much additional gain. In fact, I hope that, if we have continued peace, we may save a good deal more, but would be content with so much in the mean time.

I shall here briefly review some of the principal items of receipt and expenditure.

Review of items of receipt.

Land revenue.

The land revenue can only (except by extension of territory) be very gradually increased with the increasing wealth, population, and prosperity of the country, and through improved management on our part. In Bengal, Hindostan, and the Punjab, we cannot look for any great immediate increase. The thirty years' leases which have been granted in Hindostan, and are now being granted in the Punjab, render it necessary to await their expiry before we benefit by the extension of cultivation. I hope that an improved management of Madras and Bombay would be early beneficial to the revenue,* and am glad to find that the Court of Directors have ordered the Bombay Government to revise all the enormous allowances paid out of the land revenue of that presidency. I trust that the result will be a large increase of net receipts. I am afraid that it is too late everywhere to do full justice to Government in the matter of revenue-free tenures, but the investigation of all these holdings should be made quite complete, and they should be firmly dealt with.

I conclude, then, that the land revenue is a sure and improving income, but one not to be very rapidly and largely increased within a few years. By far the greater portion of the increases exhibited in our land revenue returns have resulted from increase of territory. The stories of sudden and miraculous increase sometimes put forth have reference only to very small localities and peculiar circumstances. The rents of no great province are to be suddenly doubled by the touch of any magician's wand; but Government may gradually do much by steady and judicious improvement. In the provinces from which by far the largest portion of the land revenue is realised, the whole land cultivated and uncultivated is assessed in blocks, so that no reduction of rates (however beneficial to the country) could possibly improve the revenue.

The opium revenue is one of a totally opposite character. It has brilliantly increased of late years, but it

* I admit, however, that a fair trial to an improved system at Madras might involve low assessments for a few years; but in the end we should be much more than repaid, and in the mean time we should make up for it by checking the extravagant waste of the Bombay land revenue.

also exhibits startling fluctuations. We must by all means make the most of it while we can, and may well from year to year spend, for the benefit of the country, or to meet extraordinary demands, the revenue which we thus realize. But it is not an income on the whole of which we can prudently rely as a permanent resource from which to defray fixed and permanent expenditure. Although, if we were perfectly assured against competition, we might restrict the sale and increase the price, that the Chinese might not be tempted to eat too much, it is hardly safe to attempt such a system when the production of opium is free to all the world beside, and it is undoubtedly our best plan to cultivate so much Bengal opium, and sell it at such a price, as to secure for it that practical monopoly to which the cheapness of its production entitles it. We should adopt stringent measures to secure ourselves against smuggled Malwa opium, and should impose on the drug, in whatever part of India produced, the same duty which is realised from Bengal opium. We might, if necessary, prohibit the cultivation of opium within a certain distance of the western coast. A duty, or profit, of about 600 rupees per chest on all opium seems to be about the best and most profitable rate; and if the Chinese will take off our hands 60,000 or 70,000 chests annually at this rate, we shall do very well. I do not know that the frequently asserted fact, that the Chinese could grow opium for themselves at a cheaper rate, is by any means ascertained. It may be so, and it also may be that the Chinese can grow tea better than we, and we can grow opium better than they. Government would do well to ascertain the facts.

Opium.

The salt revenue is the tax which presses most heavily on the masses, and which it would be our first duty to mitigate as soon as we can afford it; but in Bengal Proper, where it is most severe, it has been, in fact, considerably lightened of late years, and I do not think that we can afford to sacrifice large revenues just at present, if we would attempt expensive improvements. There is a very serious decrease in the Bengal salt receipts (including the customs on seaborne salt) of the last two years, which has been in no way accounted for, and regarding which it seems very extraordinary that the Bengal government should have furnished to the Court of Directors (as appears from the Blue Book) no explanation. It is impossible that, after having borne the pressure of a higher duty all through the present century, and having constantly increased their consumption all the while, the Bengalees should now, in times of general prosperity, suddenly break down under the salt-tax. There must be some other cause. The import of sea-borne salt has of late greatly increased, to the decrease of the manufacture of Bengal salt. I hope that the manufacturing tribes, deprived of legitimate occupation, may not have taken to smuggling. At any rate, we ought to have some explanation of the decrease, and it is to be trusted that it is only temporary. It would seem fair to make the salt-tax, as far as possible, uniform at all the presidencies, regard being had to the quality of the article, which, I believe, is of an inferior description at Madras. It does not appear why the Bombay salt-duty should be less than one-third of that of Bengal. At the time of the abolition of a variety of customs duties, the tax on the salt of Northern India was raised from one to two rupees per maund. Why, then, should Bombay escape? It would be a great saving and profit if we could arrange to get into our own hands, or surround by a smaller circle than at present, the great salt-lakes of Rajpootana. We are very fairly entitled to levy the full duty from

Salt.

the salt-pits of the Western Punjab; but while the people of Bombay and Scinde have their salt at a much smaller duty, it seems hardly worth our while to keep up the grievance on the subject of salt alleged by the Affghan border tribes. Although certain fluctuations may occur, the salt revenue, managed on a good and uniform system, is, then, a certain and large income.

Customs.

The income derived from customs (exclusive of salt-duties) is not nearly so large. In a liberal and beneficial spirit we have taken off all customs duties between the Punjab and Affghanistan, and I think that we might very well relinquish the last remnant of land customs in the continent of India. The net revenue realized from cotton and sugar (the only articles besides salt subject to duty) on the line between Hindostan and Central India does not exceed 100,000*l.* per annum, and the land customs receipts of Madras and Bombay must be much more inconsiderable. I would, then, abandon all land customs, and merely maintain a preventive line in the most convenient situation for the realization of the salt-duty.

The rates of sea customs are not exorbitant, but the revenue is very small for so great a sea-coast, the whole net receipts from customs little exceeding 800,000*l.*, of which a portion is derived from land customs. One thing should certainly be done if we would be consistent with our principles, and that is, to equalise the duties on British and foreign goods. I cannot understand how the system of charging double duties on all the most important foreign imports should have been so long continued. It would be a fine thing if we could one day make India free to the commerce of all the world, and the net loss (after deducting land and foreign differential duties) would be only about 600,000*l.* to 650,000*l.* per annum—about 5 per cent. of the cost of the army; but

I apprehend that we cannot just at present afford to do this.

Excise.

The excise on spirituous liquors is a considerable revenue, and one which it would not be expedient to reduce. Whimsically enough, however, it appears to be a subject of complaint that, while under the natives no one interfered with the manufacture and sale of spirits, we, by making it a strict monopoly, from which we derive a large revenue, have spread drunkenness through the country. I suspect that our restrictions on opium may be one reason for the progress of ardent spirits. It may still be a question whether we shall best raise a revenue on spirits by the present practice of selling monopolies, or by a fixed duty.

Abolition of moturpha and tobacco revenue at Madras.

The moturpha tax at Madras is a most obnoxious impost in every way, and a remnant of taxes which have ceased in every other part of India. It is levied on shops, tools, &c. The gross revenue is but 88,000*l.*, and I should have no hesitation whatever in at once abolishing it. I cannot imagine why such an impolitic, tyrannical, and vexatious tax should have been so long continued. The tobacco revenue is not in itself so objectionable, but it is peculiar to certain districts of Madras. If we were to impose on the people of India a new general tax, an excise on tobacco might, perhaps, be the least objectionable which could be suggested, but I hope that it will never be necessary to do so. I have seen within a few days, in a Madras Gazette, a notification that in certain territories tobacco shall henceforth be free. I do not know whether the whole revenue has been given up. If not, it ought to be so, since there can be no sufficient reason for imposing on certain districts a tax from which all the rest of India is exempt, merely because some native ruler did so before us. The net receipt is but 88,000*l.* per annum.

When I look to charges with a view to reduction, I am tempted to say that the first is military, the second is military, the third is military; that item seems so overwhelming.

Review of items of charge, and proposed savings.

In the marine establishment, if we keep the peace, I should say that 100,000*l.* per annum might very well be saved. The financial comparison which I have formerly made* will have shown that I cannot expect to save very much upon the civil establishments; but I have proposed a cheaper government, and think that the political establishments might be reduced. Those offices, on the other hand, which claim an increase, must wait till the revenue increases; and thus, in the mean time, we may put down 200,000*l.* as civil and political savings. In regard to judicial and police charges I can hold out no hope of saving. The cost of public works calls for increase, not decrease. We are not likely to gain materially by the Mint and Post-office. We ought now to get rid of the civil deficit in Scinde, and thus to save 150,000*l.* per annum.

Home charges.

I have stated generally the cost of "home establishments, including civil pensions, cost of mails, &c.," at about 709,000*l.* But I find that of this about 90,000*l.* is the cost of stores, and the amount of pensions, &c., properly chargeable to the marine department.

70,000*l.* is paid for the conveyance of mails by the P. and O. Company.

70,000*l.* is the cost of civil and Mint stores sent to India.

56,000*l.* is made up of charges connected with the Indian civil service.

* Modern India, pp. 434-7.

12,000*l.* is contributed to the cost of the mission to Persia.

20,000*l.* may be taken as the average charge for passage and outfit of governors, commanders-in-chief, bishops, and other officers.

The proper home charges are, on an average, about as follows:—

Board of Control, including pensions . . .	£30,000
Court of Directors, establishment, and contingencies	130,000
Pensions, including compensation pensions . .	200,000*
Law charges	12,000
Miscellaneous	20,000
Total home charges	£392,000

A good deal would be saved by a united home government and a less voluminous office; and it is much to be hoped that the compensation annuitants will some day begin to die out, and that the disproportionate home pensions will be reduced. Say that, in the mean time, we save on the home charges not less than 100,000*l.* per annum.

I believe that we can in no way get at the proprietors' guarantee fund, or reduce the dividend till 1874.

If we have a few years of peace, the Indian 5 per cents. may very probably be reduced, but we cannot yet calculate on this saving.

General financial result.

Supposing, then, that our present average ordinary peace charges are about equal to our average ordinary revenues, my account will stand thus:—

* This item has no reference to civil service annuities (which are paid with money remitted by the managers of the annuity funds in India). It is solely composed of home pensions. The larger portion is on account of compensation annuities to persons reduced from the establishment at home and at St. Helena in 1834, to whom India still pays considerably upwards of 100,000*l.* per annum.

Let us take the immediate net profit from the assumption of the management of Oude and an improved political system to be in the first instance only	£1,000,000	
Military saving	2,350,000	
Naval ditto	100,000	
Civil and political ditto	200,000	
Ditto on Scinde	150,000	
Home ditto	100,000	
Total financial improvement . . .		3,900,000

Against which must be set—

Sacrifice of land customs, and equalization of sea customs on foreign goods	200,000	
Sacrifice of moturpha and tobacco revenue at Madras	170,000	
Total decrease		370,000
Net surplus		3,530,000
The sum now expended on public works, exclusive of repairs, is		482,000
Total available revenue		£4,012,000

—besides what we may look to from the future gradual improvement of all the ordinary sources of revenue.

Application of surplus.

I would provide that, till the annual surplus amounts to 4,000,000*l.*, one-half shall be laid up as a provision for extraordinary contingencies (war, &c.), and towards paying the capital of the debt, and one-half shall be devoted to the improvement and benefit of the country; that, when the surplus exceeds 4,000,000*l*., the whole excess beyond that sum shall go to the latter object.

Supposing that in a few years our ordinary revenues, by good management, increase by 1,000,000*l.*; that, added to the available revenue already calculated, will make 5,000,000*l.* I would then propose to make the following reductions:—

Entire abolition of customs, net loss	£600,000
Reduction of salt-duty to an uniform rate of 1 rupee per maund (equal to about 2*s.* 10*d.* per cwt.) all over India, estimated loss	700,000
Total sacrifice	£1,300,000

There would still be a net salt revenue (allowing for a moderately increased consumption) of about 2,000,000*l.*; and if our other revenues very greatly improve, the time may come for making salt free. But in the mean time we must by all means strive to secure a revenue of at least 2,000,000*l.* annually, available for public works and general improvements.

Finance of different presidencies.

I have on a former occasion discussed the comparative financial position of the different presidencies. It is certain that, by a good system of centralisation, much would be saved, since in many things almost as great expense is incurred in the small presidencies, which were once independent governments, as in the whole of the great presidency which extends from the Bay of Bengal to the borders of Affghanistan, and comprises by far the greater portion of the resources of the empire. I must here, however, observe, that the imputation of extravagance and financial mismanagement applies much more to Bombay than to Madras; and it is well to note this fact, for I suspect that some of the sins of Bombay are visited on Madras; and, on the other hand, that excessive severity in regard to expenditure at Madras is used as an argument for removing the check which it is necessary to apply with the greatest vigour to Bombay. Bombay, having always managed to make away with more than its revenue, seems to have acquired a sort of prescriptive privilege of doing so; and deducting (to compare it with Madras), as an imperial revenue, the export duty on Malwa opium levied at Bombay, it not only contributes nothing to the general government, the home expenses, or the debt, but is upwards of a million deficient on its local revenue and charges, exclusive of the Scinde deficit; whereas Madras, from the same sources of revenue, pays its expenses, and contributes nearly half a million to the general treasury. The only charge upon Bombay, which has been very much paraded in mitigation of its financial shortcoming, is one which really covers only a small portion of it, viz. a naval charge of about 180,000*l.* per annum, which is certainly a good deal more than a due proportion of the cost of that branch of the service, and in regard to which credit for say 100,000*l.* or 120,000*l.* may be fairly given. It appears that the whole of the military expenses of the Bombay army are not debited to that presidency, and that Madras troops occupy the southern portion of the Bombay presidency. If Bombay were to realise a fair share of land and salt revenue, and to spend but a fair allowance, there might be considerable opportunity for indulgence to Madras, where the land revenue is said to be assessed more highly than a Ryotwar system can bear, where the civil expenses are (the government excepted) very moderate, and where some temporary consideration may be necessary in order to give a fair start and good basis to an improved revenue system.

Expediency of more liberal treatment of Madras.

I must say that, as regards the civil charges, Madras does certainly seem to be very hardly used. A heavy expense in collecting the revenue is a necessary result of the Ryotwar system, but the other civil charges, calculated on the sources of income common to all the presidencies, are smaller than anywhere else; and it seems to me altogether inexplicable why Madras should have been so long saddled with such abnormal imposts as the moturpha and tobacco duty, and should be denied a reasonable sum for public works, in order to make up a certain surplus, while Bombay has been permitted to get rid of all objectionable taxes, to make ducks and drakes of the land revenue, and to exhibit a deficit without any limit whatever. A fair percentage on revenue ought to be allowed to Madras for civil expenses. A study of the accounts has brought me to the conclusion that the complaints from that presidency are in a great degree well founded.

The military expenses of the subordinate presidencies should be regulated separately from their civil charges, for, if a fixed sum be allotted to them, the result seems generally to be, that the military charges increase, and complaints are made of the want of money for civil purposes. It has been so at Madras.

The Bombay and Madras armies each furnish some troops for service beyond their own domestic limits; a portion of the Bombay army serves in Scinde, and a portion of the Madras army in Central India and the Southern Mahratta country; but the numbers of troops thus employed are not more than fair quotas to the general military duties of the empire.

Finance of the Punjab.

I am sorry to say that the present financial result of the Punjab is not nearly so favourable as formerly stated. Singularly enough, the first year has turned out far more profitable than those which have succeeded it. And this is not from any shortcoming in the revenue—it has prospered and increased—but from the increased charges of increased establishments.

In 'Modern India' I stated the local charges of the Punjab beyond the Beas for 1849-50 at about 380,000*l*. I did so on extremely good authority, but it now appears that I am about 60,000*l*. in error, the true amount expended in that year (including cost of collection) being

440,000*l.* I am, however, not responsible for the subsequent increase to more than double that amount. The local charges have, in fact, increased from 440,000*l.* to 962,000*l.* (including local corps and military police), and there is still an extraordinary charge of 232,000*l.* The revenue is stated at 1,300,000*l.*, but this is *exclusive* of the acquisitions prior to 1849; and to weigh the financial result, we must undoubtedly include the acquisitions of the first war, since the first war brought on the second, and to go back to the status of 1837-8 we must have given up the whole. The whole revenue of new territory under the Punjab Board of Administration is thus fully 1,850,000*l.*, and probably rather more.

I was, perhaps, wrong in supposing it possible that the expenses could have remained at the very low figure at which they appear in the first year, but the present charges do seem very high. I suspect that part of the increase is caused by compensations for resumed jagheers and political privileges, and doubt whether it is politic to pay largely in money when a much smaller deduction from the revenue, in a more acceptable form, would better please the recipients. I believe that our management is not such as to render necessary very large establishments; and as the charges are certainly high, we may expect that when the revenue settlements and police arrangements are a little more advanced they will be reduced. We must not omit financial considerations in seeking efficiency; but at the same time we must not suppose that material saving is really effected merely by cutting the salaries of the most prominent servants. I think that the territories under the Punjab Board, after allowing for civil establishments and civil expenses, ordinary and extraordinary, on the most liberal scale, must certainly give upwards of a million sterling as clear surplus.* Say the account stands thus:—

Revenue	£1,850,000
Collecting and civil charges . .	850,000
Surplus	1,000,000

Of the 100,000 men whom it may be prudent to keep ready in Northern India, I have supposed 50,000 to be drawn from our older provinces for the defence of the common frontier, and I would charge 50,000 to the Punjab, thus:—

5,000 European foot, at 40*l*.	£200,000
5,000 irregular cavalry, at 35*l*.	175,000
40,000 Sikh and other native foot, at 11*l*. . .	440,000
Military buildings, fortifications, &c. &c. &c. .	185,000
Total . . .	£1,000,000

Compared to the times immediately previous to the Sikh war, the whole revenue of the new territory is net gain; but compared to the quiet times of 1835-6, we may well be quite content if we do not lose by our new acquisition, and have the full benefit of the improvement of our older revenues.

I think that the form of the Indian accounts should be considerably altered. There is no separate account of the Imperial Government and Imperial charges, and many things are included in Bengal which in no way appertain to that government. It only creates confusion to charge the whole Supreme Government, political expenses, and Bengal army, to

Altered form of accounts.

* The surplus last reported is but	£145,000
But deducting—of extraordinary expenses, say . .	132,000
local corps	210,000
reduced establishments on completion of settlements, &c.	200,000
And adding—net revenue of new territory cis-Beas .	400,000
We shall again have a surplus on civil expenses of .	£1,087,000

Bengal Proper. I would have it, that the expenses of the Supreme Government should be kept altogether separate; that the opium, the political receipts, and perhaps the sea-customs, as imperial resources depending on imperial policy more than on local management, should be credited to the Supreme Government; that the whole debt should be charged to the Supreme Government; that each local government should then render a separate account, in a prescribed form, of its receipts from the ordinary local sources of revenue,* of its local charges, and of its contribution to the general government and to the home expenses. If the armies remain separate, they must be separately charged; but the Bengal army will be rateably charged on the revenues of Bengal, Hindostan, and the Indus territories. If the sea-customs are taken as an imperial resource, then the naval establishments may also be charged against the Supreme Government; but if this revenue is credited to the local governments, the maritime expenses must be charged to the maritime presidencies. When the returns are made in this form, we shall see at a glance the real comparative condition of the finance of each government.

Necessity of local financial responsibility.

I would carry this farther. I would ascertain and compare the financial results of each division of each government, and, in fact, of each district. It is quite necessary to send the financial schoolmaster abroad. There has been too great a separation of the departments of receipt, disbursement, and account, and a great want of financial generalisation. I do not believe that one official in twenty understands the financial position either of his own district, his own government, or of the whole of India. There is a total absence of the wholesome obli-

* Land, excise, salt, stamps, miscellaneous.

gation to make two ends meet, in every one, from the highest to the lowest, except the Governor-General and the financial secretary. Every charge is considered intrinsically on its own merits, and without reference to the wherewithal; and the Supreme Government, unable to reconcile many contending claims, may often reject the good with the bad. It was formerly considered good service to Government to collect as much as possible, but I think that there is now rather a disposition to go the other way, to laud liberal principles both in regard to receipts and disbursements. "Oh," a man says, when he makes an assessment, "great government does not want to screw the ryots, can afford to be liberal." And again, when he proposes an establishment, he says, "Niggardly policy is a bad policy, great government must put things on a handsome and efficient footing." Now this would be all very well, and these would be very excellent sentiments, if the same men were responsible for, or knew or cared anything about, the financial result; but when every one, from the local governor downwards, goes on these principles, and the Supreme Government alone is responsible for finance, it becomes a very difficult task for the latter. I would therefore, as I have said, send the financial schoolmaster abroad, and would insist that every officer should understand and make clear to his superiors the financial result of his charge.

Proposed system of budgets and financial distribution.

I would then have a general system of local budgets, and would put the finance of each government, district, and department, on a normal and intelligible footing, and would establish standards by which the financial arrangements of each year or of each new proposition should be measured. Every departmental and divisional officer should submit to the local government a budget of proposed arrangements at the beginning, and a financial report at the end, of each year; and every local government would submit similar budgets and reports to the Supreme Government. Charges would be sanctioned by anticipation, and a certain latitude would be allowed within sanctioned limits. Every officer would thus be constantly constrained in all arrangements to keep in view the necessity of making two ends meet. I believe that in this way our finance might be rendered intelligible, uniform, and regular, and that, while much indiscreet expenditure would be prevented, much discreet expenditure would be sanctioned, which is now negatived simply because it is not understood. The local governments, while properly restrained, would have it in their power to regulate petty questions of expenditure without constant reference to a central government, unable to judge of small items, yet obliged to act as a kind of general break on the financial machine, and continually to oppose the expenditure of money. At present the local governments seem to go on the principle of asking as much as possible (on the ground that they are not likely to get one quarter of what they ask), and the Supreme Government on that of granting as little as possible, in performance of its duty as the guardian of the public purse. I would then go altogether on the principle that the Central Government should prescribe the general limits, should fix the financial landmarks, but that local governments and local officers should administer and be responsible for the expenditure of the sums assigned in the aggregate. For instance, a certain sum might be allowed for local public works for the year, on the faith of a budget previously submitted; and for any great deviation from the terms of the budget special sanction would be required.

I do not at present pretend to make an exact calculation, but give the following account as an example and approximation. I credit the net proceeds of the opium and sea customs to the Imperial Government as imperial revenues, and debit to it the imperial and marine establishments, the debt, and the home expenses. I charge the Bengal army rateably on Bengal and Hindostan, after allowing for 1,000,000*l.* charged to the Punjab, making, with 200,000*l.* which I allow for military duties in Scinde performed by the Bombay army, 1,200,000*l.* for the *local* military expenses of the Indus territory.

For the civil expenses of the Punjab and Scinde united I allow—

Charges of collection . . .	£350,000
Civil charges on net revenue . .	600,000
Total . . .	£950,000

—exclusive of the Sikh corps, hitherto local.

I expect that nearly three millions net opium and customs revenue, deducted from the local income of Bengal, would be, for the most part, compensated by political and military improvements and savings, and the deduction of imperial charges. I suppose the Madras military savings to equal the sacrifice of revenue and increase of civil expenses, and by increase of revenue and decrease of charges the Bombay finances should be improved to the extent of 1,000,000*l.*, and made at least to pay the mere local charges.

Bengal.—Net revenue		£6,000,000	
Military charges . .	£2,200,000		
Civil charges, &c. &c. .	1,100,000		
		3,300,000	
Surplus			£2,700,000
Hindostan.—Net revenue		5,000,000	
Military charges . .	1,800,000		
Civil charges, &c. &c. .	900,000		
		2,700,000	
Surplus			2,300,000
Carried forward			£5,000,000

Brought forward			£5,000,000
Madras.—Net revenue		£3,500,000	
Military charges . .	£2,000,000		
Civil charges, &c. &c. .	1,000,000		
		3,000,000	
Surplus			500,000
Bombay.—Net revenue		2,000,000	
Military charges* . .	1,330,000		
Civil charges, &c. &c. .	670,000		
		2,000,000	
Surplus			Nil.
Indus territory.—Net revenue		1,800,000†	
Military charges (including local corps, but excluding contributions from rest of India to frontier garrison) . . .	1,200,000		
Civil charges, &c. &c. (exclusive of cost of collection) . .	600,000		
		1,800,000	
Surplus			Nil.
Total surplus			5,500,000
Imperial net revenue from opium and sea customs .			4,000,000
Total imperial revenue			£9,500,000
Imperial charges.—Imperial and marine establishments . .			£700,000
Remittance for expenses incurred at home, including military expenses, but excluding dividend			1,800,000
Interest on debt and dividend on stock . .			3,000,000
Total charges			5,500,000
Surplus			4,000,000

* Besides 200,000*l.* allowed for Scinde.

† Gross revenue of Sikh territory	£1,850,000
„ Scinde	300,000
	2,150,000
Charges of collection	350,000
Net	£1,800,000

We might then distribute the surplus as follows:—

Applied to sinking fund	£2,000,000
Supreme Government for imperial works	500,000
Bengal for local works	400,000
Hindostan for ditto	400,000
Madras for ditto	300,000
Bombay for ditto	200,000
Indus territory for ditto	200,000

This distribution may seem hard on the paying presidencies, but the inequality cannot be helped.

Remittances by hypothecation.

Before concluding this chapter, I must refer for one moment to the subject of remittances from India to England. A large sum is necessarily drawn from India to meet the home expenses of the Indian Government, and this can only be met by exports exceeding the imports. The Government, therefore, on the principle of both getting their money, and, at the same time, promoting the necessary commercial result, have made a practice of advancing the money in India upon the hypothecation of goods to be exported to England; and it is repaid in England from the proceeds of the goods on their arrival there. The arrangement seems, *primâ facie*, not inappropriate: but it is not now held to be desirable to foster commerce by artificial means, and therefore, if the result as a purely commercial speculation is not favourable to Government, it cannot be justified. Under most great governments such an attempt would only lead to jobbing and loss; but I suppose it is a remnant of the old commercial aptitude of the Company that they have been able to carry on the system with signal success, and have incurred marvellously few losses. It seems to me that the question is then simply one of account. If the Government on the whole obtains (all expenses and losses deducted) a better exchange than by drawing bills, surely it is as much entitled as the meanest of its subjects to make for itself in the market the most favourable terms, especially when the result is not to retard but to promote commerce.

An opposition has, however, been made to the system, not, as I understand it, on the ground of loss to Government, but because Government is said to compete with individuals in the money market, and, through Government advances, people who have no money are enabled to compete with those who have. But is this an argument for free trade or for a monopoly? If Government, at a loss to itself, tries artificially to foster commerce, there would be good ground of complaint, but it would be very hard that, while Government has money in its hands which it wishes to remit, it should be debarred from dealing with persons who have goods to remit, upon sound mercantile principles, merely in order that certain other persons may have a monopoly. It is no new thing: Government has not come suddenly into the market, but has been always there. It is argued that the Government terms are so stringent that hypothecators had much better go to private capitalists. Then why do they not? No one forces them to deal with Government. I do not say that the hypothecation practice is a good thing, because I know nothing about it; but the sole question is, which mode of remitting is in the end most profitable to Government, treated as we would treat an individual. If otherwise, you might as well argue that it would be injurious if English capitalists were to establish a great bank in India, inasmuch as they would, for their own profit, lend money to those who have none,—and ought to have none.

CHAPTER VIII.

MORAL AND MATERIAL IMPROVEMENT.

Provision for spiritual instruction; absence of public; failure of private; state of natives, and facilities for conversion; causes of failure; mode of proceeding suggested; government interference towards this object; the most necessary means; ecclesiastical establishment; Hindoo and Mahommedan endowments; education; deficiencies of present system; nature of, recommended; schools and colleges; languages; political result of education; the press, condition of, causes of its defects; measures recommended in regard to; post-office; overland communication, and connection with Mediterranean countries; colonisation; difficulties of settlers; suggested promotion and facilities; proposed encouragement of immigration of Southern Christians; amalgamation with the natives, and gradual transformation of the masses; material improvements; agriculture and machinery; cotton; other products; tea; suggested mode of agricultural speculation; necessity of laws for protection of capital; public works; railways; reasons for preferring Bombay to Calcutta line for main route; question of interposition of companies; roads and bridges; caravanserais; tolls; Indus harbour; canals of irrigation.

Provision for the diffusion of spiritual instruction.

HAVING first provided the requisite funds, we may seriously undertake the great subjects which the title of this chapter will suggest. The parliamentary committees have announced, as one of the heads of their investigation of Indian affairs, the "ecclesiastical provision for the diffusion of spiritual instruction." The provision of chaplains for the ordinary services of European regiments and large European stations can hardly be called a *diffusion* of spiritual instruction, and Government has most assuredly made no provision for any such diffusion among the natives. On the contrary, for a very long period it regarded and treated

Absence of public.

Christianity as a most dangerous innovation, and has now admitted it to the common rights of religious freedom only under a very strict negation of all government support or countenance of any kind, direct or indirect. The question should, therefore, rather have been whether it is expedient to make any provision for the diffusion of spiritual instruction or no.

Private efforts have been made to that end; but, at least as regards the great provinces of Bengal and Hindostan, I have said, and I repeat it, that these efforts have failed—that no material religious impression on the population either has been made, or is now being made. I may add that, while the numbers of native Christians are few, we do not see, generally speaking, among those few that exalted zeal which, among the primitive Christians, was the means under God of the success of a small band, the first converts of great nations.

Failure of private.

Various reasons have been assigned for this failure. Some say that our great want is "more bishops;" some that education must precede Christianity; some that it is owing to the hardness of the hearts of the Hindoos. I by no means think that an unlimited number of bishops would mend the matter. You must get your flocks first, and then appoint your chief shepherds. I also very much doubt the assertion that Christianity depends on education. I believe that the natives of India have already quite sufficient intelligence to understand the essential doctrines of the most pure and simple of religions, and that such education as we can give them for many a long year will not bring them a bit nearer to really useful and sincere conversion. I have no hesitation in saying that it is infinitely better that a man should remain a Hindoo, than that, in a transition stage of education, he should divest himself of all religion.

When, by a very high education and great elevation of his character, you render him capable of appreciating a very perfect philosophy and very intricate historical proofs, his education may be brought to bear; but till then, you can appeal to the hearts of civilized intelligent men upon first principles, which all can understand and acknowledge, without teaching them the English language, English literature, or English ecclesiastical niceties; and it is on this ground that I am discussing religion as a separate question from that of education.

Present ethical state of the natives, and facilities for conversion.

In regard to the present state of the natives, it seems to me that practically they have wonderfully little superstition—that their idolatry is not more active than that of the Greeks and Romans. Their state is one which tends very much to rationalism. During the last few centuries they have been particularly prone to religious innovation; they are, like the Greeks, ready to listen to anything new, and I really think that they afford a particularly favourable field for religious improvement. The success of Nanak, and the wide spread of his doctrines in various forms (doubtless now much corrupted from their original purity), is alone, to my mind, a convincing proof that if a prophet were to arise, and to set about the task with sufficient energy, discretion, knowledge, and singleness of purpose, he might effect wonders.

In truth, I believe the religious state of the inhabitants of India (the Mahommedans excepted) to be really very like that of the Roman Empire at the time of the introduction of Christianity. There is the same nominal belief in an effete mythology, and the same tendency to overstrained systems of philosophy and natural religion, the refuge of acute minds seeking rest and finding none. I therefore believe that Christianity might succeed in India by the same means through which, under Divine direction, it succeeded in the Roman Empire. We shall create no impression by the paraphernalia of established churches, and the assertion of theological dogmas. The natives have already their established religions and established theologies; but if we find men fitted for the task—willing to give up everything that pertains to the world—to become what would be called in the East "Faqueers," and to devote themselves to preaching among the natives in native fashion, pure and simple, the great doctrines of the fear of God, peace and goodwill among men, and the inefficacy of all other and formal religion—I see not why, preaching a doctrine better and more easily intelligible than that of Nanak, they should not succeed better than Nanak, should not first create a sect, and then by means of that sect convert the population. The situation of the natives of the East is to a certain extent less favourable to proselytism than that of the Roman Empire, inasmuch as the eastern religions have already some infusion of good and rational principles, and their condition may, perhaps, be considered as intermediate between that of the Romans and that of the Jews. But not only have Nanak and other natives shown the possibility of the success of reformed doctrines, but the Jesuits at one time bid fair to convert both India and China, and, if their career had not been stopped by political events, would probably have finally succeeded. I am convinced, then, that there is an excellent field for the spread of Christianity.

Causes of failure.

I attribute the failure of missionary efforts, first, to the want of sufficient qualifications in the missionaries; second, to their attempting too much, insisting upon more than they can in the first instance make clear—in fact, appealing to the head with insufficient means, rather than to the heart on simple and sufficient first principles; third, to the want of any social facilities for receiving converts, such as are necessary when other conditions are not fully fulfilled.

If our missionaries and our converts were professed "Faqueers," and solely devoted to great principles like the primitive Christians, they would not stand in need of social aid; but if you do not demand an entire sacrifice of the world, you cannot disregard social considerations. Converts of the present day may be less subjected to physical persecution; but social persecution, which is still more powerful, they must submit to in its utmost rigour. The grand difficulty, then, is to get a beginning—a respectable Christian population as the nucleus to which future converts may be added. At present they become either outcasts or stipendiaries, and we can hardly expect a native without some compensation to leave all and follow a missionary who receives a fixed salary, lives in a good house, and preaches to the Hindoos a theology which seems to unenlightened men little less complicated than their own.

Mode of proceeding suggested.

I should say that, when qualified men are found to devote themselves to the work, they must commence as reformers, as it were, of the native religions. They must say, So far we agree with you—your God is our God, your natural religion is our natural religion; but beyond this you have lapsed into many absurdities. Here is a simple and beneficial reformed doctrine, which we ask you to accept on the ground of its divine wisdom, its advantage to all mankind, and its accordance with the natural reason of the heart. But they must not at first go beyond this. They must not insist on the Old Testament and the ecclesiastical histories, or on the doctrines of particular churches. They must be content with those great principles which are common to *all* Christians; they must simply preach, in the highways and byways, peace and charity as the will of God; and then, either setting an example themselves, they must create an enthusiastic sect altogether denying the world, or they must be able to say, "Come and be one of us, for we have a place in the country; you leave a native, but you are received into a Christian society."

Government interference towards this object.

I do not think that Government should make *direct* missionary efforts for the diffusion of Christianity, not that I apprehend political ruin to result from such a course, but because I think that such efforts would probably miscarry. I should place little faith in the missionary efforts of salaried retainers of Government. Those only will succeed who feel that they have a call to the service of God, and, abandoning the world, think not of any of the things of the world; while others, whose call is not so complete, may contribute out of their abundance to the subsistence of real devotees. Such efforts are better left to private enterprise. But I think that the Government may and ought to do its best to abate the social difficulties of converts. I need hardly argue the absurdity of the complaints concocted, not in native India, but in the semi-European presidency towns, on the subject of the refusal of Government to put in force an ancient law of the Hindoo hierarchy opposed to all toleration, by which persons abandoning that religion were deprived of all civil rights. It would be as reasonable if Irish Catholics were to demand, in addition to their own emancipation, the subjection of Protestants by a Protestant government to complete civil disabilities. The question has really occasioned no agitation whatever in the interior of India.

If we could obtain the nucleus of a good Christian

population, I think that some government countenance would not be dangerous, and that we might, in some degree, follow the example of the most discreet of the Mahommedan emperors, who, abandoning all systematic propagandism and religious persecution, yet regarded with political favour converts to Mahommedanism. The great step would be if we could bring over some great tribe in a body, just as the Mahommedans brought over a large proportion of the Rajpoots. It may be a question whether we should hold out direct political or pecuniary inducements to such a step, and endeavour to make a particular tribe—the Jats, for instance—our more immediate political adherents, and the commencement of a respectable native Christian population. But it is, at least, fairly open to us to form such a nucleus

The most necessary means.

by the promotion of Christian immigration and population, and the encouragement and employment of mixed and native Christians. Whether as regards religion, education, or material improvement, I believe that it is in many respects the grand desideratum to obtain a population of this kind as a commencement, and I shall shortly more particularly recur to the subject.

Ecclesiastical establishment.

When a Christian population shall exist, or wherever it now exists, Government may of course fairly provide the means for its spiritual instruction, as Mahommedan and Hindoo rulers have provided for their religions, by assignments of revenue, which are scrupulously upheld by us. With regard to the ecclesiastical establishment now maintained for the benefit of the European servants of the Government, I can hardly say anything which would not involve questions which pertain rather to this country than to India. It would be most desirable to have some test of the qualifications of chaplains (there is at present, I believe, none whatever) and some mode of recognising merit or demerit. Some arrangement for the supervision and discipline of the chaplains in the north of India is very necessary, as the Bishop of Calcutta is much too distant. The only question is, whether bishops are not inconveniently dignified superintendents. We have no bishops in her Majesty's army, and it may be that chaplains-general or archdeacons would answer the purpose, and be in more complete subordination to Government.

Hindoo and Mahommedan endowments.

An important subject, to which no attention has hitherto been paid, is the management of Hindoo and Mahommedan endowments. I have already expressed my belief that even Hindoos are better than infidels, and I may add that Mahommedanism has many very good points. We have wisely, then, upheld assignments for religious or charitable purposes. But, having done so, we have divested ourselves of all the responsibility for the due application of those funds which ought to appertain to the Government of the day, without making any other sufficient arrangement. So long as the revenues are in the hands of Hindoos or Mahommedans, we take no concern whether they are really devoted to the purposes for which they were intended or misappropriated by individuals. Hence there is often misappropriation quite as great as in our cathedral trusts. These grants were destined not only to the support of places of worship, but also, and more frequently, to charitable and educational purposes, and under native rule nothing goes so far to supply the absence of poor-laws and of national systems of education as the charitable distributions and educational facilities due to these grants.

I therefore think that all such endowments should be supervised by Government; that the conditions of tenure should be distinctly registered; that their fulfilment should be annually ascertained; and that Government should retain a power of putting them from time to time into fit hands, and, when necessary, re-distributing the funds. They should not be permitted to degenerate into mere hereditary property; and if the Government cannot be permitted to interfere with infidel funds, it should resume all grants which have been misapplied, and use the proceeds for better purposes. Educational grants in particular should be administered under the immediate supervision of Government.

Education.

Whatever be thought of the duty of Government in regard to religion, there can be no doubt that education is one of its first obligations. The people are apt scholars—they have had science and literature of their own—all their habits, institutions, and social arrangements tend to a very general spread of popular education. There is every reason to believe that, in fact, they were once very commonly educated, but a long period of war, rapine, and confusion has led to illiterate habits, and has diminished the indigenous means of instruction. It is now the duty of a great and settled Government again to develop this eastern education, and to add to it the useful knowledge of the West. Comparatively little has yet been done.

With respect to the education hitherto supplied by Government it may be observed—

Deficiencies of present system.

1. That it is deficient in quantity.
2. That it is mistaken in quality.
3. That the presidency towns have absorbed our attention rather than the country in general.
4. That the degree to which English has been made the medium of, and necessary preliminary to, education of a high order has been most injurious, and has very much confined it to particular classes.

It is impossible to allege that the education supplied

to a large extent in the presidency towns, and to a smaller extent in some of the larger towns in the interior, is such progress as should have been made during so long a period of dominion. In truth, little impression has been made on the general population. There has been hardly any attempt to educate the masses, Mr. Thomason's recent efforts alone excepted.

On the other hand, with respect to the quality of the Government education, the great mistake seems to be the preference of English literature to science. Such education (not, in truth, the most practical) as may be not altogether unfitting to English gentlemen of a certain class is preferred to the training which would be really useful to the people and the country, and for which the natives have the greatest aptitude. I except the Medical College from this general assertion (but I hope that, compared to what will be done in that department, it is yet but in its infancy). As regards all the other establishments for educating the natives, I ask where is the practical result? Where has been produced any class useful either as servants of Government or as adepts in useful arts and professions, or in any way benefactors of their country? We have a few young Hindoos who talk English and affect a semi-European style of manners and dress, but do we find a supply of useful men of any kind who owe their education and their usefulness to Government colleges? No: for all important duties we still rely upon and much prefer purely native education and talent, and for all useful arts we still have recourse to native builders, and mechanics, and weavers, educated as they were in the time of Menu. Instead of such mundane matters, we insist that the Hindoos shall appreciate the beauties of Milton,*

* Milton seems to be the favourite author, and I think that the selection is most objectionable in more ways than one. In fact, I may at once say that

and teach them a good many things which they would be quite as well without.

I would exactly reverse this system, and would substitute a practical, or what is now sometimes called a German, education for the higher classes, and reading, writing, arithmetic, and mechanics for the lower classes. I do not enter on the advantages or disadvantages of the present system of educating Englishmen who have to make their bread in the world, but I am quite sure that such a system is utterly inapplicable to Hindoos of any class, and has been injuriously substituted for that education which would be most proper to the natives, and would in every way benefit and elevate them. Whether Greek be worth the whole labour bestowed on it or no, Homer may be of *some* little use to an English gentleman, but Milton can be of *no use whatever* to a Hindoo.

Nature of education recommended.

I would therefore without delay provide a free passage to England for the gentlemen who teach Milton in the Hindoo College, and entertain in their place mechanicians and chemists and professors of all manner of useful knowledge. I would introduce a complete system of normal village schools for the education of the masses, district schools for that of the middle and better classes, and colleges of science, jurisprudence, medicine, engineering, arts, and manufactures for those who aim at the higher branches of knowledge.

The first care of Government must be that of the masses; and among a people who have so minute a distribution of property and duties there is more than usual necessity for a general diffusion of the rudiments of education. There is every

Village schools.

nothing can *possibly* be more ill chosen to set before a people whom we would convince of the folly of the Mahabharat. Not every Christian can think Milton's poems altogether removed from profanation.

readiness on the part of the people to learn or to cause their children to learn, and, if you but supply the means, education will become quite universal with much less difficulty than in this country. Government might in the first instance allow a small sum for a schoolmaster in every considerable village, and a small additional premium for every boy taught to read and write.

When the mass can read and write, many will be found who desire farther to extend their knowledge.

Schools of art and agriculture.

No class can be more skilful and intelligent than the artizans of India, and none would be more fitted to learn in schools of art. Artizans and agriculturists the most skilful of different parts of the world should be introduced into schools of art, where such things as are supposed to be fitted to the country may be fully tested, and whence those things ascertained to be so may be diffused by the medium of the village schools. If Government can only afford a reasonable expenditure, and lays out its money in the right direction, the material is ductile, and anything may be made of it. The first scholars will be sure of employment as schoolmasters, and, as the range of education extends and it becomes more cheap and general, we may expect that an increased demand for the useful arts will keep pace with an increased supply.

Higher branches of education.

I hope to see the profession of the law amply and respectably supplied from the proposed college of jurisprudence. I hope to see medicine and surgery (which the natives do of all things appreciate) introduced into every village in native dress and native language, and hedge doctors practising by the side of hedge schoolmasters. I hope to see a most ample supply of native engineers and mechanics, and a great production of articles hitherto confined to Europe for native consumption, and of native articles for

European consumption. I hope to see natives in considerable positions taking a lead in promoting all these improvements.

The most necessary means.

It must, however, be the case in regard to European education, as to European religion, that very much must depend on the presence of a nucleus of population possessed of those manners and arts with which we would indoctrinate the masses.

Education of females.

The education of females is a question of domestic manners. Some classes will have no objection whatever to send their girls to school; others will object. The higher classes of Hindoos have but borrowed from the Mahommedans a mode of treating their women which is opposed to their ancient habits and feelings, and we may well use our influence to restore the weaker sex to the place which they have lost, always provided that we at the same time instil into them such moral and social principles as shall be a sufficient safeguard against their abusing the liberty accorded to them.

Educational languages.

The question of the language in which instruction shall be conveyed to the natives has been much discussed. Some people, who advocate English, go even so far as to propose to make that language the lingua franca of all India; but I believe that such an idea has been entertained only by those who, living in Calcutta or Bombay and *realising* nothing of India beyond those places, derive their ideas of the country solely from Europeanised commercial towns. Understanding no native language themselves, they seem strangely to overlook the fact that a lingua franca of India already exists—that Hindostanee is commonly used by considerable classes throughout the whole country, and is still more commonly understood. Even the Mahommedans, whose immigration was infinitely larger than ours, and who made Persian to a great extent the language of written business, have universally adopted Hindostanee as their spoken language and the general language of India,* infusing into it a great mass of Persian words, as we may from time to time infuse into it English terms. It is quite absurd to suppose that we can ever render English general in India, although we may make it common at the chief seaports, as we do in most maritime places to which we largely trade. In the course of upwards of a thousand years we have not fully introduced English into Wales; and shall we, a petty handful of foreigners, expect to introduce it in the great continent and vast population of India? We should not do so in a geological period, and for mere mortal men to calculate on such a result is like attempting to build another tower of Babel and to reverse the consequences of the first undertaking of the kind. English must always be, as I have already said, the general language of the superior grades of the European executive; but the only common language of native intercourse must undoubtedly be, as now, Hindostanee, and I have proposed that it should be the general judicial language.

Even to people who do not perfectly understand Hindostanee it is an infinitely easier task to pick up a language habitually used by many around them, and of which a very large portion is common to all the tongues of India, than it would be to learn one which is utterly and totally foreign. For instance, Hindostanee may be among the purely Hindoo population of the most remote provinces what French is in Italy. To adopt French as a lingua franca in Italy would be a very different thing from decreeing that henceforth Sanscrit should be

* Even in the extreme South Hindostanee is the language of the Mahommedan population.

made the lingua franca of that country, and that all education should be conducted in Sanscrit.

I would then as much as possible promote Hindostanee as the lingua franca, and would infuse into it just as much English as we may at any time find useful. The vernacular of each province must of course be the common language of the village schools, but I would also give great facilities for learning Hindostanee, and I would propose that in all the higher schools (except, perhaps, the merely *local* schools of the great seaports) Hindostanee should be the *common* language; the vernacular languages being also used so far as is found necessary.

There seems to be a very great confusion of different languages in the South,—Tamul, Telagoo, Canarese, Mahratta, Oorya, and Hindostanee overlapping one another, and being spoken by different classes in the same district, sometimes almost in the same village; and each of the southern languages differing as much from the others as from Hindostanee. It is therefore almost impossible to get on well without some common medium; and if, as I believe, the idea of making English general is quite out of the question, it must be a great object to render Hindostanee as common as possible. There may be arguments in favour of Bengalee in the province of which it is the proper vernacular; but in truth Hindostanee is so commonly understood by all the classes who are likely to seek superior instruction, that I do not think it would be desirable to make an exception.

But after all, Hindostanee and English are not incompatible. There can be nothing to prevent the higher classes from also learning English if they like, whether for the purpose of communicating with Europeans, of serving as English clerks, or of gaining access to the higher branches of English science and literature. But it is quite another matter to *force* English on the natives as the sole medium of useful knowledge. In the first place, it is putting an obstacle in the way of knowledge, just as much as if we were to enact that nothing shall be taught in places of education in this country except in Greek; and secondly, I very much doubt whether it is by any means an advantage to natives to learn English. I believe that it would be much better if they could have the knowledge without the language. It may be considered unreasonable, but in the interior of the country there is certainly a very common prejudice against natives who talk English, and affect some portion of English manners. Is there no ground for this? or may it not be that the modes of thinking and acting which sit well on the Saxon character cannot be with advantage engrafted in an imperfect shape on a Hindoo stem, and that, as men are by nature more prone to the bad than to the good, those who learn English pick up without delay all our failings (shall I even venture to say our vices?), and all the misplaced ideas and anachronisms to which as regards India an imperfect acquaintance with English ideas is apt to lead, while the acquisition of the good parts of our character is postponed for a century or two? If you teach English for the sake of English literature, it must be used for other purposes also, and on the strength of an imperfect knowledge the Anglicised natives fancy that they understand, and do in fact altogether misunderstand, our character and system. They must principally derive their political ideas from the newspapers of the presidency towns, which I may make bold to say are not the safest guides. An Englishman may understand the system and circumstances under which an extreme licence of the press, unchecked by restrictive laws or by sufficient public opinion, is permitted in India; but nothing can be a worse school for the Asiatic subjects of

Political result of education.

an absolute government. They can hardly be expected to make the necessary allowances for, and deductions from, the language and statements of the newspapers.

I may here, however, at once say that I do not apprehend by any means so immediately bad a result from the spread of education and the influence of the newspapers as has been sometimes prophesied. Bengalese who learn English may become bad subjects and servants, and (if permitted to do so) they may write any amount of treason; but I do not in the least apprehend their acting upon it. The classes most advanced in English education, and who talk like newspapers, are not yet those from whom we have anything to fear; but on the contrary, they are those who have gained *everything* by our rule, and whom neither interest nor inclination leads to deeds of daring involving any personal risk. For a long time to come, if we incur any political danger, it will be from enemies of the original native stamp. As regards the general spread of education and intelligence, it seems to me to be a mistake to suppose that our rule depends on any secret which the natives being educated are at once to find out and forthwith to eject us. The natives already perfectly understand the cause of our supremacy to be in this, that they themselves are not one, but many discordant peoples and interests, and that we rule as stronger than any single political unity, and as giving greater satisfaction to the majority than the supremacy of any one native power. They know that if all natives were one we could not hold the country, but the remedy depends on great social and moral changes, rather than on the knowledge of the existence of the evil, and the natives may become perfectly well acquainted with every branch of science and literature without being a bit nearer political unity, and even without acquiring as individuals the character necessary for the highest executive offices of such a government as ours. We might still be the best and cheapest compromise among contending sects. Still education may doubtless in the end facilitate union and social amalgamation: and if, while as individuals the natives improve, we do not do justice to them; if we employ expensive European agency for duties which can in fact be as well and as impartially performed by cheaper natives, we shall give just ground of discontent, and supply an incentive to that union which the spread of intelligence has facilitated. We ought then undoubtedly, on grounds both of justice and of policy, to govern the natives in the way most advantageous to them, and if they improve both in education and in character we must elevate them accordingly. If they ever become fit for a constitution, we shall give them a constitution; or if they become fit for higher offices, they must be appointed to higher offices, till possibly there may be some day a native Governor-General. When they have very far advanced, then, in some future crisis, a constitutional government may become independent, or (perhaps more probably) a native Governor-General may become a native Emperor, and govern the country on our system more cheaply than we as foreigners can govern it.

The press.

I think that the Indian press may be more important in an educational than in a political point of view. There can be no doubt that the press is the great instrument of modern enlightenment. It is perhaps the greatest cause of the difference between European and Asiatic civilization, and it may be of the utmost consequence in India as leading and directing the native mind. It is on this account that I here notice it. Mere general principles of freedom can have no force under an absolute government, and in regulating the press we should be guided by a simple comparison of advantages and disadvantages. It is doubtless a great advantage that the acts of the officers of Government should be subjected to criticism, and that useful knowledge should be spread abroad as widely as possible; but, on the other hand, it is equally incontestably a disadvantage, if a government situated like that of India is constantly held up to the contempt of its subjects, and if unfit persons instil false ideas among a people not sufficiently advanced to judge of the facts and to appreciate the real state of things.

I believe that on a former occasion, alluding incidentally to the press (which was not then part of my subject), I have used disparaging terms too general and too sweeping. I should have admitted the existence of exceptions, particularly that very excellent paper the 'Friend of India.' My allusions had principally reference to the Calcutta papers, and were more especially provoked by certain then recent simultaneous misrepresentations of the conduct of Government. The up-country journals are more exclusively service papers, and their tone is by no means so bad. Lord Hardinge (who had principally to do with these papers), in his evidence, Commons' Report, p. 256, explains so clearly the nature of the evils which do in fact exist, that I shall not attempt to add a word on the subject, except to say that he has, perhaps, scarcely sufficiently alluded to the evil effect on the native mind of improper or indiscreet publications in such a place as Calcutta. No one can doubt that there are, in fact, some great evils connected with the Indian press. In truth its position is altogether anomalous, as a free press under an absolute government. Such a thing may succeed, but it is altogether new. Liberty of language has only been accorded where there is liberty of acts, and where, in other countries, there is freedom to abuse a free government through the press, that government also uses the press as a powerful weapon on its own side.

There are counsel for both parties,—the opposition papers attack the Government, the Government papers defend it, and attack the opposition. But in India the discussion is altogether one-sided. Government and its officers stand in the position of an accused who not only has no counsel, but who is prohibited from opening his lips in his defence. Lord Hardinge has well explained (see answer No. 2047) the difficulty under which a government labours which, for political reasons, may not be prepared to explain the facts to the press in *all* things, and is obliged to make it the rule to abstain from explanation in anything, lest in particular instances silence should be construed as consent. Such a thing as privately engaging the services of particular papers has not been known. If a Governor-General were detected in such dealings as those into which the best of Irish Lord Lieutenants unluckily entered, we should never hear the end of it.

Causes of acrimony and hostility to Government.

I believe that the Indian press is conducted with unusual acrimony and general hostility towards the Government for the following among other reasons :—

The European editors generally share the feeling of aggrieved Britons, which is the natural and chronic state of all free Englishmen living under absolute governments. This is likewise the feeling of many of their contributors and readers. The Europeans not in the service also not unnaturally resent their exclusion from important offices and employments.

The editors have not the means of ascertaining the truth, and, being obliged to find news at all hazards, they may feel themselves constrained to resort to fiction in the dearth of fact. I can conceive nothing more trying and more absolutely requiring a fertile imagination than the task of editing one of the several Calcutta dailies, and have no doubt that the excessive supply of vehicles of news, altogether disproportioned to the demand, for which Calcutta is most remarkable, is a principal reason of the objectionable tone of the press of that place.

There is too great a practical impunity to libel. No libel-laws applicable to the Mofussil courts have ever been enacted; and those who would avail themselves of the English law of libel must bring their causes to the presidency towns, and there prosecute them in many cases among a population of sympathisers on the other side. The position of Government in the Supreme Courts is somehow such that it is very unwilling to come there, and, as regards the State, press-laws are literally a dead letter. Government press prosecutions are quite unknown; and there is the utmost impunity to any language. In one or two instances private individuals have prosecuted in the Supreme Courts, and, where it has depended on the judges, justice has been done: but such prosecutions are so difficult, expensive, and rare, that they hardly appreciably interfere with the practical impunity of libel.

Recommendations in regard to.

I do not pretend to have a confident opinion as to the means by which the press evils are to be remedied, the state of things being so new and anomalous. The advantages of the press we cannot sacrifice. I trust that we shall never be deprived of our newspapers. While we encourage the use of so effective an engine of progress, some discreet censorship for the prevention of abuse would be most desirable. But then we get upon the other horn of the dilemma, for, while the use of a censorship would be advantageous, we might, by its abuse, lose more than we gain. Upon the whole, I should not *yet* advocate much direct restriction, as an ordinary rule.

I have already suggested the advantage of making public as much information as possible, and of constituting a sufficient assembly for the discussion of Indian affairs and Indian grievances in this country. As regards the European press, I would only enact a good and somewhat stringent law of libel for the protection both of Government and of individuals, to be administered by the ordinary tribunals of the country, and would attach certain disabilities to repeatedly convicted persons. But we might, perhaps, with advantage go farther in regard to the native press, and, in addition to the ordinary libel law, might make "contempt of Government" and the propagation of false intelligence penal.

I also think that the Governor-General in council must be armed with an extraordinary power to restrain the press in extraordinary emergencies, and that, both on this and on other grounds, a power of expelling from the country injurious individual foreigners (Englishmen included) should be somewhere vested.

I should say that it might be a good plan, though it may seem a strange one, to provide that no paper shall be published more than twice a-week without the permission of Government. There really is not true news to support a daily newspaper in any part of India. We should thus, then, obviate the temptation to invent highly-seasoned fictions; while the exposition of real abuses could not be materially interfered with by the delay of a day or two. It should not be permitted to evade the law which requires the registry of the real proprietors and responsible editors of all journals; and I think that, when anything appears involving a betrayal of the confidence of Government, or a breach of discipline on the part of Government servants, there should be some judicial process for determining that such is really the nature of the published matter, and compelling the editor to give up his authority.

It is practically impossible to prevent public officers from directly or indirectly defending themselves against imputations and misstatements, even when they do not amount to wilful and malicious libel; and I think that this much must be left to the discretion of individuals, provided that they do not communicate official information which ought not to be communicated. Indiscreet justifications will be considered by Government like any other indiscreet act of a public servant.

I think that we might with advantage combine a Government paper, as a vehicle of authentic news, with the usual Government Gazette—that such a paper as the 'Moniteur,' for instance, might be published in each presidency. The great advantage would be, that this paper might very largely circulate among the natives, and would be infinitely preferred by them to private and unauthorised journals, than which they have at present no other resource.

Post-office.

As connected with education and information in general, and particularly with the press, the post-office is of vast importance; and there can be no doubt that Indian rates of postage are exorbitantly high, and ought to be reduced. They are high, judged by any standard; but, compared to the value of money in the country, they are enormous. I hope that roads, improved communication, and an improved post-office discipline, will render the service much cheaper than at present; lower rates will immensely increase the use of the post-office; and we may even effect the reduction without loss of revenue. But if Government must consent to pay something for the enormous use it makes of the post-office, it should not object to do so. At present the post-office is rather for the convenience of Government than of the people; and the great mass of the mails is composed of Government despatches. But the private postage alone covers the whole cost; and the post-office pays its own expenses. I do not think that an uniform postage would answer in India; the distances are too great, and the cost of transit too considerable. To do justice to the natives, the postage for short distances must be a great deal smaller than we could afford to fix for long distances. I rather think it has been proposed to have different rates, but low ones—perhaps three rates—of which the lowest, for short distances, should be the smallest coin in common use. Stamps should certainly be introduced. The inconvenience and abuse of post-office payments is great.

As regards the overland mail communication with Europe, the present letter and newspaper rate cannot be objected to; but the excessive cost of transmitting publications (other than newspapers) and parcels is a very great grievance. I see not why printed papers should not be sent to India by post at a moderate rate, as to other parts of the British empire. The monopoly of the Peninsular and Oriental Company has certainly the effect of imposing an almost prohibitory rate on parcels; and the worst feature of the case is, that this tax is said (I do not myself know with what degree of justice) to be levied for the benefit of certain individuals connected with the Company. The communication across Egypt will soon be easy, and arrangements should be made to secure a reasonable mail-parcel rate.

Overland communication.

This brings me to the general subject of the means of direct communication between India and Europe, than which nothing can be more important, or more likely to promote the improvement of the country. The State certainly contributes liberally towards this object in the immense contract payment to the Peninsular and Oriental Company; but our present advantages are purchased by establishing a gigantic monopoly, which the Government grant secures from competition. No private speculation can contend against a company which has so great an advantage, and which, thus supported, can afford to drive any rival out of the market.

As regards the very highest class of passenger traffic, there is not at present much ground for complaining of the monopoly. There can be no doubt that great advantages have been in the first instance derived from the great and successful undertakings of the Peninsular and Oriental Company. But the cost of travelling in their vessels is certainly very high, and such as does not admit of a common and popular traffic between India and Europe. The passenger charges from India to Suez (the part of the line in which there is no competition with any other route) are in particular high; and, from what I have already said of the parcels rate, it will be seen that there is little encouragement to an overland goods traffic. In fact, nothing can be sent by this route except at an enormous expense. I think that the advantage of a very long and large contract may be doubted. It might have been better to pay so much for each letter carried, and to let the first steamer that starts have the letters; or, of two starting at the same time, the fastest. We should then have fair competition. There can be no doubt that, if the one great Government grant were now withdrawn, or split into separate payments, there would still be steamers plying from India to Suez. We might have more numerous vessels, of a somewhat inferior class, conveying a much larger traffic at much cheaper rates. I doubt whether the perfect regularity of the mail communication is worth the immense cost. True, private speculators might not run regularly twice a month in the bad season, but they would run every week in the good season; and the Government vessels might, when necessary, carry the mails at other times.

Advantage of intimate communication with Mediterranean countries.

It would be in every way most desirable to open up a cheap traffic between our Eastern possessions and the countries of the Mediterranean, and there seems to be now every facility for doing so. Anciently, the people of the Mediterranean were in close communication with the East; but, when the route of traffic was reversed, this communication almost entirely ceased. The Red Sea route has now been re-opened, but only to the magnificent arrangements and magnificent charges of the Peninsular and Oriental Company. The grand difficulty of this route was in the peculiarity of the winds, which periodically blow straight up or straight down the Red Sea, and sometimes render it impossible for a sailing vessel to get out or in for many months together. The overland journey across the isthmus would have been a comparatively trifling obstacle, and will shortly cease to be an obstacle at all. The railway from Alexandria to Cairo will soon be opened. The distance from Cairo to Suez is, I think, about eighty miles; and I should imagine that a railway between these places will be one of the cheapest in the world. The land will cost nothing. The soil is not moving sand, but good solid ground. No rain falls, and no considerable bridges will be required. I believe that the levels are very favourable, and the Pasha willing. There can therefore be no doubt of the completion of the line before long. On the other hand, auxiliary screw machinery is being rapidly introduced in the mercantile marine. To a ship so fitted, the navigation of the Red Sea is easier than that of the Atlantic. What, then, can prevent the general adoption of the direct route, if no monopoly is granted to any one, but encouragement given to all? If we can open a popular and commercial intercourse with the countries of the Mediterranean, we may become very closely connected with them, and obtain from them, with great ease, at cheap rates, and in large quantities, many things particularly well suited to India; while India may still more largely sell to them her products and those of the farther East, as in times of old. This, then, I would by every possible means promote. If there should ever be a railway through Asiatic Turkey connecting the Persian Gulf with the Mediterranean, the communication will be rendered still more quick and easy, and Europe and Asia will then be at last really united.*

Colonization and amalgamation.

The subject of colonization, and the formation of a Europeo-Asiatic Christian population, has already been alluded to as perhaps the most important means of introducing moral improvement religious and educational, and on this also principally depends the material improvement of the country. I may well, then, here notice the subject as a connecting link between those two great duties. Social improvements are not to be effected by exhortation alone —we must also have example; and, if we would really convert the natives to our manners, it must be by more or less meeting and amalgamating with them. Little has been done towards this end.

Difficulties of European settlers.

I have formerly mentioned † some of the causes of the small progress of English adventurers and capitalists in India; but I am inclined to think that I have not exhausted those causes, and that there are others capable of being re-

* There will never be in our day a connected railway to India, but there may very well be one from Smyrna to Bagdad, and the route would then be as direct and easy as could be desired.

† Modern India, p. 203.

medied. There is, in fact, great field for European enterprise, if money and practical energy be combined with skill and conduct, and aided by sufficient laws.

The imperfections of our Indian laws are, no doubt, practically, considerable obstacles, which ought to be removed, and which would be removed by good agrarian and commercial codes and good systems of procedure. The planters and merchants in the interior complain, with great reason, of our civil courts, and of the harassing litigation (especially on agrarian questions) in which they are involved; the interference of those courts in questions of landed rights, the extreme uncertainty into which they throw them, and the opportunities afforded to fraud and subterfuge, are justly regarded as great grievances. These may be remedied by an improvement of our laws, and European settlement will thus be much facilitated. Still the permanent and successful colonization, on a great scale, of pure Englishmen is, in the plains of India, impossible; and men who do not colonize must always labour under a very great disadvantage in all private enterprise. It is now, however, quite possible that, in the temperate climate of the hills, European colonization may take place to a considerable extent, and I have mentioned this result as one of the principal advantages of the formation of permanent European stations in favourable situations. I would have Government to encourage hill colonization to the utmost; and especially to hold out inducements to its servants to settle in the country. To this end they may do much by assisting in the formation of good schools in the hills. There is a very large class of the servants of Government whose income would enable them to live comfortably in India, and to educate their children there, while they are pinched to the utmost in retiring to Europe or sending their children home.

Proposed encouragement of hill colonization;

Yet there are at present few facilities for settlement and education in India, and some Government aid would be necessary to effect the desired object. The increased prevalence of marriage, and of European domestic habits, among the officers of the army, undoubtedly detract from their military efficiency, and this result can only be compensated by using it for the purposes of colonization. The European soldiers, again, have little prospect of a happy return to their native land; they frequently form native connections, and it would be alike beneficial to the country and beneficent to them, to afford to them facilities for settling in the hills.

I would use every effort to get into the hands of Government as much as possible of the land situated around European settlements and in a temperate climate. A great part of the landed rights of India are created by us, but they are much complicated and intermixed, and private individuals can only acquire them where they happen to offer. In special sites, then, the assistance of Government may be necessary, and, by making the most of its own rights, substituting grants in other places, and paying moderate compensations, Government may no doubt procure sufficient land for the purposes of colonization.

It must, however, be an indispensable condition to the settlement of Europeans, that they must adopt the political institutions of the country of their election, must submit to become the subjects of an absolute government, and must abandon claims and privileges inconsistent with our general system, with the maintenance of equal laws for all classes, and with the example which ought to be set to the natives.

There is another view which I would take of the question of colonization. Englishmen are in all their ways and habits the very antipodes of Asiatics. Make a journey from India to England by land, and step by step things become less and less Oriental, till, in this country, you reach the extreme of Occidental manners. Very many things are common to India with the countries of the South and East of Europe, which altogether disappear when you reach our colder clime. Hence Englishmen are, of all Europeans and all Christians, the least fitted to amalgamate with the natives. On the other hand, the people of Greece, Italy, Malta, Asia Minor, and Egypt, are accustomed to a warmer sun; they are content with smaller wages; their manners, arts, and agriculture more nearly approximate to those of tropical countries. If, then, they are encouraged by Government, and we have a cheap and abundant communication between India and the Mediterranean, such as I have suggested to be most desirable, it cannot be doubted that they will find their way to the East. The vine and the olive, the cotton, the poultry, and the windmills of Egypt, the arts of Italians, the enterprise of Greeks, the religion of the Asiatic churches, may flow in more readily, and take root more easily, than the colder products of our colder soil.

and of immigration from Southern Europe and Western Asia.

All this, then, I would promote. I would entertain the Southern Christians, and their arts, in the Government model schools and model farms; and would give every facility and encouragement to their private settlement.

While independent native states existed, there might have been political objections to such a course, but I think that these have now ceased. The foreign immigrants cannot serve native states without our permission; and, as individuals, the people to whom I now allude are accustomed to political servitude, and will be lost in the native mass. I do indeed suppose that, in converting and Europeanizing the natives, they will do much to fit them for future independence, but that result is one hardly to be deprecated; and, in the mean time, I should not fear political inconvenience—certainly not nearly so much from Southern Europeans as from Englishmen. At the same time, I hold the necessity of giving to an absolute government ruling a conquered country the power (to which I have already alluded in connection with the press) of expelling injurious and dangerous foreigners, when, in extreme and extraordinary instances, the supreme power of the state judges it necessary to do so. I would give this power only to the Governor-General in Council, and an appeal would lie to the Senate at home.

Amalgamation and transformation.

When we have obtained colonists who united with the mixed and native Christian population form the nucleus of change, intermixture and amalgamation with the natives will be much more easy, and should be every way encouraged. To the class which would result I would give the special countenance and support of Government, would employ and favour them to the utmost, would promote proselytism and intermarriage, and would make the position of proselyte natives and imitative artists as agreeable and profitable as possible. Once put in motion, the current of improvement will acquire volume and velocity, till it absorbs the whole country; and we may thus in the end fully introduce among the masses Christianity, education, and civilization.

Material improvements.—Agriculture and machinery.

A principal effect of colonization will be the improvement of agriculture and machinery. We have now in our Indian territories every variety of climate, food is cheap, labour is cheap and skilful, and there seems no reason why the country should not be far advanced in every description of produce and every branch of art.

We must not, however, be *too* speculative; we must

duly understand and appreciate the native arts and agriculture; we must adapt and perfect our plans in our model schools and farms, and with the aid of competent native opinion, before we attempt to impose them on the people. The natives are abundantly ready to adopt anything which will be immediately profitable, but you cannot expect them to make experiments. Some things have been introduced, or improved and extended, with great success,—for instance, tobacco in former days, and indigo in our times; to other things the climate may not be favourable. I learn that the cotton sent from India has been in reality much improved of late years, and this is, I believe, greatly owing to the mode of cleaning and packing. The climate is so dissimilar from that of America, that we can hardly be surprised if the small, quick-growing, native plant is more profitable than that fitted to a moister atmosphere. But the climate of Egypt seems very similar to that of India, and the Egyptian cotton is as valuable as any in the world. There seems, then, yet room for further experiment. Long-stapled cotton is necessary to our English cotton machinery, but if we can either render our staple long, or adapt our machinery to short staple, it is hardly possible to doubt that spinning-mills must succeed in India.

Cotton.

The potatoe seems likely to be a great staple of the hills and a favourite vegetable of the plains; but in the latter the heat of summer is too much for it, and it is so apt to be killed by the frosts of winter, that it can only be grown with great care and expense, and will never be comparatively so cheap as grain as a staple article of food.

Other products.

If the olive should succeed in the hills, it may become a great article of production; and in the valleys removed from the influence of the periodical rains we may make wine from the grape. With the aid of English capital and machinery, and French taste, the Cashmere shawl manufacture may doubtless be much improved and extended; and many other manufactures may be similarly benefited.

Tea.

After reading Mr. Fortune's most interesting work, I entertain doubts whether we shall ever supersede the teas of China. The great difficulty in the cultivation of most foreign products is the want of rain in the first half of the year, and its excess in the rainy months. In China, the genial rains of April and May seem to bring out the tea-leaves, without expense, in a way which we can hardly rival by artificial watering,* at a considerable expense. There can be no doubt that tea may be produced to a certain extent in the Himmalayas, and that for local or protected consumption it would succeed remarkably well, but it appears that under a free trade the common Chinese teas may be had so cheap as to defy the competition of less favourable climates. In Assam, however, a country bordering on China, and where the tea-plant was indigenous, considerable success seems to have been attained; and I am glad to see that a company is to try what can be done in the Himmalayas. One thing, however, I must observe in reference to their scheme, viz. that 10,000 acres of good land, favourably situated in the Himmalayas, is not so easily got. Most culturable spots are already occupied, and the hill people are by no means willing to rent their land.

Mode of agricultural speculation recommended.

In all agricultural undertakings in India I think that the best chance of success is by contracting with the cultivators for the supply of the raw material. If you make them moderate

* Mr. Fortune objects to the watering; but in most sites in India, in April, May, and June, the plants must be constantly watered or die.

advances, and bind yourself to take the produce at a fixed and profitable rate, they will cultivate whatever you like, however you like, and to whatever extent you like. In this respect they have no prejudices, and it is a mere calculation of profit. But generally they will not let you have their land, and, if they did, you would probably cultivate it at a very great loss. It is, then, by dealing with the cultivators, making advances to them, and directing their operations, that supplies may best be obtained of cotton and any other articles which our manufacturers may desire. Let them send discreet and trustworthy agents with money in their hands, and they may make the most of the capabilities of the country; but till they do so, it is absurd that they should sit at home and blame the Government for not depositing cotton at their doors.

Necessity of laws for protection of capital.

The want of stringent commercial laws is the great obstacle to the introduction of European capital. It is found that laws which are hardly sufficient to protect capital in England, under the immediate eye of the owner, and with the help of many social securities, are quite inadequate for the protection of the same capital invested in India. The majority of the great commercial and joint-stock enterprises there attempted have ended in egregious rascality, and, unfortunately, with impunity to the perpetrators. Merchant princes have recklessly, fraudulently, and feloniously, ruined thousands, and have been in no way punished, legally or socially; but on the contrary, have sometimes been set up as objects of admiration. Commercial morality is at a very low ebb, and social support too often goes with the defrauders, not with the defrauded. Hence it is that no prudent man will trust his money in private speculations in India unless he himself goes to look after it. This very few capitalists are willing to do, and those who do, think their risk and labour covered only by an enormous interest. To this cause, then, I believe may be principally attributed the smallness of the introduction of real capital and the unsubstantial character of most mercantile adventurers. The subject is one to which particular attention should be paid, and the evil should be remedied as soon as possible by laws which it may now be necessary to render somewhat severe.

We much require a good system of joint-stock partnership, containing sufficiently stringent provisions for the prevention and punishment of fraud on the part of managers, and a reasonable limitation of personal liability. If we can obtain this desideratum, people will be willing to trust their money in commercial enterprises on reasonable interest. Something of the kind is particularly required by the native community. Men, not mercantile by profession, have no means of investing their money in useful speculations; and as capital accumulates, we should undoubtedly try to bring into play the power of joint-stock machinery. It is, perhaps, from the want of tempting investments that natives who save money are induced to hoard it up in hard cash till they spend it on marriage ceremonies. If we but give them a fair opportunity, they will be found most apt to imbibe the spirit of speculation; and they have a particular proneness to the joint-stock principle. Petty and temporary private speculations are often conducted on a joint-stock system; even one's servants, and people of that kind, sometimes get up little joint-stock operations. I believe, then, we might much facilitate the application of capital in the hands of natives by good commercial laws. Their acquisitiveness is great; and if we make the temptation to speculate sufficiently absorbing, it may overcome their compensating disposition to spend on great occasions the proceeds of long acquisition. They will be immense speculators, and the result will be great material improvement of the country.

Public works.

I can neither afford space, nor am I competent, to enter into details of the great public works which a government possessed of funds should speedily carry out.

Railways.

I have said that I would make main lines of railroad an exception to the general rule of spending no more money than we can save from our revenue, inasmuch as they would be immediately profitable as a *Government* undertaking and a means of military economy. I would raise, then, without delay, money sufficient for the purpose, provision being at the same time made (as I have proposed) to devote a considerable proportion of our income to a sinking fund, to be brought into immediate and rapid operation. You cannot with advantage make trunk railways gradually; they will only be of use when the great provinces of the empire are united, and small sums expended on short lines will be nearly lost till the whole is completed. It is, no doubt, prudent at first to make experimentally short lines, sufficient to solve any engineering questions which may have arisen; but the experimental lines already far advanced must have sufficed for this purpose, and, if we are to have railways at all, we should now boldly make up our minds to spend the sum necessary to complete the great lines. If we can but keep out of war, we need not despair of paying off the capital within a reasonable time, and we shall always have the lines themselves to show for our money.

Proposed primary lines.

The railways which seem at present most necessary are as follows:—

1. Bombay to Agra, with a short branch to Saugor, in Central India;

2. Agra to Lahore and Mussoorie:
(thus forming a connected communication between Northern and Central India and the sea, as represented in the diagram).

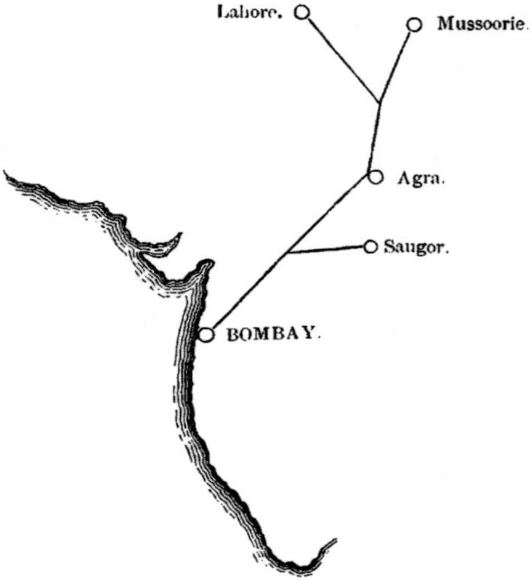

3. Calcutta to the Ganges (already commenced).

Bombay has no water communication with the interior. The damage sustained by the cotton and other articles which constitute its very large commerce, from the barbarous mode of transit and the heavy expense, are invariably represented as evils of the utmost magnitude. A railway, therefore, from Bombay into the interior of the country is most necessary, and has been projected and in part commenced. I have already suggested that it might be advantageously continued to Agra: it would pass through Malwa and other important countries. There is a large tract in Central India, part of which (known as the Saugor territories) belongs to us, and of which the products are rich and abundant, including large quantities of cotton; but they are often quite unsaleable from the total absence of any means of transport, there being in that vicinity neither navigable rivers nor good roads. Grain has been here selling for next to nothing, while there were famines in other parts of India, which would have been arrested if means of transporting the surplus products of the central territory could have been found. Doubtless, it is on this account that this tract has not been sufficiently cultivated; much of it is still in the possession of the wild aboriginal tribes. There could be no better field for European enterprise if we obtain the means of communication. A comparatively short branch of the Bombay and Agra railway, running to Saugor, will at once drain the whole of this country, and connect it both with Bombay and with Agra.

The rail between Agra and Lahore will connect our great military stations with one another and with the sea; and the whole line will open to the commerce and the traffic of Northern India the best, shortest, and quickest route to the sea, to Europe, and to Western Asia. It will then be easy to unite the Bombay and Bengal armies, and, in uniting them, to reduce their collective strength. There will be no more difficulty and hardship in finding carriage for troops and stores.

Agra already communicates with the principal towns of the Doab by a road which is almost equal to a railway, and branch and local railways may be left to future private enterprise.

It is of great importance to open the direct communication between Calcutta and the main stream of the Ganges; but, this effected, a rail along the course of the Ganges will not be of primary importance, if we have the shorter and more necessary line from Agra to Bombay. It is principally for the traffic of Northern and Central India that a railway communication with the sea is so great an object. The local commerce of the lower Gangetic provinces floats down the stream of that father of Indian rivers at a comparative small expense, and steamers can ply at all seasons between Allahabad and the point at which the Calcutta rail will join the Ganges. We shall hope in time to connect Calcutta with Agra, Bombay, and Mussoorie by rail also; but I consider this a secondary object, by no means equal to that of the shorter and more necessary line running to a better port, through rich countries possessed of no navigable rivers.

Reasons for preferring Bombay to Calcutta trunk line.

It is, then, of the utmost importance that we should speedily decide whether the great trunk rail of the first instance, connecting Northern and Central India with the sea, is to run to Bombay or to Calcutta. The greater part of the traffic has hitherto followed the circuitous route by Calcutta, because there is water carriage in that direction; but it will be a great mistake if we blindly follow a prescription which will be quite inapplicable to a land route. The water route is no reason for taking the land route by the same course, but, on the contrary, a reason for thinking a Gangetic rail less urgently necessary, and the streams are a great obstacle to the construction of a railroad, from which the other line will be comparatively free. The passage of the tributaries of the Ganges will render necessary enormous works. The bridge over the Saone is a prodigious engineering undertaking, which has never been contemplated at a less cost than a million sterling; and all the petty streams, which seem mere trifles in the dry season, require immensely large water-ways in the rain-floods.

Say that the local rails now commenced at Calcutta and Bombay are carried, in the first instance, about 150 or 200 miles each—the Calcutta rail to Rajmahal, on the Ganges; that of Bombay to the farther part of Candeish. The distance from Agra to the Candeish province will be about 450 miles; from Agra to Rajmahal, along the line of the Ganges, about 650 miles, in the course of which are several almost impracticable rivers. I should imagine that the latter rail will cost twice as much as the former, without being half so necessary or so permanently useful, and without opening up any new countries, or giving any outlet to Central India.

Madras rails.

The town of Madras has no harbour, and the presidency has so much sea-coast and sea carriage that Madras rails must be rather local than imperial, the more so as no one rail will suffice for the whole of that presidency. But, doubtless, a rail from Madras to some point in the centre of the southern portion of the peninsula will be very useful; unless, indeed, Cannanore or some western port may be preferred. Perhaps it might be a good plan to abandon Madras, fix the government at Bangalore, and have a rail to Cannanore.

Question of interposition of companies.

With regard to the mode of raising the funds for the construction of railways, it is quite clear that Government must take the risk, and in fact it has taken, and it is right that it *should* take, all material risk. Railways in India must be Government works; and it is to Government that they will certainly pay. It is equally certain that they will be largely used for private traffic, and will much benefit the country; but it is not so certain that they will pay as private speculations, for this reason, that, labour and everything else being so low priced, you must carry at very much lower rates than in this country; while the imported rails will cost more, and wooden sleepers will also be very expensive. Many expenses are, however, less heavy in India than in England, and rails will altogether cost much less; but the difference in rates of charge will be still greater. The natives will have no prejudice against travelling by rail—they are far too practical for that; but where you charge a penny a mile here, a farthing a mile will be there a prohibitive rate. A native will rather walk than pay a farthing a mile; you must carry him at a rate proportioned to the price of labour in the country. Numbers will do something to make up for low passenger rates; but still, passengers will never pay as in Europe; and, although the receipts from the carriage of valuable goods will undoubtedly be very large, private persons will not take up Indian rails as a private speculation without a Government guarantee for the interest of their money.

The question then is whether, if Government is to run the risk, it had better directly borrow money and make the railways, or act through the medium of companies. All English prescription, so far as it is applicable to such a case, is in favour of the latter course; and, doubtless, in this country, companies (in spite of all their jobbing) do great things which no government could attempt. But in India things are very different, and I very much doubt the policy of Government in embarrassing itself with companies, for this simple reason,—that the companies do nothing whatever towards the object in view, but, on the contrary, cause considerable complication and expense. The money Government could more easily raise, on at least as favourable terms, by a simple loan. But a company raising the money and Government guaranteeing the interest, it is found, first, that Government could not possibly trust the company with any independent action in India (for the money would be infallibly jobbed away by people who have everything to gain and nothing to lose by such proceedings); and second, that Government only can carry out the works. No private company could do so without Government aid. Hence a complete control and direction of the proceedings is necessarily reserved to Government, and the only result of interposing a company has been the employment of a double set of officers and considerable preliminary expenses. It is certain that the private interests of the company have had no effect in reducing the cost. I understand that the contracts for the earthwork have been entered into at a considerably higher rate than has usually been paid by the Government engineers.

If then a company can find money for a railway, and make it at their own risk, by all means give them every facility to do so; but if they do not take the risk, it is much better that Government, taking the risk, should also take the execution. An absolute government in such a country, possessed of so complete a machinery and an admirable corps of engineers (to whom additional civil engineers may be added), can very efficiently carry out such an undertaking in a way which no private company can hope to do. In truth, the guarantee to a railway company of so large a rate of interest as 5 per cent. does not seem very intelligible. I should think that abundance of money might be borrowed by the East India Company in the City as a simple loan at a much lower rate. Money is cheap and their credit is good. Then why this additional expense and embarrassment?

Roads and bridges.

In the plains of India the earthwork and bridging for great roads cost just as much as for railways, and metalling is also very expensive. The only difference of expense, then, between roads and railways, is that between the cost of road-metalling and of rails. From Allahabad to Delhi you might almost run an engine on the present road. If then we determine to go on actively with railways, we may discontinue the farther prosecution of great trunk roads; but local and branch roads will be of still greater importance than at present, and should be prosecuted to the utmost possible extent. I hope to see both the Jumna and the Sutlej bridged.

Caravanserais.

Caravanserais were among the greatest and most beneficial of the Mahommedan public works. On the great imperial road from Agra to Lahore (the line of one of my proposed railways) many of the magnificent caravanserais and gigantic mile-stones are still to be seen. At each milestone there was a well, and at each well a vendor of the most necessary articles of wayfaring consumption. The mile-towers are also said to have been used as telegraphic posts, through which intelligence was transmitted (so says native tradition) with immense rapidity. At every stage, about every ten miles, was a great caravanserai, an immense quadrangle of considerable architectural pretensions, affording space in the centre for carts, carriages, and cattle, and surrounded by arched rooms and the establishments of innkeepers aud shopkeepers. There is no pleasanter sight than the interior of a serai, and it is wonderful in how great preservation many of the old imperial hostelries still are. The brickmakers of those days made such bricks as we cannot now procure.

This mode of accommodating the travelling public is more in accordance with native opinion and habits than to trust altogether to private hostelries (which, in fact, do not exist),* and is also preferable for police reasons. I think that Government may with great advantage restore and imitate the old serais at the railway stations and principal halting-places.

* Private hotels do not seem to be understood in India, Persia, &c. Those countries do not possess these luxuries of civilization, which, according to M. Huc, would seem to be carried to as great a pitch of refinement in China as in Paris.

Tolls.

The tolls now levied at bridges (of boats) and ferries, and applied to facilitate travelling, may perhaps be continued, but I do not think that it would be desirable to levy tolls on roads. The natives had rather travel the worst than pay toll on the best road in the world; and would only look on such an impost as a new tax or a recurrence to transit duties.

Harbour at the mouth of the Indus.

A very important public work will be a harbour at the mouth of the Indus. There is no natural harbour, and the monsoon makes the coast impracticable for several months in the year. This is the great obstacle to the use of the river for navigation and commerce; and it can hardly be doubted that modern art can supply that which has not been spontaneously granted by nature.

If we cannot have a harbour on one of the mouths of the river, we must have one at Kurachee, and an artificial communication with the main stream, either by canal or by rail. Kurachee would then be to the Indus what Alexandria is to the Nile.

Canals for irrigation.

I need hardly dwell on the vast importance of canals for irrigation,—that has been amply shown by other and better qualified pens. The countries of the Upper Ganges would be many times more productive than at present if a constant supply of water could be commanded. The greater part of the plains of the Indus and its tributaries, notwithstanding the richest soil, are condemned to sterility for want of water. Meanwhile some 40,000 cubic feet of water per second, issuing from the mountains, flows unused to the ocean; and even its occupation of bearing the boats of commerce is almost to be taken from it by rails. These perennial waters are confined to great rivers, and can be made available only by great imperial works. It is merely a question of expense; if Government can find the money, all this water may be brought into use, the country may be fertilized to an immense extent, and all chance of famine may be averted. Something to this end the Mahommedan emperors did, and we have already done enough to show that the greatest rivers may yield to engineering arts, and that, as a revenue speculation, such works will amply pay. The great tracts of new land brought into cultivation by irrigation would afford great opportunity for colonization and for agricultural improvements.

All these things may be done if we have money, but without money we can do nothing.

THE END.